The '*Un*certainty of a Hearing'

Supplements

to

Vetus Testamentum

VOLUME 121

The '*Un*certainty of a Hearing'

A Study of the Sudden Change of Mood in the Psalms of Lament

By

Federico G. Villanueva

BRILL

LEIDEN • BOSTON
2008

This book is printed on acid-free paper.

Library of Congress Cataloging-in-Publication Data

Villanueva, Federico G.
 The uncertainty of a hearing : a study of the sudden change of mood in the Psalms of lament / by Federico G. Villanueva.
  p. cm. — (Supplements to the Vetus Testamentum, ISSN 0083-5889 ; v. 121)
 Includes bibliographical references and index.
 ISBN 978-90-04-16847-3 (hardback : alk. paper) 1. Bible. O.T. Psalms—Criticism, interpretation, etc. 2. Laments in the Bible. I. Title. II. Series.

 BS1445.L3V55 2008
 223'.206—dc22

                                                          2008023230

ISSN 0083-5889
ISBN 978 90 04 16847 3

To Rosemarie, Emier and Faye

CONTENTS

ACKNOWLEDGEMENTS

This book is a revised version of my dissertation submitted to the University of Bristol on November 2007, after three years (2004–2007) of research. As I reflect over these past three years, I am amazed at the number of people who have contributed towards the successful completion of this book—a reminder of the communal dimension of doing research. I would like to mention some of them here. First of all, Professor Gordon Wenham, my supervisor, whose passion for scholarship and pastoral heart has greatly encouraged me to pursue excellence in my own work; Professor John Day, my external supervisor, who helped me see important insights into my work and encouraged me to submit this work for publication and; Dr. Philip Jenson, who has assisted during the initial stages of the research. My examiners: Dr. Adrian Curtis and Dr. John Bimson, for their valuable comments and critiques into my work. My Brill readers, for their important comments and suggestions, Professor Hans Barstad for accepting the work for publication and all those with Brill who have helped towards the completion of the book, especially Mattie Kuiper and Gera van Bedaf. Hazel Trapnell, who has been so kind to read the final draft of the manuscript for proof reading and Sheila Brown, who has helped me through the entire process of writing the dissertation and then the book. Sheila and her husband, the Revd Anthony Brown, have been our parents in a foreign land.

Moving into a foreign land with your family to do PhD can be really tricky. But we survived, thanks to the wonderful communities to which we have been privileged to be a part. Trinity College Bristol, where I did my research, has welcomed my family. The postgraduate seminars have provided opportunities for me to learn from other scholars and to share my ideas. I am grateful to the administration and staff of Trinity for all their support, especially to Andrew Lucas, the executive director, for his sensitivity to the needs of students, and to Su Brown, the Librarian, for all her great efforts in finding the materials I need for my study, especially the rare ones. St Mary Magdalene church in Bristol has become for us a community which welcomed us, prayed for us and supported us in many ways. I thank Revd David Richie, the vicar, for the opportunities to take a small part in the life of the church through the worship and preaching. The Filipino church in Bristol (Jesus Cares Christian Fellowship) has been a great help to us especially during our final months in the UK.

The research would not have been possible without the financial support of organizations and individuals. Alliance Graduate School in Manila, where I teach, has granted me a study leave so I could pursue my PhD. I am grateful to the leadership and staff of AGS and to my colleagues for all the support they have given us. Overseas Missionary Fellowship (OMF) Philippines has supported us especially during our difficult times. Langham Partnership International has made it possible for me and my family to go to the UK. I especially thank Dr. John Stott, founder of Langham, Dr. Christopher Wright, Revd Howard Peskett, Canon Paul Berg and all those who are responsible in helping scholars within Langham.

My deepest gratitude goes to my family—to my father, Bishop Butch Villanueva, from whom I first learned the discipline of study; my mother, Melita Villanueva, from whom I first heard the stories of the Bible; my two brothers, Demo and Jojo, who believed in me and encouraged me; and most especially to my two children, Emier and Faye and my wife, Rosemarie, for their patience and unconditional love even in my times of lament.

To the God who hears my laments I give praise.

Rico Villanueva, March 2008
Bristol, England

ABBREVIATIONS

AB	The Anchor Bible
ABD	*Anchor Bible Dictionary* (ed. David Noel Freedman, NY: Doubleday, 1992)
ANE	Ancient Near East
ASOR	American Schools of Oriental Research
BBR	*Bulletin for Biblical Research*
BDB	*The Brown-Driver-Briggs Hebrew and English Lexicon of the Old Testament*
Bib	*Biblica*
BibKir	*Bibel und Kirche*
BibLeb	*Bibel und Leben*
BibRev	*Bible Review*
BKAT	Biblischer Kommentar Altes Testament
BN	*Biblische Notizen*
BTB	*Biblical Theology Bulletin*
BZ	*Biblische Zeitschrift*
BZAW	Beiheft zur Zeitschrift für die alttestamentliche Wissenschaft
BZWANT	Beiträge zur Wissenschaft vom Alten und Neuen Testament
CalTJ	*Calvin Theological Journal*
CBQ	*Catholic Biblical Quarterly*
ConBOT	Coniectanea biblica, Old Testament
ESV	English Standard Version
ET	English Translation
EvQ	*Evangelical Quarterly*
ExpTim	*Expository Times*
FAT	Forschungen zum Alten Testament
FOTL	The Forms of the Old Testament Literature
FRLANT	Forschungen zur Religion und Literatur des Alten und Neuen Testaments
GNB	Good News Bible
HAR	*Hebrew Annual Review*
HAT	Handbuch zum Alten Testament
HBT	*Horizons in Biblical Theology*
HKAT	Handkommentar zum Alten Testament
HTR	*Harvard Theological Review*

HUCA	*Hebrew Union College Annual*
HZAT	Handbuch zum Alten Testament
IB	Interpreter's Bible
IBS	*Irish Biblical Studies*
ICC	The International Critical Commentary
Int	*Interpretation*
ITC	International Theological Commentary
JB	Jerusalem Bible
JBR	*Journal of Bible and Religion*
JBTh	*Jahrbuch für Biblische Theologie*
JETS	*Journal of the Evangelical Theological Society*
JSNT	Journal for the Study of the New Testament Supplement Series
JSOT	*Journal for the Study of the Old Testament*
JSOTSup	Journal for the Study of Old Testament Supplement Series
JTS	*Journal of Theological Studies*
KAT	Kommentar zum Alten Testament
KHC(AT)	Kurzer Hand-Kommentar (zum Alten Testament)
LXX	Septuagint
MT	Masoretic Text
NAB	New American Bible
NASB	New American Standard Bible
NCB	New Century Bible Commentary
NEB	New English Bible
NIB	*The New Interpreter's Bible*
NIBC	New International Biblical Commentary
NIV	New International Version
NJB	New Jerusalem Bible
NRSV	New Revised Standard Version
OBT	Overtures to Biblical Theology
OT	Old Testament
OTE	*Old Testament Essays*
OTG	Old Testament Guides
OTL	Old Testament Library
OTS	*Oudtestamentische Studiën*
RB	*Revue Biblique*
RevExp	*Review and Expositor*
RSV	Revised Standard Version
SBL	Society of Biblical Literature

SBLDS	Society of Biblical Literature Dissertation Series
SBT	Studies in Biblical Theology
SJOT	*Scandinavian Journal of the Old Testament*
SJT	*Scottish Journal of Theology*
TDOT	Theological Dictionary of the Old Testament
TOTC	Tyndale Old Testament Commentaries
TynBul	*Tyndale Bulletin*
TZ	*Theologie Zeitschrift*
VT	*Vetus Testamentum*
VTSup	Supplements to Vetus Testamentum
WBC	Word Biblical Commentary
WMANT	Wissenschaftliche Monographien zum Alten und Neuen Testament
ZAW	*Zeitschrift für die altestamentliche Wissenschaft*
ZTK	*Zeitschrift für Theologie und Kirche*

CHAPTER ONE

INTRODUCTION

1.1 INTRODUCTION

Scholars have long observed the sudden change of mood in the lament psalms.[1] Popularised by Begrich in his famous article, "Das priesterliche Heilsorakel",[2] this feature has been the subject of much scholarly attention for almost a hundred years.[3] Unfortunately, the sudden change of mood has come to be understood only in terms of the movement from lament to praise. As the very phrase that has come to be associated with the discussion betrays—"Gewissheit der Erhörung"[4]—the accent falls on the element of certainty, on resolution and the overcoming of the situation of lament. Lament is always expected to move to praise and never the reverse.

Whilst affirming the presence of a movement from lament to praise, the present study seeks to draw attention to the other movements in the Psalms: the movement from praise/thanksgiving to lament, the return

---

[1] To cite some examples, observe first of all Psalm 6. This psalm begins with a petition and a plea for mercy (see vv. 2–3) which develops into a bitter lament (4–8). But suddenly it breaks into a confident declaration (9–11). Far from the mournful cry of lament, we hear the confident voice of the psalmist telling his opponents to turn away from him, "for Yahweh has heard the voice of my cry" (6:9). We see a similar pattern in Psalm 13. This psalm commences with the fourfold chiming of 'how long?' (2–3) followed by an impassioned plea for deliverance (4–5). But the psalm shifts to a declaration of trust and ends with a vow of praise (6). Yet one more example is Psalm 28. This psalm contains an imprecation in the middle (4–5), which suddenly breaks into praise: "Blessed be Yahweh!" (6). So sudden is the change of mood in this psalm that one wonders how the imprecation can turn into praise in a matter of few verses!

[2] Joachim Begrich, "Das priesterliche Heilsorakel", *ZAW* 52 (1934): 81–92.

[3] See the review of the different approaches below.

[4] "Gewissheit der Erhörung" is commonly translated in English as "Certainty of a Hearing" (A. R. Johnson, "The Psalms", in *The Old Testament and Modern Study* [ed. H. H. Rowley; Oxford: Clarendon Press, 1951], 170; W. H. Bellinger, *Psalmody and Prophecy* [Sheffield: JSOT, 1984], 23). This phrase has become a technical term for the discussion of the sudden change of mood in the Psalms (D. E. Norton, "Translator's Note", in Walter Baumgartner, *Jeremiah's Poems of Lament* [trans. David E. Orton; Sheffield: Sheffield Academic Press, 1987], 7). D. E. Orton renders the term as "assurance of being heard" in his translation of Baumgartner's book. The other technical German term associated with the subject is "Stimmungsumschwung" ("sudden change of mood").

to lament even after a movement to praise and the alternating movement between lament and praise. It is these latter movements that have
yet to receive the attention they deserve. Thus far the focus has always
been on the movement *towards* praise; the movement *from* praise has not
yet been examined. As the following review of approaches reveals, the
whole discussion of the change of mood has been narrowly treated in
terms of the movement lament-praise.

1.2   Different Approaches to the Study of
Psalms with Change of Mood

1.2.1   *Introduction*

1.2.1.1   *Pre-20th Century Scholarship*

The subject of change of mood in the Psalms has been systematically examined in the 20th century. However, it should be noted that
scholarship prior to the 20th century was not lacking in its awareness
of the presence of the sudden change of mood.[5] Four decades before
Begrich popularised the term "Gewissheit der Erhörung", Maclaren
had already used the term "certainty of the answer", noting its 'suddenness'. In his comment on Psalm 6, Maclaren writes, "But even
while thus his spirit is bitterly burying itself in his sorrows the *sudden
certainty of the answer* to his prayer flashes on him".[6] Yet even centuries
before Maclaren, Saint Augustine already noticed the change in Psalm
6. He explains that the change between vv. 8 and 9 is a result of many
prayers and tears.[7] As will be seen later, this is similar to Heiler's view
on the change of mood.

   Calvin has more to say about the subject in his commentary on the
Psalms. I will just cite the most relevant ones. Calvin notices the presence of a change of mood in a number of psalms and provides different
explanations for the psalms where he sees this feature. For Psalm 6, he

---

[5] Since the focus of the present review is on the 20th century scholarship onwards,
treatment of the pre-20th century scholarship will be brief.
[6] Alexander Maclaren, *The Psalms* (vol. 1; The Expositor's Bible; London: Hodder
and Stoughton, 1893), 55, emphasis mine.
[7] Saint Augustine, *Expositions on the Book of Psalms* (vol. 1; Oxford: John Henry Parker;
F. and J. Rivington, 1847), 41.

believes that the change of mood is due to the fact that the psalm was written after the answer to the prayer has been received[8]—a view which would resurface in subsequent scholarship.[9] For Psalm 13, Calvin thinks that the situation of the psalmist has not yet changed, but something has already taken place within him. He writes, "Although the prophet feel [op. cit.] not as yet how much he has profited by praying, yet upon trust of deliverance conceived from God's promise, he sets the shield of hope against the temptations, with the terror whereof he might be stricken through".[10] Most significant for the present work is Calvin's comment in Psalm 3:8, where he observes a *return to petition*. He comments: "But forasmuch as *it is no novelty with David in his Psalms to mingle sundry affections together*, it seems more likely that after he has introduced the mention of his trust, he *returns again* to his former prayers".[11] This observation on the return to the element of lament ["former prayers"] after expressions of confidence is one that runs through some of his comments on the Psalms.[12] Interestingly, Luther expresses a similar view of the interaction between the elements of lament and praise in one of his writings. He affirms: "hope despairs, and yet despair hopes at the same time; and all that lives is 'the groaning that can be uttered,' wherewith the Holy Spirit makes intercession for us, brooding over the waters shrouded in darkness".[13] Unfortunately this important insight into the tension between despair and hope, especially Calvin's insight into the return to lament, was lost in most of subsequent scholarship.

---

[8] John Calvin, *A Commentary on the Psalms* (trans. A. Golding; London: James Clarke & Co. Ltd., 1965), 69; cf. 75.

[9] See below.

[10] Calvin, *A Commentary on the Psalms*, 143.

[11] Ibid., 49, emphasis mine.

[12] His comments to Psalm 62 reflect his willingness to accept tension even in the midst of expressions of certainty. On the apparent inconsistency between vv. 2 and 6, in which the psalmist first declares that his soul finds rest in God (2), only to command his soul yet again to find rest in God (6), Calvin explains: "Here it is to be remembered, that our minds can never be expected to reach such perfect composure as shall preclude every inward feeling of disquietude, but are at the best, as the sea before a light breeze, fluctuating sensibly, though not swollen into billows…[T]here is no reason to be surprised though David here calls upon himself a second time to preserve that silence before God, which he might already appear to have attained; for, amidst the disturbing motions of the flesh, *perfect composure is what we never reach*" (Calvin, *Commentary on the Book of Psalms* [vol. 2; trans. James Anderson; Edinburgh: Edinburgh Printing Co., 1846], 422–23, emphasis mine).

[13] Quoted in J. L. Mays, *The Lord Reigns: A Theological Handbook to the Psalms* (Louisville, KY: Westminster John Knox, 1994), 57. I have indicated above that Luther wrote this in "one of his writings" because in his comments elsewhere he does not seem to be as prepared to see the tension between lament and praise.

1.2.1.2   20th Century Scholarship

Much of Psalms scholarship in the 20th century was dominated by
Gunkel's Form Criticism which marks a major break from previous
approaches. Past scholars, like Augustine, Calvin and Luther and others like Delitzsch and Kirkpatrick view the Psalms as reflecting actual
historical accounts of the life of David. David is viewed as the author
of the psalms which bear his name and possibly others. The psalms
are used as spiritual reflections for the edification of the life of faith.
They are read from the perspectives of the life of Christ, the ministry,
the church, and the Christian life. This would eventually change with
the introduction of Gunkel's form-critical theory. After that, the focus
shifts to historical considerations of the setting in which the individual
psalms were originally employed. Specifically in connection with the
change of mood in the Psalms, the overarching concern became the
discovery of what took place behind the lament psalm. Scholarly interest lay in knowing what occurred in between the lament/petition part
of the lament and the expression of trust/praise.

1.2.1.3   Three Major Approaches

We may identify three main approaches to the subject of the change of
mood. The first tries to answer the question, "What *caused* the sudden
change of mood from lament to praise?" This was the overarching
question for most of 20th century scholarship on the subject of change
of mood.[14] The second main approach answers the question, "What
is the *function* of the sudden change of mood from lament to praise?"
The third approach attempts to offer fresh insights into the question of
the change of mood by looking into the *nature* of the movement from
lament to praise. In what follows we discuss each of these approaches
in more detail.

---

[14] The reason for the dominance of this approach is due to the influence of the
form-critical approach, which, as noted above, seeks to discover the setting behind the
transition to praise.

1.2.2   *The* Cause *of the Movement Lament-Praise*

Three of the often cited views that fall under the present approach
are the oracle of salvation, psychological view, and covenant renewal.

1.2.2.1   *Oracle of Salvation*

The theory that an oracle of salvation was the cause for the sudden
change of mood was already suggested by Balla (1912) and Küchler
(1918).[15] But it was Begrich who advanced this theory in a more definitive and explicit manner. Reacting to the tentativeness with which the
theory had been previously presented, Begrich asserts that an answer
to the problem posed by the sudden change of mood from lament to
praise in the individual lament psalms is attainable.[16] On the basis of
similarities between some passages in Isaiah[17] and individual lament
psalms, he explains that the former are actually borrowed from the
lament psalms. It is to be assumed that the oracle originally formed the
structure of the individual lament psalms which contain the change of
mood, as Psalms 12 and 60 illustrate.

However, there is some circularity in Begrich's whole thesis, as Raitt
observes.[18] For he has already assumed the presence of a salvation
oracle in the individual lament psalms without proving it first. The way
he proves this is by demonstrating the similarities between the oracles
in Isaiah and the language of the individual lament psalms. In spite
of the circularity of Begrich's argument, the oracle of salvation as an

---

[15] E. Balla, *Das Ich der Psalmen* (FRLANT 16; Göttingen: Vandenhoeck und Ruprecht,
1912), 14–26 and F. Küchler, "Das priesterliche Orakel in Israel und Juda", in *Abhandlungen zur semitische Religionskunde und Sprachwissenschaft* (BZAW 133; ed. W. Frankenberg
and F. Küchler; Giessen: A Töpelmann, 1918), 285–301. Balla thinks that an oracle
of salvation might have formed an original part of the structure of the lament (26).
Küchler attributes the change of mood in a number of psalms to an oracle of salvation (see esp. pp. 299–300).

[16] Begrich, "Das priesterliche Heilsorakel", 81.

[17] For the specific passages in Isaiah, see Begrich, 83.

[18] Raitt, *A Theology of Exile: Judgment/Deliverance in Jeremiah and Ezekiel* (Philadelphia:
Fortress Press, 1977), 154–55; cf. A. Szörényi, *Psalmen und Kult im Alten Testament* (Budapest: Sankt Stefans Gesellschaft, 1961), who criticises Begrich's proposal on the basis
of the absence of an actual oracle of salvation in the OT (see pp. 296, 303) and asks
that, if there is indeed such a salvation oracle, why is it only the message of deliverance
that is given and not a threat, which is the more common message of the prophets in
the OT. If the prophet can only preach deliverance, and if the answer from Yahweh
is always a 'yes', what need is there for a prophet? (p. 295).

explanation for the change of mood remained the most influential view for most of the 20th century.[19]

Interestingly, although Gunkel endorses Begrich's theory, he also acknowledges that this cannot carry the whole burden of explaining the 'Gewissheit der Erhörung': "Denn man muss sich darüber klar sein, dass das priesterliche Orakel nicht die vollständige Erklärung für die Gewissheit der Erhörung bilden kann".[20] Gunkel believes that in some cases the change of mood can be explained in terms of the following view of Heiler.[21]

1.2.2.2 *Psychological view*

Heiler's view represents the second major response to the question of what causes the sudden change of mood.[22] Whereas Begrich tries to locate the answer to the question of what causes the change of mood in a more 'objective' event that occurs 'outside' the person lamenting, Heiler seeks to explain the change in terms of what happens 'within' the person praying. The view looks at the psychological aspect of the question. Heiler explains that as one articulates and pours out one's heart to the Lord, a "wonderful metamorphosis" happens. Often, a sudden change of mood occurs. But there are times, especially in extreme lamentations, when "anxiety and hope alternate. The petitioner carries on an internal conflict between doubt and certainty, hesitation and assurance, until finally faith and trust break through with victorious

---

[19] For a list of scholars who support Begrich's thesis and corresponding bibliography, see W. H. Bellinger, *Psalmody and Prophecy* (Sheffield: JSOT, 1984), 115, n. 7; 117, n. 25 and Raitt, *A Theology of Exile*, 254, n. 7. Included in the list are Gunkel, Westermann, Mowinckel, von Rad, C. Barth, G. R. Driver, and P. Harner. For an assessment of the theory of Begrich in recent German scholarship see Gregor Etzelmüller, "Als Ich den Herrn suchte, antwortete er mir", *JBTh* 16 (2001), 400–4. Etzelmüller observes that in recent years there has been a move away from Begrich's theory but nonetheless defends the salvation oracle theory, since he sees no better alternative.

[20] Hermann Gunkel and Joachim Begrich, *Einleitung in die Psalmen: die Gattungen der religiösen Lyrik Israels* (Göttingen: Vandenhoeck & Ruprecht, 1933), 247, ET *Introduction to the Psalms: The Genres of the Religious Lyric of Israel* (trans. James D. Nogalski; Macon, GA: Mercer University Press, 1998), 183.

[21] Ibid. Gunkel quotes Heiler's explanation.

[22] Friedrich Heiler, *Das Gebet: Eine Religionsgeschichtliche und Religionspsychologische Untersuchung* (München: Ernst Reinhardt, 1921), ET *Prayer, A Study in the History and Psychology of Religion* (ed. and trans. Samuel McComb; London: Oxford University Press, 1932). For an extended review of Heiler's approach see Ee Kon Kim, *The Rapid Change of Mood in the Lament Psalms: A Matrix for the Establishment of a Psalm Theology* (Seoul: Korea Theological Study Institute, 1985), 126–44.

power".[23] Interestingly, Heiler has observed the important feature of an alternation between the element of lament and praise, though he did not cite specific examples of these in the Psalms. As will be shown in this study we have in the lament psalms an alternation between the two elements.

1.2.2.3 *Covenant renewal*

The third major response to the question of what caused the sudden change of mood is Weiser's theory of covenant renewal. Weiser does not treat all lament psalms containing change of mood under one category. Instead, he distinguishes between those with transitions in the future tense (Pss. 7:12f.; 27:6) and those where the experience of deliverance is set out in the past tense. The latter reflects the practice of preserving a copy of a psalmist's experience of suffering and restoration (see Ps. 102: "Let this be recorded for a generation to come…"). The former are connected with "traditional realization of salvation in the cult; here the personal hope of salvation is based on the actualisation of the communal salvation which represents the essential theme of the festival cult."[24] A more detailed exposition of Weiser's thesis is found in his comments to Psalm 9/10. According to him, the change of mood is to be attributed to the cult where a covenant renewal highlighting God's kingship and Heilsgeschichte is re-enacted. He sees Psalms 9 and 10 as parallel. In Psalm 9, the covenant re-enaction is in the background, emphasizing what Yahweh has done. The psalmist parallels this in Psalm 10 by bringing in his own personal concerns alongside the great acts of God in the covenant. This saves his pleading in Psalm 10 from aimlessness, for it is given in the spirit of the recounting of Yahweh's deeds in Psalm 9, giving him assurance that his prayer will be answered.[25]

---

[23] Heiler, *Das Gebet*, 380, ET *Prayer*, 260. See John Day, *Psalms* (OTG; Sheffield: JSOT Press, 1990), 30–32, who favours some kind of psychological explanation for the change of mood.

[24] Artur Weiser, *Die Psalmen I* (Göttingen: Vandenhoeck & Ruprecht, 1950), 47, ET *The Psalms* (vol. 1; trans. H. Hartwell; OTL; London: SCM, 1962), 80. For an extended discussion of Weiser's view, see Ee Kon Kim, *The Rapid Change of Mood in the Lament Psalms*, 144–56.

[25] Weiser, *Die Psalmen I*, 92ff., ET *The Psalms*, 149ff. For further discussion of Psalm 9/10 see Chapter 4.

Dissatisfied with the views of Begrich, Heiler, and Weiser, quite a few scholars have submitted their own solutions to the question of what caused the sudden change of mood. The sheer number of other proposals (at least seven) demonstrates the great interest in the subject as well as the difficulty or complexity of the question.

1.2.2.4 *Divine Name*

Wevers sees the key to the enigmatic transition from lament to praise in the use of the divine name.[26] By invoking the tetragrammaton, the psalmist gains confidence that his prayer will be answered or has already been answered. Such a view is possible because, in the prevailing culture in ancient times, knowledge or access to a name gives one power over the one known.

1.2.2.5 *Vow*

Cartledge proposes a solution similar to that of Wevers.[27] Instead of the name of Yahweh, he advances the idea that vows are a motivating factor on the part of the petitioner. The vow gives the psalmist the assurance that his prayer will be heard. This, according to Cartledge, explains the sudden shift of mood in the lament psalms.

1.2.2.6 *Asseveration by Thanksgiving*

Frost explains the change of mood through what he calls "asseveration by thanksgiving".[28] The idea is that if one wants to claim the certainty of something, one formulates it in terms of a thanksgiving. Finding such a feature in Psalm 118, the prophetic literature, and even in the Gospels, Frost applies the same to the lament psalms containing change of mood. In the latter case, he explains that "to follow a lament and prayer for help by an act of praise is in fact strongly to assert that such help will be forthcoming".[29] Frost argues that we do not have to look

---

[26] J. W. Wevers, "A Study in the Form Criticism of Individual Complaint Psalms", *VT* 6 (1956): 80–96.

[27] Tony W. Cartledge, "Conditional Vows in the Psalms of Lament: A New Approach to and Old Problem", in *The Listening Heart* (ed. Kenneth G. Hoglund et al.; Sheffield: JSOT, 1987), 77–94.

[28] S. B. Frost, "Asseveration by Thanksgiving", *VT* 8 (1958): 380–90.

[29] Ibid., 383.

elsewhere for a solution to the question of what caused the change of mood. "The act of praise is to be recognised as an original part of the psalm's structure. It is the anticipatory thanksgiving, and because it is asseverative in character, there is no need to predicate, as Gunkel was inclined to do, a cultic oracle of reassurance between the two parts of the psalm. Rather, the act of praise is itself just such an assertion of the certainty of divine aid, which a cultic oracle would have given".[30]

1.2.2.7   *Trust in the warrior God*

In his published dissertation entitled, *The Rapid Change of Mood in the Lament Psalms*, E. K. Kim provides quite an extensive review of the major views on the subject; namely those of Begrich, Heiler and Weiser.[31] Employing a traditio-historical approach, he asserts that the key to the question of what caused the shift of mood in the lament psalms can be found in the holy war tradition of Israel. Kim cites Psalm 3 in particular as an example. He points out that here we find war language in key places, immediately before the occurrence of the transition to confidence (vv. 3 and 8). He concludes that "it is a faith rooted in holy war tradition that carries the psalmist over the obstacles that have been deployed against him".[32]

Relevant to the present study is his critique of Begrich's oracle of salvation theory. Commenting on the last verse of Psalm 12, he writes: "We see in this verse evidence that even after a priestly oracle a complaint can occur".[33] Citing W. O. E. Oesterley, he goes on to say: "If there is a good explanation about the complaint after a salvation oracle, it must be that 'strangely enough,' the psalmist is not wholly reassured by the 'oracle'".[34] Significantly, in his discussions of the psalms that contain an oracle of salvation (Psalms 12, 60 and 89), he explains that the reason for the inclusion of the oracle is to "point out the contrast between the ancient oracle (the Davidic victories) and the present distress

---

[30] Ibid., 385.

[31] E. K. Kim, *The Rapid Change of Mood in the Lament Psalms*. See the summarised version of the main point of his dissertation in his article, "Holy War Ideology and the Rapid Shift of Mood in Psalm 3", *ASOR* (1999): 77–93. For an evaluation of Kim's work, see the review of P. D. Miller in *Int* 41 (1987): 88–89.

[32] Ibid., 89.

[33] Kim, *The Rapid Change of Mood in the Lament Psalms*, 124–5.

[34] Ibid., 125.

of the psalmist's own day".[35] In other words, the element of certainty is introduced to highlight the incongruity between the divine response and the present situation. This comment on the return to the element of lament even after an oracle is an important insight, absent from most of the comments on the subject of change of mood.[36] However, this important feature of the return to lament after the 'certainty of a hearing' is not the focus of Kim's study. His study is aimed at providing another explanation for the question of what caused the sudden change of mood from lament to praise. In Kim's view, the solution lies in the holy war tradition of Israel in which Yahweh is depicted as the divine warrior. Victory is certain with Yahweh on their side. It is faith in Yahweh the divine warrior which gives confidence to the psalmists. Kim points out that the language of the divine warrior can be found in the communal lament. He explains that Psalms 44:5b–10, 60:12–14 (= 108:12–14) "presuppose a similar situation of national distress in early times, and they seem to be precise counterparts of the victory hymns elsewhere in the Old Testament".[37]

But a critique similar to that which Kim made of Begrich's proposal can be made of his own thesis. For we may ask: if employment of the divine warrior language is what causes the change of mood, why is there no change of mood in most, if not all, of the communal laments? On the contrary, in the case of Psalm 44, the psalm ends in a very strong lament. When we come to the individual lament psalms with change of mood, his theory only works well in Psalm 3.[38] In Psalm 6 his theory is rather forced or at least the evidence is not as obvious as he supposes. As he himself admits, it is not clear whether the setting in Psalm 6 is a military one or not.[39] By positing only one possible setting for the change of mood he has inevitably limited the scope of his approach.

1.2.2.8 *Ḥesed*

Another attempt to explain the cause for the change of mood from lament to praise is Sung-Hun Lee's 1999 dissertation entitled, "The Concept of God's *Ḥesed* as an Explanatory Feature in the Shift to Praise

---

[35] Ibid., 126.
[36] Cf. my analysis of Jer 20:7–18 in Chapter 7.
[37] Kim, *The Rapid Change of Mood in the Lament Psalms*, 184–5.
[38] In Psalm 3, he believes that "the sudden change of mood...is strongly motivated by the holy war faith" (ibid., 191; cf. 194).
[39] Ibid., 213.

in the Individual Lament Psalms".[40] As indicated in the title of his work, Sung-Hun Lee believes that the cause for the change of mood in the lament psalms is God's *Hesed*.[41] In a recently published article Lee presents a summarised form of his dissertation where he explains the centrality of *Hesed* as the ground for restoration and thus the cause for the shift to praise in the lament psalms.[42] He notes in the beginning of the article that, "The present essay proposes an answer for the transition from lament to praise in the lament psalms, in the light of several previous attempts to do so".[43] Observing scholarly interest in the subject of change of mood, he notes the presence of change of mood in Psalm 57.[44] After briefly citing the views of Begrich and Weiser,[45] he begins to establish the centrality of *Hesed* in the Psalms. First, he discusses the two main senses of *Hesed* as conditional and unconditional.[46] Then he cites instances in the Psalms where the word *Hesed* is used to speak of God's deliverance. Unfortunately, most of the passages he mentions are not lament psalms containing lament and praise but thanksgiving psalms—Psalms 119, 106, 118, 107.[47] Where he finally discusses lament psalms, he does not explain clearly how the transition occurs in relation to *Hesed*. He mentions Psalms 6, 31, 69, 109 among the lament psalms, focusing on Psalm 130. His emphasis on the latter, however, is in showing the unconditional sense of *Hesed*. Again, he does not explain how *Hesed* causes the transition to praise. Overall, he does not address the main question he has set out to pursue in the beginning of his article.

The foregoing review thus far shows various attempts to provide an answer to the question of what caused the sudden change of mood. The focus is on the psalms which contain the movement lament-praise. A noticeable shift can be seen in the following approach of Beyerlin. Whilst the concern remains the explanation of the change of mood from

---

[40] Sung-Hun Lee, (PhD Diss.; University of Manchester, 1999).

[41] Lee focuses on the following which all contain the word חסד: Psalms 5, 13, 31, 59, 130 and 69.

[42] Sung-Hun Lee, "Lament and the Joy of Salvation in the Lament Psalms", in *The Book of Psalms: Composition and Reception* (eds. Peter Flint and P. D. Miller; Leiden: Brill, 2005), 224–47.

[43] Ibid., 225.

[44] Ibid., 224.

[45] Ibid., 224–26.

[46] Ibid., 226–32.

[47] Ibid., 234–36.

lament to praise, Beyerlin's study brings into discussion for the first time the lament psalms containing the reverse movement from thanksgiving to lament and those which alternate between lament and praise.

1.2.2.9   *Visualization of Salvation*

Beyerlin reiterates Frost's view on the function of the element of praise at the end of lament psalms as an "assertion of the certainty of the divine aid" and combines it with Wevers' conception of the ancient people's use of magical formulations as a way of securing the answer to their prayers.[48] Drawing on the ANE background, he brings forward what he calls "Heilsvergegenwärtigung".[49] By this he means the capacity of people in ancient times, particularly in Mesopotamia, to anticipate what the deity will do when they declare the deity's greatness and ability to accomplish that which the petitioner has in mind.[50] Accordingly, through the process of visualization of God's attributes reflected in the divine name and character, the praying individual is enabled to claim the deliverance sought even before the answer is received.[51]

What sets Beyerlin's approach apart from the preceding ones is its attempt to include the psalms which contain the other movements into the discussion of the change of mood. Noting that previous scholarship has focused only on those laments which begin with lament and end with praise, he argues that to classify all lament psalms under one category (from lament to praise) is dubious and requires further examination.[52] Further verification is needed in the case of those psalms which contain the elements in reverse order, with thanksgiving before lament (Psalms 9/10, 27 and 40) and those which alternate between lament and praise (Psalms 86 and 71).[53] In the case of the psalms which contain an element

---

[48] W. Beyerlin, "Die Tôda der Heilsverkündigung in den Klageliedern des Einzelner", *ZAW* 79 (1967): 208–24. For Frost and Wevers' views see above.

[49] "Visualization of salvation".

[50] Beyerlin, 211.

[51] Ibid.

[52] Beyerlin writes: "Nun soll ... keineswegs bestritten werden, dass das, was in den Klagepsalmen des Einzelnen an bekennendem Lobpreis laut oder für die Zukunft angekündigt wird, in sehr vielen Fällen die *Antwort* auf das barmherzig-rettende Eingreifen Gottes ist. . . . Dass aber im Sinne dieser Folge überhaupt *alle* alttestamentilichen Klageliedtexte, in denen Worte bekennenden Lobpreises laut werden, zu verstehen sein sollten, erscheint durchaus zweifelhaft und der Nachprüfung wert" (pp. 209–10).

[53] "Insbesondere erscheint eine Überprüfung dort angebracht, wo der Lobpreis im Klagelied nicht das letzte Wort behält, sondern entweder der klage vorausgeht (Ps 9–10, 27 und 40)" (Ibid., 210).

of thanksgiving before the lament, he proposes that we understand these as acts of "visualization of salvation". The "visualization of salvation" is expressed through the thanksgiving portion of the lament, functioning as a support to the lament. The thanksgiving serves as some sort of a condition or prerequisite for a "hearing" and deliverance.[54]

Beyerlin's observation concerning the lament psalms which contain the other movements is an important one. It marks a significant step forward in terms of the scholarship on the change of mood. In the past the tendency has been to subordinate all psalms containing change of mood under one explanation of what caused the change of mood. Beyerlin is open to the possibility that there is no single explanation for all the cases of change of mood. More significantly, he brings into the discussion of the change of mood the lament psalms which contain the other movements. Where his work is lacking is in the proper consideration of these psalms containing the opposite movement from praise to lament. Since his study remains focused on explaining the change of mood from lament to praise, the lament psalms which contain the other movements have not been properly considered. The element of tension reflected in the very construction of thanksgiving—lament has not been drawn out, since thanksgiving remains the central focus. For Beyerlin, the thanksgiving portion is employed in order to encourage the lamenting individual.[55]

1.2.2.10   *Lament as Thanksgiving*

In a more recent article by H. G. M. Williamson, the lament psalms with the reverse movement thanksgiving—lament briefly resurface. Entitling his article "Reading the Lament Psalms Backwards", Williamson attempts to provide fresh insights for the present discussion.[56] Though not purely form-critical, his approach can be situated within the bounds of Form Criticism, for its concern remains the setting of the psalms concerned. The major difference is that whereas all the preceding enquiries cited above presuppose a lament setting, Williamson argues that the psalms containing change of mood actually arise from a situation when the petitioner has already received the answer to his/her

---

[54] Ibid., 220.
[55] Ibid.
[56] H. G. M. Williamson, "Reading the Lament Psalms Backwards", in *A God So Near: Essays on Old Testament Theology in Honor of Patrick D. Miller* (eds. Brent A. Strawn and Nancy R. Bowen; Winona Lake: Eisenbrauns, 2003), 3–15.

prayers.[57] We do not have to account for the sudden change of mood because the situation is already resolved. Williamson's proposal is that we read these psalms "backwards"; i.e., 'from their end'. By this he means reading the psalm from the standpoint of one who has already experienced the answer. The logical conclusion that follows is that these psalms belong not to the category of lament but to the thanksgiving psalms.[58] These lament psalms are actually composed for the purpose of thanksgiving. Consequently, we have more thanksgiving psalms than lament psalms.[59]

To support his argument, Williamson employs two non-lament psalms—Psalms 2 and 23. These psalms illustrate that the psalms become clearer when they are read from their 'end'.[60] Another passage he employs is Isa 38:10–20 which, in his view, is an example of a lament written after Hezekiah was healed, as the historical information intimates.[61] Moreover, he points out that "in both thanksgivings and laments the order in which the principal elements occur is also less stable than some textbooks imply".[62] Thanksgiving can appear before the lament (Psalms 9–10, 40). Praise and lament can alternate (Psalm 59). And there can be a return to lament even after the move to praise (Psalm 86).[63]

Like Beyerlin, Williamson has here mentioned the important feature of the reverse and alternating movements between lament and praise. Unfortunately, like Beyerlin also, he does not explain the significance of these and their implication for the whole sudden change of mood theory. Williamson does not focus on the psalms which contain the reverse movement from praise to lament and the return to lament. He only cites these to support his argument on reading the lament psalms which move from lament to praise from the situation of thanksgiving. It is not clear though how this advances his thesis. If anything, it in fact demonstrates the complexity of the relationship between the elements

---

[57] As noted above, a similar view had already been anticipated by Calvin.

[58] His idea had already been anticipated by James F. Ross, "Job 33:14–30: The Phenomenology of Lament", *JBL* 94 (1975): 38–46. Ross holds that the "psalms of lament are really another form of the psalms of thanksgiving" (45). Cf. Weiser, *Die Psalmen I*, 42, ET *The Psalms*, 70 and A. A. Anderson, *The Book of Psalms* (vol. 1; NCB; London: Oliphants, 1972), 38.

[59] Williamson, "Reading the Lament Psalms Backwards", 11.

[60] Ibid., 7–8.

[61] Ibid., 8–9.

[62] Ibid., 12.

[63] Ibid.

of lament and praise. For if we are to follow his argument—i.e. reading the psalms from their end—we would have to view the psalms which end in lament like Psalms 9/10 and 40 as arising from the setting of lament, not thanksgiving.

Williamson devotes a section in which he attempts to provide some guidelines for the application of the lament psalms in worship. He makes a distinction between "pure laments" (e.g. Psalm 88), communal laments and those laments which contain in their end an element of praise.[64] His explanation implies that the first two belong to the category of lament; the last one to thanksgiving. He explains that one application of his analysis for church worship is that personal laments should not be practised in communal worship for they belong to the realm of the private. He writes, "Individual lament…appears generally not to have been given liturgical voice. It remained private, individual: 'In my distress I cried to the Lord.' Where it became the property of the congregation's liturgy, however, was subsequently in the context of testimony leading to worship".[65] It is not clear which "individual lament" he is referring to here, whether the "pure" lament psalms or those containing both lament and praise. Certainly it is not the communal lament, since he acknowledges the place of these in the public domain.[66] He seems to be referring to the "pure" lament psalms. One is not to utilise these in the public worship. Where it would be appropriate in such a context is when the resolution has already come, such as we find in those psalms which move to praise.[67] Then it would be 'acceptable' since they can be testimonies to God's greatness. To locate the psalms which move to praise within the situation of lament would be "unrealistic". He asserts: "there is something unrealistic, even faintly ludicrous (or macabre), about the suggestion that the suffering psalmist could give voice to the kind of optimistic sentiments that we find in many of the assurances of a hearing".[68]

---

[64] It is not clear under which category he would place those psalms which contain thanksgiving before the lament and those which alternate between lament and praise.

[65] Williamson, 14–15.

[66] Ibid., 5.

[67] Williamson's view is similar to Gunkel: "it would have been quite natural for the poor suffering persons to pour out their personal pain before their God in the stillness of their own little room. By contrast, the thanksgiving songs by their very nature belong to a public setting so that the one who was delivered should give honor to God before all the world" (Gunkel, *Einleitung*, 284, ET *Introduction to the Psalms*, 214).

[68] Williamson, 6.

Williamson's approach demonstrates that the issue of the change of mood has important implications for lament. How one understands the change of mood influences how one views lament, including its practice. Those who view the sudden change of mood only in terms of the movement lament-praise will tend to emphasize the element of praise. Since lament is always understood as moving towards praise, lament comes to be regarded simply as something preliminary to praise.[69] Williamson's study which transfers these lament psalms into the setting of thanksgiving cements this emphasis on the element of praise and mutes the voice of lament. If one were to follow his suggestion, one would have to read the lament portions of the lament psalms simply as background material, the reading of which would be merely perfunctory. But the problem with this view is that, as John Day stresses, the lament portion forms "by far the largest part of the psalms, so that they are naturally understood as lament psalms".[70] Indeed, the lament can be read quite as naturally within the setting of suffering. Reading them from the setting of thanksgiving may eliminate the incongruity and tension brought about by the bringing together of the lament and praise elements in one psalm. But in the process the elements of tension and ambiguity which form the core of the lament psalms is sacrificed. When lament is removed from the setting of lament and transferred to the situation of praise, lament recedes to the background. The result is a theology which inevitably focuses only on praise, such as we find in the following approach.

1.2.3   *The* Function *of the Movement Lament-Praise*

Whereas the previous approaches try to answer the question of what caused the sudden change of mood from lament to praise, the following two approaches try to highlight the *function* of the change of mood.

1.2.3.1   *The Theology of the Movement Lament-Praise*

The first approach is by Brueggemann. But in order to understand what Brueggemann has to say on the subject of change of mood one has to go back to Westermann. We provide a sketch of Westermann's view.

---

[69] See the Conclusion.
[70] John Day, *Psalms* (Sheffield: JSOT, 1990), 30.

Westermann strongly endorses Begrich's theory on the oracle of salvation.[71] But his interest on the subject of lament is much broader than the issue of what caused the sudden change of mood. Lament, for Westermann, represents one of the two main genres in the Psalms. He declares: "In my years of work on the Old Testament, particularly on the Psalms, it has become increasingly clear to me that the literary categories of Psalms of lament and Psalms of praise are not only two distinct categories among others, but that they are the literary forms which characterize the Psalter as a whole, related as they are as polar opposites".[72] Highlighting the importance of lament in the Psalms, he writes: "it is an illusion to suppose...that there could be a relationship with God in which there was only praise and never lamentation".[73] He explains that the "cry to God [lament] is always somewhere in the middle between petition and praise".[74]

In his overall view, however, Westermann sees lament as important only in relation to praise. Although he sees lament as "somewhere in the middle between petition and praise", his view is that lament is "always *underway*...to praise".[75] He boldly claims: "There is not a single psalm of lament that stops with lamentation. *Lamentation has no meaning in and of itself*".[76] Lamentation should be read in the context of God's salvific acts. "The goal of the transition...is the praise of God. This is indicated primarily by the fact that the psalm of lament concludes with

---

[71] Claus Westermann, *Lob und Klage in den Psalmen* (5., erw. Aufl.; Gottingen: Vandenhoeck und Ruprecht, 1977), 51, ET *Praise and Lament in the Psalms* (trans. Keith R. Crim and Richard N. Soulen; Edinburgh: T&T Clark, 1981), 65 comments on the work of Begrich: "The conclusions of this work are so clear and convincing...Accordingly, as far as the lament of the individual is concerned we must reckon in every case with the possibility that the content is not only the lament and petition of the one who comes before God...but in some instances it is to be assumed that an oracle of salvation was given in the *midst* of the Psalm and that the Psalm also includes the words that follow the giving of the oracle". It should be noted that for Westermann it is not always the case that an oracle is responsible for the change of mood; he just says "in some instances".

[72] Westermann, *Lob und Klage in den Psalmen*, 5, ET *Praise and Lament in the Psalms*, 11, emphasis mine.

[73] Claus Westermann, "The Role of Lament in the Theology of the Old Testament", *Int* 28 (1974), 27.

[74] Westermann, *Lob und Klage*, 56, ET *Praise and Lament*, 75.

[75] Ibid., emphasis mine.

[76] Westermann, "The Role of Lament in the Theology of the Old Testament", 26, emphasis mine. To his claim that there is no lament psalm that ends in lament, we may point to Psalm 88, which is a "pure lament" (For a study on Psalm 88, see Juliane Schlegel, *Psalm 88 als Prüfstein der Exegeses: Zu Sinn und Bedeutung eines beispiellosen Psalms* (Biblische-Theologische Studien 72; Neukirchen-Vluyn: Neukirchener Verlag, 2005).

a vow of praise".[77] Westermann's observation that there is no lament that does not move to praise leads him to conclude that in fact in the Psalms we do not have a "preponderance of Psalms of petition" as earlier taught by Gunkel.[78] What we have rather is a preponderance of praise: "It is no longer possible to speak of an absolute predominance of petition and lament. Rather, precisely this group of heard petitions becomes a powerful witness to the experience of God's intervention, intervention that is able to awaken in the one lamenting, while his sorrow is materially unchanged, the jubilant praise of the God who has heard the suppliant and come down to him".[79]

Building on Westermann's work, Brueggemann seeks to develop a theology of the movement from lament to praise. Brueggemann does not seek to solve the question of what caused the sudden change of mood from lament to praise. This, according to him, is impossible to know.[80] What is more important is the fact that a transition from lament to praise has occurred and what this says/implies about God. Brueggemann tries to emphasize the theological function of the sudden change of mood. Accordingly, the transition to praise points to the God who answers prayers and who is able to deliver his people from their troubles. The movement from lament to praise is programmatic; Israel's history is a witness to the fact that Yahweh saves and delivers. "The people of Israel perceived their entire existence in the form of petition and thanks. They were aware of distress, but more aware of Yahweh's powerful deliverance".[81] From Israel's experience of the Exodus to the exile, "Israel's history is shaped and interpreted as an experience of cry and rescue".[82] The pattern of movement from lament to praise that we see in the Psalms points back to the God who has delivered Israel throughout all her distress. Thus, the movement that we see in the lament psalms is nothing new and should be expected: lament always turns to praise.

Brueggemann develops this idea further in his book, *The Message of the Psalms*, where he presents his grid of the cycle, orientation—disori-

---

[77] Ibid., 27.
[78] Westermann, *Lob und Klage*, 60, ET *Praise and Lament*, 80.
[79] Ibid., 60, ET 81.
[80] Walter Brueggemann, "From Hurt to Joy, from Death to Life", in *The Psalms and the Life of Faith* (ed. P. D. Miller; MN: Fortress Press, 1985), 72 [Original publication in *Int* 28 (1974): 3–19].
[81] Ibid., 77.
[82] Ibid., 82.

entation—new orientation. He explains that the "life of faith expressed in the Psalms is focused on the two decisive moves of faith that are always *underway*, by which we are regularly surprised and which we regularly resist".[83] Brueggemann's use of the word "underway" recalls Westermann's work on the lament with its assumption that lament *always* moves to praise. The same tendency to emphasize the element of praise over lament can be seen in Brueggemann's work.

As can be observed, an emphasis on the movement lament-praise can actually lead to a tendency to overemphasize the element of praise. Ironically, although Westermann tries to highlight both lament and praise, in the end we find him emphasizing the element of praise over lament as a result of his focus on the movement lament-praise. Likewise, Brueggemann's overall understanding of the movement from lament to praise leads to a lessening of the importance of lament.[84] Thus, although the movement lament-praise is crucial for it "cuts to the heart of the theological issue for faith"[85], it is important that we carefully scrutinize the movements between lament and praise. We need to ask: Is the movement only from lament to praise?

Response from Goldingay

In an important response to an earlier article by Brueggemann[86] on the movement to praise in the Psalms, Goldingay argues that the movement between lament and praise is more dynamic than Brueggemann has presented it. Goldingay explains that the movement between lament and praise is not always from petition/lament to praise; it could also be from praise to lament/petition. Initially he uses the image of a

---

[83] Walter Brueggemann, *The Message of the Psalms* (Minneapolis: Augsburg Publishing House, 1984), 20, emphasis mine. Here Brueggemann talks about the two movements of faith from orientation to disorientation and from disorientation to new orientation.

[84] For further discussion, see Conclusion.

[85] Brueggemann, "From Hurt to Joy, From Death to Life", 8. The movement lament-praise reflects a theology of deliverance, which is crucial for those who may be going through difficult situations. At such times they can be sure that the God who has delivered them in the past is able to do the same in their present situation. However, a one-sided emphasis on the 'God who delivers' actually presents a theology which is concerned only with certainty and never with ambiguity, resolution and never with tension. What makes the lament psalms particularly relevant is the fact that they are able to present the element of tension and struggle which is very much a part of human experience. For further discussion on this, see below.

[86] Walter Brueggemann, "Psalms and the Life of Faith: A Suggested Typology of Function", *JSOT* 17 (1980): 3–32. This article forms the background for Brueggemann's book, *The Message of the Psalms*.

circle to describe the movement. But he thinks that the spiral metaphor captures the idea better. Comparing the movements between lament and praise to what is commonly known as the "hermeneutical circle", Goldingay writes: "[T]he true hermeneutical circle is really more a spiral. A question provokes an answer, but the answer provokes a different question, and thus another answer, and yet another question, as we move towards the eschatological goal of understanding a text and having no more questions".[87] If I may add here, the image reminds us of the story of Abraham. Having finally reached the Promised Land, the narrator nevertheless writes, "At that time the Canaanites and the Perizzites live in the land" (Gen 13:7b). Even when we think we have already received the answer, we still do not have everything. Or, as Goldingay implies, the answer is actually another question.

Goldingay has here presented what I think is a very important insight on the dynamic movement between the elements of lament and praise.[88] As will be shown in this study the movement between lament and praise is not one-directional but interactive. The direction is not only towards 'certainty' but also towards 'uncertainty'. However, Goldingay's treatment of the subject is general and brief.[89] There is a need to test this idea of a more dynamic movement between lament and praise through actual analysis of psalms.

---

[87] John Goldingay, "The Dynamic Cycle of Praise and Prayer", *JSOT* 20 (1981), 88. Goldingay is here reacting to Brueggemann's article, "Psalms and the Life of Faith: A Suggested Typology of Function", *JSOT* 17 (1980): 3–32.

[88] Unfortunately, Brueggemann did not properly consider this important insight by Goldingay, as can be observed in Brueggemann's book, *The Message of the Psalms*. Influenced to a great extent by the form-critical framework of the movement lament-praise, Brueggemann focuses on the movement towards praise as reflected in his grid, orientation—disorientation—new orientation. Even when he admits in the introduction of his book that "life is in fact more spontaneous" than the one he depicted in his grid, the overall effect of his framework is towards resolution. Reading his book, one gets the impression that the movement is *always* from lament to praise.

[89] Goldingay does not provide an actual analysis of psalms to illustrate his point; understandably so because of the limitations of his article. In his recent commentary on the Psalms (John Goldingay, *Psalms: Psalms 1–41* [vol. 1; Baker Commentary on the Old Testament Wisdom and Psalms; Grand Rapids, MI: Baker Academic, 2006]) he is more open than other scholars to seeing the dynamic movements between lament and praise. I have cited his comments in my analysis of the relevant psalms below. But Goldingay does not actually develop the thesis he introduced earlier in his article, "The Dynamic Cycle of Praise and Prayer". One can only do so much in a commentary.

1.2.3.2 *Function of the Movement Lament-Praise for the Reader*

This next approach by J. G. McConville takes the theology of the lament psalms further by bringing into the picture the reader/worshipper. McConville explains that the key to understanding the transition from lament to joy lies not in the study of the original setting of the psalms but in their function in worship.[90] The primary focus is not on the original composer but on the reader. For McConville the important question is not how the transition occurs but why there is such a transition. Psalms of lament that move to praise function as some form of an encouragement. The key word, according to him is "remember". Through these psalms the reader is reminded of the God who delivers/saves and consequently is helped in the transition from struggle to faith. In a sense, the psalms of lament are like an inspiring 'mini-sermon' for the suffering person, reminding him of the realities of God's power reflected in the shift from lament to praise. McConville clarifies: "Here is a theology for the Psalms of lament. Their function is to draw the worshipper back to those settled convictions which are his, despite the challenges to them presented by circumstances and his own inconstancy".[91]

One contribution of this article is its focus on the reader/worshipper. Whereas the previous approaches have sought to discover the specific historical event 'behind the text' that might have triggered the turn to praise, McConville tries to focus on the effect of the transition to praise on the reader. The work by Erbele-Küster further explores to a greater extent the role of the psalms for the reader or person praying them (see below).

1.2.4 *The Nature of the Change of Mood*

The most recent approaches seek to advance the research by attacking the very foundation of the whole thesis of 'certainty of a hearing'. The works of B. Janowski (2001), B. Weber (2005) and especially by D. Erbele-Küster (2001) provide new insights into the whole discussion

---

[90] McConville, "Statements of Assurance in Psalms of Lament", *IBS* 8 (April 1986): 64–75.
[91] McConville, 73.

of change of mood. These studies look more closely into the interaction between the elements of lament and praise.

1.2.4.1   *Transition to Praise as a Process*

Although not entirely denying the presence of a movement from lament to praise, Janowski criticizes Begrich's thesis because it assumes that the transition from lament to praise is 'sudden'.[92] He does not like the term, 'Stimmungsumschwung' ['change of mood'], which has become popular along with the term 'certainty of a hearing' for explaining the change of mood. Focusing on Psalms 22 and 13, Janowski explains that what we have in these psalms is not a 'sudden' transition but a process. This view, according to him, has much to offer to pastoral theology since resolution to one's suffering may come after days, weeks, months and even years.[93] However, although Janowski's work has important implications for pastoral theology, it remains focused on 'resolution'; there is nothing on continuing lament or the preservation of the element of tension. The following approach by Weber seeks to highlight the element of tension between lament and praise.

1.2.4.2   *Tension Preserved even with the Transition to Praise*

Whereas Janowski still maintains the presence of a movement from lament to praise, Weber seeks to bring out the tension between the elements of lament and praise.[94] Using Psalm 13 as a model, Weber tries to illustrate the persistence of 'tension' between the elements of lament and praise in the first parts (1–5) and concluding section (6) of the psalm, respectively. Like Janowski, he criticizes the use of the term, 'Stimmungsumschwung', especially the qualifications, 'sudden' and 'abrupt', because according to him these do not represent what we actually find in the text.[95] But he is not satisfied with Janowski's explanation either. Weber explains that an 'easy' and simple explanation of

---

[92] Bernd Janowski, "Das verborgene Angesicht Gottes: Psalm 13 als Muster eines Klagelieds des Einzelnen", *JBTh* 16 (2001): 25–53.

[93] Ibid., 52.

[94] Beat Weber, "Zum sogenannten 'Stimmungsumschwung' in Psalm 13", in *The Book of Psalms: Composition and Reception* (eds. P. W. Flint and P. D. Miller; Leiden: Brill, 2005), 116–38. Weber builds on the work of Erbele-Küster (see below).

[95] Weber, 116, n. 1, only maintains the term 'Stimmungsumschwung' because it has been the traditional term.

the movement from lament to praise is no longer acceptable.[96] This is because "Klage und Bitte sind mit Vertrauensäusserung und Lob im selben Psalm vereint".[97] We find in Psalm 13 a certain 'simultaneity' which characterises the tension. We are not to read this lament linearly, but keep the elements together, holding them in tension.[98] Weber's emphasis on the tension between lament and praise opens the door for the other movements in the psalms. But as Weber himself admits, his work is limited to Psalm 13 and therefore has to be supplemented.[99]

By highlighting the element of tension even in the psalms which move from lament to praise, Weber's work provides a fresh approach to the question of the change of mood from lament to praise. This represents a clear attempt to move away from the more resolution-oriented approach of Begrich and others. As I will demonstrate in this study, it is possible to see the element of tension preserved even in the psalms which move from lament to praise.[100] The problem with Weber's approach is the tendency to overemphasize the element of tension in passages where there is clearly a movement towards praise.[101] The insight into the presence of the element of tension in the lament psalms is an essential corrective to the 'praise-oriented' approaches, characteristic of previous scholarship. But it is also equally wrong-headed to silence the voice of praise, especially in the lament psalms where there is a clear movement from lament to praise. I think Weber's idea of 'tension' or lack of resolution is better expressed by those psalms which move from thanksgiving/praise to lament and especially the psalms which contain a return to the element of lament even after the movement to praise. Similarly, Janowski's idea of a 'process' of movement from lament to praise is best illustrated in those psalms which alternate between lament and praise, for here one encounters the interesting series of fluctuations between lament and praise.

---

[96] Weber, 135.

[97] Ibid.

[98] Cf. Craig C. Broyles, *The Conflict of Faith and Experience in the Psalms: A Form-Critical and Theological Study* (JSOTSup 52; Sheffield: JSOT Press, 1989), 186–7, who presents a similar point.

[99] Weber, 120.

[100] See especially the discussion of Psalm 3 below.

[101] This tendency can also be seen in the work of Ottmar Fuchs, *Die Klage als Gebet: Eine theologische Besinnung am Beispiel des Psalms 22* (Munich: Kösel Verlag, 1982). For more discussion, see Chapter 3.

1.2.4.3   *'Leerstellen' and the importance of uncertainty*

Though not focused solely on the issue of the sudden change of mood, for the scope is much broader than that, Erbele-Küster's book is very important for the present study.[102] Employing the literary theories of Wolfgang Iser, Hans Robert Jauss and reader response as articulated by Stanley Fish, Erbele-Küster attempts to bring together the historically-oriented critical approaches and aesthetic reading of the Psalms. A remarkable shift in this study is the emphasis on the element of 'uncertainty'. Whereas past scholarship, dominated mostly by the form-critical approach, has always tried to pin down the one, exact setting behind the Psalms, Erbele-Küster's approach is not only appreciative of the element of uncertainty in texts but even sees this as central for the fulfilment of the function of the text—the transformation of the reader. The gaps—which are referred to as "Leerstellen"—provide windows through which the reader can take part in the formulation of meaning. The "Offenheit innerhalb der Textstruckturen der Psalmen in der Beschreibung der Notsituation und die offene Bittstruktur",[103] which enables the texts to be applied in ever fresh situations—these she calls "Leerstellen". Applying the literary and reader response insights Erbele-Küster identifies the places where one might find the Leerstellen and explains how these contribute towards a richer understanding of the Psalms. Her application of the theories is broader than the concern of the present study.[104] I will focus on those which are relevant to the issue of the sudden change of mood.

Erbele-Küster provides a critique of the previous approaches to the change of mood, especially the one by Begrich, and makes her own proposal for understanding this feature. She explains that the sudden change of mood from lament to praise represents a Leerstelle which cannot be fully filled.[105] Unfortunately, scholars are uncomfortable with uncertainties and ambiguities so they try to resolve this by focusing on the sudden change of mood and its possible cause/s.[106] Against this

---

[102] Dorothea Erbele-Küster, *Lesen als Akt der Betens* (WMANT 87; Neukirchen-Vluyn: Neukirchener, 2001).

[103] Ibid., 141.

[104] She discusses Leerstellen in the superscriptions (pp. 54–76), related narrative sections in the historical books (pp. 76–77), those reflected in the reception of the LXX and Qumran (pp. 86–107). She also talks about Leerstellen in terms of the cause of the suffering in Psalms 7, 35 and 6 (pp. 149ff.).

[105] Ibid., 161–2.

[106] Ibid., 161.

trend Erbele-Küster asserts that the element of tension between lament and praise should be preserved.[107] She finds neither Begrich's theory of an oracle of salvation nor the psychological explanation satisfactory. The problem with the latter is that it irons out the element of tension.[108] Against the former she argues that we find no basis for the presence of a salvation oracle in the Psalms.[109] Like Janowski and Weber, she finds the term 'sudden' misleading, for it implies that there is something irrational taking place.[110] For Erbele-Küster the key lies in the Psalm text itself: "Die Psalmen zeichnen einen unabgesschlossenen Prozess nach, in dessen Verlauf dem Beter durch Erkenntnisgewinn neue Erfahrungsräume eröffnet werden und er so eine veränderte Perspektive auf sich selbst und seine Welt erhält".[111] A study of the passages containing the transition to praise reveals that the issue is best explained in terms of a gaining of realisation (Erkenntnis)—realisation/discovery of the fate of the enemy, discovery of God and the receiving of the gift of speech. These, Erbele-Küster explains, are the "three triggering elements for the certainty of a hearing".[112]

Even more relevant to my work, her treatment of the psalms is not limited only to those psalms which contain the element of 'certainty of a hearing'. Arising out of her emphasis on the element of uncertainty, Erbele-Küster was able to highlight the psalms which do not contain the certainty of a hearing or which retain the element of uncertainty in spite of the certainty of a hearing. Although overlooked in most studies of the Psalms Erbele-Küster underlines the fact that we have psalms where the "petition has the last word" (Psalms 20, 25, 27, 28,

---

[107] Ibid., 162. Here she follows Fuchs, *Klage als Gebet*.

[108] Ibid., 162.

[109] Ibid., 161.

[110] Ibid.

[111] Ibid.

[112] Ibid. The discovery that God is on the side of the psalmist enables him to move on to certainty (e.g. Psalm 6; cf. Psalms 27 and 56) (pp. 163–7). For the 'discovery of God' Erbele-Küster cites Psalm 17 as an example: "Die Theophanie enthält cognitive wie sinnliche Momente und ist konstitutiver Bestandteil der Erhörungsgewissheit" (p. 168). For the third one, she explains that Stimmungsumschwung is a gift of speech and a realisation. God is the source of praise. The language of praise comes from him. In the act of praising the prayer receives a gift. As he/she declares the words of the praise a change occurs in the whole perspective of self, the world and God (see pp. 173–7). Ironically, although Erbele-Küster has criticised the other attempts to 'fill in' the 'Leerstelle', she has here actually tried to do some 'filling in' of the gap. But whereas others seek to base their explanation on events 'behind the text', she bases her explanation on the text itself.

31, 38, 39, 40 and 70).[113] This strongly contradicts the usual form-critical understanding of the structure of the lament and represents a Leerstelle.[114] In Psalm 70 in particular, where one would expect a vow of praise after the positive statement in v. 5, the psalm ended on a negative note. "Das w-adversativum des letzten Verses (6a) leitet nicht, wie erwartet, das Lobgelübde ein, sondern stellt den Frohlockenden aus v. 5 kontrastiv entgegen".[115] More significantly, Psalm 70 is joined to a thanksgiving psalm in Psalm 40. This, according to Erbele-Küster, forms another Leerstelle, which implies that even in the experience of the 'certainty of a hearing' one may still lament. Citing Spieckermann she writes: "Hinter 'der Integration ungestillter Klage in den Dank für die Rettung [steht] der theologische Gedanke, dass der Beter in Erhörungsgewissheit klagen darf' ".[116] Instead of finding the sequence, thanksgiving—lament problematic, as some form critics do, she was able to draw an important insight that stems from this: "Die eigentümliche Abfolge von erneuten Bitten und Klagen auf ein Danklied, wie sie in Ps 40 vorliegt, ist in der den Psalmen impliziten Anthropologie begründet, dass menschliche Gewissheit nie völlig eingeholt wird und immer offen ist auf Gottes sich gnädig zuwendende Gegewart hin".[117] This element of uncertainty and tension can also be seen in Psalms 12 and 38.[118]

Erbele-Küster's work, especially on the emphasis on the element of uncertainty, marks a significant development in the discussion of the subject of change of mood in the psalms. Her discussion of the psalms containing the element of thanksgiving/praise before the lament is relevant to my work. But her treatment of these passages is brief and not focused on the issue of change of mood. Psalms 27 and 40, which both have the element of thanksgiving followed by lament/petition, are

---

[113] Ibid., 152. She also mentions Psalms 12, 39 and 88 as psalms containing a Leerstelle at the end of the psalm (155).

[114] Ibid., 152.

[115] Ibid., 153.

[116] Ibid., 154.

[117] Ibid.

[118] Ibid., 155, 157. Psalm 38 is very similar to Psalm 88. Although Erbele-Küster does not explicitly say this, her discussion of Psalm 39 shows similarity to Psalm 88 in terms of its bleak ending. One of the interesting features of this psalm is its almost insulting petition at the end of the psalm (vv. 13–14). Whilst the presence of God is the aim/goal or that which the psalmist longs for in the lament psalms (expressed in the negative petition: "Do not hide your face from me" in Ps 27:9; 69:18; 102:3; 143:7 [156, n. 60]), here in Psalm 39 it is viewed as something threatening: "Das Angesicht Gottes, das der Beter gewöhnlich voller Senhsucht sucht, wird als bedrohlich erfahren" (Erbele-Küster, 156).

discussed only briefly. She uses the latter to explain both the element of uncertainty even in the midst of thanksgiving[119] and the transition from lament to praise.[120] I find this contradictory. I do not think Psalm 40 is the best text to explain the change of mood from lament to praise. Her discussion of Psalm 27 is very brief and since she is using this to explain the change of mood from lament to praise as well, the important return to petition in v. 7 even after the vow of praise in v. 6 has not been properly accounted for.[121] In the end, she does not focus on the movement from praise to lament. But this is understandable since this is not the focus of her study.

1.3 Gap in Scholarship

The foregoing survey of scholarship on the change of mood demonstrates that there remains no study which focuses on the lament psalms containing the movements *from praise to lament*. Although not escaping the notice of a few scholars,[122] the other movements in the Psalms have not been treated in any serious scholarly discussion. The whole discussion of the sudden change of mood thus far has presupposed that the change of mood is only from lament to praise.[123] The main question that scholars have sought to answer is: "what caused the sudden change of mood *from lament to praise*?" Even with the approaches which try to highlight the "function" of the change of mood and look into the "nature" of this phenomenon, the assumption remains that the change of mood is from lament to praise. Though not the concern of this study, it is revealing that there remains no study which tries to

---

[119] Ibid., 154.

[120] Ibid., 174.

[121] Ibid., see 166, in which she discusses the change of mood in terms of a process of realisation. Such realisation—expressed in the words, 'now I know'—reflects an actual experience in the life of the prayer. She does not see a return to the element of lament in Psalm 27 even with the renewed petition, since the "power relations" has already shifted in favour of the individual praying as v. 6 intimates. She writes: "Auch wenn der Beter in erneute eindringliche Bitten einstimmt, haben sich die Machtverhältnisse zugunsten des Beters gewendet: Sein Haupt erhebt sich über die Feinde" (166).

[122] See Beyerlin and especially Erbele-Küster above.

[123] Even though Weber tries to highlight the element of tension between lament and praise, he is still using a psalm which contains a movement from lament to praise. As noted above, although Erbele-Küster mentions the psalms which end in an element of lament and which contain the element of thanksgiving before the lament, the subject of change of mood is not the focus of her study.

answer the question "what caused the sudden change of mood *from praise to lament?*" Indeed, there appears to be a stubborn bent, especially among Western scholars, to impose the one-way linear movement lament-praise on every psalm where the two elements are present. Some would even go to great lengths, including changing the text and the order of a psalm just to fit them into their framework.[124] As an Asian scholar[125] approaching this subject, I cannot help but be surprised by the failure among Western scholars to see that *praise can also return to lament*. Probably the resolution-oriented, scientific and linear way of thinking which characterise many Western approaches has led to the failure to see the other movements in the Psalms. Specifically in connection with the sudden change of mood, the linear, one-way understanding of the movement from lament to praise has influenced most of the approaches on the subject. Dominated by the form-critical approach, the emphasis one-sidedly lay on the element of certainty and resolution. As noted at the beginning, the very term that has come to be linked with the whole discussion of the sudden change of mood— "Gewissheit der Erhörung"—betrays the assumption that the sudden change of mood is only from lament to praise; lament is *always expected* to move towards praise.

But is the movement only from lament to praise? Is the sudden change of mood only from lament to praise?

1.4   My Thesis

In this study I seek to demonstrate that laments are also capable of moving, and do in fact move, from praise to lament. There is in the Psalms not only 'certainty of a hearing'; we also have what I call the '*un*certainty of a hearing'.[126] Whilst not neglecting the movement lament-praise, the present work seeks to highlight the other movements in the psalms. Specifically, I seek to draw attention to the psalms[127] which:

---

[124] See the detailed analysis of Psalms 9/10 and 12 below, Chapters 4 and 5, respectively.

[125] I come from Manila (Philippines).

[126] The phrase 'uncertainty of hearing' seems to have been anticipated by Fuchs when he used the phrase, 'Nicht-Erhörung' (Fuchs, *Die Klage Als Gebet*, 154). But Fuchs' approach differs from the present study (see Chapter 3).

[127] For the specific criteria for the selection of the psalms for consideration, see Chapter 2.

- Juxtapose praise and lament, with the lament preceded by thanksgiving (Psalms 9/10, 27, 40; cf. 89)
- Move from lament to praise but then return to lament (Psalms 12 and 28)
- Alternate between lament and praise (Psalms 31 and 35; cf. 71 and 86)

Two passages outside the Psalms—Jer 20:7–18 and Lamentations 3—are also included in the study to demonstrate that the features noted above are not limited to the Psalms. I have chosen these two passages because they contain movements between lament and praise similar to what we find in the psalms I will be focusing on.[128] The psalms containing the movement lament-praise will also be discussed to affirm the presence, indeed the dominance of such a movement in the Psalms and to serve as the basis for comparison with the other movements. Specifically, the following psalms will be examined—Psalms 3, 6, 13 and 22. The last one—Psalm 22—represents an important stage in the analysis of the psalms with change of mood. It serves as a bridge between the lament psalms which move from lament to praise and those which move in the opposite direction or juxtapose between thanksgiving and lament. But the overall emphasis of the present study is on those individual lament psalms which contain the other movements.

1.5   METHODOLOGY

1.5.1   *Form Criticism*

The starting point for the present study is the form-critical framework since the whole sudden change of mood discussion stems from this methodology. My own use of the term 'lament' and 'individual lament' indicates an acknowledgment of the importance of this method for my research. Scholars generally recognise the validity of Gunkel's categories of the Psalms, though they may not agree with some of his

---

[128] For a discussion into what guided me in my choice of the passages in Jeremiah 20 and Lamentations 3, see the introduction to these passages in Chapters 7 and 8, respectively.

presuppositions.[129] However, although form criticism as a method has dominated much of the 20th century, it has come under serious attacks from many quarters in the last decades because of problems with the method itself when it comes to interpretation of the text.[130] Form criticism's attempt to determine the specific social/worship setting behind the words of the psalms has not always been successful. The sheer number of proposals as to what caused the change of mood from lament to praise demonstrates the weakness of this approach. The language of the Psalms, which by nature is metaphorical and poetic, ultimately rejects attempts to subject its words to serious historical inquiry. Gillingham explains that because of the creativity and poetic freedom exercised by those who composed the psalms, it is impossible to know the worship setting based on the study of the forms of the structure: "more often than not, poetic freedom allows the contents to dictate the form, and hence a move from analysis of form to a proposal of some particular cultic setting is impossible."[131] Historical questions posed to the text not only do injustice to the poetic nature of the psalms; they also lead to a limited appropriation of the psalms.[132] Thus, for instance, in the case of the question of the identity of the enemies in the Psalms, Miller explains: "Should one determine that most of the evildoers are sorcerers or false accusers, then the laments to some degree become capable of being appropriated only by those who are in a comparable situation, that is, being faced with sorcerers or false accusers."[133] In the same way, by identifying the specific cause of the change of mood, we actually limit the application of the psalms.[134]

---

[129] Ernest Lucas, *Exploring the Old Testament: The Psalms and Wisdom Literature* (vol. 3; London: SPCK, 2003), 1–2.

[130] See James Muilenburg, "Beyond Form Criticism", *JBL* 88 (1969): 1–18; Paul G. Mosca, "Psalm 26: Poetic Structure and the Form-Critical Task," *CBQ* 47 (1985): 212–37; David Greenwood, "Rhetorical Criticism and Formgeschichte: Some Methodological Considerations," *JBL* 89 (1970): 418–20, who cites 6 weaknesses of form criticism as a method, and Donald Berry, *The Psalms and their Readers* (Sheffield: JSOT Press, 1993), 140–41. For an in-depth analysis and critique of Form Criticism see Rolf Knierim, "Old Testament Form Criticism Reconsidered," *Int* 27 (1973): 435–68. For a recent evaluation of Gunkel's method from a canonical approach perspective, see Erich Zenger, "Von der Psalmenexegese zur Psalterexegese", *BibKir* 56 (2001): 8–11.

[131] S. E. Gillingham, *The Poems and Psalms of the Hebrew Bible* (Oxford: Oxford University Press, 1994), 224.

[132] Patrick D. Miller, Jr, "Trouble and Woe: Interpreting the Biblical Laments", *Int* 37 (1983): 32–45.

[133] Ibid., 35.

[134] Thus, for instance, if we follow Kim's argument that the cause of the change of mood is the use of the war language of the Divine warrior we actually limit the

A more serious problem with the form-critical method is the tendency to impose one framework on all the related psalms. Arising out of the preoccupation with that which is generic and typical,[135] form criticism tries to subsume texts under one common framework. Thus, in the case of the lament psalms, the one-way movement from lament to praise is applied to all the related psalms. Intriguingly, whilst they acknowledge that "there is no fixed order" for the occurrence of the elements in the individual lament psalms,[136] in the case of the lament-praise movement this has not been observed. The tendency has been to impose a one-way, linear movement from lament to praise. The overall direction of the structure of the lament, as understood by form critics, is towards the vow of praise or hymnic elements, towards resolution—away from the lament. It seems all right for the other components to occur in any order, except the elements of complaint/petition and thanksgiving/praise. For thanksgiving and complaint to occur in the reverse order—that confounds the form critic. Millard admits that "während die Formgeschichte die Umwendung des Klageliedes in ein Lob–bzw. Danklied in ihr formgeschichtliches Schema hat integrieren können, fehlt eine solche Integration der umgekehrten Wende von der Hohen Stimmung in die Klage".[137] Petition is logical only if it comes before the thanksgiving. To have petition/complaint after expressions of thanksgiving—that does not make sense.[138] Thus, Gunkel is surprised to find the lament after

---

application of the psalms to military or war situations. The same thing can be said of the oracle of salvation theory. We would have to expect a cultic prophet/priest to intervene to facilitate the change of mood. This would not work during the exile where the temple no longer exists.

[135] Muilenburg, "Beyond Form Criticism", 5.

[136] E. S. Gerstenberger, "Psalms", in *Old Testament Form Criticism* (ed. John Hayes; San Antonio: Trinity University Press, 1974), 200. The following are the common elements of the structure of an individual lament: invocation, complaint, petition, condemnation of enemies/imprecation, affirmation of confidence, confession of sins/assertion of innocence, vow of praise/thanksgiving and hymnic elements, blessings (cf. Ernest Lucas, *Exploring the Old Testament*, 3).

[137] Matthias Millard, *Die Komposition des Psalters: Eine formgeschichtlicher Ansatz* (Tübingen: J. C. B. Mohr, 1994), 58. He cites the following psalms as belonging to those which contain a shift from praise to lament: Psalm 9, 19, 27, 31, 40, 89, 90, 94, 108, 118, 119, 144 (pp. 58–59). Although he mentions these psalms he does not focus his discussion on the issue of the change of mood from praise to lament.

[138] See in particular the comment of Wilhelm Rudolph, *Das Buch Ruth. Das Hohe Lied. Die Klagelieder. Die Klagelieder* (vol. 27 [1–3]; KAT; Gütersloh: Gütersloher Verlagshaus, 1962), 236 and the discussion of Lamentations 3 in Chapter 8.

thanksgiving in Psalm 9/10.[139] Zenger observes that Gunkel would even change the text just so it would fit its Gattung.[140]

Such a tendency to change a text spills over to form criticism's uneasiness with the present form of the text, especially when it does not conform to the general form-critical framework. In the case of the psalms which contain thanksgiving in the first part followed by a lament/petition, the tendency has been to view these automatically as composite. This can be seen in the way Psalm 27 has often been discussed. The psalm is interpreted as consisting of two originally independent compositions brought together at some point. The two parts of the psalm are interpreted separately but there is generally no attempt to understand the sense of the text in its present form.[141] Moreover, since the focus is on the individual psalm, the question of the relationship of the psalm to its neighbouring context is never addressed in form criticism. Any possible purposeful ordering of the psalms is generally ignored.

1.5.2   *Canonical Approach*

1.5.2.1   *Introduction*

It is on this aspect of the present form of the text and the consideration of its present order and shape that the canonical method seeks to focus. Where form criticism has failed, the canonical approach attempts to remedy through its focus on the extant text and the present shape of the Psalter within the context of a worshipping community. Initiated by Childs, the canonical method:

> focuses its attention on the final form of the text itself. It seeks neither to use the text merely as a source for other information obtained by means of an oblique reading, nor to reconstruct a history of religious development. Rather, it treats the literature in its own integrity. Its concern is not to establish a history of Hebrew literature in general, but to study the features of this peculiar set of religious texts in relation to their usage within the historical community of ancient Israel.[142]

---

[139] See analysis of Psalm 9/10 in Chapter 4.

[140] Zenger, "Von der Psalmenexegese zur Psalterexegese", 10. He cites the following psalms as examples: Psalms 39, 63, 67, 81, 87 and 90.

[141] See the analysis of Psalm 27 in Chapter 4.

[142] Brevard S. Childs, *Introduction to the Old Testament as Scripture* (Philadelphia: Fortress Press, 1979), 73.

The canonical approach in terms of its application to the Psalms is still in its development phase.[143] Introduced by G. H. Wilson to Psalms research in 1985 through his published thesis (*The Editing of the Hebrew Psalter*)[144] under Childs, the canonical approach as a method for studying the Psalms has quickly gained a wider following.[145] As a method, it considers the overall shape of the Psalter and focuses on the final form of the text.[146] Individual psalms are viewed as individual pieces of work.[147] But unlike form criticism, the psalms are generally read in their present and final form and are interpreted in the light of their neighbouring context.[148] Further, the titles or superscriptions play an important role in the interpretation as these provide windows into how the final editor/s of the Psalter understood or applied the psalms. The very act of application reflected in the psalm titles intimates a direction from within the text itself pointing to further reception and application of the psalms. I think this is one important advantage of the method; it brings the reader back into the picture. Whereas form criticism removed the Psalms from ordinary use; the canonical approach seeks to bring it back to the community in which the Psalter was used for many generations. In addition to the context of the Psalter, the canonical approach may also consider the wider context of the Old Testament as well as that of the New Testament.[149]

In this study I attempt to employ some of the insights of the canonical approach to analyse the feature of the change of mood in the Psalter. To my knowledge no one has yet examined the feature of the *return*

---

[143] Lucas, *Exploring the Old Testament: The Psalms and Wisdom Literature*, 34. As the title of Gordon Wenham's article signifies, "Towards a Canonical Reading of the Psalms" (Paper presented in Rome, 2005), the method is still in the process of being established.

[144] Gerald H. Wilson, *The Editing of the Hebrew Psalter* (Chico: Scholars Press, 1985).

[145] Jean-Marie Auwers, *La Composition Littéraire du Psautier: Un État de la Question* (Paris: Gabalda, 2000), 6; cf. Wenham, "Towards a Canonical Reading of the Psalms", 2.

[146] For what follows, see Childs, *Introduction to the Old Testament as Scripture*, 511–22; Erich Zenger, "Was wird anders bei Kanonischer Psalmenauslegung?" in *Ein Gott, Eine Offenbarung: Beiträge zur biblischen Exegese, Theologie und Spiritualität. Festschrift für Notker Füglister* (ed. Friedrich V. Reiterer; Würzburg: Echter Verlag, 1991; cf. Erich Zenger, "Von der Psalmenexegese zur Psalterexegese".

[147] Erich Zenger, "Von der Psalmenexegese zur Psalterexegese", 11.

[148] It should be noted that there are variations in the way the canonical method has been practised. Some canonical critics, e.g., Childs and Zenger combine final form study with detailed diachronic analysis.

[149] At present, there remains no clear guideline for the specific application of the method. Scholars differ as to what to include in the study. See Wenham, "Towards a Canonical Reading of the Psalms".

to lament in the Psalms, let alone used a canonical approach to this issue. Whilst Brueggemann and quite a few others have noted the significance of the beginning and end of the Psalter as well as the overall movement from lament to praise within the Psalter, one has yet to see a study which scrutinizes the interplay between lament and praise in the in-between parts of the Psalter.

1.5.2.2   *Brueggemann's Application of Canonical Insights*

Brueggemann's article "Bounded by Obedience and Praise: The Psalms as Canon"[150] looks into the overall shape of the Psalter from a theological perspective. Specifically, it tries to explain the movement from lament to praise in the whole Psalter from a theological point of view. The advantage of this approach is that it gives us a broader perspective through which the question of the shift from lament to praise can be viewed. Following the works of Childs and Wilson, Brueggemann argues that the beginning and end of the psalm is significant and may have been placed there deliberately for a purpose. The beginning and end of the Psalter defines Israel's faith as a movement from obedience to praise. The beginning (Psalm 1) presents the life of the righteous as secure. The ending of the Psalter (Psalm 150) describes the life of the righteous as marked by praise.[151] Thus, the overall movement in the Psalter is from obedience to praise: those who live according to the demands of the Law will inevitably 'end in praise'.

But how does one move from obedience to praise?

Brueggemann explains that the way is not smooth sailing but one which is marked by much difficulty on the one hand and hope on the other. Brueggemann picks up two Psalms—Psalms 25 and 103—which express "candor" and hope, respectively. Though chosen rather arbitrarily,[152] Psalms 25 and 103 represent the various voices that we hear between the beginning and end of the Psalter. First, it is characterised by complaining. Though not in any way denying the truth declared in Psalm 1, the reality of life lived in the in-between

---

[150] Walter Brueggemann, "Bounded by Obedience and Praise: The Psalms as Canon", *JSOT* 50 (1991): 63–92.

[151] Such praise is analogous to the faith exemplified by the friends of Daniel, who decided that they would remain true to Yahweh even if he did not deliver them: Psalm 150 "expresses a lyrical self-abandonment, an utter yielding of self, without vested interest, calculation, desire, or hidden agenda" (ibid., 67).

[152] Ibid., 203, n. 25.

reflects tension and poses a challenge to the view expressed in Psalm 1. Interestingly, Brueggemann tries to relate Psalm 1 and Psalm 25 in a dynamic, interactive fashion, with the latter actively challenging the claims of the former. Although it is difficult to establish the interaction between the two psalms on a direct verbal connection, Brueggemann has here hinted at the tension-filled interaction between Psalm 1 and the laments that follow. In this study, I attempt to demonstrate a more explicit interaction between Psalm 35 and Psalm 1.[153]

Brueggemann continues that the life of faith is not only character-ised by difficulty and struggle. Surprisingly, the psalmist meets God's *Ḥesed*, as expressed in Psalm 103. As to how one moves from complaint to a deeper sense of God's *Ḥesed*, Psalm 73 points the way. This psalm serves as a bridge between Psalm 25 and 103: "This one Psalm is a powerful paradigm for Israel's often-enacted journey from obedience though trouble to praise. The speaker has traversed, as Israel regularly traverses, the path from obedience to praise, by way of protest, candor, and communion".[154] Accordingly, as one expresses his/her complaints before Yahweh, one encounters Yahweh himself, who in turn brings the individual to a renewed sense of belief that what matters is not material possession but presence and communion.[155]

Interestingly, although Brueggemann is himself not a self-professing canonical critic, his particular application of the method yields signifi-cant insights for the present study. It provides an outline of the overall movement in the Psalter. The overall shape of the Psalter is marked by the two boundaries of obedience and praise. This supplies a help-ful guide for a canonical study of the movements between lament and praise. Ultimately, the tension that is at the very heart of the lament psalms, especially those which contain a reverse movement from praise to lament, has to be interpreted in the light of the overall movement in the Psalter: towards praise. The overall movement of the life of faith is towards praise. The boundary markers—obedience and praise—are important.

But as Brueggemann reminds us towards the end of his article, Israel lives most of her life in the in-between, in "the heart of the Psalter" where lament and hope are sounded continually: "It is in the heart of

---

[153] See discussions of Psalm 35 in Chapter 6.
[154] Brueggemann, "Bounded by Obedience and Praise", 88.
[155] Ibid., 86.

the Psalter, not at its extreme edges of simple obedience and guileless doxology, where Israel mostly lives".[156] He continues: "The God of Israel's Psalter does not live safely at the two boundaries of obedience and praise. This God is situated in the heart of the Psalter, in the midst of Israel's suffering and Israel's hope".[157] Unfortunately, having emphasized the importance of "the heart of the Psalter" Brueggemann's article was content simply to describe the overall movement in the Psalter. The middle section, "the heart of the Psalter", is not given the treatment it deserves.

It is into "the heart of the Psalter" that the present work seeks to enter. Without losing sight of the overall movement towards praise, the present work highlights the 'in between' parts of the Psalter, for it is somewhere 'in the middle' that the life of faith is mostly lived. As Balentine aptly remarks:

> [T]he possibilities of what may happen in the future can never fully offset the agony of despair and uncertainty which characterize life 'in the meanwhile'... [T]he hope for future restoration, while it may be a source of confidence that things will eventually turn out for the better, is continually checked by the frustration of having to endure the present circumstance. This is life 'in the meanwhile': life lived in the period between what has happened in the past and what is hoped for in the future. This is the position of the supplicant in the lament about God's hiddenness. He senses the experience so keenly precisely because he knows that God has not always been hidden in the past; his petition for divine intervention frames his hope that God will not always be hidden in the future. But in the meanwhile he can only wait and endure and plead, 'how long O Lord?' In a real sense the significance of the shift from lament to praise cannot be fully appreciated until the uncertainty of the struggle which precedes it is given proper attention.[158]

Thus it is important that we pay close attention to the voices from within "the heart of the Psalter", for it is so easy to focus only on the overall shape of the Psalter to the neglect of the important details in between. So dominant is the form-critical framework of a one-way movement from lament to praise along with its resulting tendency to emphasize praise over lament, it spills over even into canonical approaches to the Psalter. One may discern this tendency in the canonical approach to the Psalms by Hossfeld and Zenger who write in the introduction of their commentary: "The title 'book of praises' for the Psalms is

---

[156] Ibid., 213.
[157] Ibid.
[158] Balentine, *The Hidden God*, 166–67.

appropriate even though there are more lament psalms than praise psalms". This is because "even the sharpest accusation against God is itself divine praise, because it clings fast to God and continues to seek God (even while accusing), at a time when everything seems to speak against God".[159] Though their statement is not directly made in connection to the form-critical assumption of the one-way movement from lament to praise, such a remark reflects the form-critical tendency to over-emphasize the element of praise over lament. One can actually hear echoes of Westermann in their comment. Thus, whilst there is an important element of truth in what Hossfeld and Zenger are saying, it has the potential of lessening the value of lament.[160]

1.5.2.3 *Whybray's Critique of the Canonical Approach*

Interestingly, Whybray, the first British scholar to write a book-length critique of the canonical approach, also uses the form-critical view of the lament-praise movement as one of his main arguments. Whilst he sees more potential in Brueggemann's theological reading of the movement towards praise, he finds unconvincing the more detailed applications of the method represented in the work of Wilson.[161]

Wilson's thesis, followed by others, is that there is a deliberate and purposeful editing of the Psalter. Accordingly, a careful reading of the "Royal" psalms at the "seams" of Books I–III betrays the work of an editorial hand.[162] Here one may trace the 'story' line of the Davidic kingship from its initiation through Yahweh's covenant (Psalm 2), assurance of "continued preservation in the presence of Yahweh" (Psalm 41),[163] extension to David's descendants (Psalm 72) and finally, at the conclusion of the third book, the failure of the covenant (Psalm 89). In Wilson's argument Psalm 89 occupies a prominent place, for it chronicles in agonising fashion the failure of the Davidic kingship, to which Book IV—the "editorial 'center' of the final form of the Hebrew

---

[159] Frank-Lothar Hossfeld and Erich Zenger, *Psalms 2* (trans. Linda M. Maloney; Hermeneia; Minneapolis: Fortress Press, 2005), 1.

[160] For further discussion of Hossfeld's and Zenger's view on the relationship between lament and praise, see the canonical discussions in Psalm 9/10 (Chapter 4) and Psalm 12 (Chapter 5).

[161] Norman Whybray, *Reading the Psalms as a Book* (JSOTSup 222; Sheffield: Sheffield Academic Press, 1996), 121–22.

[162] Wilson, *The Editing of the Hebrew Psalter*, 207, sees a major separation between Books I–III and IV–V.

[163] Ibid., 210.

Psalter"—forms an "answer".[164] Significantly, Psalm 89 is constructed not in the usual lament-praise pattern, but moves from hymn to communal lament. What is striking about Wilson's use of Psalm 89 is how the reverse movement from praise to lament plays a crucial role in his whole thesis. If Wilson's theory is right that the first three books of the Psalter have been edited to chronicle the failure of the Davidic kingdom, then we have in Psalm 89 an example of the use of the pattern of the reverse movement as a way of expressing a sense of failure, tension and uncertainty.[165] Wilson rightly sees depicted in Psalm 89 a strong element of tragedy: "At the conclusion of the third book...the impression left is one of a covenant remembered, but a covenant *failed*. The Davidic covenant introduced in Ps 2 has come to nothing and the combination of three books concludes with the anguished cry of the Davidic descendants".[166]

Whybray basically rejects Wilson's overall thesis. On Wilson's use of Psalm 89 as a basis for his argument, Whybray asserts that Psalm 89 does not "document the failure of the Davidic monarchy".[167] This is because laments are not actually lament but are always filled with hope. He explains:

> It is important to bear in mind that *laments in the Psalter...are not expressions of despair*. However much the psalmists may accuse God of breaking his word and becoming an enemy, hope always remains that intercession will be effective: hence the characteristic 'How long?'...Even in apparently hopeless circumstances...the psalmists continued to hope. So here in Psalm 89 the psalmist urges God not to forget the promises that he has made that the Davidic dynasty would be forever (vv. 5, 22, 29, 30) and stresses his faithfulness in passages to which he gives such prominence that they cannot have been intended merely as foils for the account which follows of disillusion and consequent loss of faith.[168]

---

[164] Ibid., 215. With Book V Wilson finds difficulty in relating a major bulk of it to the earlier emphasis on Davidic covenant. It is only in Psalms 145–146 where there is a return to this theme (see pp. 220–28).

[165] I have observed earlier that there remains no study which tries to answer the question of what caused the sudden change of mood *from praise to lament*. Could it be that one occasion for this reverse shift of mood is the deep sense of tragedy felt by the poet/s arising from their corporate experience of failure as expressed in Psalm 89? Later, in the discussion of Jer 20:7–18, I come back to this question of the possible occasion or cause for the reverse movement from praise to lament.

[166] Ibid., 213.

[167] Whybray, *Reading the Psalms as a Book*, 93.

[168] Ibid., 93–4, emphasis mine. Whybray's remarks that "laments in the Psalter...are not expressions of despair" represent the general view of lament—a view which almost disregards the value of lament.

It is striking how Psalm 89—a psalm which contains the reverse movement from praise to lament—finds itself at the centre of the canonical
discussions of the Psalter. As will be shown in this study, such a pattern
of a return to lament after praise is not confined to Psalm 89, having
been preceded by Psalms 9/10, 27 and 40. This pattern is also found
in passages outside the Psalter—Jer 20:7–18 and Lamentations 3.[169]
Unfortunately, even where we have a clear movement from *praise to
lament* as in the case of Psalm 89, the *lament-praise* framework continues
to command supremacy. Not subjected to a careful critical scrutiny, this
framework pervades much of Psalms scholarship—both among those
who try to advance a canonical reading and those who attack such an
approach. In this present work I hope to provide a stimulus through
which the scholarship on the sudden change of mood, which hitherto
has been approached mainly in terms of the movement lament-praise,
may be properly evaluated. In the process, it is hoped that a broader
perspective which takes into account the various movements in the
Psalter may be provided.

1.6   PLAN OF THE BOOK

Using the form-critical framework of the one-way movement from
lament to praise as a starting point, I employ relevant insights from the
canonical method to examine the subject of change of mood in the
Psalter.[170] Specifically, I focus on the psalms which contain the reverse
movement from praise/thanksgiving to lament, return to lament even
after the movement to praise and alternate between the two elements.[171]
I highlight these other movements as a necessary corrective to the one-
sided emphasis on the movement to praise. It is not the purpose of
this study to provide an alternative thesis for the editing of the Psalter,
though the movement lament-praise and the alternation between the
two elements may be an attractive idea and may have been possibly one
of the organising principles used by the editor/s. I will not be tracing
the development of the change of mood throughout the Psalter. Rather,
I employ relevant insights from the canonical approach to emphasize

---

[169] See Chapters 7 and 8, respectively.
[170] At present, there remains no clear guideline for the specific application of the
method (Wenham, "Towards a Canonical Reading of the Psalms"). Scholars differ as
to what to include in the study.
[171] For the specific psalms under each of these three categories, see above.

the element of lament in the Psalter. The role of the superscription/
title for the analysis of the psalms will be considered only in Psalm 3,
since it is only here that we find a biographical element among the
psalms to be examined; the rest simply have "A psalm of David" or
simply "Of David". I have limited the scope of my study to Book I of
the Psalter because it is here where we find most of the psalms which
contain change of mood. Outside the Psalter, I only cite passages from
Jeremiah and Lamentations, since my goal is not to try to trace the
topic at hand throughout the rest of the Old Testament.

Specifically, the present work:

1. Affirms that the overall movement in the Psalter is from lament to
   praise (see discussions above) through the study of representative
   psalms which contain the movement lament-praise.
2. Focuses on the present form of the text. Where a psalm exhibits the
   presence of two originally independent compositions, the focus will
   be on the text as we now have it. Discussions about various scholars'
   perspectives on the composition of the psalm will be provided. But
   the focus is on the overall sense of the present form of the text.
3. Provides an analysis of the relevant psalms. This includes:
   a. textual notes[172]
   b. a brief introduction, discussing relevant issues about the psalm
   c. structural analysis
   d. detailed analysis, focussing on the interaction between the ele-
      ments of lament and praise
   e. summary/conclusion
4. Seeks to discern possible connections with neighbouring psalms to
   see how these contribute towards a richer understanding of the
   text. There is no attempt to provide discussions on the context of
   neighbouring psalms for each of the psalms. This will be provided
   at particular parts of the book in a summarised form. The neighbouring contexts will be considered only as they shed light on the
   interplay between lament and praise in the psalm/s being studied.
   Where possible, connections and interplay between psalms, not

---

[172] For the textual notes only the ones which have a direct bearing on the interpretation of the psalms are included.

necessarily close to each other, will also be considered (e.g. Psalms 1 and 35; see below).

5. Explores relevant materials outside the Psalms, specifically in Jeremiah and Lamentations.

In the following chapter (Chapter 2) I examine representative psalms containing the movement lament-praise. This serves as a backdrop for the discussions of the other movements in the rest of the book. Chapter 3, which focuses on Psalm 22, forms an important bridge between the psalms which move from lament to praise and those which contain the other movements. The juxtaposition between lament and praise in Psalm 22 prepares us for the juxtaposition between the two elements in Psalms 9/10, 27 and 40—the focus of Chapter 4.

Chapter 5 highlights two psalms—Psalms 12 and 28—which contain a return to lament despite a movement to praise. Chapter 6, which focuses on Psalms 31 and 35, demonstrates that the movement to praise is not a one-time event but may involve a series of swinging back and forth between lament and praise. Chapters 7 and 8 are explorations of the features found in the previous chapters (Chapters 2–5) outside the Psalter, specifically in Jeremiah and Lamentations—two books which show affinities with the lament psalms. Finally, a summary and conclusion of the overall thesis is provided at the end.

CHAPTER TWO

FROM LAMENT TO PRAISE

2.1 INTRODUCTION

In the previous chapter, we have seen how the subject of the sudden change of mood has come to be viewed narrowly in terms of the movement lament-praise; thus, the need for a study which highlights the other movements. At the same time, I have registered my observation that there is also a tendency in recent works on the subject to deny that there is a movement to praise.[1] Whilst the main focus of the present study is on the other movements, one has to be careful not to over-emphasize these movements to the neglect of the important movement lament-praise. As will be seen below (Table 2), this movement is the most common in the individual lament psalms. It is thus important that we include this movement in our analysis, both to affirm that there is indeed a movement from lament to praise and to provide us with the necessary background for the consideration of the other movements.

In this chapter, we come to the actual analysis of the psalms, beginning with representative psalms which contain the movement lament-praise. But before that, it is necessary first to establish our criteria for the selection of the psalms to be considered in this chapter and for the rest of the book. As will be seen in the overview of scholars' views of which psalms contain a change of mood (see Table 1), the task of identifying the relevant psalms is not as easy as it may seem.

2.1.1 *Criteria for the Selection of the Psalms*

As can be observed below, scholars differ in their list of which psalms contain a change of mood. In most cases we are not sure whether they are giving us an exhaustive list of what they think should belong to this

---

[1] See the previous chapter and the discussion of Psalm 13 below.

Table 1: *Lament Psalms with a Change of Mood as Identified by Various Scholars**

Psalm	AJ	BA	CB	CW	EK	HG	HK	HZ	JD	JE	SF	WB	Total
3	x	x		x	x	x		x			x	x	8
4		x											1
5					x	x					x		3
6	x		x	x	x	x	x	x	x	x	x	x	11
7					x	x			x				3
10		x		x	x								3
12					x							x	2
13	x		x	x	x	x	x		x	x			8
14												x	1
16										x			1
17					x								1
20						x							1
22		x	x				x	x					4
26		x			x								2
27				x	x					x		x	4
28		x	x	x	x			x	x			x	7
30		x					x						2
31	x	x	x	x	x	x	x		x				8
35	x				x	x							3
36	x							x			x		3
41		x					x						2
51											x		1
52						x			x				2
54			x	x			x			x			4
55	x		x		x	x	x		x		x	x	8
56		x	x	x	x	x	x		x	x			8
57					x				x				2
58					x								1
59					x					x			2
60					x							x	2
61		x			x	x	x		x				5
63	x	x					x				x		4
64		x	x	x	x		x						5
69		x			x		x			x			4
71		x			x	x	x						4
79					x								1
80												x	1
86	x		x		x	x	x						5
94			x				x		x				3
102			x				x						2
126												x	1
130			x		x	x			x				4
140	x				x	x			x		x		5
Total	10	8	19	11	26	16	19	4	13	8	8	10	

* Scholars

AJ = A. R. Johnson	EK = Ee Kon Kim	JD = J. Day
BA= W. Baumgartner	HG = H. Gunkel	JE = J. Eaton
CB = Christoph Barth	HK = H.-J. Kraus	SF = S. B. Frost
CW = C. Westermann	HZ = Hossfeld and Zenger	WB = W. Bellinger

category.[2] The overriding principle for the selection is the movement towards praise.[3] Since the understanding of the concept of change of mood is limited in terms of the movement lament-praise, the psalms containing other movements are not properly accounted for. So for example, Psalms 9 and 40, which clearly contain a change of mood, albeit from thanksgiving to lament, were not included in the list.[4] Psalm 12, a psalm which contains a divine oracle, only receives two points. In view of the popularity of Begrich's theory on the oracle of salvation for explaining the change of mood, it is striking that Psalm 12 does not feature prominently in the list of psalms with change of mood. This is probably because this psalm is considered by many as a communal lament. But more likely, this is because Psalm 12 does not end on a positive note.[5] As will be shown in our analysis of Psalm 12, scholars expect a lament to end on a positive note, so that a negative ending will be deemed as anticlimax, if not unacceptable.

Finally, in some cases the identification of the psalms is influenced by the particular scholar's view as to what caused the sudden change of mood. Thus, it is important that one is aware of a scholar's perspective on the issue of change of mood when reading his/her own list of psalms.

2.1.2   *My Own Criteria for the Selection of the Psalms*

My own perspective in this study is not limited by the lament-praise framework. Rather, I try to approach the subject of change of mood with the aim of showing that we do not only have *one* movement in the Psalter but several. The change of mood is not only from lament to

---

[2] John Day, *Psalms* (OTG; Sheffield: JSOT Press, 1990), 30. John Day admits that in his own listing he was not sure whether he was intending it to be 100% complete (personal correspondence, 15 April 2005). Gunkel does not provide a list of what he considers are psalms with 'certainty of a hearing' or change of mood. One has to go to his commentary (*Die Psalmen*) and his *Einleitung* to gather the 'scattered' information. Seybold did not have his own list of psalms with change of mood, which is why he is not included in the list above (Table 1).

[3] Christoph F. Barth, *Introduction to the Psalms* (trans. R. A. Wilson; Oxford: Basil Blackwell, 1966), 17; Westermann, *Lob und Klage*, 60, ET *Praise and Lament*, 80, remarks concerning the psalms he selected that these are "*no longer mere lament, but lament that has been turned to praise*"—Pss 3; 6; 10; 13; 22; 28; 31A; 54; 56. To these he also adds: Isa 38:10–20; Pss 27A; 64).

[4] Psalms 9 and 10 are considered as one psalm, which makes it wrong to identify only Psalm 10 as some scholars do (see Table 1).

[5] See discussions of Psalm 12 in Chapter 5.

praise but also vice-versa. As such, my criteria for the selection of the psalms and the way I group these differ from those mentioned above. Specifically, I use the following criteria for the selection of psalms with change of mood:

1. Individual lament, though not limited to this genre (see below)
2. Presence of both the elements of lament and praise
3. Change of mood *not* only from lament to praise but more importantly the reverse movement from praise to lament

First, the psalm should be an individual lament psalm, since it is with the individual lament psalms where the issue of the sudden change of mood has been discussed. This is generally the case among the psalms I will be looking at, though the study is not restricted to this since its main focus is not whether a lament is individual or not. Rather, my central concern is on the interplay between lament and praise. Secondly, it should be one where there is a clear presence of both the elements of lament and praise. Thus, Psalm 88 is excluded from the list even though it is one of the individual lament psalms where the element of lament probably finds most expression, since it has no element of praise in it, being a "pure lament".[6] More crucially, the third and most important criterion for my selection of the psalms is the presence of a change of mood between the elements of lament and praise, especially the change of mood from praise/thanksgiving to lament. This is because the focus of the present study is on those psalms which contain what I call an 'uncertainty of a hearing'; i.e., those psalms which contain a reverse movement from praise/thanksgiving to lament. Thus, Psalm 12 is included in the list even though its status as an individual lament may be in doubt.[7] I included this psalm because it contains a change of mood from certainty to uncertainty in spite of an oracle of salvation. As such, this psalm provides a clear example of how a lament can return to lament even in spite of an oracle of salvation and its consequent 'certainty of a hearing'.

---

[6] For the use of "pure lament", see Williamson above. Another reason for the exclusion of Psalm 88 is that, as mentioned in the previous chapter, I have limited the scope of this study to Book I of the Psalter.

[7] For discussions on the specific genre of Psalm 12—whether individual or communal, see Chapter 5.

Using these criteria, we may group the psalms containing change of mood as follows:

1. Those which move *from lament to praise*
2. Those with the reverse movement *from praise to lament*
3. Those contain a *return* to lament after the movement to praise
4. Those which *alternate* between lament and praise

Following Westermann and others, I employ the term *praise* to include the elements of praise, thanksgiving, 'certainty of a hearing', expressions of trust and vow of praise. Westermann notes: "confession of trust, certainty of being heard, and praise of God cannot be clearly distinguished here but merge with one another".[8] Likewise, I use the word *lament* to include the element of petition and complaint.[9] Elsewhere, Westermann calls lament "the Psalm of petition".[10] Praise and lament broadly represent two differing moods—joy and sorrow, thanksgiving and petition, expressions of confidence and uncertainty, respectively.

---

[8] Westermann, *Lob und Klage*, 55, ET *Praise and Lament*, 74. Cf. Brueggemann, *The Message of the Psalms*, 54–57, who tries to simplify Westermann's categories: 1. Plea—under this category are: a) address to God; b) complaint; c) petition; d) motivations; e) imprecation; 2. Praise—"The *praise* element tends to include three factors": a) assurance of being heard; b) payment of vows; c) doxology and praise. Broyles, *The Conflict of Faith*, 35–6, writes: "Even a casual reading of the Psalms reveals that their basic forms of speech may be described most generally as praise and lament, or praise and petition". Note he uses lament and petition interchangeably. Cf. Erbele-Küster, *Lesen als Akt der Betens*, 152, who seems to understand petition and lament as interchangeable: "Bitte bzw. Klage". Likewise, E. S. Gerstenberger, *Psalms: Part I with an Introduction to Cultic Poetry* (vol. 14; FOTL, ed. Rolf Knierim and Gene M. Tucker; Grand Rapids, MI: Eerdmans, 1988), 169 and Samuel Terrien, *The Psalms: Strophic Structure and Theological Commentary* (Grand Rapids, MI: Eerdmans, 2003), 338, both use praise and thanksgiving interchangeably. See also M. Millard, *Die Komposition des Psalters: Eine formgeschichtlicher Ansatz* (Tübingen: J. C. B. Mohr, 1994), 53, who assumes that praise and thanksgiving belong to the same category, speaking of the "elements of praise and thanksgiving".

[9] Westermann, *Lob und Klage*, 5, ET *Praise and Lament*, 11. He uses petition and lament interchangeably (see pp. 25, 27 [ET 31, 33]) and links them closely: "The petition which is meant here receives its distinctive character from the lament" (27 [ET 34]). Cf. Westermann, *The Living Psalms*, 12, where he sets lament and petition together opposite praise and thanksgiving. Cf. Erbele-Küster, *Lesen Als Akt Der Betens*, 152, who classifies lament and petition together. For a differing opinion, see Gunkel, *Die Psalmen* (HKAT; Göttingen: Vandenhoeck & Ruprecht, 1926), who distinguishes between lament and petition in his comments on Psalms 6 (p. 13) and 9/10 (p. 77).

[10] Westermann, *Lob und Klage*, 5, ET *Praise and Lament*, 152.

The present work is basically concerned with psalms where there is a marked change of mood.[11]

Using the criteria above, I have identified the psalms which contain a change of mood and have grouped them according to their particular movement/s between lament and praise (see Table 2).

As can be observed below (Table 2), the movement lament-praise is the most common of all the movements in the Psalter. Previous scholarship is therefore justified in emphasizing this movement. Where it faltered is in its sole focus on this movement. As can be seen, although the movement lament-praise is the most common movement, there are also other movements, which, though not as numerous, are nevertheless important for our overall understanding of the sudden change of mood and lament in general. That is why we are considering all these movements in this study, beginning in this chapter with the movement to praise. Specifically, we focus here on Psalms 3, 6 and 13.

2.2   PSALM 3

2.2.1   *Introduction*

Gunkel considers this psalm as the "Muster eines 'Klageliedes eines Einzelnen'".[12] The other psalm to which he applies such a designation is Psalm 13. But I think it is in the latter that his genre category is worked out more clearly. The movement from lament to praise is more clearly spelled out in Psalm 13, whereas in Psalm 3 we get the petition (8a) even after the statements of confidence (4–7), before finally ending in a note of confidence. In a way the elements are mixed up in Psalm 3. It contains various motifs: lament, confession of trust, thanksgiving, and wish for blessing.[13] It also uses various modes of speaking: a recorded speech of the enemy (3b), a direct cry for help (8a), a statement of trust (4), a lament (2–3).

---

[11] Cf. Robert Alter, *The Art of Biblical Poetry* (NY: Basic Books, 1985), who understands the transition in the lament psalms not in terms of the occurrence of an actual resolution but more an emotional one. Commenting on the transition of Psalm 13, he writes: "In the psalm, there is less resolution than surprising emotional reversal impelled by the motor force of faith" (66).

[12] Gunkel, *Die Psalmen*, 13.

[13] Klaus Seybold, *Die Psalmen* (HZAT I/15; Tübingen: J. C. B. Mohr, 1996), 34.

Table 2: *Individual Lament Psalms with Change of Mood*

Individual lament psalms with a change of mood:
Psalms 3, 6, 9/10, 13, 22, 27, 28, 31, 35, 54, 55, 56, 57, 59, 69, 71, 86, 94, 109, 130, 140; cf. Psalm 89[14]

Psalms which move from *Lament to Praise*

Psalm	*Lament*	*Praise*
Psalm 3	vv. 2–3	vv. 4–7
	8a[15]	8b–9
Psalm 6	vv. 1–7	vv. 8–10
Psalm 13	vv. 2–5	v. 6
Psalm 22[16]	vv. 2–22a	vv. 22b–32
Psalm 54	vv. 3–5	vv. 6–9
Psalm 55	vv. 2–19	v. 20
Psalm 56	vv. 2–10a	vv. 10b–14
Psalm 57	vv. 2–7	vv. 8–11
Psalm 69	vv. 2–30	vv. 31–37
Psalm 94	vv. 1–17	v. 18–23
Psalm 109	vv. 1–29	vv. 30–31
Psalm 130	vv. 1b–6	vv. 7–8
Psalm 140	vv. 2–12	vv. 13–14

Psalms which move from *Praise to Lament*

Psalm	*Praise*	*Lament*
Psalm 9/10	9:2–19	9:20–10:18
Psalm 27	vv. 1–6	vv. 7–12
Psalm 40	vv. 1–11	vv. 12–18
Cf. Psalm 89	vv. 2–38	v. 39–52

Psalms which contain a *Return to Lament* after movement to Praise

Psalm	*Lament*	*Praise*	*Lament*
Psalm 12	vv. 2–5	vv. 6–8	v. 9
Psalm 28	vv. 1–5	vv. 6–8	v. 9
Psalm 86	vv. 1–7	vv. 8–13	vv. 14–17

Psalms which *alternate between Lament and Praise*

Psalm	*Lament*	*Praise*	*Lament*	*Praise*	*Lament*	*Praise*
Ps 31	vv. 2–7a	vv. 7b–9	vv. 10–14	vv. 15–17		
Ps 35	vv. 1–8	vv. 9–10	vv. 11–17	v. 18	vv. 19–26	vv. 27–28
Ps 59	vv. 2–8	vv. 9–11	vv. 12–16	vv. 17–18		
Ps 71	vv. 1–13	vv. 14–16	vv. 17–19a	vv. 19b–24		

[14] I have included Psalm 89 in the list although it is a communal lament because of the similar movement from praise to lament in the psalm.

[15] After the movement from lament to praise in vv. 2–3 and 4–7 respectively, the psalm goes back to lament and then to praise. But ultimately, the overwhelming emphasis in this psalm is on the movement to praise, so I included this psalm under the category lament-praise.

[16] As will be shown below, Psalm 22 is unique in that it can be grouped under the psalms which move from lament to praise and also under the psalms which contain the reverse movement. In a way, Psalm 22 forms a bridge between these two movements. See discussion of Psalm 22 in the following chapter.

2.2.2 *Structural Analysis*

Overall, the psalm reflects the following structure:

[Superscription (1)][17]
Invocation (2a)
Lament (2–3)
Praise (4–7)
   Assurance (4)
   'Certainty of a Hearing' (5)
   Sense of Security (6–7)
Lament (Cry for help) (8a)
Praise
   Statement of Confidence (8bc)
   Ascription (9a)
Blessing (9b)

Except for the last colon (9b), which is probably a liturgical addition,[18] the whole psalm presents a unity. It forms an inclusio with the invocation, "O Yhwh" at the beginning (2a) and the ascription, "To Yhwh" (9a) at the end. The tetragrammaton is the most repeated word in the entire psalm, occurring 6x. It is found in all the parts of the structure: in the invocation and lament (2), assurance (4), 'certainty of a hearing' (5), sense of security (6), cry for help (8) and ascription (9a).[19] But the employment of repetition as a literary device in this psalm is not confined to the divine name. Another word that is repeated quite a number of times is רב, occurring 3x in vv. 2–3 and alluded to in v. 7 with the image of a very large number of enemies (רבבה). An implied contrast can be detected in the play on words between vv. 2–3 and v. 7: Whereas the psalmist is complaining about the 'many' who are

---

[17] For a discussion of the superscription, see below.

[18] H.-J. Kraus, *Psalmen I* (vol. 15/1; 4th ed.; BKAT; Neukirchen-Vluyn: Neukirchener, 1972), 24, ET *Psalms 1–59* (trans. H. C. Oswald; Minneapolis: Augsburg, 1988), 137, thinks that the whole of v. 9 is a liturgical addition; cf. Gunkel, *Die Psalmen*, 13; Leslie, 348. On the basis of the structural analysis here, I think 9a originally belongs to what precedes it.

[19] Interestingly, the places where tetragrammaton does not occur are in those lines where an allusion to the enemies of the petitioner is found. In v. 3, instead of 'Yhwh' we find 'באלהים', since it is the 'quoted' speech of the enemy. The same is true in v. 7 where the enemy is alluded to and in v. 8bc which speaks of the destruction of the enemy.

assailing him (2–3), he stands confident even before tens of thousands of them (7).

Another important word is ישׁועה. The word ישׁועה appears in vv. 3, 8 (as a verb), and 9a (as a noun). A sense of progression is discernible in the use of this word. Denied as a possibility by his enemies (3), the psalmist cries out for it (8a) and receives it (9a).[20] The help that comes from Yhwh is his salvation. Thus, we see the pattern: salvation denied—begged for—received.

Two other words which are relevant for the present discussion are אלהים and קום.[21] The latter occurs in vv. 2 and 8a; the former in vv. 3 and 8a. Here we see similar progression in terms of intensification with the use of the word אלהים: from "there is no help *in God*" (3b), to "Deliver me *my God!*" (8a). Notice that ישׁע and אלהים occur in both vv. 3 and 8a. This establishes the internal connection between v. 8a and the preceding section. Adding the words, יהוה and קום, which both occur earlier (2), further seals the connection and denies the claim made by some that 8a is an intrusion.[22]

2.2.3 *Detailed Analysis*

2.2.3.1 *The interaction between lament and praise in Psalm 3*

Psalm 3 begins with an invocation (2a), followed by a lament (2–3). Following this is a statement of the psalmist's declaration of trust in Yhwh even in the midst of his difficult situation: "But you, O Yhwh, are a shield around me…" (4).[23] He lifts up his voice in prayer, resulting in an experience of God's answer: "My voice I lifted to Yhwh, and he answered me…" (5). As a result of God's answer, the psalmist is able to rest even in the midst of danger. Presumably, the actual danger has not yet vanished; the assurance that the psalmist experiences is more

---

[20] Cf. Seybold, *Die Psalmen*, 36: "Was nach 3 von den Vielen nicht für möglich gehalten, ja geleugnet und nach 8 hilfesuschend erbeten wird, das wird nach 9 als Realität bekannt und proklamiert".

[21] See F.-L. Hossfeld and E. Zenger, *Die Psalmen I. Psalm 1–50* (Die Neue Echter Bibel Kommentar zum Alten Testament mit der Einheitsübersetzung [Nechb. At]; Würzburg: Echter, 1993), 58, for the connection between vv. 2 and 8 with the word קום: "JHWH soll sich erheben in Antwort auf das Aufstehen der Feinde".

[22] Duhm, *Die Psalmen*, 15.

[23] LXX has ἀντιλήμπτωρ for the MT's מגן ידעב.

of an internal one. In vv. 6–7, he is able to sleep and rest, with no fear whatsoever. He can boldly say that even when confronted by a great host of enemies, he will not fear.

Immediately after these statements of confidence, however, the Psalmist utters a cry which contrasts sharply with the preceding note of confidence (8a).[24] Readers could almost hear the shaking in his voice as it were. Our psalmist suddenly drifts into a state in which he is desperate for God's help. Even in the midst of all his confident utterances, he still admits his great need for help. He cries out: "Arise, O Yhwh, save me, O my God!" If we follow a strict linear/chronological way of reading, we may wonder, "I thought he had already received the answer to his prayers". The overall movement in the psalm is from lament to praise; the psalm is undeniably full of expressions of trust and the overall accent falls on the note of confidence in Yhwh's salvation. But it is interesting to see how the element of lament in the form of the cry for help manages to find its way even towards the end (8a). Below we devote substantial space to a discussion of the interplay between lament and praise in v. 8.

2.2.3.2   *The tension between lament and praise in vv. 7–8*

The structural analysis above has shown the unity of the whole psalm with the exception of 9b. It has also established the close verbal connection between v. 8a and the preceding sections. The difficulty with v. 8a is that it seems to contradict the overall positive tone of the preceding sections which contain expressions of trust, assurance and certainty (vv. 4–7). The cry, "Arise, O Yhwh, save me, O my God!" (8a) shatters the rather serene mood of the previous sections. The cry comes so suddenly and without any preparation that some scholars consider v. 8a either as an intrusion or that at least some kind of inversion of the order should be done. Duhm considers v. 8a as an intrusion and not a genuine part of the psalm since v. 8bc flows more smoothly from the confident and secure mood of v. 7.[25] The problem with this view is that it has no textual support. It reflects rather an attempt to iron out the element of tension reflected in the present arrangement of the text. One may also detect here the influence of the one-way move-

---

[24] Cf. Hossfeld and Zenger, *Die Psalmen I*, 55.
[25] Duhm, 15; Cf. Seybold, *Die Psalmen*, 34.

ment from lament to praise. The general understanding is that once lament has moved to praise there is no more turning back. But as will be demonstrated in this study the movement from lament to praise is not uniform and one-directional. Often, that which scholars think 'disturbs' the flow of the text actually forms an essential part of the passage. Such incongruity actually creates an 'empty space'. 'Leerstellen' or gaps, as Erbele-Küster calls them, engage the reader and create a more active participation.[26]

In vv. 7–8, we find an alternation between confidence and cry for help as illustrated in the following diagram:

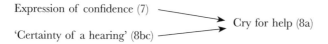

Expression of confidence (7) ⟶ Cry for help (8a)
'Certainty of a hearing' (8bc) ⟶

In this alternation we observe not only the 'sudden' shift from the expression of confidence (7) to the cry for help in 8a but also the 'sudden' transition from the cry for help (8a) to the 'certainty of a hearing' in 8bc. Immediately after the cry for help (8a), we find a statement in the perfect tense:

‎כי־הכית את־כל־איבי לחי שני רשעים שברת.

The transition from 8a to 8bc and the relationship between the two have proved to be a challenge for scholars. Anderson admits, "It is difficult to determine the relationship between verse 7a [8a] and 7bc [8bc]".[27]

Scholars have tried to find ways of explaining the relationship between vv. 8a and 8bc. One of the ways of explaining the connection between the two is to adjust either one of them to fit the other. Oesterley tries to do this by reading 8a not as an appeal/petition but as an affirmation of trust. He writes: "*Arise, Yhwh, save me, my God,* is an exclamation denoting the psalmist's affirmation of trust, rather than in the nature of an appeal; this is evident from the statement of Yhwh's action in the words which follow".[28] Moving towards the opposite direction, Buttenwieser adjusts 8bc to fit 8a. He interprets the perfect tense in 8bc as a precative perfect and reads 8bc as petition, similar to 8a.

---

[26] Erbele-Küster, *Lesen als Akt des Betens*, 41–48.

[27] Anderson, *The Book of Psalms* (vol. 1; *NCB*; London: Marshal, Morgan & Scott, 1972), 74.

[28] W. O. E. Oesterley, *The Psalms Translated with Text Critical and Exegetical Notes* (London: SPCK, 1939), 129.

Buttenwieser translates the whole verse as follows: "Arise, O Lord, help me, O my God. Yea, smite all mine enemies upon the cheek, Break the teeth of the wicked".[29] Buttenwieser explains that the precative perfect is similar to the perfect of certitude; it has its background in "primitive man's belief in the magic power of the word" which later developed as a means of professing one's faith in God.[30]

The problem with Oesterley and Buttenwieser's proposals is that they tend to read the Hebrew sentence in a rather unnatural way. It is better to take 8a as a petition since it reflects the tone of lamentation.[31] "Arise, O Yhwh" occurs here and in Pss 7:7; 9:20; 10:12; 44:27; 74:22.[32] And in all of these instances, the statement is a petition, representing the integral part of lamentation. It is thus unlikely, as Oesterley suggests, for 8a to be read other than as a petition. Likewise, Buttenwieser's suggestion which takes 8bc as a petition to make sense of its connection to 8a is unlikely. The particle כִּי here is best translated in the sense of 'for', since it provides some form of a substantiation to 8a. Moreover, a statement in the perfect tense is not uncommon for psalms containing movements towards praise (see Pss 6:9–10; 28:6f.).

But if we take 8a as a petition and 8bc as a statement set in the perfect tense, how do we explain the relationship between the two? If the psalmist had just cried out: "Arise, O Yhwh, save me, O my God", how can he suddenly move to the following statement of certainty: "For you have smitten all my enemies…"? What is the sense of the latter in relation to the former?

There are three main ways of explaining the relationship between the two. The first understands 8bc as a reference to a future reality. Broyles holds that 8bc should be read as an anticipation of what Yhwh will do. He comments: "The past tense of the Hebrew 'for you have struck' all my enemies on the jaw might seem odd…unless we observe that prayer psalms sometimes give thanks in anticipation of Yhwh's deliverance".[33] Similarly, Anderson mentions what he calls a "prophetic

---

[29] Moses Buttenwieser, *The Psalms Chronologically Treated with a New Translation* (Chicago: University of Chicago, 1938), 396.

[30] Buttenwieser, 24.

[31] Anderson, *The Book of Psalms*, 75. Hossfeld, *Die Psalmen I*, 55 understands v. 8a as a "Notschrei".

[32] Samuel Terrien, *The Psalms: Strophic Structure and Theological Commentary* (Grand Rapids, MI: Eerdmans, 2003), 92.

[33] Craig C. Broyles, *Psalms* (NIBC; Peabody, Massachusetts: Hendrickson Publishers, Inc., 1999), 50; cf. S. B. Frost, "Asseveration by Thanksgiving," *VT* 8 (1958): 380–90.

perfect" as a possible explanation for the perfect tense.[34] Coming from a different perspective, though nonetheless similar, is Eaton. He argues that the speaker of the Psalm is a king and views 8bc as a prophetic declaration of the defeat of the enemy.[35]

Delitzsch rejects the prophetic perfect, and proposes what he calls the "retrospective perfect".[36] According to him 8bc is to be taken as a reference to past experiences of God's deliverance which forms the basis for the petition in 8a. He avers, "The cry for help...justifies itself with כִּי and a retrospective perfect. The perfects here are not perfects of prophetically assured hope...for in our passage the logical connection demands an appeal to what has already been experienced".[37] Kirkpatrick's view is similar. He writes that what we have here is an appeal to past experience which serves as the "ground of prayer".[38] Likewise, Schmidt sees in 8bc a statement that contains "die triumphierende Gewissheit aus einer *erfahrenen* Hilfe".[39] Kittel connects 8bc with vv. 4–5. He explains that in vv. 4–5 the psalmist recalls the many experiences of God's help in the past and in 8bc a specific example of how God had delivered him in the past is provided. It reflects the psalmist's faith that as God had been his helper before, so he now believes he will be the same helper to him.[40] Two of the recent scholars who adopt this view are Anderson and Kraus, though the latter combines it with the next view.[41]

Kraus does not explain 8bc as a reference to the *future* ("prophetic perfect"). However, in his discussion of Psalm 3, Kraus signifies that 8bc points to both *past* experiences of God's help ("retrospective perfect") and to a *present* reality. In his introductory comment, he says that 8bc "looks back upon Yahweh's intervention".[42] But then he goes on to

---

[34] Anderson, 75.

[35] J. H. Eaton, *Psalms: Introduction and Commentary* (London: SCM, 1967), 35.

[36] Franz Delitzsch, *Biblischer Commentar über die Psalmen* (Leipzig: Dörffling und Franke, 1883), 86, ET *Biblical Commentary on the Psalms* (trans. D. Eaton; vol. 1; London: Hodder and Stoughton, 1887), 140.

[37] Ibid.

[38] A. F. Kirkpatrick, *The Book of Psalms* (Cambridge: Cambridge University Press, 1903), 16.

[39] H. Schmidt, *Die Psalmen* (vol. 15; HAT; Tübingen: J. C. B. Mohr, 1934), 7, emphasis mine.

[40] D. Rudolf Kittel, *Die Psalmen* (3rd and 4th ed; Leipzig: A. Deichertsche Verlagsbuchhandlung, 1922), 13.

[41] Anderson, 75; Kraus, *Psalmen I*, 24ff., ET *Psalms 1–59*, 137ff.

[42] Kraus, *Psalmen I*, 24, ET 137. Kraus makes it clear through this statement that he agrees with the preceding view. What is not clear is his additional comment that since 8bc is a reference to past experiences of Yhwh's help it must be "separated from the

explain that "between these two parts of the verse lie the occurrence of actual intervention and aid on the part of Yahweh".[43] By this statement Kraus is implying that 8bc is not just a reference to a past experience of Yhwh's deliverance as he has intimated in his former comment. He is saying that what we have here is something that belongs to the realm of the present. He has just experienced something decisive, causing the sudden change of tone, from lament (petition) to confidence. It seems that Kraus has here mixed the past with the present. It is not clear whether 8bc refers to the past or to the present. But the element of ambiguity may actually be an indication that what we have in 8bc is more than meets the eye. Something decisive has transpired in between the cry for help and the answer in 8bc. As to what it is specifically, the text does not tell us. Seybold is of the opinion that we have the presence of a "Zäsur", a pause, in between 8a and 8bc which signifies that something decisive has happened to the psalmist. Seybold believes the setting here is that of a falsely accused individual who at this particular point finds asylum and justice.[44] The pause is required by the decision.[45] Gunkel also thinks that something decisive has occurred before 8bc. Although he does not explicitly mention here what caused the transition, we may infer that it is due to a pronouncement of a priestly oracle. According to him, the perfect must be understood as a Gewissheit.[46] Kraus basically agrees with Gunkel on this point.[47]

The foregoing discussion demonstrates the difficulty of making sense of the relationship between 8a and 8bc, let alone determining what actually took place behind these verses. Trying to pin down the exact sense of the verses is something that easily slips one's grasp. Verse 8bc could be a reference to the *future* as an expression of faith in what Yhwh will do, to the *past* as a recollection of what Yhwh has done before, or to the *present* as an account of an actual experience of deliverance. Here lies the openness of the poetic language of the psalms. The very construction of the verse creates a 'gap'. Scholars, who are often uncomfortable

---

preceding" (ibid.). In what sense is 8bc to be separated from 8a? He cites Schmidt's comment that 8bc is "the triumphant certainty based on help experienced" (27–28, ET 141). But Schmidt thinks that 8bc belong to another setting, i.e. a thanksgiving prayer added later. Kraus does not explicitly say he agrees with Schmidt on this point.

[43] Ibid., 28, ET 141.
[44] Seybold, *Die Psalmen*, 34.
[45] Ibid.
[46] Gunkel, *Die Psalmen*, 14.
[47] See discussion of Psalm 6 below.

with the presence of ambiguity and uncertainty, almost automatically try to fill in the gap. However, in the process they have actually blurred the element of tension and ambiguity which the very construction of the text intimates. A better alternative is to remain open to the various possibilities of interpreting the passage. The text can actually contain the multiple senses which scholars have attributed to it. As Weiser very well captures it: "The past, the present, and the future intertwine at this moment; God has already helped, he has already wrought deliverance, and yet at the same time his help and his deliverance are prayed for and hoped for by man".[48] Psalm 3:8 reflects certainty and uncertainty, assurance and ambiguity at the same time. Although the element of trust dominates the entire psalm,[49] the voice of lament nevertheless finds its way in even towards the end of the psalm.

2.2.3.3   *The contribution of the Superscription*

A consideration of the superscription helps us see this element of tension and uncertainty in Psalm 3. Historical critical approaches have generally ignored the psalm titles/superscriptions in the interpretation of the Psalms. But whilst it may be true that these do not provide historical information as to the origin of the psalms, they are relevant for they "give an important glimpse into the way the psalms were interpreted".[50] Whether they originally formed a part of the psalm or have been added later by the redactor/s, the titles provide a specific angle through which a particular psalm had been viewed in the process of its reception. In the case of Psalm 3 the presence of the superscription is significant because it provides us with a background for the presence of tension even in a confidence-filled psalm like Psalm 3. Psalm 3 is the first psalm which contains a superscription.[51] Even more importantly, Psalm 3 is the first of only 13 psalms which include a biographical element.[52] In most cases, the superscription is simply "A Psalm of David" or "Of David". In Psalm 3 we find the following words in the title: "A psalm

---

[48] Weiser, *Die Psalmen I*, 73, ET *The Psalms*, 118.

[49] Gunkel, *Die Psalmen*, 13.

[50] Wenham, "Towards a Canonical Reading of the Psalms", 7.

[51] Psalms 1 and 2 do not have titles; the former being the introduction to the whole psalm and the latter, a probable continuation of Psalm 1.

[52] The psalms with brief biographical notes in them are: Psalms 3, 7, 18, 34, 51, 52, 54, 56, 57, 59, 60, 63, 142 (Lucas, *Exploring the Old Testament: The Psalms and Wisdom Literature*, 20–21).

of David, when he fled from Absalom his son". This gives a program-matic function to Psalm 3, setting the stage for the laments that follow. A closer examination of the psalms with biographical elements reveals that most of these refer to a difficult situation in the life of David.[53] The image of David painted in these superscriptions is not the David who is successful and triumphant. Rather we see the human David, strug-gling, a fugitive running for his life, hiding in a cave (e.g. Psalm 57). In most cases they speak about events before David became king; and those which relate to the time when he is already king are mostly about difficult times in his life such as we find in Psalm 3, with David fleeing from his own son Absalom.[54] Scholars usually point to the passage in 2 Sam 15:13–18 as the possible background for the title in Psalm 3.[55] By relating the psalm to this particular situation in the life of David, the redactor/s sees something in the psalm which captures the struggle experienced by David. Reading the psalm with the superscription enables us to see why the psalm, even though it is full of confidence, still expresses uncertainty and tension. Conversely, the expression of the element of tension makes the depiction of David's suffering in the superscription more realistic.[56]

2.2.4 Summary

The overall movement in Psalm 3 is from lament to praise. Although there is a movement back to the element of lament in v. 8a, it is the tone of trust and confidence that dominates in the psalm. The psalm

---

[53] Martin Kleer, *Der liebliche Sänger der Psalmen Israels* (vol. 108; Bonner Biblische Beiträge; Bodenheim: Philo, 1996), 116.

[54] Jean-Marie Auwers, *La Composition Littéraire du Psautier: Un État de la Question* (Paris: Gabalda, 2000), 150.

[55] Auwers, *La Composition Littéraire du Psautier*, 138; For the contextual and verbal connection between Psalm 3 and the account in 2 Samuel see Jean-Luc Vesco, *Le Psautier De David* (Paris: Cerf, 2006), 98–99.

[56] One may compare here the experience of reading Daniel Defoe's *Robinson Crusoe*. As Crusoe writes in his journal his initial experiences of being a castaway in an unin-habited island, he does so as one who remains composed, almost unshaken in spite of his situation. The reader wonders whether he/she would ever find a section which tells of Crusoe's struggles. When the reader finally finds this in the book, somehow he/she experiences a sense of relief: the hero is also human; he struggles just like us. Indeed, the humanness of the presentation is one of the book's abiding gifts to the many generations who have read it. The same thing can be said of Psalm 3. If we only read the psalm without the superscription, we would not be able to appreciate fully the element of tension in the text.

begins with a lament (vv. 2–3) which is immediately followed by expressions of trust and confidence (vv. 4–7). The psalm ends with a note of deliverance. That is why this psalm can be rightly counted among psalms which move from lament to praise. Yet interestingly, in this psalm one encounters the important feature of the return to lament. I have devoted a substantial space to this since this is the focus of the whole study. As will be seen below, this feature of the return to lament can also be found in a number of lament psalms.

2.3 PSALM 6

2.3.1 *Introduction*

Gunkel remarks that "Psalm 6 is perhaps the most illustrative example" of a 'certainty of a hearing' that moves directly from the lament.[57] Whereas in Psalm 3 the expression of confidence (8bc) stems directly from the petition (8a), here it flows directly from the lament (see Ps 6:8 and 9–11).

So sudden is the transition from lament to the 'certainty of a hearing' that some scholars regard vv. 9–11 as a later addition. Oesterley holds that vv. 9–11 have been added after the petitioner has been healed.[58] Similarly, Weiser thinks that the verses have been recited later "within the setting of the cult after the worshipper had obtained the assurance that his prayer had been answered".[59] Schmidt considers vv. 9–11 as a "new prayer" that belongs to a different setting.[60] He argues that since it is a different composition, we are not to see the statement as an expression of the certainty of the hearing of the prayer. Taking the psalm as a prayer of a sick person, Schmidt explains that the prayer for sickness has already ended with v. 8; what follows is an entirely new prayer. Accordingly, the composition belongs to a different setting, written

---

[57] Gunkel and Begrich, *Einleitung in die Psalmen*, 247, ET Gunkel and Begrich, *Introduction to Psalms*, 182. Gunkel distinguishes between petition and lament. However, in both cases, be it in terms of petition or lament, the situation envisaged is similar: both reflect a situation of difficulty. Thus, I prefer the broader understanding of lament which includes petition (see above).

[58] W. O. E. Oesterley, 135.

[59] Weiser, *Die Psalmen I*, 80, ET *The Psalms*, 130.

[60] H. Schmidt, *Die Psalmen* (vol. 15; Handbuch zum Alten Testament; Tübingen: Verlag von J. C. B. Mohr, 1934), 11.

beforehand and spoken after the hearing of his prayer. "Man hat hier
neben dem Flehgebet aus dem Munde eines Kranken ein kurzes Dank-
gebet für seine Heilung aufbewahrt; wahrscheinlich weil das eine wie
das andere immer wieder gebraucht und gefordert worden ist".[61]

In contrast, Seybold sees Psalm 6 as a unity. He understands the
psalm as the prayer of a sick person employing a ritual for healing
as its setting. Accordingly, the psalm is to be regarded as consisting of
two parts: vv. 2–8 and 9–11.[62] The first part deals with the ritual for
sickness, consisting of an appeal to Yhwh. The second part contains
an appeal to the enemy. Both are to be interpreted from the setting
of penitence.[63]

Whatever the specific setting of the psalm might have been is now
lost to us. As to the question of what caused the sudden change of
mood, we also do not know for certain. The majority view is that a
priestly oracle is delivered in between vv. 8 and 9. Gunkel believes that
a priestly oracle is what brings about the sudden change.[64] Although
he does not explicitly state it, Kraus basically agrees with Gunkel's
and Begrich's view. In his comment on Psalm 3, he writes: "Between
these two parts of the verse lies the occurrence of actual intervention
and aid on the part of Yahweh...Was a word of God issued in the
form of an 'oracle of salvation'?"[65] His comment on Psalm 6 is more
revealing: "The petitioner has heard the 'Fear not'".[66] Seybold, after
citing two other possible explanations for the sudden change of mood,
in the end considered the oracle of salvation as the most likely view.[67]
Interestingly, in his commentary written 20 years later, he does not seem
to hold the same position as tightly as he used to, but counts the oracle
of salvation as only one possibility among other options.[68] Kittel thinks

---

[61] Ibid.
[62] Klaus Seybold, *Das Gebet des Kranken im Alten Testament: Untersuchungen zur Bestimmung und Zuordnung der Krankheits- und Heilungspsalmen* (BZWANT 19; der Ganzen Sammlung Heft 99; Stuttgart: Kohlhammer, 1973), 154ff.; cf. C. A. Briggs, and E. G. Briggs, *A Critical and Exegetical Commentary on the Book of Psalms* (vol. 1; ICC; Edinburgh: T & T Clark, 1906), who writes, "The congregation have not been overwhelmed by their grief and the divine chastisement; their prayer receives its answer *while they are making it*" (48, emphasis mine). Briggs sees the 'I' of this psalm as a reference to the community.
[63] Ibid., 158.
[64] Gunkel, *Die Psalmen*, 22; cf. Begrich, "Das priesterliche Heilsorakel," *ZAW* 52 (1934): 81–92.
[65] Kraus, *Psalmen I*, 28, ET *Psalms 1–59*, 141.
[66] Ibid., 28, ET 162.
[67] Seybold, *Das Gebet des Kranken im Alten Testament*, 157.
[68] Seybold, *Die Psalmen*, 44.

that the change occurred as a result of the psalmist's own struggle as he pours out his heart in prayer, but nonetheless endorses Gunkel's view.[69] Other scholars simply note the change but do not attempt to explain the cause of the change.[70] Weiser holds that such a transition is a "gift from God. It is only and solely God himself who has brought about what has here come to pass...The complete change which has taken place in the worshipper's mind proves the power of that God-given assurance of faith".[71]

The cause of the sudden change of mood is not certain; what is certain is that we have a sudden change of mood.

2.3.2 Structural Analysis

There is in Psalm 6 a clear movement from lament to praise. The psalm consists of two main parts: lament (2–8) and praise (9–11). Both the elements of lament and praise are clearly marked. Here, we analyse the passage in terms of its movement from lament to praise. As noted above, there are those who hold to the view that the psalm is composite because of the suddenness of the change of mood in the psalm. But as the following detailed analysis of the psalm demonstrates, what we have here is a unified psalm. Broyles is of the opinion that the two parts of the psalm, vv. 2–8 and 9–11 "show strong linguistic ties, and the introduction of the enemies in v. 8b provides a suitable transition into this assurance of being heard".[72] The following analysis further supports this.

2.3.3 Detailed Analysis

2.3.3.1 The Lament (vv. 2–8)

Whereas we find the petition only towards the end in Psalm 3 (v. 8a), Psalm 6 moves directly into the petition, formed by two consecutive parallel requests. The first one is constructed in the negative, reinforced

---

[69] Kittel, Die Psalmen, 21.
[70] Briggs, 48; Delitzsch, Biblischer Commentar über die Psalmen, 106, ET Biblical Commentary on the Psalms, 174.
[71] Weiser, Die Psalmenn I, 82, ET The Psalms, 133.
[72] Broyles, The Conflict of Faith and Experience in the Psalms, 183.

by a beautiful parallelism (2). This is followed by a positive, but forceful request: "Be gracious to me…heal me", each colon supported by a motivation, beginning with כי (3). This first part of the psalm, particularly v. 2 is identical to Ps 38:2, which is a penitential psalm. This has led scholars to regard Psalm 6 as a penitential psalm;[73] Psalm 6 being the first of what the church traditionally considered as the seven penitential psalms: 6, 32, 38, 51, 102, 130, and 143. Gunkel does not deny the presence of the element of penitence in Psalm 6, but does not consider it as a dominant feature.[74] Weiser holds a similar view and rightly points out that "the actual confession of sin is entirely lacking".[75]

The petition (2–3) is followed by a description of the pitiful condition of the psalmist (4a). He repeats the word בהל (3b), which in Ps 2:5 means 'terrify' to describe the agony of his soul. Notice the addition of the adverb מאד, which further highlights the intensity of the psalmist's expression of suffering. These two words will be significant in the discussion below.

What follows 4a is a construction whose beginning can easily be identified with a statement of trust similar to Ps 3:4's "ואתה יהוה". But instead of a declaration of confidence in Yhwh, we find a lament: ואתה יהוה עד־מתי (4b). It seems as though the psalmist wanted to break into a confident trust in Yhwh in spite of his situation, but has been unable to do so; at least not yet at this point. One can sense the struggle between faith and doubt here. Weiser notes, "He stretches out his arms towards God whenever he is overcome by his misery, and the unfinished question 'but thou, O Lord,—how long?'—in which *hope and doubt contend with each other*—sounds like the gasping of a stammerer".[76]

Verses 5–6 are similar in construction to vv. 2–3. The following petitions: Return, deliver, and save (5) are followed by a motivation which begins with the particle כי (6). The first petition (שוב) is to be understood in the sense of 'turn again toward'.[77] This word is particularly

---

[73] Briggs, *A Critical and Exegetical Commentary on the Book of Psalms*, 45; Delitzsch, *Biblischer Commentar über die Psalmen*, 102f., ET 167f.; Oesterley, *The Psalms*, 135; Leslie, *The Psalms*, 391f.

[74] Gunkel, *Die Psalmen*, 21.

[75] Weiser, *Die Psalmen I*, 80, ET *The Psalms*, 130. The central feature of confession of guilt which characterises the prayer of confession (cf. Ezra 9, Nehemiah 1, 9, and Daniel 9; Cf. Ps 38:19) is not present in Psalm 6.

[76] Weiser, *Die Psalmen I*, 81, ET *The Psalms*, 131, emphasis mine.

[77] Cf. Kraus, *Psalmen I*, 49–50, ET *Psalms 1–59*, 162.

relevant in Psalm 6 because the poet employs the word again later in v. 11 (see below).[78]

After providing a motivation as to why God should act on his behalf (6) the psalmist continues his lament, further describing his suffering through the use of poetic images (7–8). In 7b, he simply says, "I flood my bed all night long". Flood it with what? The answer is given in 7c, in the form of an ellipsis: "with tears, I soak my couch". At the end of v. 8, the psalmist refers to his enemies as the cause of the wasting of his eyes in grief.[79] With the mentioning of the enemy, the lament reaches its lowest point.

2.3.3.2 *Transition to Praise: 'Certainty of a Hearing' (vv. 9–11)*

Yet precisely at the lowest point of the lament we encounter a sudden change of mood in v. 9.[80] From the lamenting cry of vv. 2–8, the psalmist addresses his enemies and tells them to turn away from him. He declares to them with complete boldness that his prayer has been heard. Notice the twice repeated verb שמע (9b–10a) and לקח. Finally, the psalmist anticipates the destruction of his enemies (11).

As already mentioned above, one of the issues about vv. 9–11 is its connection with the preceding section. But does the sudden change of mood mean that vv. 9–11 is a later addition? The linguistic link with the preceding section shows the unity of the psalm. There is evidence that we have here a single composition rather than a conflation of two originally separate compositions. The psalmist uses two significant words: בהל and שוב. The latter is mentioned in v. 5 as part of the psalmist's petition: "return, O Yhwh". He uses this word again in v. 11b to speak of his enemies' "turning back". There is a movement from

---

[78] Interestingly, the petition שוב also occurs in a thanksgiving psalm (Psalm 116). If in 6:5, it says, "return, O Yhwh"; in 116:7, it says *"return* my soul to rest". Even in a thanksgiving psalm the element of uncertainty persists.

[79] Scholars discuss what specifically causes the suffering of the psalmist in Psalm 6. Seybold, *Das Gebet des Kranken im Alten Testament*, 154, believes it is primarily his sickness which is psychological in nature, only secondarily does he mention the psalmist's enemies as the cause. In contrast, Kittel, *Die Psalmen*, 19, argues that the enemy is the primary cause of the suffering. Gunkel, *Die Psalmen*, 21, stays in the middle in saying that it is both the psalmist's sickness and enemy that is inflicting difficulties on him.

[80] That there is a sudden change of mood in vv. 9–11 is generally recognized by scholars: Briggs, 48; Delitzsch, *Biblischer Commentar über die Psalmen*, 106, ET 174; Leslie, 393; Weiser, 80, ET 130. As illustrated in Table 1, 11 out of 12 of the scholars see a change of mood in Psalm 6.

petition (5) to response (11), from imperative to indicative. It seems as if the psalmist is saying, "Because the Lord has already 'returned' to me (5), my enemies will 'turn back' (11b). The other significant word—בהל is used twice in the first section to describe the psalmist's miserable condition (vv. 3, 4). In v. 3 he describes his bones as being "terrified". In v. 4 the agony intensifies with the addition of the qualifying מאד. Interestingly, the psalmist repeats exactly the same words in v. 11a; this time to depict the anticipated destruction of the enemy: ויבהלו מאד. If, earlier, it was the psalmist who is 'terrified'; here it is his enemies who will be greatly terrified. These linguistic links between the two parts of the psalm show the active interplay between lament and praise. The progression of thought as well as the strong element of reversal in the psalm point to a clear movement from lament to praise.

2.3.4 *Summary*

Psalm 6 is a clear example of an individual lament psalm which moves from lament to praise. Both elements are clearly marked in the psalm, with lament occupying the first part and praise the second. The transition from one to the other is sudden. But as demonstrated above, this does not make the psalm composite. Although there is no mention of an actual occurrence of deliverance, the overall tone and movement of the psalm is towards certainty and praise.

2.4 PSALM 13

2.4.1 *Introduction*

As noted earlier, Gunkel considers Psalm 13 as a "Muster eines Klageliedes eines Einzelnen.[81] The psalm is a classic example of an individual lament psalm where the elements are presented and arranged in a perfect form-critical way (see Structural Analysis below). The three subjects

---

[81] Gunkel, *Die Psalmen*, 46.

of lament—God, self, and enemy—are all present in the psalm.[82] One can trace very clearly in the psalm a movement from lament to praise. Westermann writes:

> On reading the psalm through several times, from the first sentence to the last, one observes a marked change in the course of it. By the end, the situation of the supplicant has altered; he does not stand where he stood at the beginning. The psalm is a lament but the final words have moved away from lament and the psalm closes with an expression of sure and certain confidence in the future.[83]

2.4.2 *Structural Analysis*

Psalm 13 combines elements from Psalms 3 and 6. The first part resembles Psalm 3. The question, "How long?" (Ps 13:2), is analogous to Psalm 3's, "how many are my foes" (2). Both are constructed using a beautiful parallelism: Psalm 13, with the repeated "how long?" and Psalm 3 with the word "how *many* are my foes". It is similar to Psalm 6 in that after the psalm reaches its nadir, a sudden change of mood occurs. In Psalm 6, a transition occurs after the mentioning of the enemies—the darkest moment in the lament. In Psalm 13 the psalmist speaks of 'death' in v. 4 and in v. 5 of enemies exulting over his downfall. Precisely at the lowest point of the psalmist's experience,[84] the psalm moves to "but I will trust in you..." (13:5).

Overall, the psalm has the following structure:

1. Lament (2–3)
2. Petition (4–5)
3. Declaration of Trust (6a)
4. Vow of praise (6b)

---

[82] Westermann, *Lob und Klage*, 128, ET *Praise and Lament*, 169, identifies the three subjects of lament. Cf. Alexander Maclaren, *The Psalms* (vol. 1; The Expositor's Bible; ed. W. Robertson Nicoll; London: Hodder and Stoughton, 1893), 118: "Very significant is the progress of thought in the fourfold questioning plaint, which turns first to God, then to himself, then to the enemy".

[83] Claus Westermann, *The Living Psalms* (trans. J. R. Porter; Edinburgh: T & T Clark, 1989), 69; cf. 73.

[84] Alter, *The Art of Biblical Poetry*, 65, is of the opinion that the enemy is the main cause of the psalmist's misery.

2.4.3 *Detailed Analysis*

The psalm begins with the question "how long?" (עַד־אָנָה), which is repeated 4x (vv. 2–3). In these verses, the psalmist complains about:

- Yhwh's apparent inaction ("how long will you *forget* me?") or absence ("how long will you *hide* your face?") (v. 2);
- His own struggles ("how long must I be confused and have sorrow in my heart all day long?") (v. 3a).
- His enemy (v. 3b).

In view of his situation, the psalmist pleads before Yhwh that He might "look" (i.e., upon his condition) and "answer" him (4a). He asks for some sort of a 'reviving'; "give light to my eyes," he prays (4b). Following these petitions are a series of motivational statements, aimed at moving the heart of God towards responding to his request (vv. 4b–5):

- "Lest I sleep in death"
- "Lest my enemy triumphs over me; lest my enemy rejoices because I am shaken"

We observe the following pattern:

Lament directed to God (2–3a)
Lament over one's *enemies* (3b)
 ➤ Petition
Petition for God's response with corresponding motivation (4–5)
 Motivation: 'lest I die'
 Motivation: 'lest my *enemy* . . .' (5)
  ➤ Assurance

As can be observed in the pattern above, whenever the enemy is mentioned a transition occurs in the prayer; first, towards petition, then to assurance. This indicates to the reader the main issue confronting the psalmist. But more importantly, it is during the darkest moment of the petitioner's struggle that a movement towards assurance takes place. From the lowest point (5), the psalm suddenly moves upward to a note of confidence, highlighted by the adversative waw at the beginning of v. 6: "But as for me" (וַאֲנִי). The psalmist declares his trust in Yhwh's steadfast love. Because of the Lord's goodness, his heart will exult in the salvation that Yhwh brings. Again similar to Psalm 6, Psalm 13 employs significant words to assert his faith and trust in Yhwh. The word heart ('inner being' in v. 3, לבב)[85] which is full of sorrow/grief is repeated in v. 6 to speak of his rejoicing (יגל לבי) in 'his salvation'. Such a rejoicing also recalls the rejoicing of his enemies in v. 5: צרי יגילו. If earlier it was his enemies' rejoicing that he was fearful of, here he is certain that his will be the last laugh "because of your salvation" (6b). Commenting on the transition in v. 6, Mays remarks:

> So certain is his confidence of the reality of God's salvation that he sum- mons his heart to sing of it... The hymn lays bare the foundation upon which the whole prayer is based. Somewhere, sometime, the psalmist has encountered the graciousness of God, and confidence in that grace has become the ground and support of his life. It is the reality that no other experience can diminish and with which he undertakes to live through every other experience.[86]

2.4.3.1 *The movement to praise as a process*

Although the idea of a sudden change of mood from lament to praise in Psalm 13 has always been assumed in the past, this has been chal- lenged in recent scholarship. Reacting to Begrich's theory, some schol- ars have started to question the idea of 'suddenness' in the change of mood. As mentioned in the previous chapter, Janowski questions the notion of a 'sudden' transition to 'certainty of a hearing' in Psalm 13.[87] Instead of the term 'sudden' he proposes the idea of a 'process' as a more apt description of what takes place in the transition from lament to praise. He writes: "hinter der Wende von der Klage zum Lob eine Prozess, genauer: ein *Gebetsprozess* steht, der von Anfang an, d.h. mit Beginn des Betens, in Gang kommt und den ganzen Text durchzieht".[88] Accordingly, a progression is discernible in Psalm 13; from the invocation "Yhwh" (2a) to "Yhwh, my God" (4a), and finally, to the expression of confidence in v. 6.[89] Through the lament psalm itself, i.e. the text, one is able to go through the process of transition

---

[85] William L. Holladay, *A Concise Hebrew and Aramaic Lexicon of the Old Testament* (Leiden: E. J. Brill, 1971), 172, notes that לבב is "semantically like" לב.
[86] James Luther Mays, *The Lord Reigns: A Theological Handbook to the Psalms* (Louisville: Westminster John Knox Press, 1994), 56.
[87] Ibid., 45–46.
[88] Ibid., 46.
[89] Ibid., 50.

from lament to praise: "Der einzelne Klagepsalm ist die zeitlich geraffte Darstellung eines *Prozesses*, d.h. eines Durchgangs durch die Stadien: Not—Bitte—Gewissheit".[90]

2.4.3.2 *'Simultaneity' between lament and praise*

Moving even further from the idea of a 'sudden' change of mood, Weber argues in his analysis of Psalm 13 that actually what we have in the psalms of lament with change of mood is a "simultaneity". Following Markschies' view, he explains that the element of trust is actually present in all parts of the psalm.[91] One does not move from lament to praise, for even in the lament the element of trust is already present. There is both "discontinuity" (Absetzung) and "continuity" (Anknüpfung) between Ps 13:6 and the preceding sections.[92] Weber tries to demonstrate the continuity in v. 6 by pointing out that the three subjects of the lament in the previous sections—God, self and enemy—are also present in v. 6.[93] What Weber is suggesting is a kind of reading which considers the whole of the psalm—both the lament and praise 'at the same time'.[94] Although he sees the importance of Janowski's proposal of a 'process', he nonetheless prefers reading the psalm 'simultaneously', preserving the element of tension between the various elements in the psalm.[95] Although he does not mention it, Weber has here presented an idea similar to that of Broyles, who earlier commented concerning the movement from lament to praise in Psalm 13:

> [T]he psalm does exhibit a progression from lament to petition and finally to anticipatory praise. Nonetheless, though the psalm ends on the high note of a vow of praise, it must be regarded as just that, a promise and not necessarily a 'change of mood'. There is nothing to suggest that the psalmist has dropped his protest against God's adverse disposition. Simultaneous with the psalmist's confession of present trust is his complaint of God's hiddenness.[96]

---

[90] Ibid., 52.

[91] Beat Weber, "Zum sogenannten 'Stimmungsschwung' in Psalm 13", in *The Book of Psalms: Composition and Reception* (ed. P. W. Flint and P. D. Miller; VTSup 99; Leiden: Brill, 2005), 133.

[92] Ibid.

[93] Ibid., 126–27.

[94] Ibid., 135.

[95] Ibid.

[96] Broyles, *The Conflict of Faith and Experience in the Psalms*, 186. It should be noted, however, that Broyles presents the element of tension more than Weber does. Broyles

2.4.4 *Summary*

In view of the emphasis on the element of tension and the movement from praise to lament in the present study, Broyles and Weber's idea of tension in Psalm 13 presents an attractive reading for this psalm. One has to be careful, however, that one does not read too much of the element of 'tension' into the psalms of lament which contain a clear movement from lament to praise such as we find in Psalm 13.[97] Whilst it is a mistake to highlight one-sidedly the movement lament-praise, it would be wrong-headed to deny it totally. The movement from lament to praise is very clear in this psalm as demonstrated in the analysis above. Alter observes that the movement in Psalm 13 is more regular and "stable".[98] One can trace a development and a heightening throughout the psalm.[99] The movement might not be as 'sudden' as Psalm 6, and one may agree with Janowski's reading of Psalm 13 in terms of a process, but overall the direction of the psalm is towards praise.[100] We may conclude then that Psalm 13 contains a movement from lament to praise.

2.5 CONCLUSION

We started this chapter by establishing our criteria for selection of the psalms for the present study. We have tried to group them under one of the movements in the Psalms: from lament to praise, from praise to lament, return to lament after praise and alternation between lament and praise. We then proceeded with the actual analysis of the psalms themselves, beginning in this chapter with those which move from lament to praise; specifically, Psalms 3, 6 and 13. We have observed

---

highlights the element of lament and tension in his presentation. Weber seems to highlight the element of praise more than the lament.

[97] One of the mistakes of previous approaches is the tendency to impose the single movement lament-praise to all the lament psalms. It would be a similar mistake to read the element of tension into all the lament psalms.

[98] Alter, *The Art of Biblical Poetry*, 69.

[99] Ibid., 65.

[100] Cf. Alter, 67, who sees at the end of the psalm "a paradoxical swing of faith that enables the speaker at the nadir of terror to affirm that God will sustain him, indeed has sustained him".

that there is indeed a movement from lament to praise.[101] Among the three psalms we have looked at Psalm 13 is probably the most straight-forward in terms of the movement from lament to praise. Here we can see a clear progression from lament to praise. Indeed, as Gunkel remarks, Psalm 13 is the "Muster eines 'Klageliedes eines Einzelnen'".[102] Psalm 6 also contains a movement from lament to praise; the two elements are clearly marked, with lament first followed by praise. But the transition from lament to praise is more sudden in Psalm 6. There is almost no preparation for it, except for the fact that the psalmist has expressed his lament. We observe a similar 'suddenness' in Psalm 3, though here the interplay between lament and praise is more dynamic. Overall, Psalm 3 moves from lament to praise but it also contains a 'return' to the element of lament towards the end before finally ending in a note of praise. In a way Psalm 3 gives us a glimpse of the more active interplay between lament and praise which will be discussed in the next chapters.

Thus, we may conclude that there is a movement from lament to praise. This movement is not uniform but varies from psalm to psalm. The distinguishing characteristic is that the psalm ends on a note of praise. The transition from one to the other is rather sudden, though it is possible to see some form of a process in the transition (Psalm 13). More importantly for the purpose of the present study, the movement is not always straightforward but can be complex as in the case of Psalm 3. In the next chapter we are introduced to the more complex nature of the relationship between lament and praise.

---

[101] Although the movement lament-praise has always been assumed in the past and therefore my statement above may sound obvious, there is a need to reiterate this fact to avoid the tendency to deny the presence of this movement (see Weber above).

[102] Gunkel, *Die Psalmen*, 13.

CHAPTER THREE

THE TENSION BETWEEN LAMENT AND
PRAISE IN PSALM 22

3.1 INTRODUCTION

We started our analysis of the psalms in the previous chapter with three psalms which contain the Psalter's most common movement, from lament to praise: Psalms 3, 6 and 13. Psalm 22—the focus of the present chapter—can actually be grouped under this category. Read as a whole, Psalm 22 contains a movement from lament to praise. What sets this psalm apart from the previous ones, however, is that here we have a juxtaposition of what appear to be two independent compositions.

Scholars generally view Psalm 22 as consisting of two main parts:[1] vv. 2–22 and vv. 23–32, which from this point on will be referred to as Ps 22A and Ps 22B, respectively. The two sections differ remarkably in tone, representing two genres; the former being a lament and the latter, praise/thanksgiving. In fact, one can easily assign the two parts to two entirely different settings. This has led some to regard the psalm as originally consisting of two separate compositions which have been joined together.[2] Others see the passage undergoing a series of redactions before finally reaching its present form.[3] Specifically for the

---

[1] Kraus, *Psalms 1–59*, 292; Weiser, *Die Psalmen I*, 139, ET *The Psalms*, 219.

[2] See Scott Arthur Ellington, "Reality, Remembrance, and Response: The Presence and Absence of God in the Psalms of Lament", (PhD Diss, University of Sheffield, 1999), 104.

[3] Briggs, *A Critical and Exegetical Commentary on the Book of Psalms* (vol. 1; Edinburgh: T & T Clark, 1906), 188, is of the opinion that Psalm 22 originally consisted of vv. 1–23, 26 to which vv. 24–25, 27 were added and then extended further by the addition of vv. 28–32; cf. Gerstenberger, *Psalms Part I with an Introduction to Cultic Poetry*, 112. Becker, *Israel deutet seine Psalmen*, 38–9, sees vv. 2–27 as originally a unity, with 28–32 as a reinterpretation. In his discussion of the various redactional developments that the passage has undergone, Spieckermann, *Heilsgegenwart: Eine Theologie der Psalmen*, 242–43, believes we have the work of an editor in vv. 4–6 as reflected in the collective voice of the words. The next redactional supplement (Nachtrag) is in v. 10f. (p. 243). But the most expansive redaction occurs after v. 23, which is the original ending. To v. 23 is added the quite unusually long 'promised song of praise' vowed in v. 23 (p. 244). Broyles, *Psalms*, 113; cf. 120–22, tries to discern a development in the psalm to

present study, our concern is to understand the interaction between lament and praise in Psalm 22. How are the elements presented in the psalm? What overall effect does the present arrangement have for understanding the relationship between lament and praise? Although we no longer have access to what originally constituted Psalm 22, whether it was originally composite or not, our view on the composition of the psalm is crucial for the understanding of the interplay between lament and praise. Does Psalm 22 reflect a unified whole or do we have here a juxtaposition of two compositions? If the former then the movement between lament to praise is easier to discern; like the previous psalms at which we have looked, the movement from lament to praise would be easier to see. But if Psalm 22 exhibits traces of a joining of two compositions, then the task of understanding the interaction between lament and praise becomes more complex or at least not as readily apparent as in the previous psalms we have examined. The juxtaposition of the two creates a certain disjuncture. A 'gap' is created in which the making sense of the whole becomes more challenging and the reading of it more engaging.

The understanding of the composition of Psalm 22 is therefore crucial for our understanding of the interaction between lament and praise. To determine the nature of the composition of the psalm we analyse its structure and contents. We begin with an analysis of the structure of Psalm 22A and Psalm 22B to see whether the two parts represent two self-contained units. If they do, then we have some indications of a joining together of two compositions. A more extended textual discussion of v. 22 is provided, as this is significant to the discussion of the relationship between the major parts of the psalm. Finally, a summary and conclusion is provided at the end.

---

make sense of the lack of uniformity, particularly vv. 28–32, which is different from the rest of the psalm. According to him, the psalm originally consisted of vv. 2–22 which is a prayer psalm of an individual. Initially for individual use, the lament was later applied to the nation of Israel during the exilic period. In the post-exilic period, vv. 23–32 have been added, representing the thanksgiving of the people. As support for this thesis, Broyles notes the similarity between Ps 22:28–32 and Psalms 69, 51 and 102 which all speak of Israel's restoration (pp. 120–22). Hossfeld, *Die Psalmen I. Psalm 1–50*, 145 also attempts to recover the text which originally constituted Psalm 22. In his view, the text at its core consisted originally of vv. 2–3, 7–23, to which vv. 4–6, 24–27 (first redaction) were added as an expansion and much later on, 28–32 (second redaction). The latter reflects the theology common in the Hellenistic period with its emphasis on the resurrection or a possibility thereof.

3.2   STRUCTURAL ANALYSIS: PSALM 22A

In the diagram below I have tried to sketch the flow of the overall structure of Psalm 22A.

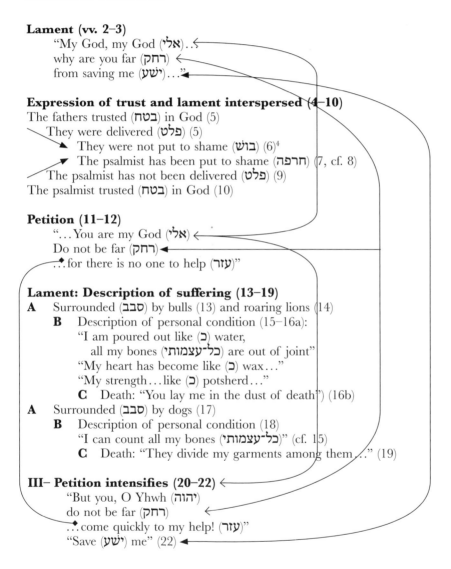

Lament (vv. 2–3)
   "My God, my God (אלי)..
   why are you far (רחק)
   from saving me (ישע)..."

Expression of trust and lament interspersed (4–10)
The fathers trusted (בטח) in God (5)
   They were delivered (פלט) (5)
      They were not put to shame (בוש) (6)[4]
      The psalmist has been put to shame (חרפה) (7, cf. 8)
   The psalmist has not been delivered (פלט) (9)
The psalmist trusted (בטח) in God (10)

Petition (11–12)
   "...You are my God (אלי)
   Do not be far (רחק)
   ...for there is no one to help (עזר)"

Lament: Description of suffering (13–19)
A   Surrounded (סבב) by bulls (13) and roaring lions (14)
   B   Description of personal condition (15–16a):
      "I am poured out like (כ) water,
         all my bones (כל-עצמותי) are out of joint"
      "My heart has become like (כ) wax..."
      "My strength...like (כ) potsherd..."
      C   Death: "You lay me in the dust of death") (16b)
A   Surrounded (סבב) by dogs (17)
   B   Description of personal condition (18)
      "I can count all my bones (כל-עצמותי)" (cf. 15)
      C   Death: "They divide my garments among them..." (19)

III– Petition intensifies (20–22)
   "But you, O Yhwh (יהוה)
   do not be far (רחק)
   ...come quickly to my help! (עזר)"
   "Save (ישע) me" (22)

---

   [4] It should be noted that בוש (v. 6) and חרפה (v. 7) differ. Unlike in the rest of the presentation here, what binds the inner structure of vv. 6 and 7 is a similarity of ideas not of key words.

3.3 Detailed Analysis

3.3.1 *Keyword of Psalm 22A:* רחק

As I have tried to demonstrate through the diagram above, Ps 22A exhibits a well-structured unit. Overall, it is linked by the keyword רחק, which appears in three significant places—in the beginning, middle and end:[5]

> "*My God, my God, why have you forsaken me? [Why are you]* **far** *from saving me? [Why are you far from] the words of my groaning?* (2)

> "*Do not be* **far** *from me, for trouble is near and there is no one to help!"* (12)

> "*But you, O Yhwh, do not be* **far***, my strength, come quickly to my help!"* (20)

Together with אלי—which is also repeated three times (vv. 2 [2x] and 11)—and the name יהוה in v. 20, רחק captures very well the tension between intimacy and distance in the psalmist's relationship with God, between past experience of salvation and its absence in the present. It aptly depicts the inscrutable absence of God and the torturing sense of abandonment felt by the psalmist. The one to whom the psalmist cries as '*my* God' is also said to have abandoned him and is *far* from him. Thus, Fuchs is justified in seeing the whole psalm as already contained in the cry of v. 2: "Der Textanfang ist gleichsam das Tor, das mit seinem 'Namensschild' und seiner Gestaltung viel von dem dahinterstehenden Gebäude verrät".[6] As Gunkel writes, "der Psalmist klammert sich an den, der ihn zu verlassen droht: du hast mich verlassen, aber ich lasse dich nicht, du bleibst 'mein Gott'!"[7]

The whole lament is developed around this tension. It begins with the cry 'My God, my God, why have you forsaken me?' which is reinforced in the following verse by a merismus. The words 'day' and 'night' are employed in the two parallel lines of v. 3 to express the growing agony of the psalmist who is at the point of frustration. He

---

[5] Ridderbos, *Die Psalmen*, 185, divides Ps 22A into three parts: 2–11; 12–19; 20–22. Observing the occurrence of רחק in all three, he considers רחק as the keyword (189).

[6] Otmar Fuchs, *Die Klage als Gebet: Eine theologische Besinnung am Beispiel des Psalms 22* (Munich: Kösel Verlag, 1982), 69.

[7] Gunkel, *Die Psalmen*, 91.

complains that his pleas are continually ignored even though they are uttered unceasingly.

But the employment of the words 'day' and 'night' is not only a contrasting literary device; it also signals the contrast that follows between Yhwh who is "enthroned in the praises of Israel" (4) and the psalmist who describes himself as "a worm and not a man" (7). The contrast is unmistakeable as reflected in the use of ואתה and ואנכי in vv. 4 and 7, respectively. Gunkel captures the contrast very well: "Ein schrecklicher Gegensatz: hier der armselige Dulder, der sich in seinen Schmerzen windet; dort der majestätische Gott, thronend im Heiligtum, gepriesen von den Lobliedern Israels!"[8]

3.3.2 *Expression of trust and lament interspersed (4–10)*

The contrast is not only between Yhwh and the psalmist, but also between the forefathers' experience of Yhwh's salvific acts and the appalling absence of such for the psalmist. This is reflected in the structure I have sketched above:

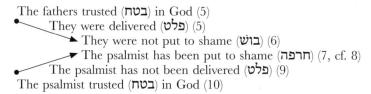

The fathers trusted (בטח) in God (5)
    They were delivered (פלט) (5)
        They were not put to shame (בוש) (6)
        The psalmist has been put to shame (חרפה) (7, cf. 8)
    The psalmist has not been delivered (פלט) (9)
The psalmist trusted (בטח) in God (10)

The palistrophe shows that the high note falls on the middle part, the experience of shame. The following close examination of the pattern in vv. 5–6 demonstrates that the word בוש represents the peak:

Line 1: Our fathers trusted (בטח); they trusted (בטח) and were delivered
Line 2: They (i.e. 'our fathers) cried and were rescued
Line 3: In you they trusted (בטח) and were *not* put to shame (בוש)
    Trusted in God   ⟶   Deliverance
    Cried out to God   ⟶   Rescue
    Trusted in God   ⟶   *Not* put to shame

The diagram demonstrates how every act of coming to God on the part of the forefathers has been met with divine response. Each action

---

[8] Ibid.

in column A is matched by a positive description in column B. The fathers trusted (2x in v. 5 for emphasis), cried out (6a) and trusted (6b). In all three the object is God, as the prepositional phrases, "in you" (בך) and to you (אליך) reveal. Interestingly, the word 'cried' is parallel to and enveloped by the word בטח. This implies that crying out to God is actually an act of trusting. Lamenting is an act of bold faith! Each time the fathers came to God, they received an answer. As can be noticed, however, there is a difference with the third response. Whereas the first two responses are positive ('delivered' and 'rescued'), the last one is negative ('*not* put to shame'). Why the change? I think the change is deliberate to highlight the contrast between the experience of the fathers and that of the psalmist. This contrast is carried on in the following verse which also contains the negation לא and חרפה—a word synonymous with בוש: "But I am a worm and *not* a man, a *reproach* of men" (7).

3.3.3 *Expression of trust and petition (10–12)*

The analysis thus far shows that Psalm 22 begins with a lament, followed by a construction where lament and expression of trust are interspersed. From the combination of lament and trust comes a full expression of the psalmist's trust in vv. 10–11. These verses form an ABB'A' structure:

A "For you (אתה) brought me forth from the womb (מבטן) (10a)
    B You caused me to trust (בטח)[9] even on my mother's breast (10b)
    B' On you[10] I was cast[11] (שלך) from birth (11a)
A' From my mother's womb (מבטן) you (אתה) are my God" (11b)

---

[9] The MT has the Hiphil participial form (מבטיחי) whilst the LXX has the noun form (מבטחי = ἡ ἐλπίς μου). The MT should be preferred in the light of the previous participle (גחי) in the first part of the verse and the parallelism with the verb in the next verse (שלך).

[10] The prepositional phrase, "on you" (עליך) looks back to the series of similar phrases in vv. 5–6 (בך and אליך). As in the latter, עליך clearly signifies trust. Thus, although the word בטח is not used in 11b, the sense of trust is very much present.

[11] בטח is parallel to שלך. Although the former is active (Hiphil) and the latter passive (Hophal), both point to God as the main actor. In the former, God is said to have caused the psalmist to trust in him. In the latter, the psalmist is said to have been cast on God. The parallel line shows that it is God himself who did the 'casting off': "from my mother's womb, you are my God". For a discussion of the peculiar function of the Hophal, see Bruce K. Waltke and M. O'Connor, *An Introduction to Biblical Hebrew Syntax* (Winona Lake, Indiana: Eisenbrauns, 1990), 447–49.

The statement, "you are my God", especially the form אלי, prepares us for the petition that follows (12) and recalls v. 2's double אלי אלי and רחק (see overall structural outline above).

The first direct petition in Psalm 22 occurs in v. 12. As he had used contrast to formulate the previous section, so the poet employs the same to construct his petition. The words 'far' and 'near' ring loudly in the ears: "Do not be *far* from me, for trouble is *near*, for there is no one to help!" The first two cola should be enough, since they form a perfect parallel and contrast. But interestingly, another colon is added in "for there is no one to help (עזר)". The addition further underlines the difficult situation in which the psalmist finds himself and anticipates the series of petitions in vv. 20–22, where the word עזר reappears (20).

3.3.4   *Lament: Description of suffering (13–19)*

The parallel section that follows builds on the motivation mentioned in the petition. The psalmist pleads with Yhwh not to be *far* from him, for trouble is *near* and there is no one to help. Verses 13–19 depict the situation when God is far and trouble is near. The clue to identifying the structure of these verses is the repetition of the word סבב in vv. 13 and 17 and the shift from external to internal descriptions of the psalmist's situation. In the following, I try to outline the structure of vv. 13–19.

A   Surrounded (סבב) by bulls (13) and roaring lions (14)
    B   Description of personal condition (15–16a):
        "I am poured out like (כ) water,
            all my bones (כל־עצמותי) are out of joint"
        "My heart has become like (כ) wax…"
        "My strength…like (כ) a potsherd…"
        C   Death: "You lay me in the dust of death" (16b)
A   Surrounded (סבב) by dogs (17)
    B   Description of personal condition (18)
        "I can count all my bones (כל־עצמותי)" (cf. 15)
        C   Death: "They divide my garments among them…" (19)

3.3.4.1   *External trouble*

We begin with the description of the situation of the psalmist 'from outside' (external). Instead of the nearness of God, the psalmist experiences the 'nearness' of hostile forces. Bulls surround him (13). Lions—described as 'devouring' and 'roaring'—are threatening him

(14). Interestingly, the word translated 'roaring' is the same word used for 'groaning' in v. 2. By repeating the word שאג the poet creates a subtle contrast between God's 'farness' and the closeness of danger: the roaring (שאג) of the lion is near (14) whilst God is far "from my groaning" (שאגה) (2). In the parallel section in v. 17, the psalmist continues to describe his 'external' situation. Corresponding to the bulls and lion (13–14), the dogs are also said to be surrounding (סבב) the psalmist (17). There is a movement in the latter from the metaphor towards a description of who these people are ("a company of evildoers", 17b) and what they do to the psalmist (17c).

3.3.4.2 *Description of personal situation*

From the external dangers, the psalmist moves on to describe what happens within him.[12] As in the foregoing, we find here parallel descriptions of the psalmist's 'internal' situation in vv. 15–16a and 18. The psalmist employs a series of similes to depict his condition. Three times the preposition כ is repeated: "like water", "like wax", "like a potsherd". He speaks of "all my bones (כל-עצמותי) as out of joint". In the parallel verse, he employs exactly the same phrase (כל-עצמותי) (v. 18), confirming the connection between vv. 15 and 18.

3.3.4.3 *'Dying' situation*

The last parallel statements in the present section are linked through the idea of 'death'. Though not as closely-knit as the previous ones, vv. 16b and 19 reflect some affinity. They both speak of death/dying. In the former, the psalmist accuses God of 'laying me to the dust of death'. In the latter, the psalmist depicts the final stages of a person about to die or already considered dead.[13] A further support for considering

---

[12] Gunkel, *Die Psalmen*, 90, observes a similar movement from a reference to the psalmist's enemies in vv. 13–14 and 17 to a description of his own condition (eigenes Ergehen) in vv. 15–16; i.e., a movement from the external to the internal situation of the psalmist (cf. Gese, "Psalm 22 und das Neue Testament", 9). The difference is that I see v. 18 as a description of the psalmist's own condition whilst Gunkel sees in it and in v. 19 a combination of the psalmist's enemies and personal condition. A more radical difference is my observation of the structural parallelism between vv. 16c and 19, both of which focus on the feature of death/dying. See below.

[13] H.-J. Kraus, *Psalms 1–59*, 298, sees v. 19 as reflecting a situation of death. He quotes a song from Mesopotamia: "The coffin lay open, and people already helped themselves to my valuables; before I was even dead, the mourning was already done".

v. 16b as a separate element in the structure is its dissimilarity from the construction preceding it. As already noted, the preceding verses form a series of similes describing the situation of the psalmist. Suddenly, in v. 16c the language shifts from 3rd person to 2nd person address to God. This marks a transition to a new element in the structure.

3.3.5 *Intensified petitions*

The extended descriptions of the external and internal situations of the psalmist (13–19) lead into the final set of petitions (20–22). It is interesting to note that two words from v. 2 reappear in the final petitions in a sort of envelope fashion: רחק and ישׁע[14] reappear in vv. 20 and 22, respectively. This demonstrates the self-contained character of Ps 22A. The repetition also implies a pointing back to the lament. *The cry of lament at the beginning is sustained towards the end.*

Verse 20 functions as a transition to the series of petitions that follows. The verse alludes to earlier sections through the employment of earlier mentioned words; foremost of which is ואתה. The last time we encountered this word was in v. 4. There ואתה functioned as an instrument for the expression of both lament and trust. Preceded by the cry of lament (v. 2–3), the psalmist struggles to cling on to God, holding on to his trust: "But you". Yet the ואתה also serves the purpose of the lament in facilitating the contrast between the 'you' (Yhwh) (4) and the 'I' (psalmist) (7) and that of the experience of the fathers (5–6) and the psalmist (7–9). Here in v. 20, there is an indication that in the ואתה the psalmist had swung more to the side of trust, though not quite letting go of the rope of lament. The psalmist no longer comes with the intensity of the earlier complaints; yet at the same time he is desperate. Having described the worst in the preceding verses, he no longer has anyone to go to but God. If we compare the preceding section (vv. 13–19) with vv. 4–10, we will notice that the former is darker and bleaker. We do not find any recollection of what Yhwh did in the past; there is only the awful present situation. DeClaissé-Walford thinks vv. 13–19 is the lowest point of the lament.[15] As demonstrated above, the

---

[14] The word appears as a noun in v. 2 and as a verb in v. 22.

[15] Nancy L. deClaissé-Walford, "An Intertextual Reading of Psalms 22, 23 and 24", in *The Book of Psalms: Composition and Reception* (ed. P. W. Flint and P. D. Miller; VTSup 99; Leiden/Boston: Brill, 2005), 146–47.

parallel construction ended with the sound of death (16c and 19). What is worse than a situation in which death is already being experienced? And what is more, the one who should deliver the person from such a condition is also viewed as the one responsible for it. Yet it is interesting that the one whom the psalmist accuses of laying him to death (16b) is also the one to whom he now comes, pleading for mercy. This exemplifies what Westermann explains about the characteristic nature of the biblical lament. It is always directed to God. No matter how terrible the situation is, how utterly hopeless, still, everything is brought to God.[16] Even when the problem is God himself, the lamenting person nevertheless clings on to God.[17]

The intensity of the petitions is further illustrated in the psalmist's address to God. The psalmist addresses God as יהוה for the first time in v. 20. The first time יהוה appeared was in v. 9 in the mouth of those who are taunting the psalmist. Three times the address has been אלי (2 [2x], 11). Two other words repeated are רחק and עזר. The former occurs earlier in vv. 2 and 12; i.e., in the lament and petition, respectively. With its repetition here, the main concern of the whole lament is pinned down. The repetition of עזר recalls the petition of v. 12. But one notices a deeper sense of urgency in v. 20: "Come quickly to my help!"—a further deepening of v. 12's "there is no one to help".

Verses 21–22 form a parallelism. Both follow the pattern: Verb (Vb)—Indirect Object (I.O.)—Direct Object (D.O.):

Verse 21:
   Deliver (Vb)—from the sword (I.O.)—my life (D.O.)
   (Deliver)[18]—from the hand of the dog (I.O.)—my only one (D.O.)

---

[16] What I like about what Westermann said is that *lament becomes only a true one in its biblical sense when it is brought before God.* He writes that lament "is the means by which suffering comes before the one who can take it away" (Westermann, "The Role of Lament in the Theology of the Old Testament", *Int* 28 [1974], 32.

[17] Westermann, *Lob und Klage*, 128, ET *Praise and Lament*, 169, mentions the three subjects of lament—"God, the one who laments, and the enemy". The most challenging is the last one, since the one being called is apparently also the one who is causing the problem. Yet, the psalmist still directs his lament *against* God *to* God.

[18] There is clearly an ellipsis here where the verb 'deliver' should be carried into the next line.

<u>Verse 22</u>:
Save (verb)—from the mouth of the lion (I.O.)—me[19] (D.O.)
  (Save)[20]—from the horns of the wild oxen (I.O.)—my poor [soul] (D.O.) /
  he answered me

A textual issue which is important for the present analysis is the question
of the form of the last word in v. 22. The issue is significant because
it affects our understanding of the relationship between lament and
praise in the whole of Psalm 22. If the last word reflects some form of
resolution then the transition into the second part of the psalm (Psalm
22B) is somehow facilitated and shows an indication of the unity of the
psalm. But if the last word of v. 22 betrays an absence of resolution
then Psalm 22A remains a "pure" lament and the transition to the
thanksgiving part of the psalm (Psalm 22B) becomes rather too abrupt
and sudden; the relationship between the two parts becomes strained
and explaining the sense of the overall psalm in relation to the movement between lament and praise becomes less apparent. So we devote
the following excursus to this important textual issue.

3.3.6   *Excursus: The Textual issue of Ps 22:22b*

3.3.6.1   *Difficulty of the textual issue in Ps 22:22b*

The textual problem in v. 22b is particularly challenging for two reasons.
The first is the difference between the MT and the LXX readings. The
former has the verb, עניתני ("and you have answered me"), whilst the
latter reflects the reading, עניתי ("my poor" [soul/life]). As can be seen,
the two readings are very similar. Consonants-wise, the LXX reading
presents no problem.[21] Relevant to the present study, the MT reflects
some form of resolution to the previous lament, whereas in the LXX
the lament remains, ending on a rather sombre note. Somehow, the
transition to the second part of the psalm is facilitated by the reading
in the MT. The LXX leaves the matter unresolved; no explanation
for the change of mood in the second part of the psalm (Psalm 22B)
is provided.

---

[19] The object 'me' is already in the verb, 'save', so there is no need to produce
one here.
[20] Another case of an ellipsis where the verb 'save' is extended to the second line.
[21] Kilian, "Psalm 22 und das priesterliche Heilsorakel", *BZ* 12 (1968), 173.

These differing effects which the two readings create actually arise
from the nature of the composition of Psalm 22 itself which consists of
two entirely distinct genres—an individual lament psalm and a thanksgiving psalm. This is the second reason why the issue of the textual
problem in v. 22b is rather complicated.[22] Each of the two main parts of
the psalm exhibits a self-contained unity. The problem is how one goes
from the lament to the thanksgiving part. The MT reading somehow
facilitates the transition from the lament to praise. In the case of the
LXX, the lament is left hanging and the connection between the two is
rather strained. There is a "gap" that is created. It is here that Begrich's
theory offers an 'attractive' solution. It is attractive because it provides
a 'way out' of the problem; it 'fills in' the 'gap'. Gerstenberger's candid
comment betrays the real motive behind many scholars' decision on
the proper translation of v. 22b: "The arguments pro and con usually
reflect only the interpreter's prior position regarding the so-called salvation oracle".[23] A review of some of the scholars who adopt the MT
reading confirms Gerstenberger's observation.

3.3.6.2   Scholars' adoption of the MT reading based on the oracle of salvation theory

Ridderbos follows the MT because, according to him, it represents the
'certainty of a hearing' which presumably occurred before v. 23ff.[24] As
further support for his view, he points out that the word עָנָה forms an
inclusio with v. 3.[25] Ellington affirms Ridderbos' latter point, explaining that the "strongest argument for maintaining the reading of the
Masoretic Text...is structural. The repetition of the verb עָנָה in this
particularly strategic place seems unlikely to be accidental as it functions
to close out the lament portion of the psalm by resonating with the
opening cry of 'you do not answer me' and by providing an explana-

---

[22] We may add here the difficulty of the word עֲנִיתִי. This retrojected form never
occurs in the MT. Hatch and Redpath admits the difficulty of the occurrence in Ps
22:22, marking it as 'uncertain'. Of the 33 instances where the word ταπεινωσις occurs,
the majority (18x) derives it from the root עֲנִי (Edwin Hatch and Henry Redpath, eds.,
A Concordance to the Septuagint and the Other Greek Versions of the Old Testament, vol. 3. (Graz-
Austria: Akademische Druck- U. Verlagsanstalt, 1954), 1307–08). It is understandable
that the copyists would prefer the more common, 'and you have answered me'.

[23] Gerstenberger, *Psalms: Part I with an Introduction to Cultic Poetry*, 112.

[24] N. H. Ridderbos, *Die Psalmen: Stilistische Verfahren und Aufbau mit besonderer Berücksichtigung von Ps 1–41* (BZAW; ed. G. Fohrer; Berlin: Walter de Gruyter, 1972) 191.

[25] Ibid.

tion for the abrupt transition to praise".[26] Ellington cites the work of Kselman,[27] who himself adopts Begrich's thesis.

Kselman sets out his study with the aim of heeding Muilenburg's call for something "Beyond form criticism". A closer scrutiny of his work, however, reveals that although he tries to approach the text rhetorically, it remains very much within the scope of form criticism. In his textual comments on v. 22, he writes: 'you have answered me' "stands as the psalmist's response to a salvation oracle pronounced by some cultic official".[28] Like Ridderbos, Kselman's decision on the textual issue of v. 22 is determined by his decision to adopt Begrich's thesis.

Craigie likewise translates 22b as 'you have answered me', assuming an oracle of salvation.[29] He writes: "In participating in such a liturgy, the worshiper hoped for a priestly oracle favorable to his plea, which would enable the great declaration of confidence".[30]

Kraus believes that an oracle of salvation caused the shift of mood and thus prefers the MT reading which reflects the reception of such an answer.[31] Interestingly, he admits that עניתני (MT) is a "makeshift emendation" of the Hebrew verb. Unfortunately, though he admits that the MT reading is a "makeshift emendation", he opts for this reading because it expresses the certainty of being heard.[32] Similarly, although Anderson views the oracle of salvation as only one of the possibilities for explaining the change of mood, he nevertheless adopts the MT reading because, according to him, it provides an explanation for the change of mood in v. 23.[33]

---

[26] Ellington, "Reality, Remembrance, and Response", 110.

[27] John S. Kselman, "Why Have You Abandoned Me?: A Rhetorical Study of Psalm 22", in *Art and Meaning: Rhetoric in Biblical Literature* (ed. David J. A. Clines et al; Sheffield: JSOT Press, 1982). For his explicit support for Begrich, see ibid., 180.

[28] Ibid., 179.

[29] Peter C. Craigie, *Psalms 1–50* (Waco, Texas: Word Books, Publisher, 1983), 195–98, 201.

[30] Ibid., 198. The problem with Craigie's proposal is that we do not have support for the idea that the worshipper coming to the temple anticipates an oracle. Craigie explains that the reason we do not have the actual words of the cultic priest is because presumably he is around the corner waiting for the specific response from God for the individual (200).

[31] Kraus, *Psalms 1–59*, 292.

[32] Ibid.

[33] Anderson, *The Book of Psalms* (vol. 1), 191. He believes that the change of mood is due to the fact that the psalm is actually a thanksgiving psalm, with the lament inserted to recall the previous situation prior to deliverance.

Seybold goes a step further, transporting the last word of v. 22 to v. 23. He translates v. 22 as follows: "Save me from the mouth of the lion; and from the horns of the bull", and joins "and you answered me" with the thanksgiving in vv. 23ff.[34] According to him, 'and he answered me' is a "signature" (Unterschrift) added later along with the thanksgiving after the experience of deliverance, characterizing it as a "heard prayer".[35]

Weber's position is very similar to Seybold's. In his translation, Weber removes עניתני from the rest of v. 22.[36] The reason for his adoption of the MT is that it brings out the certainty of hearing in v. 22b. He writes: "Das abschliessende עניתני 'du hast mich erhört' stellt wohl eine Erhörungbezeugende Unterschrift des Psalmisten dar".[37]

Seybold's joining of עניתני to the following section has already been suggested by Schmidt. But Schmidt follows neither the MT nor the LXX. He explains that the MT's rendering would contradict what was stressed in the preceding parts of the psalm. As for the LXX rendering, he says that the parallelism demands no new expression for the object. What is needed instead is some kind of a verb, like, פלט. What he decides to do is to move עניתני to the second half of the psalm.[38]

As demonstrated in the foregoing there is a strong 'pressure' to explain the sudden change of mood between vv. 22 and 23 and Begrich's thesis has proved to be an attractive explanation.[39] Unfortunately, most schol-

---

[34] Klaus Seybold, *Die Psalmen* (vol. I/15; Handbuch zum Alten Testament; Tübingen: J. C. B. Mohr, 1996), 95–96.

[35] Ibid., 97.

[36] Beat Weber, *Psalmen Werkbuch I: Die Psalmen 1 bis 72* (Stuttgart: Kohlhammer, 2001), 121.

[37] Ibid., 123.

[38] Schmidt, *Die Psalmen*, 36, 38. The problem with Schmidt's suggestion is that it disrupts the parallelism between vv. 21 and 22 by adding the verb פלט. Verse 21 only has one verb which creates an ellipsis with the second part of the verse.

[39] There are a few scholars who adopt the MT reading not on the basis of the oracle of salvation theory. Hossfeld also follows the MT (Hossfeld, and Zenger, *Die Psalmen I*, 145), though he prefers a more internal explanation for the change of mood rather than an external one as in the oracle of salvation. In his view, it is more likely that the change of mood arises from an internal change which flows from a heart full of trust; cf. J. Clinton McCann Jr., "Psalms", in *NIB* (vol. 4; Nashville: Abingdon Press, 1996), 764. Rudolf Kilian, "Psalm 22 und das priesterliche Heilsorakel", 183, follows the MT's reading of Ps 22:22b, but interprets it not as a perfect in the sense of an event that has already transpired, but rather as what he calls, "Perfectum confidentiae". Nothing has occurred yet but the psalmist hopes and trusts in the Lord that something will happen. He uses as his support the emphasis on trust in the whole psalm (esp. vv. 4–6 and 10–11). Such trust fuels the faith of the psalmist, enabling him to construct his prayer in such a manner as if the event had already transpired. He applies the

ars' decision to follow the MT is dictated more by the need to resolve the apparent tension in the text rather than by a consideration of the context and language of v. 22. We will discuss this point below. But before that let us turn to the other option—the LXX reading.

3.3.6.3   *The LXX reading*

As mentioned above, the LXX translation indicates the presence of a word which appears something like this: עָנִיתִי. Conspicuously, this view is actually the minority view among scholars. I think Begrich's explanation of the cause for the sudden change of mood in the lament psalms as well as the whole form-critical method has been greatly influential in promoting the MT rendering.[40] As noted above, Begrich's theory offers an attractive alternative to the problem posed by the sudden transition to thanksgiving in v. 23.

Among the scholars who defend the LXX reading are Briggs, Kittel, Gunkel, Spieckermann, and most recently, Curtis. Briggs prefers the LXX reading for the following three reasons: a) the MT copyists misread what may have been originally, עֲנִיָּתִי ('my afflicted' [one]), interpreting it as a perfect verb;[41] b) the MT creates a too abrupt a transition and c) makes it difficult to explain the meaning of 'from the horns of the ox'.[42] Kittel's argument in favour of the LXX is similar to Briggs' second point. He thinks the MT reading is rather "premature".[43] Interestingly, Gunkel also prefers the LXX reading over the MT. He prefers the LXX reading because the statement of certainty—"you have heard me"—does not match the parallelism in 21. "My poor [soul]"

---

same reading of the perfect tense in Ps 3:8—a passage which has been commonly used as a support for the sudden change of mood in Ps 22:22b (p. 173). Recognizing the potential hindrance to his view in the perfect verb in v. 25, he likewise reads the perfect here as he did in v. 22b (p. 184). Kilian's view has already been anticipated by Delitzsch, who likewise understands v. 22b as a *"perf. confidentiae"* (Delitzsch, *Biblischer Commentar über die Psalmen*, 235, ET *Biblical Commentary on the Psalms*, 395). Finally, M. Dahood, *Psalms I (1–50)* (vol. 16; AB; Garden City, NY: Doubleday, 1966), 142, following Buttenweiser, understands the word in the MT as a "precative perfect". He thinks that the word 'triumph' brings out the sense of the word better, for it balances the imperative at the beginning of the verse: 'save me'.

[40] See Gerstenberger's comment above.
[41] Briggs, *A Critical and Exegetical Commentary on the Book of Psalms* (vol. 1), 197.
[42] Ibid.
[43] Kittel, *Die Psalmen*, 82.

is parallel to יחידתי in v. 21. He writes: "das Pf. der Gewissheit passt nicht zur Parallele".[44]

Spieckermann favours the LXX reading because according to him, the MT rendering "has neither syntactical nor internal connection with the preceding".[45] He cites Symmachus (κακωσιν μου) along with the LXX. Like Briggs, he believes that the MT copyist has misread a noun for a verb: "Dieser Rückbezug, der auch schon bei יחידתי 'meine einzige' vorlag, ist später nicht mehr erkannt und deshalb zur Bestätigung der Erhörung umgeschrieben worden".[46] The change seems likely to have occurred in the MT since the word, "you have answered me" would have provided a more suitable link between the petition (22) and the vow of praise (23).[47]

If Spieckermann is correct that the change occurred in the MT, *then we have in the MT the first attempt to make sense of the change of mood in Psalm 22B*. Ironically, as the reading in the LXX testifies, even the MT's very own attempt is not certain after all!

Intriguingly, whilst most scholars follow the MT, quite a few modern translations adopt the LXX,[48] one of which is REB which translates v. 22 as follows: "Save me (21a [22a])...(save) this poor body (21b [22b])". Curtis follows the REB on the basis of the parallelism with the previous verse.[49] Although he is open to the possibility of an oracle which could explain the shift of mood, he nevertheless remarks: "But such transition from lament to praise occurs in the psalms without any textual indication of an oracle, and the REB rendering makes good

---

[44] Gunkel, *Die Psalmen*, 96.

[45] Hermann Spieckermann, *Heilsgegenwart: Eine Theologie der Psalmen* (FRLANT 148; Götingen: Vandenhoeck & Ruprecht, 1989), 241, n. 7.

[46] Ibid.

[47] Ibid.

[48] Among those which follow the LXX are the RSV ("Save me from the mouth of the lion, my afflicted soul from the horns of the wild oxen!"), JB, NJB, NAB, and REB; cf. the New American Catholic Bible ("Save me from the lion's mouth; from the horns of the wild bulls, my wretched life"). The *The Psalms: A New Translation for Worship* by William Collins and *The Revised Psalter* (The amended text as approved by the Convocations of Canterbury and York in October 1963 [London: SPCK, 1964]) also follow the LXX. For modern translations which adopt the MT, see NRSV and NASB; cf. NJPS. The NIV treats the verb as an imperative: "save me from the horns of the wild oxen" (cf. TNK). Although this provides a good parallelism with the verb הושיעני, it does involve unsubstantiated emendation: ענני (John Day, in a personal conversation, March 2006).

[49] Adrian Curtis, *Psalms* (Epworth Commentaries; Peterborough: Epworth Press, 2004), 48.

sense as it stands". His comment affirms the nature of the movement from lament to praise. As observed in the analysis of Psalms 3 and 6, the movement from lament to praise is 'sudden'; the change of mood from lament to praise *simply occurs*; no explicit transition is given.

3.3.6.4 *Which reading is the more likely to be original*

Having presented the two alternatives for the textual problem in v. 22, we may ask, which of the two readings represents the more likely original form of the Hebrew word—עניתני (MT) or עניתי (LXX)?

Admittedly, the issue is far from easy, which is why some scholars remain undecided.[50] A decision to adopt the LXX reading would require an emendation. Further, one cannot deny the possibility that what we actually have in Ps 22:22b is the one contained in the MT: here we have a clear witness to the possible original Hebrew word. Tov, in his article on textual criticism, explains the problem with a retroverted Hebrew of the Versions like the one in the LXX. He writes: "Very few elements in the Versions can be retranslated with absolute certainty to specific Heb variants. In general, it is uncertain whether a deviation in a translation is due to a Heb variant or, for example, is the result of a free translation or of exegesis".[51] Nevertheless, he also notes that the LXX of the Psalms is among those he considers "slavishly literal" in its translation.[52] Further, in his discussion of how to evaluate the evidence, he explains: "all Heb readings in principle are of equal value and this applies also to reconstructed variants, provided the reconstruction is trustworthy".[53] Among the criteria for evaluating the evidence, he mentions the importance of "context". By context he refers broadly to a "complete exegesis of the passage as well as to an analysis of the language and style of the OT as a whole and the specific scriptural unit under investigation".[54] In addition, he mentions two other 'subjective'

---

[50] Gerstenberger and Mays view the issue as debatable/uncertain. The former thinks the LXX has the support of the parallelism, but could not deny entirely the MT reading (Gerstenberger, *Psalms: Part I with an Introduction to Cultic Poetry*, 112). The latter confesses, "Neither of these problems is subject to any certain solution" (Mays, *Psalms* [Interpretation; Louisville: John Knox Press, 1994], 111).

[51] Emanuel Tov, "Textual Criticism (OT)", *ABD* 5: 403.

[52] Ibid.

[53] Ibid., 410; cf. Bruce K. Waltke, "The *New International Version* and Its Textual Principles in the Book of Psalms", *JETS* 32 (1989): 17–26, for a helpful guide in doing textual criticism.

[54] Ibid.

criteria: the preference for the shorter reading (*lectio brevior*) to a longer one, and the 'more difficult' reading (*lectio difficilior*) to easier ones".[55]

Using these criteria for deciding on the issue at hand, we may register first of all that on the basis of the 'subjective' criteria the LXX is the shorter reading. It is also the more difficult reading. As explained above, in the MT the rather rough transition to Psalm 22B is somehow smoothed. With the LXX the first half of the psalm is left without a proper closure and the transition to the next is rather strained. This is probably the reason why the MT is the more popular option among exegetes, for it provides an explanation along with the oracle of salvation theory to what would otherwise be a 'hanging' case.

On more objective grounds, we note that the "context" of Psalm 22 favours the LXX reading. As demonstrated in the analysis above, Psalm 22A is full of contrasts; the element of tension persists throughout, so that a reading which sustains and preserves the element of lament fits better with the context. In terms of "language" and "style", the LXX reading has the advantage. The LXX preserves the parallelism with the previous verse (see my analysis of the structure of vv. 21–22 above), as Gunkel rightly points out. This is important, for as will be seen below, maintaining the parallelism leads to the creation of an ellipsis in the second half of v. 22. This ellipsis brings out the element of tension, thus further establishing the contact with the preceding context.

With the MT reading, we not only have the 'easier' reading which makes it an unlikely option on the basis of the subjective criterion; we are also confronted with the difficulty of explaining the language of the verse if we follow the MT. I am referring here to the problem of making sense of the meaning of "from the horns of the wild ox". If we take "and he answered me" with this phrase, it may imply that God was located on "the horns of the wild ox". Seybold and others thus propose that we treat "and he answered me" as an isolated word. The problem with this proposal is that it results in an unusual Hebrew construction in which one word is isolated. Moreover, transporting 'and he answered me' to the next verse not only destroys the parallelism with the previous verse (v. 21), it also disturbs the present construction of v. 23.

It is more likely then that the LXX reading represents the original reading of the Hebrew of v. 22b. Even though this involves emendation,

---

[55] Ibid.

it is only a slight one, as the two readings are identical consonants-wise.[56] More importantly, the context of Psalm 22A as well as the language and style of vv. 21–22 support the LXX reading.

The decision on the textual issue above has important implications for how we read Psalm 22. The first part of Psalm 22 (Psalm 22A) ends with the noun "my poor [soul]", not with the verb, "you have answered me". This means that the last word of v. 22 is not one of certainty but of uncertainty. The employment of the noun instead of another verb (cf. v. 21a) creates an ellipsis in v. 22b. On the significance of an ellipsis, Alter explains: "from the viewpoint of the poet, what is accomplished through this simple syntactic manuever is a freeing of space in the second verset...which can then be used to elaborate or sharpen meaning. This freeing of space, moreover, nicely accords with the formal focusing effect of the absence of the verb in the second verset, which has the consequence of *isolating for attention* this second object of the verb".[57] By employing an ellipsis in v. 22 the focus shifts from God's act of deliverance to the lamentful situation of the petitioner. The ellipsis focuses the attention on 'my poor [soul]'. With this word the whole of Psalm 22A ends...on a note of despair. Though the psalmist desperately clings on to God, resolution and deliverance remains a distant memory.

This makes the transition in v. 23 sudden; there is nothing in the text that prepares us for the change of mood. In v. 23 everything has changed; it seems as though we have been transported into a different world. Indeed, the reversal is so conspicuous that the temptation to resolve the tension is very strong, as reflected in many scholars' decision to follow the MT reading. Yet if we follow the LXX reading, there is no need to resolve the tension. This very 'gap' created by the absence of a clear resolution may actually be one of the main ingredients in the text added to facilitate a more active reading of the text. We may see here what Erbele-Küster calls a "Leerstelle". We will come back to this below. Before that let us look at the structure of the second part of Psalm 22.

---

[56] As noted by Kilian, "Psalm 22 und das priesterliche Heilsorakel", 173.
[57] See Alter, *The Art of Biblical Poetry*, 24, emphasis in the original.

3.4   STRUCTURAL ANALYSIS: PSALM 22B

The structure of Psalm 22B is not as unified as Psalm 22A, showing
more signs of redaction.[58] Nevertheless, one is able to detect some organising principle with the word הלל. The verb הלל is repeated 4x (3x as
verb [23, 24, 27] and 1x as a noun [26]), indicating the emphasis in the
entire section. Praise/thanksgiving is evidently the focus of the second
half of Psalm 22. Overall, Psalm 22B may be outlined as follows:

> Vow of praise (23)
> Call to worship (24)
> Motivation for praise (25)
> Fulfilment of vow (26)
> Yhwh will be praised (27)
> Yhwh will be praised beyond the limits (28–32)
> > By all the ends of the earth (28a)
> > By families of the nations (28b)
> > By those already dead (30)
> > By those yet to be born (31–32)

Verse 23 forms a chiastic structure:

> I will declare your name to my brothers
> > In the midst of the congregation
> I will praise you

3.5   DETAILED ANALYSIS OF PSALM 22B AND
COMPARISON WITH PSALM 22A

The first two lines of v. 24 are parallel, with the second forming a
chiastic structure with the third line:

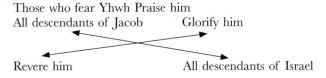

Those who fear Yhwh   Praise him
All descendants of Jacob   Glorify him

Revere him   All descendants of Israel

Verse 25 provides the motivation for vv. 23–24. There is a significant
change in the construction of v. 25. Whereas the preceding is mostly
parallel, v. 25 contains a series of three negations:

---

[58] Becker, *Israel deutet seine Psalmen*, 39 is of the opinion that vv. 28–32 is a latter
interpretation and application of the psalm to a more communal context.

He has *not* despised, he has *not* abhorred   the affliction of the poor
He has *not* hidden his face from him
When he cried to him, he heard

Clearly the threefold repetition of לא is for emphasis; the employment of two verbs in line 1 differs from the preceding verses which have one verb in each colon. Here we have one object and two verbs; both verbs are directed to the object—the 'affliction of the poor'. This forms a contrast with the earlier double negation in the first part of the psalm (vv. 6–7). We may recall the contrast between 'they were *not* put to shame' (6) and 'But I am *not* a man' (7). Observe as well the occurrence of the word בזה in vv. 7 and 25. This indicates an attempt to link the two main parts of the psalm,[59] though in a rather contrastive way. The interplay between the two parts is marked by a contrasting movement between vv. 5–6 and v. 25. The movement is opposite: from positive to negative in vv. 5–6 (he has delivered, he has rescued and 'he has *not* put to shame'); from negative to positive in v. 25: "He has *not* despised, he has *not* abhorred, he has *not* hidden his face...*he heard*").

The contrast between Psalms 22A and 22B is further illustrated in the following verse. Verse 26 repeats the word, תהלה, which occurs earlier in v. 4. The employment of the word, according to Kraus is a clear indication of contact with v. 4. By using תהלה instead of the expected תודה, the poet draws attention to his earlier reference to the word in v. 4.[60]

Verse 27 is linked to v. 23 with the word הלל, but does not indicate any allusion to Ps 22A. Instead, it alludes to some passages in Deuteronomy which employ the same language to speak of what the Israelites would eventually do when they reach the promised land. The words אכל and שבע are the same as in Deut 8:10–12; cf. 31:20. Moses tells the Israelites that when they enter the land that the Lord is giving them, they will eat (אכל) and be satisfied (שבע) and bless (ברך) the Lord (Deut 8:10).[61] The word ברך is similar to הלל (praise) in Ps 22:27.

---

[59] The first possible allusion to Ps 22A occurs in v. 23 with the word ספר which probably alludes to v. 18, though the connection is not as direct as in v. 25.

[60] Kraus, *Psalms 1–59*, 299.

[61] These words are to be understood in the context of the warning that follows in v. 11: "Be careful, lest you forget the Lord..." The repetition of the two words, אכל and שבע in v. 12 highlights the importance of the exhortation. The structure of Deut 8:10–12 yields a chiasm with the warning to 'be careful' in the middle and the words אכל and שבע enveloping it. For as the story of Israel relates the people indeed forgot the Lord (Deut 31:20; cf. Neh 9: 25–26).

The difference is that whereas in Deuteronomy the Israelites "turned to other gods" (31:20), here "all the ends of the earth will remember and turn to Yhwh" (28). Verse 29 provides the motivation for v. 28. Verse 30 repeats the word אכל. The mentioning of the "fat of the earth" recalls Deut 31:20, which speaks of the people eating, having their fill and getting fat. But in Ps 22:30 again the difference is that here the people will be worshipping Yhwh.

An interplay with the first half of the psalm resumes in v. 30b with the word, עפר. The word is used earlier in the lament (v. 16c). The psalmist complains that Yhwh himself brought him to the extreme depths of human suffering possible, i.e. death. Here (v. 30b), he speaks of the extreme heights of praise with the dead bowing down to God. Here we find what Davis calls "exploding the limits".[62] Extending the limits further, the psalmist embraces even the generation yet to be born within the scope of the worship of Yhwh (31–32).

As can be seen above and in the diagram below (Table 3), Ps 22A and Ps 22B contrast sharply with each other.

Table 3: *Comparison Between Psalm 22A and Psalm 22B*

Psalm 22A	Psalm 22B
Keyword: רחק (occurs 3x in vv. 2, 12 and 20), corresponding to the theme of lament	Keyword: הלל (occurs 3x in vv. 23, 24 and 27), corresponding to the theme of praise
Isolation: the 'I' in isolation (see esp. vv. 7 and 12)	Community: the 'I' in community ("my brothers", the קהל (23; cf. 26)
"I can count (ספר) all my bones..." (18)	"I will tell (ספר) of your name..." (23)
"Despised (בזה) by men" (7)	"He did not despise (בזה) the affliction of the poor" (25)
עניתי (22, LXX)	ענות עני (25)
Emphasis on the negation: Yhwh did *not* put his forefathers to shame (6); "I am *not* a man" (7)	Emphasis on the negation: "He did *not* despise, he did *not* abhor, he did not hide his face" (25)
"You are...enthroned in the praises (תהלה) of Israel" (4)	"From you comes my praise (תהלה) in the great assembly" (26)
"You lay me to the dust (עפר) of death" (16)	"...all who go down to the dust (עפר) will bow down before you" (30)

---

[62] Ellen F. Davis, "Exploding the Limits", *JSOT* 53 (1992), 93–105.

The tones are completely different as reflected in the keywords: רחק and
הלל. The former brings out the emphasis on lament and the latter the
focus on praise. There is also a contrast between the 'I' and the 'we',
between the 'I' who is in isolation and the 'I' within the community.
The lack of experience of deliverance which the psalmist complains
about (7) is considered as an item for praise in the thanksgiving part of
the psalm (25). His lament that he is 'despised by men' is met with the
testimony that God "did not despise the affliction of the poor". One
can also observe the use of play on words and repetition as a means
of bringing out the contrast between the two parts of the psalm. The
employment of the word ספר in the thanksgiving part of the psalm
(23) recalls one of the lowest points of the lament (18). Formerly used
in the context of lament (18), ספר is now employed in the context of
worship and praise (23). Another possible play on words can be seen
in vv. 22 and 25. If we are correct in our textual decision that what
we have in 22b is the one preserved in the LXX, then we have here
an interesting play on word with the phrase, ענות עני ('affliction of the
afflicted') in v. 25. Verse 25 forms a powerful response to the ending of
Psalm 22A: To the cry, "deliver...my poor [soul]" (עניתי) of v. 22b, we
find the words "He has not despised...the affliction of the afflicted"
(עני ענות) (25). A further connection is intimated by the word תהלה.
The word is used with almost the same sense in the two parts of the
psalm—vv. 4 and 26; the difference is that in the latter תהלה becomes
my praise and not just Israel's praise as in the former. Finally, we notice
the repetition of the word עפר (16, 30). Davis believes that "the unusual
wording here may be a deliberate echo of v. 16, where dust is specifically identified with death".[63]

We thus have a psalm which reflects the presence of two compositions
as indicated by the self-contained nature of the two parts. At the same
time there are indications of a purposeful and creative bringing together
of the two as evidenced by the verbal and thematic links between
them. The connections, however, are not strong enough to justify the
conclusion that what we have in Psalm 22 is a unified composition.
As mentioned above, scholars believe that the psalm has undergone a
series of developments. What is significant for the present study is the
arrangement of the text as we now have it. How do we explain the
relationship between lament and praise in Psalm 22? Is the movement

---

[63] Ibid., 102.

from lament to praise or are there other ways of viewing the relationship between the two elements?

3.5.1   *The interplay between lament and praise in Psalm 22*

The more common and traditional way of envisaging the interplay
between lament and praise in Psalm 22 is to see here a movement from
lament to praise. As shown in the comparative analysis above, there is a
stark contrast between the two parts of the psalm, between the lament
and praise. The lament can be read in the light of the assertions of
the second part of the psalm. Especially with the change of the word
from "my poor [soul]" to "and you have answered me" in the MT such
a reading is facilitated. But as shown in the discussion of the textual
problem in v. 22, it is more likely that the original reading is the one
represented in the LXX. In that case, the transition from the first part
of the psalm to the second becomes rather abrupt and sudden. When
we add to this the self-contained nature of the two parts of the psalms,
the result is a reading which is not self-evident. The rather familiar
movement that we always assumed (from lament to praise) turns out to
be not as simple after all; the relationship becomes more complicated.
For in this case we have a juxtaposition of two compositions which
differ remarkably from each other. The very act of juxtaposition makes
the reading of the movement in the psalm complex. A 'gap' is created
in the process.

   As remarked at the start of this chapter, explaining the relationship
between lament and praise becomes more complex in the case of a
juxtaposition. It is possible to see a movement from lament to praise so
that the overall direction and focus is on the element of praise. But it
is also possible in a juxtaposition to see an element of tension between
lament and praise, between Psalm 22A and Psalm 22B. In recent
discussions of Psalm 22 it is the latter view that has been presented,
particularly by Fuchs.

   Fuchs's book of more than 300 pages, *Die Klage als Gebet*, focuses
on a detailed analysis of the movement between lament and praise in
Psalm 22.[64] The approach is still within the form-critical method, as his
three-fold structural outline of lament, petition and praise shows. Fuchs

---

[64] Fuchs, *Die Klage als Gebet*.

divides the psalm into three main sections: vv. 2–11; 12–22; 23–32, corresponding to the three-fold form-critical structure. He believes that the second section ends with a 'certainty of a hearing'.[65] However, Fuchs does not agree with all of Begrich's theory. Like Janowski, Weber and Erbele-Küster, he criticises the whole idea of 'sudden' change of mood, arguing that what we have in Psalm 22 is not a sudden change of mood from lament to praise but a gradual movement. His thesis can be described by the word *process* (cf. Janowski above). He explains that what we have in Psalm 22 is a slow process from lament to more trust, before finally reaching the peak where the lament gives way to praise (section 3).[66] But even in the praise section, the element of lament persists. The reason why this is so is because actual deliverance has not yet come. Fuchs reads the third section as an expression of trust but not as thanksgiving for deliverance, which has not yet actually occurred. He explains that unless an explicit answer comes, "the beginning question remains unanswered up to the end".[67] "Das *Rätsel der Not* bleibt".[68] Rather than considering a movement from lament to praise then, Fuchs sees the element of tension preserved in the juxtaposition of lament and praise in Psalm 22.

Fuchs' view is affirmed by Paul Ricoeur in his article on Psalm 22 entitled, "Lamentation as Prayer".[69] Ricoeur maintains the presence of a tension between the two parts of the psalm. He quotes LaCocque, who writes: "The praise remains a lament right to the end".[70] Ricoeur proposes a reading of the lament from the perspective of the exile. It is important that the explanations of God's abandonment offered in the narrative of the OT and the prophets be complemented by the 'Word' preserved in the lament. The former offers explanations in terms of God's delivering act (narrative; e.g. Exodus) and retribution for sin. But the theology that arises from the lament is from the perspective of suffering. This too needs to be heard. Ricoeur notes that "we need to be attentive to the diversity of ways this theology of history gives

---

[65] Ibid., 86.
[66] Ibid., 102.
[67] Ibid., 138.
[68] Ibid.
[69] Paul Ricoeur, "Lamentation as Prayer", in *Thinking Biblically* (ed. André LaCocque and Paul Ricoeur (Chicago and London: The University of Chicago Press, 1998), 211–32. O. Fuchs, *Die Klage als Gebet: Eine theologische Besinnung am Beispiel des Psalms 22* (Munich: Kösel Verlag, 1982).
[70] Ibid., 219.

the cries of distress a place that is proportional to the place it gives to the theme of deliverance".[71] We need to consider the experience of exile. He writes:

> We must not, therefore, confine ourselves to giving the framework of traditional history, where deliverance in fact answered the people's supplication, as the background of the dynamism that leads from lament to praise. The lament has to be set within the context of an exile *where one does not know whether it will repeat the Exodus.*[72]

Ricoeur sees a 'simultaneity' in Psalm 22: "Looked at from the point of view of its end, the movement from lamentation to praise seems to unfold within a single 'being-with-God'. Looked at from its beginning, the prayer is a movement that starts from the silence of God and never loses its aspect of being a struggle for renewed trust. In this sense, the starting point remains contained within the end point, despite the reversal to regained trust".[73] He continues: "The paradox of reversal from the one to the other is inseparable from this struggle whose outcome is never guaranteed. The divine inscrutability is not lessened by the conversion of the *Urleiden* into jubilation".[74]

Fuchs and Ricoeur's readings show that the task of grasping the relationship between lament and praise is not straightforward. Indeed, their reading, which differs from the usual form-critical view, proves the complexity of the interplay between lament and praise. Both see the element of tension preserved even with the movement to praise in Psalm 22. Where I differ from Fuchs is in the 'source' of the tension.[75] For Fuchs the element of tension is derived from the fact that we do not have a clear indication of an actual deliverance from the passage. In a way, his explanation is 'historically oriented'; i.e. the absence of an objective, external resolution points to the continuing experience of lament. My explanation of the presence of tension is derived more from the text itself (text oriented), particularly from the way the text as we now have it has been arranged. As noted above, we have in Psalm 22 a juxtaposition of two apparently separate compositions. The jux-

---

[71] Ibid., 223.

[72] Ibid., (emphasis mine).

[73] Ibid., 231. This is similar to Weber's view though Ricoeur's emphasis is more on the element of lament whilst Weber's is on the element of praise.

[74] Ibid., 231–32

[75] In the case of Ricoeur's approach, his treatment is general and he does not provide a detailed analysis of the passage, understandably so because that is not his focus.

taposition opens up various possibilities for the interpretation of the interplay between lament and praise. Though it is possible to see here a movement from lament, this is not the only way of explaining the interplay between lament and praise. It is also possible to see a preservation of the element of tension as the very nature of the composition of Psalm 22 intimates.

A consideration of the neighbouring context of Psalm 22 supports a reading which maintains tension between lament and praise.

3.6   Psalm 22 in its Canonical Context

3.6.1   *Psalm 22 and its surrounding context*

Even long before the canonical method became fashionable Delitzsch had already made some 'canonical' observations concerning Psalm 22. He notes the contrast between Psalm 22 and Psalm 21: "Psalm 22 is a plaintive Psalm, whose deep complaints occasioned by the most shameful humiliation...stand in striking contrast with the calm and cheerful mood of Ps. 21".[76] A proper canonical criticism scholar—McCann—would later affirm Delitzsch's observation. Without denying that the connection may just be coincidental, McCann avers that it is significant that three key words from Psalms 20–21 recur in Ps 22:2–6: ישׁע (v. 2; see Ps 20:6–7, 9; 21:2, 6), ענה (v. 3; see Ps 20:2, 7, 10) and בטח (vv. 5–6; see Ps 21:8).[77] He writes: "In Psalms 20–21, there is the certainty that the sovereign God will answer and help the king, who lives by his trust in God. Thus the canonical sequence emphasizes the sharp contrast; there is no help and no answer for the psalmist".[78]

Hossfeld likewise observes that if we compare the royal thanksgiving prayer in Psalm 21 and the Prayer of trust in Psalm 23, Psalm 22 stands out through its extended lament.[79] Both Psalms 21 and 22 revolve around the theme of Yhwh's help (21:2, 6; 22:2, 22).[80] The

---

[76] Delitzsch, *Biblischer Commentar über die Psalmen*, 222, ET *Biblical Commentary on the Psalms*, 372.
[77] McCann, "Psalms", in *NIB* (vol. 4; Nashville: Abingdon Press, 1996), 762.
[78] Ibid.
[79] Hossfeld, F.-L., and E. Zenger. *Die Psalmen I. Psalm 1–50*, 145.
[80] Ibid.

description of the psalmist of himself as a worm contrasts sharply with
the kingly description, 'majesty and splendour' (Ps 8:6; 21:6).[81] As for
the connection between Psalms 22 and 23, Hossfeld notes that both
prayers are faced with death (22:16; 23:4) and hope in the deliverance
of life (22:21; 23:3).[82] Further, the promised praise of Yhwh's name in
22:23 is performed in 23:3. Above all, the feast of the poor (22:27) is
further carried out in 23:5.[83]

    The element of tension between lament and praise can also be
observed in the broader context of Psalm 22. Psalm 22 is placed
within a redactional unit dominated by expressions of trust and praise.
DeClaissé-Walford observes that the series of royal psalms that begin in
Psalm 18 is actually preceded by a long series of lament (Psalms 3–17,
except 8 and 15).[84] Lament resumes in a series of 10 laments in Psalms
25–28, 31, 35–36, 38–40. This makes Psalms 18–24 significant, for we
have here a short redactional unit which is focused more on the element of praise and not on lament.[85] This makes the position of Psalm
22 within the redactional unit of Psalms 18–24 significant. For in the
midst of expressions of trust, we have the cry of lament in Psalm 22A.
The position of Psalm 22 within its redactional unit is comparable to
the position of Psalm 8 within its own redactional unit. But whereas the
latter is a psalm of praise in the midst of laments, Psalm 22 is a lament
in the midst of praise.

3.7   Conclusion

Psalm 22 represents an important development in our study of the
sudden change of mood in the lament psalms. Whilst most of previous
scholarship has always assumed a linear movement from lament to praise
in the psalm, our analysis has shown that the interplay between lament
and praise is not limited to this movement. In view of the overall structure of the psalm and its content, Psalm 22 can also be read in terms
of a tension between lament and praise. The juxtaposition between

---

[81] Ibid.
[82] Ibid., 146.
[83] Ibid.
[84] DeClaissé-Walford, "An Intertextual Reading of Psalms 22, 23 and 24", in *The Book of Psalms: Composition and Reception*, 140–41.
[85] Ibid.

lament and praise opens up other ways of reading the movement in the psalm. It makes a pure linear/chronological reading of the movement rather simplistic, for the act of juxtaposition inevitably makes the task of grasping the interplay between lament and praise more complex. The juxtaposition creates a 'gap' which cannot be fully filled.[86] Psalm 22 then marks a development from the psalms which move from lament to praise. It also forms a bridge into the psalms which juxtapose between lament and praise in the next chapter.

---

[86] Cf. Erbele-Küster (see above).

CHAPTER FOUR

FROM PRAISE TO LAMENT

4.1 INTRODUCTION

In the previous chapter we have focused on Psalm 22—a psalm which juxtaposes lament and thanksgiving. Although it is possible to read Psalm 22 in terms of the movement lament-praise, I have tried to argue that it is also possible to read the psalm as a composition in which the elements of lament and praise are held in tension. The juxtaposition of two apparently independent compositions is open to various interpretations, creating a "Leerstelle" which cannot be fully explained.

In the present chapter we will also be considering other psalms which juxtapose the two elements of lament and praise. Only this time the arrangement is the other way around. For instead of the order lament// praise, we have praise//lament. The psalms we will consider contain thanksgiving at the beginning followed by the lament—the reverse of Psalm 22. Specifically, we will focus on Psalms 9/10, 27 and 40. In two of these (Psalms 27 and 40) there is a clear juxtaposition of thanksgiving and lament. Psalm 9/10 also juxtaposes thanksgiving and lament, though here the two elements are held together by the acrostic. Through these psalms I hope to demonstrate that in the Psalter we do not only have the movement from lament to praise; we also have the reverse movement from thanksgiving/praise to lament in which the tension between the two elements is given prominence.

An introduction dealing with interpretative issues relating to the psalm will be provided, followed by an analysis of the structure and a detailed analysis of the psalm, focussing on the interaction between lament and praise. Questions relating to canonical context will also be addressed, though only in a limited way.[1] A brief summary is provided at the end of each psalm. The chapter ends with a conclusion.

---

[1] Of the three I will only provide a proper discussion of the canonical context of Psalm 9/10. Psalm 40 will be discussed with Psalm 70. Psalm 27 will have to wait until we discuss Psalm 28 (Chapter 5).

4.2   Psalm 9/10

4.2.1   *Introduction*

Scholars generally accept the unity of Psalm 9/10, as evidenced by
the following: 1) the use of the acrostic pattern, not uncommon in the
Psalms; 2) the absence of a title for Psalm 10; 3) the fact that the LXX
combines the two psalms.[2] But because Psalm 9 and 10 belong to two
entirely different genres, thanksgiving and lament, respectively, and
because the order is from thanksgiving to lament, some have thought
otherwise.[3] Delitzsch remarks that although the language of the two
chapters is similar, they are to be considered as separate because they
belong to different genres.[4] Gunkel considers the psalms as a unity until
the question 'why?' of 10:1 which goes beyond the boundaries of the
thanksgiving genre. He could tolerate the presence of a petition at the
end of Psalm 9 (vv. 18–21), for we also find elsewhere cases where
petition appears at the end of thanksgiving psalms. But the למה at the
beginning of chapter 10 cannot be accommodated into this genre, for
it represents the characteristic cry of the lament psalm. Gunkel writes,
"Von ל an ist also der Verfasser ganz ins Klagelied geraten und hat

---

² Kirkpatrick, *The Book of Psalms* (Cambridge: Cambridge University Press, 1903),
41; Briggs, *A Critical and Exegetical Commentary on the Book of Psalms*, 68–70; Weiser, 92ff.,
ET 149f.; Anderson, 104–5; Kraus, *Psalmen I*, 77, ET *Psalms 1–59*, 191; Terrien, *The
Psalm* (Grand Rapids, MI: Eerdmans, 2003), 138; Dirk Sager, *Polyphonie des Elends: Psalm
9/10 im konzeptionellen Diskurs und literarischen Kontext* (vol. 21; FAT, 2. Reihe; Tübingen:
Mohr Siebeck, 2006), 23–24.

³ Anderson, 104–5. John Strugnell and Hanan Eshel, "Psalms 9 and 10 and the
Order of the Alphabet", *BibRev* 17 (2001): 41–4, posit a rearranging of the two
psalms on the basis of what they argue as an evidence for the existence of an alphabet
consisting of two halves (*lamed* to *tav* and *aleph* to *kaf*, respectively) and the occurrence
of the same in the reverse order. But the real motivation for their proposal is what
they find as a rather problematic arrangement of the psalm as it now stands. "The
pieces seem to stand back to back, reversed thematically. From the standpoint of literary flow and the regular forms of the Book of Psalms, Psalm 9 should *follow* 10"
(42). The problem with this position is that we have a clear evidence in the MT and
the LXX that the arrangement is as it now stands. There is also no evidence within
the Psalter itself, especially among the other acrostic psalm of such an arrangement.
More importantly, as will be shown in this study, lament can follow a thanksgiving;
such an arrangement is not unique to Psalm 9/10 as I will demonstrate in my analysis
of Psalms 27 and 40 below.

⁴ Delitzsch, *Biblischer Commentar über die Psalmen*, 125, ET *Biblical Commentary on the
Psalms*, 222; cf. Kittel, 32.

seinen ursprünglichen hymnischen Anfang völlig vergessen".[5] He adds
that had the poet been more extensive and had he been more conscious,
he would have made changes at least in material (Stoffmassen), and
begun with the lament and ended with the praise.[6]

Clearly, it is here that we see the limitations of form criticism. The
problem is with trying to fit every element into a particular form. And
if it does not fit into it, then the unity of the text is questioned. Had
there been only one genre (either lament or thanksgiving), and had the
arrangement been the other way round, i.e. from lament to thanksgiving,
there would have been no question about the unity of the two psalms.
It is the presence of two differing moods, set parallel to each other and
moving in the opposite direction, which disturbs the commonly known
order of the elements. This has led to various attempts to explain the
tension caused by the juxtaposing of the elements of thanksgiving and
lament in such an arrangement.

Dahood implies that the movement from thanksgiving to lament
posits "logical difficulties".[7] Following the suggestion of Buttenwieser he
resolves this by interpreting the verbs in 9:5–7 as "precative perfects".
He explains: "In this analysis the poem can be seen to be a lament
throughout. The opening verses become a promise to thank Yhwh on
condition that he put the psalmist's enemies to flight. Once the nature
of the verbs in 9:5–7 is correctly appreciated, the long-standing grammatical and logical difficulties are quickly resolved".[8]

Weiser explains the relationship between the two psalms in terms of
his cult renewal theory. If anywhere, it is in the discussion of Psalm
9/10 that his thesis on what caused the change of mood in the lament
psalms is demonstrated. Such confidence is derived from the cult, where
a covenant renewal highlighting God's kingship and *Heilsgeschichte* is re-
enacted. Viewing the two psalms as a unity, he explains that they are
parallel to each other. In Psalm 9, the covenant re-enactment forms
the background, calling attention to what Yhwh has done. In Psalm 10
the psalmist brings his own personal concern alongside the recitation
of God's great acts reflected in the covenant. In this way, the recollection of Yhwh's deeds serves to inspire and guide the prayer in Psalm
10, giving assurance to the psalmist that his prayer will be answered.

---

[5] Gunkel, *Die Psalmen*, 33.
[6] Ibid.
[7] M. Dahood, *Psalms I (1–50)* (vol. 16; AB; Garden City, NY: Doubleday, 1966), 54.
[8] Ibid.

The occasion for the recitation of the psalm is understood to be the "celebration of the feast of Yhwh's Covenant".[9]

A slightly different approach from Weiser is Beyerlin's view. Beyerlin basically sees that the focus of Psalm 9/10 is on the prayer of lament. The purpose of the first chapter is to back up or support the lament through what he calls "visualization of salvation".[10] Here the psalmist thanks Yhwh for his past acts as revealed in the salvation history. But implicit in the act of thanksgiving is the longing that experiences of deliverance will be a present reality.[11]

Kraus does not agree with Beyerlin's view on two grounds: first, the psalms which he chose in order to explain what he calls 'visualization of salvation' do not demonstrate congruity, and secondly, because Psalm 9/10 is an "artificial construction".[12] What is significant about Kraus' interpretation of Psalm 9/10 for the present study is the way he sees the element of tension presented in the composition of the psalm—a view closest to the one espoused in this Chapter. In contrast to the scholars above who finds the material in Psalm 9/10 'illogical' or needing explaining, Kraus accepts that what we have here is a psalm which presents the tension between lament and praise. This tension is reflected in the juxtaposition of lament and praise. He writes:

> On the one hand, Psalm 9/10 lets it be known what miracles (Ps. 9:1 [2]) or rescue and bestowal of salvation are performed for the יודעי שמך (Ps. 9:10 [11]). But on the other hand, the psalm also indicates what anguish then is precipitated when the signs of God's help fail to appear (Ps. 10:1–11). And so the 'didactic extension' of the individual song of thanksgiving is characterized, on the one hand, by hymnic expressions, and by lamenting and pleading on the other. Godforsakenness and triumph are juxtaposed in one and the same psalm, and that quite abruptly. Jubilation and lament permeate the song. Two experiences lie adjacent to each other, just as they are met with under the world reign of God on Zion: *Wondrous rescue and incomprehensible delay.*[13]

---

[9] Weiser, *Die Psalmen I*, 92ff., ET *The Psalms*, 149ff.

[10] W. Beyerlin, "Die Tôdā der Heilsverkündigung in den Klageliedern des Einzelner", 221.

[11] Anderson, 105.

[12] Kraus, *Psalms 1–59*, 193. For my own evaluation of Beyerlin's view, see the review of the different approaches to the change of mood in Chapter 1.

[13] Kraus, *Psalmen I*, 86–7, ET *Psalms 1–59*, 198–9. For a helpful presentation of the tension between lament and praise in the Psalm 9/10, see Alison Lo, Alison Lo, *Job 28 as Rhetoric: An Analysis of Job 28 in the Context of Job 22–31* (vol. 97; VTSup; Leiden/Boston: Brill, 2003), 239–42. A comprehensive treatment of Psalm 9/10 can be found in Sager, *Polyphonie des Elends: Psalm 9/10 im konzeptionellen Diskurs und literarischen Kontext.*

Where I differ slightly from Kraus is in his interpretation of the final verses of the psalm. In his view, the overall movement of Psalm 9/10 is towards the element of praise and resolution (see below). He writes: "in the hymnically oriented closing words (Ps. 10:16–18) the anguish of the waiting sufferer is incorporated in the eschatological hymn. It is not blended in hymnically, but it is taken up in a definitive solution of all mysteries that lie with the מלך Yahweh".[14] In my analysis below, I have tried to demonstrate that the element of tension is sustained throughout the psalm.

In what follows, we look at the overall structure of the psalm with the focus on the elements of praise and lament and how the two interact throughout.

4.2.2 *Structural Analysis*

Overall, the structure of Psalm 9/10 can be outlined as follows:

1. Thanksgiving (9:2–19)
   a. Declaration of praise (2–3)
   b. What Yhwh has done (4–7)
   c. Yhwh's eternal reign (8–9)
   d. The God of the lowly (10–11)
   e. Call to praise (12–13)
   f. (Petition) (14–15)
   g. Destruction of the wicked (16–19)
2. Lament (9:20–10:18)
   a. Petition (9:20–21)
   b. The cry of lament (10:1)
   c. Description of the wicked (2–11)
   d. Petition (12; cf. 9:20)
   e. Alternating expressions of lament and trust (13–18)
      i) Lamenting question (13)
      ii) Affirmation of trust (14)
      iii) Petition (15)
      iv) Certainty and uncertainty (16–18)

---

[14] Kraus, 87, ET 199.

4.2.3 *Detailed Analysis*

4.2.3.1 *Thanksgiving*

As shown in the overall structure above, Psalm 9/10 is divided into two main parts—thanksgiving and lament. The first part begins with a declaration of praise to Yhwh (9:2–3), followed by a recounting in general terms of what Yhwh has done to his enemies (4–7),[15] which all reflect Yhwh's eternal reign as judge over all the earth (8–9).[16] Even though Yhwh is the great God, he is also the protector of the lowly (10). In the context, those who are lowly know who Yhwh is, and Yhwh in turn does not abandon them (11). He is therefore to be praised; his wonderful works are to be declared (12–13). At this point a petition is inserted (14–15), probably as a creative way of exploiting the acrostic because the next letter is ח.[17] The psalm continues with the account of the destruction of the nations (16–19), which contains a powerful statement depicting the certainty of the destruction of the wicked (18). Verse 19 is connected with vv. 16–18, with the כי providing a substantiation for the statements just made. But it also forms a subtle transition from the thanksgiving to the lament. The tone is still one of assurance since it speaks about the fact that the needy will not be forgotten. It uses the word שכח, which is mentioned earlier in 9:13. But there is a difference: whereas 9:13 is constructed using the perfect tense and the active voice (לא־שכח), 9:19 is constructed in the imperfect tense, with the passive voice and, as used in the context, implies that the needy are presently being forgotten: כי לא לנצח ישכח אביון.

---

[15] V. 6 forms a parallelism: גערת—to rebuke // אבדת—to destroy/perish
גוים—nations // רשע—wicked
Linguistic and thematic affinity also binds v. 6 to v. 7. The word אבב occurs in 6a and 7b; their name will be blotted out forever (6b) and v. 7a speaks about perpetual ruin; name (6b) and the remembrance of them (v. 7b).

[16] V. 8 forms a contrast with the preceding verses: enemies will be destroyed forever, along with their cities and their name/memory, "but Yhwh sits (enthroned) forever".

[17] Contra Kraus, *Psalmen*, 78–9, ET 192–93, who seems to imply that the shift to petition is necessitated by the acrostic, implying a lack of poetic creativity on the part of the psalmist.

4.2.3.2 *Lament*

a. *Petition*

The psalm turns into the element of lament with the petition in 9:20–21. As I have indicated above (Chapter 2), I am using the term lament in a broader sense to include both the elements of lament and petition. Gunkel distinguishes between petition and lament. Normally, in the form-critical framework the lament is followed by the petition. But this does not fit in with the present order of Psalm 9/10, for here it is the other way around: the petition is followed by the lament. Here we can see that the two elements do not appear in one fixed order; the two cannot be totally separated because they are intertwined. Actually, even before the cry of the lament in 10:1 the psalm has already shifted to the element of lament in the last two verses of chapter 9. The cry of v. 20 is reminiscent of the cry in Ps 3:8a: "Arise, O Yhwh!"[18] As noted above, there is already a discernible shift from the confident disposition of the thanksgiving into a more unsettled state (see v. 19). With the petition in vv. 20–21 the movement away from the thanksgiving becomes more explicit. Verse 20 employs a word play with the repetition of שפט and פניך. Both words occur earlier in vv. 5 and 4, respectively. The repetition reflects a subtle contrast between the earlier settled condition and the more uncertain state of the psalmist's present condition. Whereas the experience of justice is a received reality in the past ("you have maintained my just cause" [5]), such has to be sought for urgently in the present ("Arise, O Yhwh... let the nations be judged before you!" [20]). The last word (פניך) in v. 20 recalls v. 4 and betrays a contrast similar to that between v. 20 and v. 5. If the enemy stumbled "before you" (מפניך) in v. 4, now the psalmist appeals to Yhwh to do the same. Another word that is repeated twice here and appears again in 10:18 is אנוש.

b. *The cry of lament (10:1)*

In 10:1, the move away from the thanksgiving is complete, with the characteristic cry of the lament, "why?". Conspicuously, the psalmist employs the same phrase, לעתות בצרה. This phrase occurs in 9:10b, used in the context of protection and security (Yhwh is described

---

[18] The cry for help is exactly the same in Ps 3:8 and 9:20: קומה יהוה.

using the metaphor "refuge/stronghold", 10a). He is a refuge for the oppressed "in times of trouble". But in the present verse, the psalmist is questioning the earlier affirmation. He does not see the reality of the earlier declaration. It seems as though the earlier thanksgiving is recited only to be questioned at this point. One can see here a pattern similar to that of Psalm 44.[19] There is a clear movement from thanksgiving to lament, a movement which disturbs the usual form-critical framework of the movement lament-praise. Unfortunately, instead of becoming open to the possibility that praise can also move into lament, some form critics continue to impose the one-way movement from lament to praise into the text. And where this does not apply, they resort to other explanations.

As mentioned above, Gunkel attributes the shift to lament here to the use of the acrostic pattern. The next letter is ל, and thus the question, "למה?".[20] In effect Gunkel blames the use of the acrostic for the transition to lament in Psalm 9/10. This is clearly a reflection of the limited view of the movement between lament and praise. As seen in the review of the different approaches in Chapter 1, the subject of change of mood is understood only in terms of the movement lament-praise. Psalm 9/10 demonstrates that the change of mood is not only from lament to praise but also from praise to lament. The genius of the poet of Psalm 9/10 is that he is not limited by one particular line of thought. The power of poetry is such that it is able to shatter established norms and expectations. Gunkel's interpretation has actually undermined the creativity of the psalmist. Ironically, the psalmist's decision to employ the acrostic, which naturally led to certain limitations, has actually become a means whereby he could freely pour out his heart before Yhwh! The employment of the acrostic actually facilitated the move from thanksgiving to lament. As a modern day poet states, "the human-insight of the poem, and the *technicalities* of the poetic devices are inseparable".[21] What we think are mere accidents or technicalities may actually be reflections of the creative intuition of the poet.

---

[19] Cf. Weiser, *Die Psalmen I*, 94, ET *The Psalms*, 152.

[20] I wonder whether there may have been a better Hebrew word which the psalmist could have employed to avoid the move to lament.

[21] John Ciardi, *How Does a Poem Mean?* (Boston: Houghton Mifflin Company, 1959), 676, emphasis mine. He refers here to the use of rhyme by modern poets and how it fuses into the art of composing a poem. He cites as an example Robert Frost's poem, "Stopping by Woods on a Snowy Evening". He explains how Frost's decision to use full

c. *Description of the wicked (10:2–11)*

10:2–11 consists of a series of descriptions of the oppressive activities of the wicked (2–3, 6–11) and their success (5) despite the fact
that they "do not seek God" (4). This section corresponds to Psalm
9. The word עני occurs twice in Psalm 9 as an affirmation that Yhwh
will not abandon the poor/afflicted[22] (13) and as a petition that Yhwh
consider "my affliction" (14). Both of these statements are challenged
by the complaint in 10:2. A more significant word is repeated in
10:4. דרש occurs twice earlier as a reference to the righteous whom
Yhwh will not abandon (9:11) and as an image describing Yhwh as
the "one who seeks blood" (13). With this as background, the psalmist
complains that the "wicked does not seek".[23] The word also appears
later in 10:13, 15. Another loaded word is שכח. Like דרש this word
occurs 5x in Psalm 9/10. It appears earlier as an assuring statement
that Yhwh does not forget the cry of the afflicted (9:13), that he will
destroy those who forget him (9:18). As implied in 9:19, however, it
seems that the poor are now being forgotten. The word occurs next
in 10:11 as part of the speech of the wicked: "The wicked says in his
heart, 'God has forgotten'". The wicked speaks 3x in these psalms.
The first is in 10:6, boasting of his security, here in v. 11 and in 13.
Interestingly, the psalmist places his own complaint in the mouth of
the wicked.[24] What the wicked says in v. 11 is actually the concern of
the psalmist, as indicated in 9:19, 10:1, and in the entire description
of the wicked (2–10). The psalmist is lamenting over the incongruity
of the earlier affirmations about Yhwh's abiding protection for the
weak and what he sees in his own situation. By employing the word
שכח the psalmist expresses his own complaint through the voice of
the wicked in v. 11. But in v. 13, he becomes more direct, telling God:
אל־תשכח ענוים.

---

rhyming in all his lines has led to an unexpected turn towards the end of the poem,
whereby he repeats one line. The result was a profound composition which creates
space for further reflection.

[22] The Hebrew could be read as the noun עני or the adjective עני.

[23] The verb does not have an object in the MT; cf. 10:13.

[24] Cf. Erbele-Küster, *Lesen als Akt der Betens*, 119–20.

d. *Petition (12; see discussion of 9:20 above)*

e. *Alternating expressions of lament and trust (10:13–18)*
The description of the wicked is followed by a series of verses which
alternate between lament and expressions of trust. Verse 13 begins with
another question, similar to 10:1. Both are translated 'why?' in English,
though they are different words in Hebrew, עַל־מֶה (13) and לָמֶה (1). The
psalmist is here asking God why he is allowing the wicked to despise
God through his belief that God "does not seek".[25] In v. 14 we find the
psalmist struggling to refute what the wicked says. Although there is no
adversative waw, the sense of "but" is implied in the context. For the
first time since 9:19, we hear a statement which reflects trust in Yhwh
from the psalmist: "But you, you do see..." (10:14). But the expression
of trust is short lived for the mood immediately returns to lament with
the petition in v. 15. Interestingly, the word דרשׁ is again employed;
this time the psalmist is asking for Yhwh to "seek out" the wickedness
of the evildoer until there is no more. This is the last occurrence of
the word in Psalm 9/10. We note how the use of the word דרשׁ flows
through the psalm:

9:11—Yhwh will not abandon those who **seek** (דרשׁ) him
9:13—Yhwh is referred to as the one who **seeks** (דרשׁ) blood
10:4—The wicked does not **seek** (דרשׁ)
10:13—The wicked himself speaks, "You will not **seek** (דרשׁ)"[26]
10:15—The psalmist asks God to **seek** (דרשׁ) (the evil person's wickedness)

In v. 15, even though the psalmist has been trying to affirm his trust in
Yhwh earlier (14), his struggle remains. Finally, in v. 16 he breaks into
the mood of certainty. Leslie thinks that we have here, between vv. 15
and 16, a pronouncement of an oracle of salvation.[27] There is noth-

---

[25] There is ambiguity here.
[26] This verb is left without an object. I think this is a deliberate ambiguity. In 10:4,
the construction is similar, for which the NASB has to supply the object, "does not seek
him". Similarly here, NASB adds the object *it* in 10:13. But literally the Hebrew is just
simply: "you do not seek". It is probably left open to call the attention to 9:11—"those
who seek you" as well as 9:13—the one who avenges blood remembers them; he does
not forget the cry of the afflicted. Paul R. Raabe, "Deliberate Ambiguity in the Psalter," *JBL* 110 (1991): 213–27 proposes the presence of "deliberate ambiguities" in the
Bible that calls for multivalent readings. He mentions three areas in which these can
be found: lexical, phonetic, and grammatical.
[27] Leslie, 222.

ing in the text that indicates the presence of an oracle; what we have rather is a juxtaposition of lament and thanksgiving. Yhwh's kingship, already cited in 9:8 is repeated here. Ps 10:17 contrasts with 10:3: the latter speaks of the תאוה of the wicked; the former of the fact that the longing (תאוה) of the poor has been heard. The psalm ends with a statement similar to 9:20–21. The psalmist hopes that as a result of Yhwh's intervention mortal humans (אנוש; cf. 9:20–21) will no longer cause terror on earth (10:18). The repetition of אנוש parallels the end of the petition in 9:20–21 and creates a sense of tension. As Terrien notes, "The repetition of the words 'mortal man', at the beginning and end of the same strophe (vv. 20a, 21b), reveals both the certitude and the doubt of the poet".[28] Having begun with thanksgiving the psalm ends with the element of tension between trust and doubt, certainty and uncertainty.

4.2.4 *Summary*

Psalm 9/10 contains strong linguistic ties reflecting a complex but unified composition. The movement goes against the usual form-critical view of lament-praise. When read as a whole we see a composition that is full of tension.[29] A consideration of the canonical context of the psalm, specifically the preceding neighbouring context, further underlines the element of tension between praise and lament.

4.2.5 *Canonical Context*

Maclaren observed more than a century ago the connection between Psalms 7 and 9: "Psalms vii and ix are connected by the recurrence of the two thoughts of God as the Judge of nations and the wicked falling into the pit which he digged. Probably the original arrangement of the Psalter put these two next each other, and Psalm viii was inserted later".[30] With the application of the canonical approach to Psalm research, further explorations into the connection of Psalm 9 with its

---

[28] Terrien, *The Psalms*, 142.
[29] Balentine, *The Hidden God*, 54–55.
[30] Alexander Maclaren, *The Psalms* (vol. 1; The Expositor's Bible; ed. W. Robertson Nicoll; London: Hodder and Stoughton, 1893), 78.

neighbouring context, particularly with the preceding psalms, have been introduced. Wilson observed that in the Psalms as well as in the ANE similar phraseology at the beginning and end of certain compositions serve as a basis for their placement alongside each other.[31] Building on this insight, Miller tries to show the connection between Psalms 7, 8 and 9. He observes how the ending of Ps 7:18 is picked up later in Psalm 9: "The formulations at the end of 7.18 and at the end of 9.2 are exactly the same, including the reference to 'Most High'...Psalm 9.1–2 thus refers back to the praise rendered in Psalm 8 in accordance with the vow at the end of Psalm 7 and also continues to praise the name and recount the wonderful deeds of the Lord".[32] In this view Psalm 9 continues to fulfil the vow made in 7:18 which Psalm 8 has already started.

Similarly, Zenger sees a close connection between the three psalms. In his view, one of the reasons for placing Psalms 7, 8 and 9 beside each other is the presence of key words within the psalms themselves which link them together.[33] Thus, he observes how the end of Psalm 7 contains key words which link it to Psalm 8 and Psalm 9. The vow at the end of Ps 7:18 is realised in Psalm 8. The chorus of Psalm 8 which occurs at the beginning and end contains key words similar to Ps 7:18, "*your name* in all the earth". This prepares us for Ps 9:2f. which contains very similar language with Ps 7:18: "*I will thank YHWH*...I will sing *of your name*, O Most High". Zenger believes that "Durch die Verkettung wird Ps 8 ausdrücklich zum hymnishcen Lobpreis der Verfolgten (Ps 7) und der Armen (Ps 9)".[34]

Scholars have rightly pointed out the connection between Psalm 9 and the two preceding psalms—Psalms 7 and 8. Where their efforts fell short was in their failure to bring Psalm 10 into the discussion. The emphasis in the preceding contexts of Psalms 7 and 8 is on thanksgiving. Psalm 9 continues this through its own declarations of thanksgiving to Yhwh. However, Psalm 9 does not stop with thanksgiving, but continues with the lament in Psalm 10. When we consider the emphasis on thanksgiving in Psalms 7 and 8 and their link to Psalm 9, the transition to the lament in Psalm 10 becomes more striking. Indeed, the canonical

---

[31] Wilson, *Editing of the Hebrew Psalter*, 175.

[32] P. D. Miller, "The Beginning of the Psalter", in *The Shape and Shaping of the Psalter* (ed. J. Clinton McCann; Sheffield: Sheffield Academic Press, 1993), 90.

[33] Erich Zenger, "Von der Psalmenexegese zur Psalterexegese", *BibKir* 56 (2001), 12.

[34] Ibid., 13.

context highlights all the more the shift to lament. It tells us that even in spite of the vow of thanksgiving in 7:18 and the actual realisation of such a vow in Psalm 8, the thanksgiving in Psalm 9 nonetheless turns to lament. Unfortunately, in the canonical discussions above, Psalm 10 was not included. Having considered the surrounding context of Psalm 9, scholars have generally ignored the context of Psalm 9 itself, which as demonstrated above is closely linked with Psalm 10.[35] I think the link is crucial. For if we only relate Psalm 9 with the preceding psalms, the emphasis falls on the element of thanksgiving. Bringing Psalm 10 into the picture changes the emphasis altogether. If anything, it makes the connection all the more in favour of an emphasis on the lament. For in this case the emphasis shifts from thanksgiving to lament. The canonical consideration further brings out the tension between lament and praise.[36]

4.3   Psalm 27

4.3.1   *Introduction*

Like Psalm 9/10 the unity of Psalm 27 has been questioned by scholars. In the case of Psalm 27 the argument against the unity of the psalm is even more strongly advanced by scholars. For unlike Psalm 9/10, Psalm 27 does not have the advantage of an acrostic. The psalm consists of two parts—vv. 1–6 and 7–14—which can both stand on their own.[37] The two parts, which will be referred to from this point as Psalm 27A

---

[35] An exception is Sager, *Polyphonie des Elends: Psalm 9/10 im konzeptionellen Diskurs und literarischen Kontext*, 242, who insists that Psalm 9/10 should not be separated in canonical discussions of the psalm. His point is similar to my view, though I arrived at this position independent of his work.

[36] This weakens Hossfeld and Zenger's argument that the centre of the redactional unit in Psalms 3–14 falls on the element of praise (Psalm 8) (Hossfeld and Zenger, *Die Psalmen I*, 12). For if we read Psalm 8 itself in the context of its surrounding context (Psalms 7–9/10) we would have to reckon that the accent falls, in this case, on the element of lament, not praise. For an alternative view which sees Psalm 9/10 as the centre of Psalms 3–14, see Sager, *Polyphonie des Elends*, 235–37.

[37] John Goldingay, *Psalms* (vol. 1; Baker Commentary on the Old Testament Wisdom and Psalms; Grand Rapids, MI: Baker Academic, 2006), 396.

and Psalm 27B, respectively, reflect two entirely different tones.[38] The first can be easily categorised as an individual thanksgiving, the second an individual lament psalm.[39] Further, the way in which the two parts have been arranged is "rather unusual":[40] the thanksgiving comes first followed by the lament. Had the order been the other way around; i.e., lament then thanksgiving, such as we find in Psalm 22, the unity of the psalm would not have been doubted as strongly as it has been. For in this case it would follow the usual form-critical understanding of the movement in terms of lament to praise. But as it stands we have a composition in which two apparently different psalms have been combined in such a way that thanksgiving moves to lament.

In view of the factors cited above, many scholars have regarded the psalm as composite.[41] Gunkel considers Psalm 27A and 27B as independent and in his comments he discusses the two separately without any attempt to make sense of the present arrangement of the psalm.[42] For him, the two have been joined together by mistake.[43] Kittel reasons that had Psalm 27B exhibited the tone of confidence as in Psalm 27A, we could consider them a unity.[44] Weber thinks Psalm 27B can be interpreted as an insertion of an earlier petition to which vv. 1–6 is the answer.[45]

---

[38] Weiser, *Die Psalmen I*, 156, ET *The Psalms*, 245, writes concerning the two parts of the psalm: "[they] differ from each other in mood and subject-matter. They cannot have been written in the same circumstances, and also they can hardly have been composed by the same author". Cf. Emmanuel Podechard, *Le Psautier: Traduction littérale et explication historique* (vol. 1; Lyon: Facultès Catholiques, 1949), 132: "Les deux poèmes réunis dans le Ps. 27 sont très différents".

[39] Cf. Hossfeld and Zenger, *Die Psalmen I*, 171.

[40] Anderson, *The Book of Psalms* (vol. 1), 219; cf. 223–24.

[41] Briggs mentions that majority of the 19th century commentators consider the psalm as composite (C. A. Briggs, and E. G. Briggs, *A Critical and Exegetical Commentary on the Book of Psalms* [vol. 1; ICC; Edinburgh: T & T Clark, 1906], 237). He cites the following scholars: Horsley, Cheyne, Kirkpatrick, Dyserinck, Ewald, Olshausen, Reuss and Delitzsch. He includes himself in the list. In 1933, Birkeland, "Die Einheitlichkeit von Ps 27," 221, points out "dass Mowinckel...der einzige moderne Forscher ist, der die Einheitlichkeit verficht".

[42] Gunkel, *Die Psalmen*, 112–18.

[43] Ibid., 116.

[44] Rudolf Kittel, *Die Psalmen* (3rd and 4th ed.; Leipzig: A. Deichertsche Verlagsbuchhandlung, 1922), 107, writes: "Tatsächlich passt unser Stück zu jenem Liede nur insofern, als auch hier wie dort das starke Vertrauen auf Jahwe einen Grundton bildet. Darin mag Grund der nachtraglichen Verbindung liegen. Im übrigen ist die Lage und die Stimmung in beiden doch recht verschieden und man hat allen Grund, zwei ehedem selbständige Gedichte anzunehmen".

[45] Beat Weber, *Psalmen Werkbuch I: Die Psalmen 1 bis 72*, 141.

Others have attempted to argue for the unity of the psalm using ANE background,[46] various settings,[47] and verbal correspondences between the two parts of the psalm.[48] However, ultimately we no longer have

---

[46] Sigmund Mowinckel, *The Psalms in Israel's Worship* (trans. D. R. Ap-Thomas; vol. 1; Nashville: Abingdon Press, 1962), 97, argues that we actually find support in the ANE background for the joining together of lament and praise, and especially the lament which is preceded by an extended hymn. A. H. van Zyl, "The Unity of Psalm 27", in *De Fructu Oris Sui. Festschrift A. Van Selms* (eds. I. H. Eybers *et al.*; Leiden: E. J. Brill, 1971), 233–51, attempts to prove the unity of Psalm 27 by further developing the thesis of Mowinckel. He supports his argument on the basis of the Sumerian *šu'illa*, which he argues is similar to Psalm 27 in its extended address containing praise that precedes the lament. He notes, however, the difference in tone between the Sumerian and Hebrew poetry. The former formulates the extended address with praise for the purpose of gaining attention from the gods, whereas the latter reflects personal faith and trust in Yhwh, not in a coercive and magical way as does the former. Having established the possibility that in ANE a lament is preceded by extended praise, he goes on to show that even in the Psalms, particularly Psalms 41, 62 and 40, we find a similar pattern. Finally, he also appeals to the example in Jeremiah 17 (242–43).

[47] Gerstenberger, *Psalms Part 1 with an Introduction to Cultic Poetry*, 126, argues for the unity of the psalm, explaining the differing tones as reflective of the various parts of a ritual; possibly a "complaint ceremony". He envisages the situation in the first verses of the psalm (vv. 1–6) as belonging to the setting where the psalmist is reciting the psalm before his enemies as a "militant complaint ritual". H. Schmidt, *Die Psalmen* (vol. 15; HAT; Tübingen: Verlag von J. C. B. Mohr, 1934), 50–51, explains that the differing tones in Psalm 27 can be explained in terms of the particular setting in which the psalm was written. Accordingly, the first part corresponds to the situation in which the psalmist makes his way from the sanctuary into the court. During this time, the psalmist recites the first part of the psalm which is a psalm of trust. It represents the psalmist's inner resolve, in which he imagines Yhwh to be his help. Apparently, he has been falsely accused. But in the midst of this difficult situation he still trusts in the Lord. On the question of the move into petition and lament in vv. 7ff., Schmidt clarifies that we have at this point a movement in the setting. Now the hour of actual confrontation, where his enemies would stand against him has come. This accounts for the change of tone in v. 7ff. For here the real battle begins. Left all by himself, he stands before the mysterious moment, in which it must be decided whether Yhwh will show his countenance or whether he will be allowed to be in the land of the living. Kraus, *Psalmen I*, 221–22, ET *Psalms 1–59*, 332–33, basically follows Schmidt's view. The major problem with Kraus and Schmidt's view as well as other attempts to explain Psalm 27 in terms of an actual setting is that we do not have evidence from the text to support such an imagined setting. As Weiser, *The Psalms*, 251, writes, "The attempt made by H. Schmidt and accepted by Kraus to adhere to the view of the psalm being a literary unit is based on imaginative additions derived from the situation of an accused man, which, however, have no basis in the text itself". A variation of the above is Broyles' (*Psalms*, 142) suggestion of a liturgical setting for Psalm 27. Accordingly, the first part "confesses the faith that one resolves to attain, not that one has attained". The second part represents the resolve to work out such a goal in the present moment when the psalmist is confronted by his enemies. Cf. Derek Kidner, *Psalms 1–72: An Introduction and Commentary on Books I and II of the Psalms* (Tyndale Old Testament Commentaries; London: Inter-Varsity, 1973), 121.

[48] Peter C. Craigie, *Psalms 1–50* (Waco, Texas: Word Books, Publisher, 1983), 231, notes some significant verbal connections between the two parts of the psalm (see below).

access to what constituted the original text or the setting from which the text arose. What is important for this study is the present form of the text. In its present form the psalm indicates the presence of two different compositions. At the same time, a close examination of the two parts shows significant verbal connections. The analysis below suggests that what we have in Psalm 27 are two different compositions which have been creatively and deliberately brought together. Whatever the reason for the joining together of the two might have been, one striking effect of the present arrangement is that it brings out the contrast or tension between thanksgiving and lament. The mere juxtaposition of thanksgiving and lament powerfully communicates the element of tension in the text.

4.3.2　*Structural Analysis*

Structurally, Psalm 27 can be divided naturally into two distinct parts. As noted above, the psalm consists of thanksgiving (Psalm 27A) and lament (Psalm 27B). The presence of a vow in v. 6 is a clear indication of an ending.[49] With the introduction of the petition in the next verse we have the "rather unusual"[50] arrangement in which lament follows thanksgiving. It is interesting, however, that although the two sections are distinct there are significant correspondences between them. As the following comparative analysis will demonstrate, there is a dynamic interplay between the two parts of the psalm.

4.3.2.1　*Verbal Connections between Psalm 27A and 27B*

An important aspect noted by both Craigie and Broyles is the close correspondence between the two parts of Psalm 27. Craigie cites the following verbal connections: ישע (1, 9); צר (2, 12); לב (3, 8, 14); קום (3, 12); בקש (4, 8); חיים (4, 13).[51] We find in both sections (vv. 1–6 and vv. 7–14) employment of similar/the same words.

In v. 4, the psalmist intimates that which he really wishes to experience—to "seek (בקש) him in his holy temple". The verb בקש occurs

---

[49] Westermann, *Lob und Klage*, 56, ET *Praise and Lament*, 75.
[50] Anderson, 219.
[51] Craigie, *Psalms 1–50*, 231; cf. Broyles, *Psalms*, 141.

Table 4: *Similarities Between Psalm 27A and Psalm 27B*

Psalm 27A	Psalm 27B
V. 1—Yhwh…my salvation (ישעי)	V. 9—"My God, my salvation" (ישעי)
V. 2b "my enemies (צרי) will stumble and fall"	V. 12—"Do not give me to the desire of my enemies" (צרי)
V. 4 "This is what I seek" (בקש)	V. 8—"Seek (בקש) his face; your face, O Yhwh, I will seek (בקש)
V. 4 "To behold the beauty of Yhwh" [similarity of image and thought]	V. 8—"your face…I will seek" V. 13—"to see the goodness of Yhwh"
V. 5—He will hide (סתר) me in the shelter (סתר) of his tent.	V. 9—"Do not hide (סתר) your face from me"

in v. 4 in the thanksgiving section of the psalm. In v. 8, the verb is repeated 2x, but this time in the context of lament. The word סתר is mentioned in v. 5: "he will hide me in the shadow of his tent". In v. 9, he uses the same word but this time in a negative sense: "Do not *hide* your face from me". Further, if in Psalm 27A Yhwh is referred to as "my salvation" (ישעי) (1), he repeats the same word in his lament. In v. 9 he pleads, "…do not forsake me, O God of my salvation (ישעי)". Interestingly, the structure of v. 1 sets apart ישעי from the rest. Notice the parallelism in v. 1. In both lines we observe the following pattern: 1) Name of Yhwh; 2) a metaphor describing who Yhwh is for the psalmist; 3) a rhetorical question.

יהוה אורי וישעי ממי אירא
יהוה מעוז־חיי ממי אפחד

Notice that the second line only has 'stronghold' of my life, whilst the first line has two descriptions: 'my light and my salvation'; the first one a metaphor corresponding to the 'stronghold' in the second line. The metaphor 'light' is not qualified unlike the 'stronghold'. Instead, what we have is a non-metaphor word, 'salvation'. It is possible that the slight change here is deliberate, for later on in the prayer, the same word turns up again; this time in the petition in v. 9.[52] The psalmist declares Yhwh as his salvation both in praise and lament.

---

[52] Hossfeld, *Die Psalmen*, 174, notes that ישע is unusual with the metaphor 'light'.

4.3.3   *Detailed Analysis*

4.3.3.1   *Thanksgiving*

As demonstrated above, the two parts of the psalm are linked by significant verbal correspondences. We now consider the overall flow of
the passage in its present form. The psalm begins with an assertion
of trust. Verse 1 forms a parallelism (see above) which expresses the
psalmist's confidence in Yhwh. Yhwh is referred to as "my light and
my salvation" in the first line and "the stronghold of my life" in the
second. This provides the basis for the confidence expressed in the
double rhetorical question in the second colon of each line: "whom
shall I fear/dread?" The psalmist is not afraid of anyone. Even when
wicked people "assail me...they will stumble and fall" (2).[53] Such is
his confidence that he declares that even if a host encamps against
him, or war breaks out, he will not be afraid (v. 3). The language is
similar to Ps 3:7.

Ps 27:3 forms another parallelism, though the last colon is somewhat
ambiguous. בזאת (3b) could be a reference to the preceding statement,
further declaring the psalmist's confidence. Or it could refer to the next
verse. If the latter, it signifies that the foundation for his confidence
lies "in this"; i.e., "that I may dwell in the house of Yhwh all the days
of my life..." (4). The psalmist expresses the one thing that he seeks:
"to dwell in the house of Yhwh...to behold the beauty of Yhwh". He
believes that in the house of the Lord, he is safe. There, the psalmist
finds protection and security (5). The first colon of the two lines in
v. 5 forms another perfect parallel: Yhwh "will hide me in his shelter/
hide me (סתר) in the secret place of his tent". Both the second cola of
each of the two lines of v. 5 are also parallel though not as closely as
the preceding cola. The last colon forms a transition into v. 6 with the
word רום: "He will set me high (רום) on a rock" (5b). Because of the
confidence that Yhwh will "set me high" (רום) (5) the psalmist can now
declare, "And now my head is lifted up (רום) above my enemies..."
(6). Thus, the psalmist offers a vow of thanksgiving. The vow marks
a clear conclusion to the preceding thanksgiving. Westermann asserts:
"almost without exception the vow of praise maintains its fixed place

---

[53] The language here is similar to Ps 9:4.

at the end of the petition".[54] Goldingay comments that vv. 1–6 "would make a complete testimony psalm".[55] We would expect at this point some form of praise or thanksgiving.[56]

4.3.3.2 *From Thanksgiving to Lament*

But instead of turning into praise or an expression of thanksgiving comparable to that which we find in Psalm 22B, Psalm 27 suddenly shifts to lament. Instead of a climactic shout of praise, we have a cry for help in v. 7 as the psalm turns from thanksgiving to lament. Having climbed its way towards the peak, the psalm unexpectedly dips into the depths. Indeed, as Goldingay remarks, we are "not prepared for vv. 7–12".[57] If in Psalm 22 we have a sudden change of mood from lament to praise, here we have a sudden change of mood from thanksgiving to lament. The psalmist pleads for a hearing in v. 7a: "hear my voice, O Yhwh". He asks for mercy (7b). Verse 8 contains a difficult text but the overall sense of the verse is discernible.[58] The verse recalls v. 4 through its double repetition of the word בקש (8). The one thing which the psalmist is seeking (בקש) as intimated in v. 4 is to "dwell in the house of Yhwh…to behold the beauty of Yhwh". Here similar language is used: "your face, O Yhwh, I seek". Interestingly, as בקש is used in v. 4 followed by סתר in v. 5, so also the double occurrence of בקש in v. 8 is followed by the reappearance of the word סתר in v. 9. Clearly, we have here a close correspondence between Psalm 27A and 27B. But the repetition of the significant words is for the purpose of

---

[54] Westermann, *Lob und Klage*, 56, ET *Praise and Lament*, 75.

[55] Goldingay, *Psalms I*, 396.

[56] Weber, *Psalmen Werkbuch I*, 141.

[57] Goldingay, 396.

[58] The textual problem is with בקשו פני. BHS proposes that we read the verb as singular—בקש (seek [singular] his face). LXX takes the verb not as an imperative but as an aorist indicative singular: "he sought my face". As it stands the MT is in the form of a plural. It may be reflective of the communal aspect of worship, so that even though the statement is being addressed to an individual person, such is formulated in the plural form (cf. Weiser, *Die Psalmen I*, 160, ET *The Psalms*, 252). Interestingly, where one would expect a plural in v. 14, one finds a singular verb (קוה). Except for the plural form of the imperative, the text does not seem to contain difficulty in terms of understanding its sense. The psalmist is saying: "to you [Lord] my heart says, 'seek his face'. In the OT, there are only 5 occurrences of the verb 'to seek' in the plural imperative: Here in Psalm 27; I Sam 28:7; I Chron 16:11; Ps 27:8; 105:4; Zeph 2:3. Except for I Sam 28:7 (seek for a woman), each of the passages is a command in the plural to seek the Lord. Ps 105:4 is exactly the same as Psalm 27.

drawing a contrast between the two sections of the psalm. Whereas the words connote a strong sense of security and protection in vv. 4–5, the employment of the words in vv. 8–9 signify an element of insecurity, even of abandonment (the word עזב occurs 2x in the context [9–10]). The statement in v. 8 betrays a hint of complaint. Set in the context of v. 9 where the psalmist is asking Yhwh not to hide (סתר) his face, there is an implicit complaint in the formulation of the words. The psalmist seems to be saying: "I have sought your face, but why are you hiding yourself from me?". Indeed, instead of experiencing the sense of security resulting from Yhwh's protective presence (v. 5) the psalmist has been experiencing divine absence. The words "יסתרני בסתר אהלו" (5) and אל־תסתר פניך ממני (9) contrast sharply. Instead of 'being hidden' in the shelter of Yhwh's tent, Yhwh himself is 'hiding'.[59] And the series of negative petitions that follow are clear indications of a troubled soul: the psalmist feels abandoned. The construction of the following lines follows the pattern of a lament, where the second line is shorter than the first:[60]

אל־תט־באף עבדך עזרתי היית
אל־תטשני ואל־תעזבני אלהי ישעי

One gets a further glimpse of the extent of his experience of turmoil when one reads the first part of v. 10: "For my father and my mother have forsaken me". The repetition of עזב links 10a with the preceding verse. The particle כי can thus be taken with the preceding verse. But the second colon of v. 10 adds another function to the particle. From the element of lament in the preceding verses the psalm shifts into an expression of confidence in Yhwh (10b). Here כי has the sense of "if" or "though", indicating a movement back to the earlier thanksgiving: "Though my father and mother forsake me... Yhwh will take me in" (10).[61] But just as the psalm has moved quite quickly into the element of confidence, so it turns back to petition in the following verse (11). The alternation between the elements of lament and praise reminds us of Ps 3:8 (Chapter 2). Another psalm which contains an alternation

---

[59] At least that is how the psalmist feels as expressed in the words of the psalm.

[60] Cf. Goldingay, 391 who observes that even the lines in the earlier verses of the first part of the psalm (Psalm 27A) contain shorter lines, characteristic of the structure of lament.

[61] There is a beautiful Tagalog word which captures the sense of the verb אסף here: "*kakalingain/kukupkopin* ako ng Panginoon".

similar to Psalm 27 is Psalm 86. The latter is a psalm which moves from lament (Ps 86:1–7) to praise (8–13) and back to lament (14–17). Psalm 27 moves into a petition using similar words to those in Psalm 86: 11. The petition, הורני יהוה דרכך ("teach me your way…" [Ps 27:11]), is exactly the same as in Ps 86:11. After this petition, the psalmist returns to his earlier lament: "Do not surrender me up to the desire of my foes, for false witnesses have risen against me…" (Ps 27:12). Interestingly, the words are also similar to Psalm 86:14: "O God, insolent men have risen up against me".

The last two verses (13–14) of Psalm 27 which contain the overall ending for the entire psalm fall short of the confident note with which the psalm began. Goldingay notes: "The statement of trust [in v. 13] is incomplete as well as implicit".[62] Similarly, the exhortation in v. 14 indicates that the struggle continues. In his study of the teaching function of the admonition in the lament in Psalm 130, Firth explains that "Admonition…suggests that the psalmist does not believe that Israel currently acts in the way requested, which is why the climax in vv. 7–8 contains both the admonition proper and additional reasons why Israel should decide to express such hope".[63] I think a similar point can be made with the admonition to "Wait on Yhwh…" in the last verse of Psalm 27. The statement expresses hope yet at the same time it implies that the element of struggle remains; the audience remains in the situation of lament.

4.3.4   *Summary*[64]

Psalm 27 consists of two distinct parts, which may have originally existed independently of each other. The different tones, reflective of two distinct genres (thanksgiving and lament) and the clear indication

---

[62] Goldingay, *Psalms I*, 399. Goldingay translates v. 13 as follows: "Unless I believed in seeing good from Yhwh in the land of the living". Cf. JPS: "Had I not the assurance that I would enjoy the goodness of the LORD in the land of the living…"

[63] Ibid., 400. Cf. David Firth, "The Teaching of the Psalms", in *Interpreting the Psalms* (eds. P. S. Johnston and D. Firth; Leicester, England: Apollos, 2005), 168, who comments on the sense of the admonition in Psalm 130: "Admonition…suggests that the psalmist does not believe that Israel currently acts in the way requested, which is why the climax in vv. 7–8 contains both the admonition proper and additional reasons why Israel should decide to express such hope".

[64] For discussions on the canonical context of Psalm 27, see Psalm 28 in the next chapter.

of an ending in v. 6 indicate the presence of two compositions. But
whatever may have been the history behind the psalm's development,
we have here compositions which have been creatively joined together
to bring out the element of tension between lament and praise. As
the analysis above has shown, there are significant correspondences
between Psalm 27A and 27B. Such correspondences, however, are not
simply for aesthetic purposes; more importantly these serve to convey
the contrast between the element of thanksgiving and lament. The
overall movement in the psalm from thanksgiving/praise to lament
further underlines the element of tension in the text. Even at the end
the psalm leaves its readers 'hanging in the air' as it were, with no sure
resolution, only an admonition to keep waiting (קוה) on Yhwh.

4.4   Psalm 40

4.4.1   *Introduction*

As if responding to the admonition to "wait (קוה) on Yhwh" at the
end of Psalm 27, Psalm 40 begins with the declaration "I waited (קוה)
patiently on Yhwh..." (2). Like Psalm 27, Psalm 40 is the reverse of
Psalm 22: it has an "unusual order",[65] which begins with thanksgiving
and ends with lament. Consisting of two main parts—vv. 1–11 (Psalm
40A) and vv. 12–18 (Psalm 40B)—the psalm moves from thanksgiving to lament, respectively. Like Psalm 27A and 27B, Psalm 40A and
40B can each stand on their own.[66] What distinguishes Psalm 40 from
Psalms 9/10 and 27 is that here we have an indication of a more
explicit attempt to combine two independent psalms. The major part
of Psalm 40B (vv. 14–18) actually occurs as a separate psalm—Psalm
70. This contributes to our understanding of psalms which exhibit
some form of juxtaposition like Psalms 22 and 27, providing evidence
for the practice of joining two compositions together.

Unfortunately, because Psalm 40 is composite and because the
sequence goes against the usual form-critical view of the movement
lament-praise, the two parts of the psalm have often been discussed

---

[65] Terrien, *The Psalms*, 338.
[66] Goldingay, 568.

independently of each other.[67] Kraus, for instance, discusses only Psalm 40A for his comments on Psalm 40 and refers his readers to Psalm 70 for his comments on Psalm 40B.[68] But as Zenger avers one ought not to silence the strong element of tension inherent in the very construction of the psalm in its present canonical form.[69]

Here in our last passage for the present chapter on psalms which juxtapose thanksgiving/praise and lament, we try to compare Psalms 40 and 70 to see the significant differences between the two and how this contributes to our understanding of Psalm 40. An overall outline of the structure is provided, followed by a detailed analysis of the passage. The focus of the latter is on the interplay between the elements of lament and praise. As will be shown in the following analysis, although Psalm 40 exhibits the presence of two compositions, the two parts of the psalm and the overall flow of the psalm reflect a creative and deliberate juxtaposition. The analysis of the middle verses of the psalm (10–12) demonstrates the close link between Psalm 40A and 40B.

4.4.1.1 *Psalm 40 and Psalm 70*

As noted above, Ps 40:14–18 occurs as a separate psalm in Psalm 70. Scholars are divided as to which psalm did the borrowing. Weiser holds that the author of Psalm 40 employed an existing psalm, in this case, Psalm 70. He explains that the inability of the psalmist of "seeing things clearly" as a result of his situation may have led to the borrowing of a "current liturgical text which appeared to him appropriate to his personal circumstances and suitable for the purpose of working out his supplication in more detail".[70] Gerstenberger, on the other hand, thinks the author of Psalm 70 made use of a portion of Psalm 40—a practice which, according to him, people still do today.[71] If this is correct then it is remarkable indeed that it is the lament that is borrowed and not the thanksgiving part! (Usually, we copy the 'happy bits' and leave out the 'sad parts'.)

---

[67] Zenger (Hossfeld and Zenger, *Die Psalmen I*, 252) observes that often commentators simply refer to their discussion of Psalm 70 for their comments to Psalm 40B.

[68] Kraus, *Psalmen I*, 310, ET *Psalms 1–59*, 424; noted by Millard, *Die komposition des Psalters*, 57.

[69] Hossfeld and Zenger, *Die Psalmen I*, 252.

[70] Weiser, *Die Psalmen I*, 220, ET *The Psalms*, 340.

[71] Gerstenberger, 169. This implies that Psalm 40 is originally a unity and that only a part of it has been used to form Psalm 70.

As will be shown below, the question of the relationship between these two psalms has important implications for the present study. Although we do not have a way of knowing with certainty which psalm is more original,[72] the analysis below indicates that it is more probable that Psalm 70 has been joined to Psalm 40, but the psalmist/redactor did so in a creative and deliberate manner, making subtle changes to link Psalm 40B (the lament) with 40A (the thanksgiving).

Table 5: *Comparative analysis between Ps 40:14–18 and 70:2–6*

Psalm 40:14–18	Psalm 70:2–6
רצה יהוה להצילני יהוה לעזרתי v. 14	אלהים להצילני יהוה לעזרתי v. 2
יבשו ויחפרו יחד מבקשי נפשי v. 15 לספותה יסגר חורא ויכלמו חפצי רעתי	יבשו ויחפרו מבקשי נפשי v. 3 יסגו אחור ויכלמו חפצי רעתי
ישמו על־עקב בשתם האמרים v. 16 לי האח האח	ישובו על־עקב בשתם האמרים v. 4 האח האח
ישישו וישמחו בך כל־מבקשיך v. 17 יאמרו תמיד יגדל יהוה אהבי ת שועתך	ישישו וישמחו בך כל־מבקשיך v. 5 ויאמרו תמיד יגדל אלהים אהבי ישועתך
ואני עני ואביון אדני יחשב לי v. 18 עזרתי ומפלטי אתה אלהי אל־ תאחר	ואני עני ואביון אלהים חושה־לי v. 6 עזרי ומפלטי יהוה אל־תאחר

Differences:

1. רצה (40:14) is lacking in Psalm 70.
2. Instead of יהוה Psalm 70 has אלהים. The same is the case in Ps 40:17 (יהוה) and 70:5 (אלהם). Psalm 70 belongs to the group known as the elohistic psalms.
3. Ps 40:18 has אדני for Psalm 70's אלהם.
4. Where we finally find יהוה in Ps 70:6, Ps 40:18 has 'my God' (אלהי). This is the only occasion in Psalm 70 where יהוה is used.
5. יחד and לספותה (40:15) are missing in Psalm 70, as well as לי (40:16) in 70:4.
6. The first word in Ps 40:16 (שמם) and 70: 4 (שוב) is slightly different.
7. Ps 40:18 has יחשב whereas 70:6 has חושה. The latter appears earlier in 70:2, whereas the former appears in verbal form in 40:6.

---

[72] Anderson, 314; Craigie, 314; Curtis, *Psalms*, 90.

From the above, we can see that Psalm 40 includes four words not found in Psalm 70: לספותה, יחד, רצה and לי. If we may use the insight in textual criticism of the rule of the 'shorter reading', the likelihood is that Psalm 40 has made the addition to what is an original piece in Psalm 70. The change in the divine name from אלהים to יהוה can be explained on the basis of the use of יהוה in Psalm 40.[73] In Psalm 40 יהוה is employed 9x; 6x in the section which does not appear in Psalm 70. This indicates that the composer of Psalm 40 made the change to fit the use of the divine name with the rest of the psalm. Two significant changes are with the words רצה and חשב which both occur in the earlier parts of Psalm 40. In the case of the latter it is more likely that the חושה is original in the light of its earlier use in Ps 70:2. Psalm 40 made the change to allude to the earlier use of the verb in 40:6. Similarly, with רצה, it is more likely that the author of Psalm 40 added the word to make a connection with v. 9 where the same word occurs (see below).

4.4.2 *Structural analysis of Psalm 40*

Structurally, the psalm is divided into two main parts, representing the elements of thanksgiving and lament. The two main parts interact with one another through the use of similar or contrasting language/imagery, repetition/play of words and overall structure.

I—Thanksgiving
Thanksgiving (2–4)
Praise (5–11)
  Declaration of praise (5–6)
  Praise through obedience (7–9)
  Declaration of praise (10–11)
II—Lament
Petition (12)
Lament (13)
Petition (14–18)

---

[73] Explaining the change as due to the elohistic group to which Psalm 70 belongs is rather weak since in Ps 70:6 the name יהוה occurs as well. Interestingly, Psalm 70 employs יהוה where Psalm 40 has אלהם.

4.4.3   *Detailed Analysis*

4.4.3.1   *Contrast between the beginning and end*

The beginning and end form a thematic unity, beginning with the idea
of waiting and ending with the plea for God not to tarry.[74] One can
sense the contrasting correspondence between "I waited patiently" (2)
and "my God, do not delay" (18). The sense of contrast increases as
the psalm proceeds. Delitzsch observes the close connection between
the parallel lines of v. 3: "The high rock and the firm steps are opposite
of the deep pit and the yielding, miry bottom".[75] One may extend the
thematic contrast to v. 13. The image of "troubles without number
encompassing (אפפו)" the psalmist (13) recalls the "pit of destruction"
and "miry clay" (3) from which Yhwh has rescued the psalmist. The
word אפפו recalls Ps 18:5 and implies the image of a flood.[76] Whereas
the movement in v. 3 is upwards (from the pit to the "high rock"), the
movement between vv. 13 and 3 is downwards: having been taken out
of the pit of destruction (3) the psalmist now speaks of being 'drowned'
by a flood of troubles (13).

4.4.3.2   *Transition from thanksgiving to lament in the middle section*

A close analysis of the middle section (10–12) of the psalm reveals
a creative attempt to relate Psalm 40A and 40B. Verses 10–12 are
crucial because they form the transition from thanksgiving to lament.
Verses 10–11 belong to Psalm 40A; v. 12 forms the introduction of
Psalm 40B. Scholars are divided as to whether to take v. 12 with the
preceding or following section. The difficulty with v. 12 is that it shows
a close link with both sections. In vv. 10–11, the psalmist declares what
he did through the employment of positive and negative statements:
he declared the good news of God's deliverance (10), spoke of Yhwh's
salvation (11) and draws attention (see הנה) to the fact that he did not
shut up his mouth (10) and did not hide Yhwh's חסד and אמת. The
negative statements outnumber the positive ones, indicating where the

---

[74] Cf. Brueggemann, *The Message of the Psalms*, 131.

[75] Delitzsch, *Die Psalmen* (5th ed.; Giessen: Brunnen Verlag, 1984), 308; ET *Biblical Commentary on the Psalms* (vol. 2), 41.

[76] Kirkpatrick, I: 213; Briggs, I: 356.

emphasis/stress of the statements lies. In v. 12 the psalmist employs 4 words from vv. 10–11. אתה (12) is emphatic, recalling the אתה in v. 10b which is also emphatic: "You, O Yhwh, *you* know" that "I did not shut up my mouth". Since the psalmist did not shut up (כלא) his mouth, the expectation/request is that Yhwh also would not withhold (כלא) his mercy but guard him with his חסד and אמת (12).

Clearly, there is a strong correspondence between vv. 10–11 and 12 representing the elements of praise and lament respectively. In addition, we see in v. 11 a chiastic structure:

> Your deliverance I did *not* hide within my heart
>> your faithfulness and salvation I have declared
> I did *not* hide your *Ḥesed* and truth to the great assembly

Notice the negation in the first and third lines and the positive in the middle highlighting the psalmist's action: what he did. One cannot miss the interaction with the following verse (12) which speaks of Yhwh not withholding his mercy.

At the same time v. 12 is structurally linked with v. 13. Grammatically v. 13 flows from v. 12 with the word כי. Verse 13 can be read naturally with v. 12; the כי at the beginning of the verse as well as the images in both verses 12 and 13 correspond closely.

This ambiguity of the connection of v. 12 makes it difficult to ascertain whether v. 12 is an affirmation or a petition. The ambiguity here is due to the presence of two compositions on the one hand and the attempt to relate the two together. Those who view the psalm as composite tend to read v. 12 with the preceding section as an affirmation.[77] In contrast, those who view the psalm as a unity view read v. 12 as a petition.[78] One can detect in the former the tendency to impose a positive ending to a thanksgiving psalm. Taking v. 12 as a petition makes the transition from v. 11 to v. 12 rather uneven. But one does not need to read v. 12 as an affirmation to argue for the composite view of the psalm. As demonstrated above, there are some indications that Psalm 70 has been added to Psalm 40. Further, as shown in the analysis of Psalms 9/10 and 27, it is not uncommon to have a sudden transition from thanksgiving to lament. The grammatical connection between

---

[77] Kirkpatrick, 213; Oesterley, 236; Dahood, 244–45; Kraus, 310, ET 423.
[78] Weiser, *Die Psalmen I*, 219, ET 339; Gerstenberger, *Psalms Part I*, 172; Broyles, *Psalms*, 192.

v. 12 and v. 13 shows that it is more likely that v. 12 is a petition introducing the transition to the lament in the second part of the psalm.
As a continuation of v. 12, v. 13 adds an element of urgency to the
petition. For instead of the חסד and אמת guarding the psalmist (12),
it is many troubles that surround him! (13).

4.4.3.3   *Tension between thanksgiving and lament*

One can see the element of tension not only between the beginning and
end and the middle section of the psalm but also between the whole of
Psalm 40A and 40B. A study of the key words occurring in both parts
brings out the strong contrast between them. In Psalm 40A, the psalmist
praises Yhwh, describing his wonderful deeds as beyond measure (עצמו
מספר) (6). In Psalm 40B, the psalmist repeats these two words later to
lament over the troubles that have encompassed him, describing these as
"without number (מספר)" and "more than (עצם) the hairs of my head"
(13). Twice he employs the verb חפץ in Psalm 40A to speak about what
Yhwh does not desire (7) and what he desires (9). He repeats the word
in Psalm 40B (v. 15b) to speak of those who "desire (חפץ) my hurt/
ruin". But as he has asserted earlier, his desire is to do the will (רצון) of
God (9); thus he asks Yhwh to "Be pleased (רצה) to deliver me" (14).
Briggs considers רצה as an unlikely original part of the psalm since it
is not found in Psalm 70.[79] The problem with this view is that there is
no textual evidence to support it. In view of the literary style of the
composer thus far demonstrated, it is more likely that the occurrence of
the word here is deliberate: it is repeated in order to make an allusion
to רצון in v. 9. The absence of the word in Psalm 70 in fact reinforces
the thesis that what we have here is a deliberate change on the part of
the poet to fit his intended purpose. As Ridderbos rightly points out, the
use of רצה here has particular force particularly because in v. 14 the
word is used in quite an unusual way.[80]

Another word that is lacking in Psalm 70 which has been employed
here is חשב (Ps 40:18). I think the word has been added to Psalm 40
to allude to מחשבה (6). In the first section, the psalmist speaks about
the many things that Yhwh has done, his "thoughts (מחשבה) towards

---

[79] Briggs, 357.
[80] Ridderbos, 290, n. 3. He cites Köhler here.

us" (6). In v. 18 he employs the verbal form of the word which was earlier used in the context of praise, applying it in the context of lament. One can sense here a contrast between the reference to Yhwh's thoughts (מחשבה) "towards *us*" (6) and the petition, "may the Lord think (חשב) of *me*" (18).

4.4.4 *Summary*

The foregoing analysis of the two main sections of the psalm demonstrates a creative and deliberate linking of Psalm 40A and Psalm 70. The comparative analysis has helped us see significant deviations from Psalm 70, which further bring out the contrasting nature of the relationship between the two sections. Indeed, the very act of adding a lament (Psalm 70) to a composition focused on thanksgiving is in itself a powerful indication of the element of tension in the text. As Erbele-Küster observes we have in Psalm 70 a psalm which is left open, without any sign of resolution. Instead of the expected vow of praise after the positive statement in Ps 70:5, the psalm ends with an adversative waw which brings out the sense of tension in the psalm: "Das ו-adversativum des letzten Verses (6a) leitet nicht, wie erwartet, das Lobgelübde ein, sondern stellt den Frohlockenden aus V5 kontrastive entgegen".[81] There is here a beautiful play on words with the effect of joining the sufferer with his suffering: ואני עני: "Auf der auditiven Ebene kann er kaum mehr zwischen sich selbst und seinem Elend unterscheiden. Die Lage des Beters ist in der Schwebe. Seine Worte bekräftigen Zuversicht hinsichtlich Gottes Eingreifen zugunsten aller Bedrängten (V5), und doch gleichzeitig muss er seine verzweifelte Situation konstatieren".[82] The joining of this tension-filled psalm into Psalm 40A—a psalm centred on thanksgiving—reminds us that the '*un*certainty of a hearing' remains even in spite of the 'certainty of a hearing'. Citing Spieckermann, Erbele-Küster writes: "Hinter 'der Integration ungestillter Klage in den Dank für die Rettung [steht] der theologische Gedanke, dass der Beter in Erhörungsgewissheit klagen

---

[81] Erbele-Küster, *Lesen als Akt der Beten*, 153.
[82] Ibid.

darf'"".[83] The movement between lament and praise cannot be explained in a simple linear schema; the relationship is complex, more dynamic, more alive, reflecting the realities of human existence.[84]

4.5   CONCLUSION

In this chapter we have tried to demonstrate that lament psalms do in fact move from praise to lament. We do not only have a sudden change of mood from lament to praise, we also have a sudden change of mood *from praise to lament*. We have examined three psalms—Psalms 9/10, 27 and 40. In Psalm 9/10 we have seen how the movement from thanksgiving to lament was facilitated by the employment of the acrostic. The application of the acrostic to what may clearly have been two compositions along with the employment of repetition (e.g. לעתות בצרה) certainly holds Psalm 9/10 together. The elements of praise and lament are held together in such a way that we have a clear movement from praise to lament in the psalm. In Psalms 27 and 40 we have indications of a deliberate juxtaposition of thanksgiving and lament. I have sought to demonstrate that the juxtaposition is not arbitrary but deliberate, purposeful and creative. The striking thing is that the redactor or whoever was responsible for the present form of the text has so arranged the psalms in such a way that thanksgiving comes before the lament. Commenting on the rather "unusual" arrangement in Psalm 40, Terrien writes that "no satisfactory explanation has been found to justify an editorial combination of praise followed by lament".[85] But as I have tried to demonstrate in this chapter, the analysis of the psalms containing the reverse movement from praise to lament in this chapter

---

[83] Ibid., 154; cf. Brueggemann, *The Message of the Psalms*, 131, who comments on the movement in Psalm 40: "Understood logically, the sequence is wrong. A complaint should not come after the joy of the new song, but experientially the sequence is significant. It reminds us that the move from disorientation to new orientation is not a single, straight line, irreversible and unambiguous...In our daily life the joy of deliverance is immediately beset and assaulted by the despair and fear of the Pit. So the one who hopes has to urge God against the delay. The one who has not 'withheld' praise has to ask that Yahweh not 'withhold' mercy". Unfortunately, whilst Brueggemann acknowledges that the movement is "not a single, straight line", in his overall presentation of his grid the emphasis is clearly on the one-way movement from lament to praise. See further below.

[84] Cf. Erbele-Küster, 154.

[85] Terrien, *The Psalms*, 338.

signifies that the editorial arrangement is deliberately made in order
to highlight the tension that characterises the life of faith. The reverse
movement from praise to lament shows that the 'blessed life' promised
to those who would follow the Torah is also marked by uncertainties.
It is interesting how the first part of Psalm 40 "echoes the sentiments
of Psalm 1".[86] The two psalms are linked by a number of significant
words: אשרי (Ps 40:5; Ps 1:1); חפץ (Ps 40:9; Ps 1:2); תורה (Ps 40:9;
Ps 1:2). The first part of Psalm 40 clearly recalls Psalm 1. But it does
so not in order simply to affirm it. Rather, in a subtle way, the connections are made in order to draw a sharp contrast with the present
experience of the author of Psalm 40 as shown in the incorporation of
Psalm 70 into Psalm 40. Psalm 1 is alluded to in order to highlight the
contrast between the 'blessed life' and the experience of the author of
Psalm 40. Interestingly, Psalm 40 is not the only psalm which alludes to
Psalm 1 in this manner. A consideration of the context of the following
psalm—Psalm 41—indicates that this tension between the blessed life
and the present experience of the psalmist is not confined to Psalm 40.[87]
Another psalm which alludes to Psalm 1 in the manner in which Psalm
40 does is Psalm 35. We will discuss this in Chapter 6 below. But before
that, we will see in the next chapter how the tension between lament
and praise builds up, as the sense of uncertainty amidst expressions of
certainty becomes more marked.

---

[86] Wenham, "Towards a Canonical Reading", 5.

[87] See the comments of Will Soll, *Psalm 119: Matrix, Form, and Setting* (vol. 23; The
Catholic Biblical Quarterly Monograph Series; Washington, DC: The Catholic Biblical Association of America, 1991), 73–4. Here he compares Psalm 119 and Psalm 41
which both begin with the statement on the blessedness of the righteous. Yet in both,
the statement is set in contrast to the present experience of the psalmist. He comments
on Psalm 41: "There is anxiety as well as hope in this *'ašrê*; the psalmist believes in
the promise, but is also aware that in his present condition that promise has yet to be
fulfilled ('But as for me...,')" (73).

CHAPTER FIVE

THE RETURN TO LAMENT

5.1 INTRODUCTION

We have tried to show earlier that lament psalms also move from praise to lament. Here we try to advance this thesis further by demonstrating that laments can return to lament even after they have already moved to praise. We focus on two psalms which contain a *return* to lament after praise—Psalms 12 and 28. One cannot overestimate the significance of these psalms, especially Psalm 12. In this psalm we have a clear example of the occurrence of an oracle.[1] As mentioned earlier (see Chapter 1), the most common explanation for the change of mood from lament to praise is the theory of Begrich on the oracle of salvation. Conspicuously, as will be seen below, even despite the presence of an oracle, indeed even despite the 'certainty of a hearing' that flows from the reception of an oracle, the psalm ends in lament. There is an '*un*certainty of a hearing' despite the 'certainty of a hearing'. It is for this reason why Psalm 12 is included among the passages for this study, even though its status as an individual lament psalm is in doubt.[2] As explained earlier,

---

[1] Küchler, who introduced the idea of an oracle of salvation as the cause of the sudden change of mood in the lament psalms, cites Psalm 12 as one of the passages where an oracle is explicitly given ("Das priesterliche Orakel in Israel und Juda", 299). He also believes an oracle is present in Ps 60:8–10 as well as in those passages in which there is a change of person in the verb and the pronoun (298). But as Williamson, "Reading the Lament Psalms Backwards", 6, rightly points out, it is only in Psalm 12 where a "clear example" of an oracle can be found in the Psalter.

[2] Majority of scholars consider Psalm 12 as a communal lament psalm (P. S. Johnston and D. G. Firth, eds., *Interpreting the Psalms: Issues and Approaches* [Leicester: Apollos, 2005], 296), though some are unsure. Anderson, *The Book of Psalms*, I: 123, thinks the psalm could be communal lament although it is also possible to read it as an individual lament psalm (cf. Craigie, *Psalms 1–50*, 137). The question arises because of the difference between the MT and the LXX in Ps 12:2: MT simply has the imperative 'save' (הוֹשִׁיעָה) without the first person personal pronoun 'me' while LXX has the personal pronoun added to the imperative: 'σῶσόν με'. In most cases, where the LXX has 'σῶσόν με', the MT has הוֹשִׁיעֵנִי (3:8; 6:5; 7:2; 22:22; 31:17; 54:3). It is only in Ps 12:2 that the personal pronoun is missing where the LXX has it. It is possible that what we have in the LXX is a case of an addition under the influence of frequent usage (P. Kyle McCarter, *Textual Criticism: Recovering the Text of the Hebrew Bible* [Philadelphia:

my primary criterion for the selection of the psalms is the presence of a sudden change of mood, especially the change from thanksgiving/ lament to praise.[3]

As I have done in the previous chapters, I will focus here on how the elements of lament and praise interplay in Psalms 12 and 28. I will examine the structure of the psalm as well as its contents. Here I provide a longer discussion of the canonical context of Psalm 12. A consideration of the canonical context for both Psalm 28 and 27 will be provided. This supplies the discussion of the canonical context for Psalm 27, promised earlier.

5.2   PSALM 12

5.2.1   *Structural Analysis*

Psalm 12 is developed using elements of contrast, chiasm, inclusio and repetition, to name the main structural components. I have sketched below the overall structure of the psalm:

> A   *Absence* of the upright/faithful (2)
>   B   Words of the wicked—*vain* (3)
>   C   Petition/wish: that the wicked be cut off (4)
>   D   Speech of the wicked (5)
>   D'   Speech of Yhwh (6)
>   B'   Words of Yhwh—*pure* (7)
>   C'   Assurance: Yhwh will protect us (8)
> A'   *Presence* of the wicked (9)

The inner structure is developed using contrast:

1) The words of the wicked, described as שׁוא (3), are contrasted with the words of Yhwh, exalted as 'pure' (7). שׁוא is singled out in verse 3, highlighting its significance. Encased by the word, ידברו, verse 3 is formulated in such a way that שׁוא stands out. In contrast to the

---

Fortress Press, 1986], 28–29). The context of v. 8 further supports the MT reading. In v. 8, the LXX itself translates the verse using the first person plural pronoun: "σὺ κύριε φυλάξεις ἡμᾶς καὶ διατηρήσεις ἡμᾶς".

[3] See Chapter 2 for a discussion of my own criteria for the selection of the psalms.

speech of the wicked, the "words" of Yhwh are described as "pure" and compared to a well-refined silver (7).

2) The wish/petition (4) corresponds to the assurance of God's protection in v. 8. Here the tone of petition (lament) is matched by the voice of certainty (praise).

3) In the centre of the structure, the quoted speech of the wicked (5) is set in contrast to the quoted divine speech (6).

This leaves us with the outermost structure. The beginning and end of the psalm form an inclusio, with the repetition of the phrase, בְנֵי אָדָם (2 and 9). Interestingly, whereas the rest of the psalm is developed through contrast, the outermost structure is not. Rather, it expresses the same thing from two different angles, representing as it were the two sides of a coin. In v. 2, the psalmist complains about the *absence* of the upright/righteous. In v. 9, he laments over the *presence* of the wicked. Where one would expect the *presence* of the righteous or the *absence* of the wicked in v. 9 so as to form a contrast with v. 2, one finds neither.[4] The train of thought expressed at the beginning remains unaltered. If anything, it has in fact been reinforced.

But why drop the contrast in v. 9? I think such subtle change is deliberate in order to make an important point. Through this alteration, the psalmist is able to communicate the tension between the promised deliverance on the one hand and the present reality on the other. Even with the divine response in v. 6, there remains struggle. The divine response represented by the divine word in the middle of the psalm is being challenged by the reality confronting the psalmist in the present. Thus, we see the tension between the middle of the psalm and its beginning and end. What takes primacy—the central part or the inclusio—is a matter worth exploring.[5]

---

[4] Where one would expect some form of a positive statement in light of the divine response in the middle, conspicuously, one finds a negative statement instead.

[5] On this issue of which takes primacy, the middle part or the ending, cf. the discussion of Lamentations 3 in Chapter 8.

5.2.2   *Detailed Analysis*

5.2.2.1   *Petition (2–4)*

Alarmed by the absence of the upright/faithful, the psalmist cries for
help: 'save, O Yhwh!' Immediately following the cry is the motivation represented by כי (1b). The parallelism that follows underlines the urgency of the situation: כי־גמר חסיד is followed by
כי־פסו אמונים. The use of חסיד signals that we are to read in אמונים not
a quality (faithfulness) but a reference to people (faithful people).[6] More
importantly, one may discern here a development through heightening:
from חסיד (singular) to אמונים (plural). The move towards generalization
is affirmed in the use of the phrase, 'sons of man', which is a "poetic
expression for the human race".[7]

Such a widening of scope is further seen in vv. 3–4. In these verses,
the psalmist describes what it is that he complains about in the wicked.
Here the subject changes from the righteous (2) to the wicked (3–5).
Absence of the righteous implies the presence of the wicked. But here,
curiously, the psalmist complains mainly of the use of the tongue or
speech by the wicked. Gordon Wenham observes that "of all the sins
in the Decalogue it is surely that of the ninth commandment which
receives the fullest treatment [in the Psalter]: 'You shall not bear false
witness against your neighbour' (Exod 20:16)".[8] It is not clear why the
Psalter emphasizes the misuse of the tongue so much.[9] One has to
examine the Psalter as a whole to give a definitive answer. But my own
observation of Psalm 12 indicates a similarity between its structure as
well as some of its key words to Genesis 11.[10] Structurally, the speech
of the wicked is matched by the speech of God in both passages:

---

[6] See David J. A. Clines, ed., *The Dictionary of Classical Hebrew* (vol. III; Sheffield:
Sheffield Academic Press, 1996), 282, where חסיד is rendered as 'loyal one or godly
one' and אמונים as 'faithful one'.

[7] H. Haag, "בני", *TDOT*, 161.

[8] Gordon Wenham, "The Ethics of the Psalms", in *Interpreting the Psalms* (eds. P. S.
Johnston and David Firth; Leicester: Apollos, 2005), 186.

[9] Ibid., 187. Wenham notes some observations to the question of why the topic of
the misuse of the tongue is so popular in the Psalms but gives no definite answer.

[10] To my knowledge, no commentator has made the connection between Psalm
12 and Genesis 11. Alexander Maclaren, *The Psalms*, in W. Robertson Nicoll, ed.,
The Expositor's Bible (vol. 1; London: Hodder and Stoughton, 1893), 111, mentions
Babel in his comment but only as an allegorical allusion describing the situation in
Psalm 12; he does not explicitly relate Psalm 12 with Genesis 11. Even the book by

Speech of the wicked (Ps 12:5; Gen 11:3–4)
Divine speech (Ps 12:6; Gen 11:6–7)

Both speeches form the central part of the structure. Understandably the two passages will have differences: Genesis 11 is constructed as a narrative whilst Psalm 12 is formulated as a prayer. Whereas in Genesis 11 the wicked experienced judgment as a result of the divine action, in Psalm 12 the wicked remain free, prowling around as they used to, in spite of the divine speech. But the differences are minimized when one considers the numerous similarities between the two in terms of the significant words employed.[11] "Sons of Adam" occurs in both (Ps 12:2, 9; Gen 11:5). The phrase, "they speak each one to his neighbour" (Ps 12:3) is also used in Gen 11:3 (cf. v. 7). The two words, בלב ולב (Ps 12:3b), when read together, sound like the famous play on words between בבל and בלל (Gen 11:9). Moreover, one of the most repeated words in Psalm 12—שפה (Ps 12:3, 4, 5)—is a central term in Genesis 11, repeated 4x (6, 7 [2x], 9). The verb אמר also shows up in significant places in both passages (Ps 12:5, 6; Gen 11:3, 4, 6). Finally, the climactic עתה appears in both (Ps 12:6; Gen 11:6).

Although we cannot be certain whether what we have in Psalm 12 is a direct allusion to Genesis 11, it is remarkable how much similarity the two passages have in both their wording and structure (see below). Interestingly, Psalm 12 is not the only psalm which shows some links with a passage in Genesis. Psalm 8 is a meditation on the glorious creation of humans. McCann also recognizes Psalm 150 as a psalm "reminiscent of the early chapters of Genesis".[12] More specifically, Psalm 12 is not the only passage in the Psalms which makes use of the story in Genesis 11. The imprecatory prayer of Ps 55:10 also alludes to the story. As Weiser comments: "Disgusted by the oppression and fraud which have taken control of the market-places quite openly, he prays that that place of vice may be overtaken by a divine judgment similar to the one which is reported in the tradition of the confusion

---

W. H. Gispen, *Indirecte Gegevens voor het bestann van den Pentateuch in de Psalmen?* (Zutphen: Drukkerij Nauta & Co., 1928), which discusses the passages in the Pentateuch linked to the Psalms does not include Psalm 12 (Gordon Wenham mentioned this to me in a personal conversation).

[11] For a list of the key words in Psalm 12, see Martin Buber, *Right and Wrong: An Interpretation of Some Psalms* (trans. Ronald Gregor Smith; London: SCM Press, 1952), 12.

[12] J. Clinton McCann, Jr., *A Theological Introduction to the Book of Psalms* (Nashville: Abingdon Press, 1993), 56.

of tongues at the building of the tower of Babel".[13] In Psalm 12 we
see a similar concern. The psalmist is asking that God would judge
the wicked as he has done in the past. This is indicated in his petition
in v. 4. Here he asks that Yhwh "cut off all smooth tongues". Notice
the intensification here. The phrase, שפת חלקות, mentioned in v. 3,
is here repeated but with the qualification, כל (4). What the psalmist is
asking then, in the light of allusions to Genesis 11, is that Yhwh perform
judgment on the wicked similar to what he did in Genesis 11.

5.2.2.2   The Divine response (5–6)[14]

The answer to the petition is given in vv. 5–6. Formulated in a similar
fashion to Genesis 11, Ps 12:5 represents the quoted speech of the
wicked. One notices here the repetition of the words, שפה and לשון,
which have been mentioned in the preceding verse, forming an A-B-
B'-A' structure:

שפה
לשון
לשון
שפה

---

[13] Weiser, *Die Psalmen I*, 272, ET *The Psalms*, 419–20.

[14] There is a textual problem in v. 6, specifically with the last two words, which in
the MT reads, יפיח לו. The MT and LXX agree with the rest of v. 6 except with
these last two words. The last four words of the MT and LXX read as אשית בישׁע
יפיח לו and θήσομαι ἐν σωτηρίᾳ παρρησιάσομαι ἐν αὐτῷ, respectively. The difficulty
here lies in determining the meaning of the last two words of the MT (יפיח לו) and
its relationship to its immediate context. LXX basically follows the first two words but
differs in meaning with the last two. The verb פוח can mean "to blow/snort/blow"
or "to long/pant" (I) or "to declare" (II) (Ludwig Koehler and Walter Baumgartner,
The Hebrew and Aramaic Lexicon of the Old Testament [vol. 2; Leiden: Brill, 2001], 917).
The second meaning is similar to the LXX meaning. The various attempts to resolve the
textual difficulty here can be summarised into three: 1) Those which understand פוח
in the sense of longing and לו as the object of longing: "I will set in security him who
longs for it (Gesenius; cf. RSV, NASV, NJB). 2) Those who take the whole phrase,
יפיח לו, as the object of the verb 'to set': I will set in security him against whom one
blows" (Kohler II: 917; Mowinckel, *Psalmstudien* II:173. Here Mowinckel interprets the
sentence as a reference to magical curses hurled against the righteous). 3) Although
the second proposal is possible syntactically, Miller proposes that reading יפיח not as
a Hiphil verb but as a substantive with the meaning 'witness' fits better syntactically:
"I will place in safety the witness in his behalf" (P. D. Miller, "Yāpîaḥ in Psalm xii
6", *VT* 29 [1979], 498–99. He develops here the work of Pardee on the word Yāpîaḥ
(Dennis Pardee, "Yph 'Witness' in Hebrew and Ugaritic", *VT* 28 [1978]: 204–13). One
cannot be certain as to the actual Hebrew word here. What is clear is that the sentence
expresses assurance to the righteous who, presumably, is suffering from the blows of
the wicked. This explains the shift to a positive tone in verses 7–8.

As the speech of the wicked is paralleled by the divine speech in Genesis 11, so in v. 6 we find a divine speech. It forms a powerful response to the words of the wicked in v. 5. Erbele-Küster calls it a rejoinder.[15] We have here a climactic event. Scholars generally see the presence of a divine oracle at this point.[16] Not only is the oracle situated in the middle of the psalm along with the speech of the wicked, one also finds the decisive עתה and the important word קום.

For God to "arise" (קום) is an important plea for the lamenting person (see Ps 3:8; 7:7; 9:20; 10:12). What the psalmist has been asking from Yhwh; i. e. that he arise and deliver them, is here finally answered in the most direct manner. In his canonical discussion of Psalms 3–14, Zenger notes the development of the usage of the petition, "arise": what is mentioned a number of times is answered directly in 12:6.[17] The big difference here is that in comparison with the other preceding psalms where the petition 'arise' occurs, it is only in Psalm 12 where we find a divine response. After a series of petitions, finally, God says "I will arise". But more than just a rejoinder, the divine speech forms a significant contrast with the words of the wicked. Whereas the speech in v. 4 is all focused on 'us' ("*our* tongue", "*our* lips", "our own"), the divine speech is oriented towards and has as its motivation *others*, specifically the poor and the needy.[18] In contrast to humanity's self-centredness, we find the self-giving character of God. As McCann writes, "Just as the speech of the wicked reveals their character, so also God's speech reveals the divine character. God acts...to help the poor and needy".[19]

5.2.2.3   *The psalmist's response (7–8)*

One can only respond with an 'Amen' to the divine word just uttered. Delitzsch remarks, "In v. 6 the psalmist hears Yahve Himself speak, and in v. 7 he says Amen to what He says".[20] The psalm talks a lot about

---

[15] Erbele-Küster, *Lesen als Akt der Betens*, 155.

[16] Westermann, *Lob und Klage*, 54, ET *Praise and Lament*, 73; Anderson, *The Book of Psalms*, I:124.

[17] Cf. Erich Zenger, "Was wird anders bei kanonischer Psalmenauslegung?" in Friedrich V. Reiterer, ed., *Ein Gott, Eine Offenbarung: Beiträge zur biblischen Exegese, Theologie und Spiritualität. Festschrift für Notker Füglister* (Würzburg: Echter Verlag, 1991), 405.

[18] The perspective of the wicked person focused on himself is very similar to that of the rich man in Luke 12:16–19.

[19] McCann, "Psalms", 724.

[20] Delitzsch, *Biblischer Commentar über die Psalmen*, 149, ET *Biblical Commentary on the Psalms*, 247; cf. Ridderbos, *Die Psalmen: Stilistische Verfahren und Aufbau mit besondere Berücksichtigung von Ps 1–41* (BZAW; ed. G. Fohrer; Berlin: Walter de Gruyter, 1972), 149.

speaking. It is significant to note that the word אמר is repeated 4x in Psalm 12, twice as a verb and twice as a noun. The word is used in vv. 5 and 6 of the wicked and Yhwh's speech, respectively. As the wicked speaks (5), so Yhwh also speaks (6). Here in v. 7, the psalmist takes up this 'speaking' to meditate on the words of Yhwh. This verse is reflective in mood, praising the reliability of the words of Yhwh. אמר occurs twice in v. 7. The "words of Yhwh" are described as "pure" in contrast to the words of the wicked which are "vain" (3). This reflection signifies a shift of focus from the wicked to Yhwh. Out of this shift of focus comes a change of mood, from complaint about the wicked to praise of Yhwh's reliable words. From despair...to hope.[21]

5.2.2.4   *A return to lament (9)*[22]

Psalm 12 could have ended with v. 8, on a note of hope. However, the psalm moves unexpectedly to a statement in v. 9 which basically

---

[21] Whereas in v. 2 the psalmist complains, "the upright are no more", in v. 8 he confidently declares, "You will keep them, you will guard us".

[22] Textual note: v. 9. The difficulty here is with translating כרם זלות. The meaning of זלות is uncertain (Koehler, I: 272). Two of the attempts to resolve the textual problem here are P. Wernberg-Møller and W. E. March's text-critical works on Ps 12:9 (P. Wernberg-Møller, "Two Difficult Passages in the Old Testament", *ZAW* 69 [1957]: 69–73 and W. E. March, "A Note on the Text of Psalm 12:9", *VT* 21 [1971]: 610–12). Through his comparative study based on the findings from LXX, the 'Secunda', Hebrew dialect of the Dead Sea Scrolls, and the Accadian dialect of Mari, Wernberg-Møller concludes that כרם is actually כֶּרֶם (vineyard), and זלות, originally גזלת, suffered from haplography. He translates the sentence as follows: "the wicked who '*walk about (in) the vineyard with spoils belonging to* (or: *taken from*) *the children of men*'" (Wernberg-Møller, 71). As a further support for his thesis he cites Isa 3:14. According to him, Psalm 12 uses the same metaphor as Isaiah does and the context of Psalm 12 affirms this reading because of the presence of the poor in the passage. March argues that we need not make changes to the vowel pointing nor to the letters found in the MT. All we need to do is to redivide the text. He writes: "Instead of maintaining the text as it has been received and reading סביב רשעים יתהלכון כרם זלות לבני אדם, the text should be redivided and read סביב רשעים יתהלכו נכר מזלות לבני אדם" (p. 611). He translates the verse as follows: "Wicked ones prowl around; the Star (or Constellation) is acknowledged (or possibly 'scrutinized', 'consulted') among the sons of men" (p. 612). Terrien follows the proposal of March (Terrien, *The Psalms*, 156). But the majority of modern translations follow the MT in reading כרם as an infinitive construct and translating זלות as 'vileness/depravity' (see Revidierte Lutherbibel, NASB, RSV, NJB). They either translate the phrase as, "*when* vileness is exalted" or "*as* vileness is exalted". Translating the preposition as 'when', however, makes the sentence conditional: "Wicked people prowl on every side/around, *when* vileness is exalted among the sons of men". I prefer translating the preposition as "as" since this fits more with the sense of the verse which is a return to lament: "Wicked people prowl on every side/around, *as* vileness is exalted among the sons of men" (see further discussion below).

expresses the threat of the wicked found earlier in v. 2. Broyles admits: "Verse 8 [9] sounds like a disappointing anticlimax".[23] Curiously in his earlier book, *The Conflict of Faith and Experience in the Psalms*, he highlights the capacity of a poetic composition to maintain tension. Commenting on the movement from lament to praise in Psalm 13, he stresses that "though the psalm ends on the high note of a vow of praise, it must be regarded as just that, a promise and not necessarily a 'change of mood'. There is nothing to suggest that the psalmist has dropped his protest against God's adverse disposition. Simultaneous to the psalmist's confession of present trust is his complaint of God's hiddenness".[24] A poetic composition as such should be read differently from a narrative. Whereas the sequence may be clear in the latter, one ought to read a psalm "simultaneously". One does not drop each line as the poem progresses.[25] Reacting to Weiser's interpretation of Psalm 13, Broyles writes: "Weiser's interpretation is possible, but it assumes that the psalmist 'drops' each line as he leaves it for another. Rather, in light of the 'wholeness' of poetry, it seems more likely that he holds on to each line until he has gathered the whole. All the lines of the poem would be voiced, as it were, in a single breath. Each part of the psalm would be experienced *simultaneously*".[26]

If Broyles can make such a comment on Psalm 13, however, one wonders why he is surprised at the way Psalm 12 ends.[27] If the element of lament is sustained even in spite of the statement of assurance in Psalm 13, why is it not possible for Psalm 12 to return to lament? But Broyles is not alone in his reaction. Another author who is surprised at the ending of Psalm 12 is Ridderbos. In fact he finds Ps 12:9 "odd", describing it as a "dark contrast" from the preceding statement.[28]

Because of the difficulty of making sense of v. 9, some interpret it not as lament but as an expression of affirmation. Baethgen takes v. 9 as a continuation of the statement of assurance in v. 8. He views it not as an independent statement but as a concessive clause connected to v. 8.

---

[23] Broyles, *Psalms*, 84.
[24] Broyles, *The Conflict of Faith and Experience in the Psalms*, 186–87.
[25] Ibid., 30–31.
[26] Ibid., 31–32, emphasis mine.
[27] Unfortunately, even though Broyles made the above remarks on the presence of tension in the lament psalms, in his actual work on the lament psalms he does not apply what he 'preaches'. In his discussions of other lament psalms he does not demonstrate the tension present in the psalms.
[28] Ridderbos, *Die Psalmen*, 150.

His reason for taking such a stance is revealing: "Da eine Rückkehr zu der Schilderung des Tuns der Frevler am Schluss des Psalms nicht wahrscheinlich ist, so fasst man 9a besser nicht als Aussage, sondern als Konzessivsatz zu 8".[29] He basically believes that a lament should end in praise or at least in a positive note. He thus translates the verse beginning with the word "trotz" (in spite of/although). Similarly, Kissane feels that the psalm should 'appropriately' end on a positive note. Verse 9 is literally translated as, "Round about wicked men walk as depravity arises for the sons of men".[30] But in his view, this translation "forms a weak conclusion to the poem. One would rather expect a statement on the overthrow of the wicked".[31] He thus opted for a translation which contains a note of affirmation: "Though wicked men stalk round about, Like a worm Thou contemnest the sons of men".[32] To support his translation, he appeals to the LXX translation, which according to him, reads, "as Thou risest up Thou wilt make little of the sons of men", and also the Targum, which has, "like a worm" for "as Thou risest up". But even though he tries to support his argument on the basis of appeals to textual notes, his conclusion betrays the real motivation for his translation. He writes: "On the basis of G and Targ. we get the text translated above which *gives an appropriate sense*".[33] The basic idea that a lament in the manner of Psalm 12 must end in a positive note remains the determining factor in his interpretative decision.[34]

Others are not as explicit as Baethgen and Kissane, but nonetheless view v. 9 as an expression of the psalmist's trust in Yhwh in spite of the situation. This is generally done by translating the verse the same as in the above, supplying the concessive particle, 'even though'. The dominating mood remains the assurance in vv. 7–8. Gunkel notes that even though the wicked continue to boast, in the end it is Yhwh who wins.[35] Anderson likewise writes concerning v. 9: "this seems to suggest that even when the godless *surround* the righteous, God is fully able to protect them".[36] Weiser also has the same view. He writes: "Taking their

---

[29] Baethgen, *Die Psalmen*, 34.
[30] Kissane, *The Book of Psalms*, 51.
[31] Ibid.
[32] Ibid., 50.
[33] Ibid., emphasis mine.
[34] What is alarming for me here is that he is willing to adjust the text to fit what he thinks is an appropriate ending. But who decides what the appropriate ending should be?
[35] Gunkel, *Die Psalmen*, 44.
[36] Anderson, 127.

stand on the foundation of the truth of the Word of God, those who have faith can firmly hold their own. They can look around without fear at the illusive glamour and haughty pretence of men's boastful vileness which surrounds them".[37]

The emphasis in the above arguments lies on the side of the element of praise. Whilst the element of lament is not denied, its force is softened, its voice muted. But reading v. 9 as a concessive clause is a lesser alternative than taking the verse as it stands—as a plain statement. Grammatically, it is better to translate v. 9 as a statement. Those who render the verse using 'even though' generally do not explain their basis for doing so. But translating the verse with a concessive sense makes it different from v. 2. This is rather unlikely, for v. 9, like v. 2, is clearly a lament. Terrien rightly comments that v. 9 restates the problem in v. 2, expressing it in a more forceful manner.[38] Gerstenberger sees v. 9 as formulated in "true lament fashion".[39] Likewise, Broyles acknowledges that v. 9 is a "lament that echoes the opening verses".[40] McCann, notes that v. 9 "recalls v. 1 [2], and the effect is a reminder that the promises of God are always surrounded by the apparent triumph of the wicked".[41] As the Structural Analysis above demonstrates, vv. 9 and 2 form an inclusio with the former developing the thought of the latter.

Thus, we see the element of uncertainty even at the end. Schmidt recognizes that in spite of the announcement (Ankündigung) of the word of Yhwh, there remains uncertainty. He explains that although Yhwh might now fulfil his word, it is not yet evident. I like the way Schmidt ends his comment on v. 9: "Bitter, wie sie begonnen, endet die Klage".[42] Similarly Kidner observes the following about the structure of Psalm 12: "The pattern is an alternation of prayer—promise—prayer; it contains an assurance of relief, but ends with the conditions still outwardly unchanged".[43] He finds no problem relating v. 9 to the whole of Psalm 12 because he recognizes the tension in the psalm.

---

[37] Weiser, *Die Psalmen I*, 100, ET *The Psalms*, 161.

[38] Terrien, *The Psalms*, 156.

[39] Gerstenberger, *Psalms Part I*, 81.

[40] Broyles, 84.

[41] McCann, "Psalms", 725.

[42] Schmidt, *Die Psalmen*, 21, emphasis mine. My translation: "Bitterly, as the lament began, so it ends".

[43] Derek Kidner, *Psalms 1–72: An Introduction and Commentary on Books I and II of the Psalms* (Tyndale Old Testament Commentaries; London: Inter-Varsity, 1973), 74. Although Kidner is aware of the tension in Psalm 12 he did not elaborate on the significance of this feature. Cf. Curtis, *Psalms*, 26, who notes that the psalm "might be expected to end on the positive note of v. 7 [8]", but acknowledges that the text as we

Such tension in the psalm has long been noted by Delitzsch. He comments about v. 9: "Thus even at the last, and while the psalmist is avowing his assured hope, the depressing view of the present asserts itself. The present is gloomy. But in the hexastich of the middle of the Psalm the future is lighted up as a source of consolation against this gloominess".[44] Very interestingly, Delitzsch here draws upon the two elements of lament and praise and puts them in lively interaction with each other. I have earlier remarked in the Structural Analysis on the tension between the middle point of the psalm and the inclusio (beginning and end). I asked which takes primacy, the middle part of the psalm or the end. In Delitzsch's comment, the former takes precedence. Even in the midst of a situation filled with darkness one may see light. But is it also possible to see here a sustained tension?

Erbele-Küster answers in the affirmative. Employing literary anthropology and reader response theories, she argues that in the psalms we find a "Leerstelle", an 'empty space' which refuses to be fully 'filled' or explained, reflecting ambiguity and absence of complete resolution. This 'Leerstelle' is found in a number of Psalms, including Psalm 12.[45] What is remarkable about Erbele-Küster's work is that, as noted above,[46] she does not deny the presence of tension in the lament psalms; in fact she sees profound value in it. Whilst other scholars simply mention the occurrence of lament in Psalm 12 without elaborating on it, Erbele-Küster demonstrates the significance of the lack of resolution, specifically for the act of reading the psalms. Another scholar who sees the element of tension sustained in Psalm 12 is Mandolfo. Her study is about the shifts in voices in the lament psalms as proof of the presence of a 'dialogic' feature in these psalms. According to her, Ps 12:8 belongs to the "didactic discourse" which aims at encouraging the people. But she points out that in spite of the encouragement, the psalm still returns to lament. Commenting on Ps 12:9, she writes: "the central objective of the didactic discourse (along with the oracle) is to

---

now have it actually ended in a negative note: "it ends with the wicked and the *esteem* that is won through *what is of little worth*".

[44] Delitzsch, *Biblischer Commentar über die Psalmen*, 151, ET *Biblical Commentary on the Psalms*, 251.

[45] Erbele-Küster, *Lesen als Akt der Betens*, 155. Other passages where she finds Leerstellen are Ps 40/70, 39, 88 (ibid.).

[46] Chapter 1.

eliminate any concern on the part of the supplicant, *but the voice of doubt and complaint gets the last word anyway*".[47]

5.2.3 *Psalm 12 and its surrounding context*

When we consider the canonical context of Psalm 12, the element of tension in Psalm 12 becomes all the more clear. The major gap in past scholarship in terms of the reading of Psalm 12 is the lack of an alternative framework through which the return to lament can be properly evaluated. It is only in recent years that the possibility of maintaining the tension in the lament psalms has been explicitly set forward. The works of Erbele-Küster and Mandolfo help pave the way for such a reading, although their methods differ from each other and from that employed in this study.[48] In order to facilitate the way for an alternative explanation for the return to lament in Psalm 12, we need to consider not only Psalm 12 but also the context of the neighbouring psalms as well as the Psalter as a whole. I will attempt to show that a canonical reading of Psalm 12 will demonstrate that the return to lament is not 'odd' after all but a normal part of the prayer.

One of the dominant themes that run through the preceding psalms (Psalms 1–11) is the contrast between the righteous and the wicked. Psalm 1 introduces the Psalter as a whole and specifically Psalms 3–12 by setting the righteous and the wicked in contrast to each other.[49] Psalm 1 declares that the righteous and the wicked stand on opposite side of

---

[47] Carleen Mandolfo, *God in the Dock: Dialogic Tension in the Psalms of Lament* (JSOT Supp. 357; London/New York: Sheffield Academic Press, 2002), 52, emphasis mine. Examining the changes in the use of voices in the Psalms, Mandolfo seeks to argue that the change in voice represents a change in speaker.

[48] In addition to a difference in methodology, the two works, by Erbele-Küster and Mandolfo, deal only to a limited extent on the issue of the sudden change of mood in the lament psalms, since that is not the focus of their research.

[49] The idea that Psalm 1 forms an introduction to the whole Psalter has become a well-accepted view in recent years (see Brevard S. Childs, *Introduction to the Old Testament as Scripture* [Philadelphia: Fortress Press, 1979], 512–14; Wilson, *The Editing of the Hebrew Psalter*, 204–7; Brueggemann, "Bounded by Obedience and Praise: The Psalms as Canon", in P. D. Miller, ed., *The Psalms and the Life of Faith* [Minneapolis: Fortress Press, 1995], 190–2]). For the function of Psalm 2 a part of the introduction of the Psalter, see P. D. Miller, "The Beginning of the Psalter", in J. Clinton McCann, ed., *The Shape and Shaping of the Psalter* (JSOT Supp. 159; Sheffield: Sheffield Academic Press, 1993), 83–92.

the extremes in terms of defining the better life; the former prospers
whilst the latter perishes. Immediately after this assertion, however,
we read a series of psalms which, when read together, contradict the
truth claimed in the introduction of the Psalter. McCann observes
the apparent contradiction between what is set out at the beginning of
the Psalter, in which the blessedness of the righteous is asserted, and
what follows. He explains that this is a reflection of the psalmist's view
of reality. "The psalmist knew about the 'real world' ".[50] When the
psalms preceding Psalm 12 are read together, they present a tension
between the claims of Psalm 1 and the present realities confronting the
'righteous'. Wenham rightly acknowledges that although "the righteous
enjoy ultimate prosperity and vindication, they may well have to suffer
in the short term. The many laments in the Psalter are prayers of the
righteous, who are suffering from illness, oppression and persecution
(e.g. Pss. 3–7)".[51]

Thus, we see that the psalmist laments over the great number of those
who rise up against him (3:2–3) and complains about those who "love
vain words and seek after lies" (4:2) and those who "flatter with their
tongues" (5:10).[52] The stress on the use of empty words and flattering
tongues in Psalms 4 and 5, respectively, introduces the similar emphasis
in Ps 12:3–4. In Psalm 6, the psalmist speaks of his suffering (3–8) and
his confrontation with the "workers of evil" (9). Even more significant
is Psalm 7 which exhibits verbal connections with Psalm 12.

5.2.3.1   Psalm 12 and Psalm 7

Psalm 7 has been composed from the standpoint of one who is righteous
or at least one who claims to be such. The psalmist's innocence and
righteousness as well as God's righteousness fill the whole passage (see
vv. 5–6, 9b, 12 and 18). A comparative analysis between Psalms 12 and
7 intimates an interaction between the two. Indeed, it may be possible
to read Psalm 12 as a response or reaction to Psalm 7. Whereas the
latter takes refuge (חסיתי) in Yhwh (Ps 7:2), the former complains that
the חסיד is no more (12:2). Note the similarity in sound between חסיתי

---

[50] McCann, Jr., *A Theological Introduction to the Book of Psalms*, 34.
[51] Wenham, "The Ethics of the Psalms", in *Interpreting the Psalms*, 188–89.
[52] Maclaren, *The Psalms*, 111, observes how "sins of speech are singled out" in
Psalm 12 as in Psalm 5.

and חסיד. Both cry out to God, "help!" (7:2; 12:2).[53] One hears the petition "*arise*, O Yhwh" in 7:7 and the response in 12:6: "Now I will *arise*". Most important is the occurrence of the word גמר in connection with the רשעים. גמר occurs only 5x in the Psalms (7:10; 12:2; 57:3; 77:9; 138:8). Of these it is only in Psalms 7 and 12 where the word is employed in the context of the relationship between the righteous and the wicked. The psalmist pleads in 7:10: "O let the malice of the wicked come to an end (גמר), but establish the righteous". It is to be noted that the petition for the destruction of the wicked is formulated using the jussive, whereas the request for the establishment of the righteous is formed with the imperative. This reflects the intensity of the psalmist's desire for God to 'establish' the righteous. The emphasis lies on the second petition. But whilst Psalm 7 asks for the banishment of the wicked and the establishment of the righteous, Psalm 12 gives utterance to the woeful state in which the poet finds himself: "the upright are no more (גמר)" (2). And whilst Psalm 12 answers the petition in Psalm 7 through the divine oracle in v. 6, the return to the lament in v. 9 creates a tension between that which the psalmist has been longing for and the present reality. It seems as if Psalm 12 is saying to Psalm 7: "your petition has already been answered—but not yet". For instead of the righteous being established, they have been banished (12:2). Instead of the wicked being destroyed, they remain very much present (12:9). And all this in spite of the divine response in v. 6.

5.2.3.2   *Psalm 12 and Psalm 9/10*[54]

As discussed earlier Psalm 7 is related canonically to Psalm 9/10.[55] But unlike Psalm 7, Psalm 12 does not show deliberate verbal connections to Psalm 9/10. It only contains a similar concern about the destruction of the wicked (9:6–7, 20; cf. 12:4) as well as the petition "arise", which is mentioned 2x (9:20; 10:12). The relevance of Psalm 9/10 lies in its presentation of the elements of lament and praise. In this psalm we find for the first time in the Psalter the reverse movement from thanksgiving to lament. The other laments that precede it all move from lament to

---

[53] Ps 7:2 has the first personal pronoun 'me' whilst 12:2, as discussed above, does not.

[54] Psalm 8 belongs to another category from that of Psalm 12 and the preceding psalms. It does not lament but expresses praise. It shows resemblance to Psalm 12 in terms of its reflection of the first parts of Genesis and its mention of 'son of man' (8:5).

[55] See the discussion of the canonical context of Psalm 9/10 in Chapter 4.

praise (e.g. Psalms 3 and 6). This gives Psalm 9/10 a significant role. As the canonical discussion of this psalm demonstrates (see above), the reversal from praise to lament is central to Psalm 9/10. In a way, reading Psalm 12 from the perspective of Psalm 9/10 prepares us for the *return* to lament even after the movement to praise in Psalm 12. I think the failure to see the significance of the ending of Psalm 12 lies in part in the failure to pay close attention to the preceding canonical context of Psalm 12, especially Psalm 9/10. A reading of these psalms one after another shows some form of a 'progression', from the movement lament-praise (Psalms 3, 6), to the opposite movement from thanksgiving to lament (Psalm 9/10) and now in Psalm 12, the return to lament after praise.

5.2.3.3 *Psalm 12 and Psalm 11*

As noted earlier, it is interesting that long before the idea of a canonical reading of the Psalter became fashionable, Delitzsch had already made some 'canonical' observations.[56] Although not as explicit as Hossfeld and Zenger[57] in their consideration of a particular psalm's surrounding context, Delitzsch had already registered the following observation: The order—Psalm 12 following 11—is appropriate, for the two are similar.[58] An analysis of Psalm 11 confirms Delitzsch's point. Psalm 11 sets the righteous in contrast to the wicked. The former is referred to using several terms: ישר־לב (2b), צדיק (3, 5) and ישר (7). The latter is referred to generally as רשע (2, 5, 6), though he is also described as "one who loves violence" (5).

Structurally, Psalm 11 exhibits a pattern very similar to Psalm 12:

> Expression of trust in Yhwh (1a)
> Complaint directed to the wicked (1a)
> Lament about the activity of the wicked (2–3)
> Yhwh's response (4–5)
> Statement of assurance (6–7)

---

[56] Erich Zenger, "Was wird anders bei kanonischer Psalmenauslegung?", 399, n. 9; cf. Wenham, "Towards a Canonical Reading of the Psalms", 2, observes that Delitzsch "noted how consecutive psalms were linked together by key words".

[57] I have in mind here the commentaries by Hossfeld and Zenger on the Psalms.

[58] Delitzsch, *Biblischer Commentar über die Psalmen*, 147, ET *Biblical Commentary on the Psalms*, 244.

Immediately after the expression of trust ("In Yhwh I take refuge",
1a), the psalmist directs his attention (complaint?) to the wicked. The
language is similar to Ps 6:9, where the psalmist turns to his enemies
and rebukes them, although such an element features in different places
in the two psalms. In Psalm 6, it comes after the assurance has been
received; in Psalm 11, it comes at the beginning. Similar to Psalm
12, the psalmist describes the activity of the wicked (Ps 11:2–3; cf. Ps
12:3–5). This is followed by a report on the activity of Yhwh (Ps 11:4–5).
As the 'words' of the wicked are matched by the 'words' of Yhwh in
Psalm 12, so the actions of the wicked are matched by Yhwh's action
in Psalm 11. In both there is a shift in perspective—from down here
below to up there in the heavens. Ps 11:4–5 is from the perspective of
transcendence. Yhwh is in his "holy dwelling", "seated on his throne"
whilst he examines the "sons of man". Like Psalm 12, there is similarity between Psalm 11 and Genesis 11. The description of Yhwh's
action in vv. 4–5 is similar to Genesis 11. Both speak of Yhwh looking at the "sons of man". The latter reveals Yhwh's decision to come
down *in order to see* that which the *sons of man* are trying to build (Gen
11:5). The former mentions that "his *eyes examine* . . . the *sons of man*"
(Ps 11:4b). We have already noted the significance of the phrase "sons
of man" in the structure of Psalm 12. What Psalm 11 does is provide
us with a background for the term. In the context of Ps 11:4–5, we
know that the "sons of man" refers to humans in general—including
the righteous and the wicked. See the repetition of the word בחן in
vv. 4 and 5. In v. 4 the psalmist says that Yhwh tests (בחן) the "sons
of man"; employing the same word (בחן) in v. 5 the psalmist speaks of
Yhwh's testing of both the righteous and the wicked.

The action of Yhwh is followed by a statement of assurance. Like
the 'Amen' of Ps 12:7–8, Psalm 11 speaks of the destruction of the
wicked and the preservation of the upright (6–7). Employing significant
repetition, the poet repeats חזה (4b) to highlight the blessed state of the
righteous (7). The major difference is that whereas Psalm 11 finishes off
with a positive note, Psalm 12 returns to the element of lament. Read
in their present canonical order, these two psalms exhibit strong interaction. Psalm 12 forms a response to Psalm 11, albeit in the negative
sense. For whereas Psalm 11 declares the triumph of the righteous over
the wicked, Psalm 12 laments the banishment of the upright. Similar
to the interaction between Psalms 12 and 7, Psalm 12 reflects a note
of challenge to the claims of Psalm 11.

5.2.3.4 *Psalm 12 and Psalm 13*

The canonical order of Psalms 12 and 13 is striking. When read together with Psalm 12, especially its ending, the opening words of Psalm 13 become more poignant. As underlined above, despite the divine response in the middle of Psalm 12, the psalm nonetheless ended in lament: the "wicked prowls around" (12:9). Indeed, the situation remains unchanged, one only wonders for how long. Then comes the opening words of Psalm 13: "How long, O Yhwh, how long…?" One can hardly ask for a more powerful presentation of lament than this one. Psalm 13 recalls the presence of Yhwh (lit. 'face of Yhwh') mentioned at the end of Psalm 11. But whereas Psalm 11 speaks about the upright beholding the face of Yhwh (v. 7) Psalm 13 laments the absence of Yhwh (v. 2).

Zenger discusses the function of Ps 12:9 in relation to Psalm 13. He sees a close connection in Psalms 12–14 as part of the broader redactional unit of Psalms 3–14.[59] He basically views 12:9 as a redactional expansion to introduce Psalm 13. The redactor employs words from Psalm 11 and 13 to form Ps 12:9, drawing connections with Psalm 13. Specifically, the word רשע is taken from Psalm 11 (vv. 2 and 6). Such is the case since רשע occurs nowhere in Psalm 12. From Ps 13:3b, the redactor employs the word רום, shedding further light on the lament in Psalm 13. On the whole, Zenger claims that Ps 12:9 is not originally part of Psalm 12. In addition to his arguments above, he explains that v. 9 should be seen as a later addition because the phrase, לעולם (8) seems to be an appropriate ending and the syntax of 12:9 is difficult.[60] Unfortunately, although Zenger tries to read the psalms canonically, he performs some 'exegetical surgery' which is unnecessary in order to establish the connection between specific psalms. There is no need to resort to such actions; the thematic and linguistic connections between Psalms 12 and 13, as well as Psalm 11 are strong enough to support a close connection between these psalms which properly reflect a canonical reading. Further, the tension between the elements of lament and praise in Psalm 9/10 prepares us for the lament in Ps 12:9.

My hunch is that Zenger's decision is guided more by the general assumption about the movement from lament to praise. This is reflected in his analysis of Psalms 3–14. He proposes that this redactional unit

---

[59] Zenger, "Was wird anders bei kanonischer Psalmenauslegung?", 401–2, 405–6.
[60] Ibid., 401.

forms a unity with Psalms 3 and 14 as its frame and Psalm 8 as the "theological centre of the composition".[61] He also sees a similar pattern in the redactional unit of Psalms 25–34, where Psalm 29 is the centre. Both Psalms 8 and 29 are praise psalms, reflecting the emphasis of the Psalter as a whole. Such emphasis on praise is further shown in the commentary which Zenger writes with Hossfeld. As mentioned earlier in Chapter 1, Hossfeld and Zenger believes that the title 'book of praises' is appropriate for the Psalms because even though there are more lament psalms it is the element of praise that dominates. To quote their comment again: "even the sharpest accusation against God is itself divine praise, because it clings fast to God and continues to seek God (even whilst accusing), at a time when everything seems to speak against God".[62] Furthermore, we find the movement towards praise not only in the lament psalms themselves (except for Psalm 88) but also in the Psalter as a whole. We see that from Psalm 91 onwards "praise has the upper hand".[63] As I have observed earlier (Chapter 1), we see here how the elements of lament and praise are set over against each other with the latter winning.[64]

A close analysis of the Psalms, however, indicates that the picture is not as simple as that drawn by Zenger and Hossfeld. As we have seen, there is a strong sense of tension between what was claimed at the beginning of the Psalter and the laments that followed. In the redactional unit of Psalms 3–14 and 25–34 they have to make sense of at least three Psalms contained in each of these units which clearly demonstrate an emphasis on the tension between lament and praise. Specifically, I refer to Psalm 9/10 and Psalms 27, 28 (see below), respectively. These passages reflect deliberate redactional arrangement to highlight the tension between the elements of lament and praise. To be added here is Psalm 31 (see below), where lament and praise alternate. Interestingly, as Hossfeld and Zenger's own analyses show, such alternation

---

[61] Ibid., 405.

[62] Hossfeld and Zenger, *Psalms 2*, 1 (already quoted in Chapter 1). This statement is similar to what Westermann said elsewhere. But as Ellington avers, such a perspective reflects an overly positive approach which tends to relativize "all expressions of Israel's doubts and questions" and "does not fairly represent the full dilemma of the psalmist at the time of the lament" (Scott Arthur Ellington, "Reality, Remembrance, and Response: The Presence and Absence of God in the Psalms of Lament" [PhD diss, University of Sheffield, 1999], 94–95).

[63] Hossfeld and Zenger, *Psalms 2*, 1.

[64] See my survey of literature in Chapter 1.

between the elements of lament and praise is manifested not only in individual laments but also in groups of psalms.

Using various organizing principles, Hossfeld and Zenger observe the following alternation between lament and praise in a cluster:[65]

> For Psalms 51–72:
> Petition (51)—Lament (52–55)—Confidence (61–64)—Praise/Thanksgiving (65–68)—Lament (69–71)—Petition (72).
> Within Psalm 73–83: "The compositional arc is repeated twice":
> Teaching (73; speaker: 'I')—Lament (74; speaker: 'we')—Oracle/God's Response (75–76)—Lament (77; speaker: 'I').
> Teaching (73[66] [78?]; speaker: 'I')—Lament (79–80; speaker: 'we')—Oracle/God's Response (81–82)—Lament (83; speaker: 'I').

In the first grouping we see alternation between lament and praise. More interestingly, in the second set of psalms (73–83), there is a movement from lament to oracle/God's response and then back to lament—a pattern similar to Psalm 12.[67] Unfortunately, Hossfeld and Zenger did not elaborate on their observation, nor discuss the theological implication of the alternation between lament and praise and, more relevantly, the return to lament even after the divine response. As can be seen, the pattern that we see in Psalm 12 is not an isolated case but one which runs through the whole Psalter. McCann also observes lament and hope alternating in Book III.[68] It would certainly make a lot of difference to the way we look at these psalms when the lively interaction between the elements of lament and praise is properly considered.

5.2.3.5 *Psalm 12 and Psalm 14*

Psalm 14 is linked to both Psalms 13 and 12. Psalm 14 repeats two words from Ps 13:6—לב and גיל (Ps 13:6). The words show up at the beginning (v. 1) and end (7) of Psalm 14, respectively.[69] But whereas

---

[65] Hossfeld and Zenger, *Psalms 2*, 2.

[66] There seems to be a mistake in Hossfeld's psalm numbering here. It should be Psalm 78, not 73.

[67] It is also possible to see the pattern teaching—lament—oracle—Response in Psalms 1–12: Teaching (1, 2)—Lament (3–11, except 8)—oracle (12:6)—Lament (12:9).

[68] See his table in McCann, "Books I–III and the Editorial Purpose of the Psalter", in McCann, ed., *The Shape and Shaping of the Psalter*, 97.

[69] Cf. Zenger, "Was wird anders bei kanonischer Psalmenauslegung?", 402. Zenger sees Ps 14:7 as a redactional expansion to establish the connection with Psalm 13. He notes the employment of ישועה and גיל in Ps 14:7 which recall 13:6.

the two words are used in the context of praise in Psalm 13, here the words are used in the context of lament. Psalm 14 turns the movement to praise in Psalm 13 back to lament. Indeed, a reading of these psalms beginning with Psalm 11 creates a certain movement towards resolution and back to lament. Psalm 11 ends with a statement of assurance, with the righteous winning. Psalm 12 brings this upward movement down through its complaint. Psalm 13 continues with the lament, turning into praise in the process. But then we have Psalm 14 again which brings back the element of lament. More relevant is the emphasis on negation throughout Psalm 14. Three times the word, "there is none" (אֵין) is repeated in vv. 1 (2x), and 3 (2x). What is negated specifically is any sign of the presence of anyone who does good. Twice, the statement "there is no one who does good" is repeated (1, 3). Clearly, this recalls the similar cry in Ps 12:2. The close link between Psalm 12 and 14 is further enhanced by the repetition of the phrase "sons of man" (14:2; 12:2, 9) and the word "poor" (עָנִי) (14:6; 12:6). Yhwh's looking down from heaven (14:2) reminds us of the transcendent perspective of 12:6. Finally, the wish expressed in Ps 14:7 presents an open scenario. That which the psalmist longs for is restoration for Israel. But whether such has actually transpired remains open. Thus like Psalm 12, albeit not as grim, Psalm 14 ends in a not-so-clear-resolution. Israel will "rejoice". Yes. But that will happen "*when* Yhwh restores his people" (14:7).

5.2.4 *Summary*

Psalm 12 marks a significant development for the present study. It begins with the lament, "the godly are no more". A more 'appropriate' and encouraging ending would be, "the wicked are no more". Instead, the psalm ends on a rather disappointing note. For instead of the wicked vanishing from humankind, they are in fact very much present, "prowling on every side". What is more, the negative ending comes despite the clear divine response in the middle of the psalm, creating a tension between what God says and the present reality confronting the psalmist. On the one hand the psalmist would like to believe that God has already acted. On the other hand, he could not help but wonder why it is that in spite of the divine response the situation remains the same. Even more strikingly, this tension is left unresolved: we have in Psalm 12 a psalm which ends in a lament. The analysis of the canonical context of Psalm 12 brings out further the sense of tension between lament and praise.

5.3 Psalm 28

5.3.1 *Introduction*

Another psalm which contains a return to the element of lament is Psalm 28. The psalm is often included in the list of psalms which contain the movement lament-praise. That the psalm contains such a movement is certain. But as can be seen in the analysis below, there is a return to lament after the movement to praise.

5.3.2 *Structural Analysis*

Psalm 28 starts with the element of lament, opening with a series of petitions for oneself, then moving to petitions directed to others (imprecations). Suddenly, in v. 6 the psalm moves into praise and expressions of confidence. Unexpectedly, at the end, the psalm utters another petition. Structurally, Psalm 28 can be outlined as follows:

1. Lament
   a. Petition (1–3)
   b. Imprecation (4–5)[70]
2. Praise
   a. Praise (6)
   b. Declaration of Confidence (7–8)
3. Lament
   a. Petition (9)

5.3.3 *Detailed Analysis*

The psalm begins with an invocation, followed by four related petitions which alternate between negative and positive:

---

[70] Verse 5 is not easy to categorise and will be discussed in more detail below.

Invocation: "To you (אֵלֶיךָ) O Yhwh, I call"
1. Negative: "Do not be deaf to me…" (1b)
2. Positive: "Hear the voice of my supplication when I cry to you (אֵלֶיךָ) for help" (2)
3. Negative: "Do not drag me away…" (3)
4. Positive: "Repay to them according to their work…" (4)

As can be seen the first positive petition in v. 2 is similar to the invocation, with its repetition of the phrase, "to you" (אֵלֶיךָ). As the psalmist cries, "*To you*, O Yhwh, I call" in v. 1a, so in v. 2a, he says: "Hear the voice of my supplication when I cry *to you* for help". The phrase, "to you" will be significant rhetorically as the direction shifts from Yhwh to his enemies in v. 4; from "to you" (אֵלֶיךָ) (1–2) to "to them" (לָהֶם) (4). Interestingly, לָהֶם is repeated 3x in v. 4.

Similarly, the first negative petition yields some points of contact with the third through its employment of the particle עִם. Both are constructed in the negative. The first one simply has the petition, "Do not be deaf to me" (1b), followed by a motivating statement, indicating that if Yhwh remains silent, he will be counted (lit. "he will become like") with (עִם) those who go down to the pit.[71] The third petition repeats עִם 3x in v. 3, qualifying what he means by "those who go down to the pit". Who are these people? They are the "wicked, the workers of evil, who speaks peace with their neighbour but there is evil in their hearts" (3). Verse 3 is then developed through the play on word with פֹּעַל as shown in what follows.

Having described the wicked as "workers (פֹּעַל) of evil" (3), he now asks that Yhwh "Give to them according to their works" (פֹּעַל) (4).[72] This petition is actually the first one that directly focuses on the 'wicked'. In the previous requests, the concern has been the concern of the psalmist *not* to suffer the same fate as the wicked.

---

[71] One can sense here the desperation reflected in the petition that if Yhwh does not do anything (i.e. if he remains silent), then the psalmist is 'finished'. Unfortunately, such total dependence is something that is missing in today's society, especially in the West.

[72] The word comes up again in the following v. 5. For this play on words, see N. H. Ridderbos, *Die Psalmen*, 215–16.

5.3.3.1 *Relationship of v. 5 with preceding and following section*

In between the petition (1–4) and the next section (vv. 6–7), we have a verse that stands out—v. 5. It differs from the preceding section grammatically and functionally. Whereas the preceding verses employ a second person address, v. 5 is constructed in the third person. Yhwh is addressed directly in vv. 1–4 whilst in v. 5, he is talked about. The former functions as a petition whilst the latter as a statement about what Yhwh will do to the wicked. It is not clear how one should understand the relationship between 5a and the preceding verse as well as 5a and 5b.

The כִּי at the beginning of v. 5a can be connected with v. 4 as a substantiating statement: "Give to them according to what they have done…(4), for they show no regard to your works…" (5a). Or it can be linked to what follows as most modern versions do: "Because they do not regard the works of Yhwh…(5a) he will tear them down and not build them up" (5b). I think both are possible and we may well have here what Raabe calls a deliberate ambiguity. As mentioned earlier, Raabe proposes the presence of "deliberate ambiguities" in the Bible that call for multivalent readings. He points out three areas in which these are found: lexical, phonetic and grammatical. To avoid excesses, he suggests three controlling guides—context, theological significance, and Hebrew usage.[73] Reading the כִּי with the preceding context has as its support the earlier construction in v. 1. There we find a petition followed by a substantiating statement. Likewise here, one can read v. 5 as providing a motivation for the petition in v. 4. God should give to them according to what their actions deserve, for they do not show regard to the works of Yhwh. The word translated 'works' (פֹּעַל), repeated in v. 5a, further supports the connection between the two verses. We may see some sort of a progression here. The "workers (פֹּעַל) of evil" (3) need to be recompensed for their works (פֹּעַל) (4) because they do not show regard for the works (פֹּעַל) of Yhwh (5a).

Taking v. 5a with v. 4, however, leaves the statement in 5b bare, hanging by itself as it were. This may be part of the reason why the majority of translators join the כִּי with what follows: "Because they do not show regard to the works of Yhwh and the works of his hands, he will break them down and not build them".[74] A further difficulty with

---

[73] Paul R. Raabe, "Deliberate Ambiguity in the Psalter," *JBL* 110 (1991): 213–27.
[74] But one can also say that the difficulty of making sense of the relationship between v. 5a and v. 4 is actually a support for reading the two together.

reading the כי with the preceding verse is the shift in voice. Whereas
v. 4 addresses Yhwh directly (second person), v. 5 talks about Yhwh
(third person).

Both possibilities have their own advantages and problems. Scholars
try to make sense of the passage by drawing on a possible reconstruction of the setting of the psalm. Most believe that v. 5 represents the
words of a cultic prophet addressed to the praying individual. But it
could also be the petitioner's own words reflecting his own conviction
which he may have acquired in the process of his praying. In the end,
one cannot really know for sure what the psalmist has actually intended
here or the historical setting behind the text. Probably he himself does
not fully understand the matter. But such a sense of ambiguity prepares
us for the next section.

5.3.3.2 *Sudden Change of Mood from Lament to praise*

In the second main section of the psalm, we are immediately confronted
with a sudden shift of mood, where the tone changes from lament to
praise (6). The imprecation (4) turns into a ברכה (6). Through employment of the phrase קול תחנוני (see v. 2), the connection between the
two main sections of the psalm is made explicit. But the personal tone
of the psalm in vv. 1–7, which contrasts with the more corporate tone
of vv. 8–9, has led some scholars to regard the latter as an addition.
Cheyne holds that the psalm consists of insertions and additions by a
later editor. Verse 5 is viewed as a "fragment"; vv. 6–7 an addition; and
vv. 8–9 as a "liturgical appendix".[75] Kittel sees vv. 8–9 as an addition
(Zusatz).[76] Briggs sees v. 9 as a liturgical addition.[77] Oesterley thinks vv.
8–9 do not belong here but may have been taken from the liturgy of
worship: "These verses can hardly be an original part of the psalm;
they represent the *people* and the king…whereas in the rest of the psalm
it is the individual psalmist".[78] But to judge the unity of a section of
a psalm on the basis of the personal and communal elements in the
psalm is a dichotomy that does not do justice to the biblical writers'
worldview. Weiser describes such a practice as a "carrying too far the

---

[75] T. K. Cheyne, *The Book of Psalms: Translated from a Revised Text with Notes and Introduction* (vol. 1; London: Kegan Paul, Trench, Trübner & Co., 1904), 119.
[76] Kittel, 109.
[77] Briggs, 245.
[78] Oesterley, 199.

modern fashion of contrasting the individual and the community".[79]
A more promising ground is provided for us by the text itself. A close
examination of the structure of vv. 6–9 indicates that what we have
here is a unified section. My analysis of the structure of these verses
yields the pattern, A B B' A':

> Blessed (ברך) be Yhwh...(6)   A
>   Yhwh is my strength (עז) and my shield...(7) B
>   Yhwh is the strength (עז) of his people...(8)   B'
> Save...bless (ברך) your inheritance...(9)   A'

In this section, the psalmist expresses his praise to Yhwh for the answer
received (6), declares his confidence in Yhwh (7), applies this confidence
to the people and the anointed one (8) and, significantly for this study,
moves on to another petition (9). Linguistically, one can see that the
psalmist has employed key words in each line to draw important connections. Thus we see the words עז and ברך are repeated in vv. 8 and
9 respectively. As Yhwh has been his strength, so he declares the same
for his people. Interestingly, while he repeats the word ברך, the function
of the word changes here from praise to petition. As he blesses Yhwh,
so now he asks Yhwh to bless his people. What makes the employment
of ברך in v. 9 more conspicuous is the fact that in the Psalms the word
is never used elsewhere as a petition for God to bless others. The word
is normally used in the same sense as in Ps 28:6—that of praising
Yhwh or calling others to bless Yhwh. Clearly, the psalmist has here
employed the word creatively for his own purposes. The 'certainty of
a hearing' reflected in the praise (6) is developed into another petition
through the repetition of the same word.

One can outline the overall structural movement of the second section as follows:

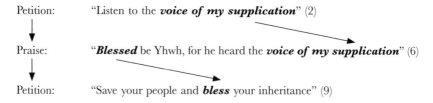

Petition: "Listen to the ***voice of my supplication***" (2)

Praise: "***Blessed*** be Yhwh, for he heard the ***voice of my supplication***" (6)

Petition: "Save your people and ***bless*** your inheritance" (9)

---

[79] Weiser, *Die Psalmen I*, 165, ET *The Psalms*, 258–9.

5.3.3.3 *Return to Lament after Praise*

From the diagram above, one can observe a movement from lament to praise and then another transition from praise to lament (petition).[80] The return to the element of lament comes almost unexpectedly in the light of the previous movement to praise and the declarations of confidence that flow from it. The psalm could have ended on a high note with the praise in v. 6 or the confident assertions of vv. 7–8. But the psalm moved on into another petition. We are reminded here of what Goldingay said about the movements between lament and praise: "A question provokes an answer, but the answer provokes a different question, and thus another answer, and yet another question, as we move towards the eschatological goal of understanding a text and having no more questions".[81] Psalm 28 started with a lament which receives an answer as reflected in the praise and expressions of confidence. But then, interestingly, praise returns to the element of lament: the answer provoked a "different question".[82]

5.3.4 *Canonical Context*

5.3.4.1 *Psalm 27 and 28*

In my own analysis of the overall pattern of Psalms 27 and 28 I have observed a number of similarities between the two psalms (see Table 6

---

[80] For this understanding of petition as lament, see Chapter 2.

[81] Goldingay, "The Dynamic Cycle of Praise and Prayer", 88.

[82] This movement into petition after expressions of confidence is not unique to Psalm 28. Ridderbos, *Die Psalmen*, 96, observes: "es kommt gelegentlich vor, dass auf die Äusserung der Erhörungsgewissheit wiederum eine erneute Bitte folgt". Along with Psalm 28, he cites Pss 20:10 and 14:7 as examples. Unfortunately, rather than leaving the issue of what caused the turning from praise to another petition open, Ridderbos tries to 'fill-in' the 'gap'. In the case of Psalm 28 he believes that in v. 5 a servant of the sanctuary comes in and delivers in the name of Yhwh an answer to the prayer. The speaking of Yhwh is a deed; he speaks and it happens (Ps 33:9). Thus the prayer can now say: "I am helped" in v. 7b. But he clarifies that what we find in 6f. is an anticipation of faith: the enemies are not yet actually punished (216). This explains why at the end of the prayer we find a petition. Interestingly, he also cites the presence of petition at the conclusion of psalms of thanksgiving and praise as found in Ps 9:20; 21:14; 68:29–31; 118:25; 138:8c. Such arrangements should not surprise us, according to Ridderbos; petitions must always be joined to the thanksgiving and praising, for humans remain dependent; they are totally dependent on the help of Yhwh in every following step (96).

below).[83] A comparative analysis of the Psalms 27 and 28 yields the following overall structure:

Praise/thanksgiving (27:1–6)   A
   Lament/petition (27:7–14)   B
   Lament/petition (28:1–5)   B'
Praise (28:6–8)   A'
   Lament/petition (28:9)   C

Table 6: *Comparative analysis between Psalm 27 and 28*

Psalm 27	Psalm 28
First part (Praise) (1–6)	**First part (Lament) (1–5)**
3rd person form of address	2nd person form of address
Yhwh is my light and my salvation (1a)	O my rock (צור) (1)
Yhwh is the stronghold (מעוז) (1b)	Hear (שמע) the voice (קול) of my
My heart (לב) will not fear (3)	supplication (2)
In this I will be confident (בטח) (3b)	To you (אליך) I call (קרא) (1)
He will set me high upon a rock	Do not be deaf to me (1)
(צור) (5)	Who speak peace...
	but evil is in their hearts (3)
Second part (Lament) (7–14)	**Second part (Praise) (6–8)**
2nd person form of address	3rd person form of address
Hear (שמע), O Yhwh my voice (קול) (7)	Yhwh is my strength and my shield
I call (קרא) (7)	(7)
to you (לך) (8)	My heart (לב) trusts (בטח) (7)
Do not hide your face (9)	Yhwh is the stronghold (עוז) of his
False witnesses (12)	anointed one (8)

Psalms 27 juxtaposes the elements of praise and lament. Psalm 28 follows the usual form-critical movement lament-praise, but then turns into the element of lament at the end.[84] Together, Psalms 27 and 28

---

[83] Cf. Hossfeld and Zenger, *Die Psalmen I*, 172.

[84] It is interesting that whereas the unity of Psalm 28 is not questioned, the unity of Psalm 27 is doubted. This is because Psalm 28 follows the usual form-critical framework of the movement lament-praise. Had the elements of praise and lament been reversed in Psalm 27, as in Psalm 28, I reckon its unity would not have been questioned. This betrays a rather limited view of the movements between the two elements. The comparative analysis shows that the movement is not only from lament to praise but also vice versa. As we have seen, even in the case of Psalm 28 where the lament moves on to praise,

form an A-B-B'-A'-C structure. As can be observed, the structure would have made a perfect chiasm had it not been for the petition at the end of Psalm 28. But I think this variation is significant for it adds to the emphasis on lament in the present ordering of the two psalms. There is an active interplay between the two psalms as can be observed in the correspondences between the two.

The first part of Psalm 27 demonstrates verbal correspondence with the second part of Psalm 28, both of which correspond to the element of lament in each psalm. Both employ third person address. In both there is a declaration of who Yhwh is to the psalmist as an expression of trust (27:1a; 28:7). The word לב and בטח occurs in both chapters (27:3; 28:7), as well as מעוז (27:1b; 28:8). Likewise, the second part of Psalm 27 exhibits similarities with the first part of Psalm 28. Both employ the second form of address. The petition for Yhwh to hear the voice of the psalmist is very similar in the two psalms as can be observed in the terms used—שמע and קול. The preposition 'to' (ל and אל) plus the second person suffix coupled with the verb appear in both (27:7–8; 28:1). The petition, אל־תסתר פניך ממני ("do not hide your face from me" [27:9]) is similar to אל־תחרש ממני ("do not be deaf to me" [28:1]). Finally, the idea of "false witnesses" (27:12) is the same as the description, "who speak peace with their neighbor but evil is in theirs hearts" (28:3).

5.4 SUMMARY AND CONCLUSION

In this chapter we have focused on two psalms which contain a rather more complicated movement than the usual form-critical understanding of the movement lament-praise. For here we have laments which move *beyond* praise into another lament or form of petition. In Psalm 12, we encounter a *return* to lament even in spite of a clear response from Yhwh. This psalm is a classic example of the presence of uncertainty even in spite of the 'certainty of a hearing'. There is a clear tension between the elements of lament and praise. On the one hand, God's response is highlighted in the middle of the psalm. On the other hand, this response is challenged by the reality that confronts the psalmist at

---

it is possible to see a movement back to the element of lament as indicated by the presence of the petition at the end.

the present, intimated at the beginning and end of the psalm. What surprised me in the process of working with this psalm is the lack of a framework which is able to embrace the unexpected return to lament in the psalm.[85] The general trend has been to impose the form-critical perspective of the one-way movement from lament to praise on Psalm 12. This has resulted in the failure to appreciate and understand the return to lament in v. 9. I have tried to demonstrate in my analysis that a better way of approaching Psalm 12 is by becoming open to the possibility of a return to lament even in spite of a resolution.

This openness to the possibility of a return to lament enables us to appreciate the movements in Psalm 28. In this psalm we have a sudden change of mood from lament to praise. But where one would expect the psalm to end on a note of praise, the psalm carried on, turning into another form of petition. Although the return to lament is not as dramatic as in Psalm 12, the shift from praise to lament at the end of Psalm 28 illustrates how the answer to one petition can lead not only to praise but that the answer itself can turn into another petition. This further demonstrates the complex movement and interaction between lament and praise. The movement is not a simple 'lament to praise'; it is more dynamic. As the comparative analysis between Psalms 27 and 28 has shown, there appears to be a deliberate attempt to juxtapose lament and praise not only in a single psalm but also in two neighbouring psalms. The fact that an editor saw fit to juxtapose lament and praise in Psalms 27 and 28 and in addition, to arrange the two psalms in such a way that praise moves to lament, signifies something of the perspective of the psalmist with regards to the relationship between these two elements. We do not only have the movement lament-praise. We also have the reverse movement as shown in the previous chapter, and here, a return to lament even after the movement to praise. Psalms 27 and 28 are arranged in such a way that lament and praise alternate. As we have seen in the study of the canonical context of Psalm 12, this alternation between lament and praise is a common feature in the Psalms. In the following chapter we explore further this alternation between the two elements within a psalm.

---

[85] Erbele-Küster's approach is an exception to the general trend.

CHAPTER SIX

THE ALTERNATION BETWEEN LAMENT AND PRAISE

6.1 Introduction

Our journey thus far has taken us to consider three movements between lament and praise: 1) the movement from lament to praise (Chapter 2); 2) the reverse movement from praise to lament (Chapter 4) introduced by the juxtaposition between lament and praise in Psalm 22 (Chapter 3) and 3) the return to lament after praise (Chapter 5). In this chapter, we present the fourth one—the alternation between lament and praise. This brings together the different movements thus far presented. Since we find alternation between the two elements, we have more opportunities to examine the movement from lament to praise, the reverse movement and the return to lament. Specifically, we focus on Psalms 31 and 35—two psalms which contain an alternation between lament and praise.

6.2 Psalm 31

6.2.1 Introduction: 'Tension in time'

What makes any study of Psalm 31 challenging is that here one is confronted with a composition in which chronological flow is difficult to discern. Broyles sees in the psalm what he calls "tension in time". He writes: "The transition from the first to the second prayer reflects a tension in time. In anticipation of Yahweh's hearing the prayer, the speaker has just claimed, 'you...knew the anguish of my soul. You...have set my feet in a spacious place.' But he now laments, 'I am in distress'".[1] Similarly, Mandolfo comments:

---

[1] Broyles, *Psalms*, 157.

One area of difficulty seems to revolve around attempts to make chronological sense of the poem. The tenses seem to jump back and forth in such a way as to make it difficult to know if the supplicant is offering thanks for a prayer already answered (v. 22), vowing praise for future assistance (vv. 8–9), or simply asserting confidence in the deity's assistance (vv. 15–16).[2]

A common resort is to regard the psalm as composite. Taylor views the psalm as a "combination of three laments, each of which is representative of a distinct class".[3] Kraus sees the psalm as consisting of two parts: vv. 1–8 [2–9] and vv. 9–24 [10–25]. These two parts represent two originally separate compositions. He argues that here "we would have to think of two different songs"; structural unity is hardly imaginable.[4] Hossfeld acknowledges the difficulty of putting together the various elements of the psalm. Through redaction criticism, he tries to discern the development of the psalm. Originally, the psalm consisted of vv. 10–19 to which the beginning part (2–9) and the thanksgiving (20–25) have been added later in the post-exilic period.[5]

It may be that what we have in Psalm 31 is a combination of two or three originally independent compositions. A closer examination of the psalm, however, reveals that we have here a composition that has been deliberately put together. There are significant verbal correspondences throughout the psalm.[6] What is more striking is the way in which the elements of lament and praise alternate in the psalm.

6.2.2   Structural Analysis

The psalm may be divided into three main parts:

First part: Lament to praise (2–9)
    Lament (2–7)
    Vow of praise (8–9)

---

[2] Mandolfo, God in the Dock: Dialogic Tension in the Psalms of Lament, 71–72.
[3] R. W. Taylor and W. S. McCullough, "The Book of Psalms," in The Interpreter's Bible (vol. 4; NY: Abingdon Press, 1955), 162.
[4] Kraus, Psalmen I, 247, ET Psalms 1–59, 360.
[5] Hossfeld, and Zenger, Die Psalmen I, 192. The idea that Psalm 31 originally constituted of a core (the middle part) to which the beginning and end parts have been added has been proposed earlier by Kirkpatrick, 156–58.
[6] See Léo Laberge, "A Literary Analysis of Psalm 31", Église et Théologie 16 (1985): 147–68.

Second part: Return to lament (10–19)
   Lament (10–14)
   Expression of trust (15)
   Petition/imprecation (16–19)
Third part: (20–23): Praise
   Thanksgiving/praise (20–23)
   Admonition (24–25)

Each major section involves a shift in mood. In the first section we see a build-up from a series of petitions (2–7) to expressions of confidence (8–9). But just when the psalm has reached its peak with the vow in v. 8 and the note of resolution in v. 9 the psalm suddenly falls back to lament in the second section (vv. 10ff.). We may recall here the similar movement from vow to lament in Psalm 27 (see above). The second section in turn reaches its height with the imprecations in vv. 18b–19. Then suddenly, the psalm moves to praise (vv. 20ff.). The transition from imprecation to praise is similar to the movement in Psalm 28.[7] There is a clear alternation between lament and praise in the psalm. The psalm as a whole ends with an admonition (24–25).

6.2.3 *Detailed Analysis*

6.2.3.1 *The tension between lament and praise in the first two parts of Psalm 31*

There is a close link between the first two parts of the psalm. The first part begins with the petition for Yhwh not to allow him to be put to shame: אל־אבושה (v. 2). The psalmist repeats exactly the same phrase in the second part (18): "O Yhwh, do not allow me to be put to shame" (אל־אבושה). This clearly links the first two parts of the psalm. Relevant to our study, the repetition highlights the contrast between the two parts. In the first part, the psalmist has already claimed that his petition not to be put to shame has been answered. This can be understood from v. 9: "you have not delivered me into the hand of my enemy". The repetition of the phrase אל־אבושה in the second section

---

[7] Like Ps 28:4–6, Ps 31:18–23 moves from imprecation to praise. The praise expression ברוך occurs in both after the imprecation (Ps 28:6; 31:22).

(18) contradicts such an affirmation, creating a tension between the two sections. This element of contrast and tension between the two sections is further seen in the interplay between vv. 8–9 and 10ff.

1. חסד (8) and חנן (10)—Although not exactly the same, these two words overlap in meaning, particularly in the present context. In v. 8 the psalmist declares and praises the gracious acts of Yhwh, whilst in v. 10 he asks Yhwh to be merciful/gracious to him.
2. חסד (8, 17)—This word appears in vv. 8 and 17. But whereas Yhwh's חסד is praised in the former, such is used as a basis for petition in the latter.
3. צרה (8) and צר (10)—In v. 8 the psalmist praises Yhwh because he has seen (lit. "knew") his distress (צרה). But in v. 10 the psalmist laments over his distress (צר). Using a play on words, צר (10) and צרה (12), he further complains about his enemies in v. 12.
4. ביד־אויב (9) and מיד־אויבי (16)—The interplay between these two phrases further illustrates the contrast between the two sections. As mentioned above, there is in the psalm a 'tension in time' which makes it difficult to make sense of its unity. On the one hand, the psalmist has already been delivered; on the other hand, we find him still struggling. One could ask, for instance, with regard to the relationship between vv. 9 and 16: "I thought his distress has already been dealt with?" For here there is a tension between the assertion, "you have not delivered me *into* the hand of my enemy (ביד־אויב)" (9) and the appeal, "deliver me *from* the hand of my enemy" (מיד־אויבי) (16). Note the interesting difference between the prepositions used: "into" (ב) and "from" (מן).

How do we account for the contradiction between the two parts of the psalm? How do we make sense of the 'tension in time'? Mandolfo and Broyles try to make sense of the 'tension in time' and contradictions of thought between the first and second parts of the psalm by reading the vow (8–9) as some sort of a promise or an anticipation.[8] Similarly, Ridderbos explains that what we have in the first part should not be read as an 'actual/complete deliverance' from the trouble besetting the psalmist. He writes, "In v. 8f. spricht der Dichter, als habe die Errettung bereits stattgefunden. In Wirklichkeit aber befindet er sich

---

[8] Mandolfo, 72, sees vv. 8–9 as a promise and Broyles, 157, as anticipation.

noch in derselben Not. In v. 10ff. scheint seine Not noch schwerer auf ihm zu lasten als zu Beginn".[9] He understands vv. 8–9 as a motivation (Beweggrund); the thanksgiving in 8f. is not for actual experience of deliverance but some sort of a motivation.[10]

I think a better alternative is to see here a juxtaposition between the two parts of the psalm, deliberately designed in such a way as to create a sense of disjuncture, even of discomfort resulting from the incongruity between the two parts. The easier thing to do is to silence the voice of the praise to fit into the lament that follows it. Ridderbos' proposal enables a smooth transition from the vow to the lament. But it somehow eliminates the strong element of tension between the two parts. Verses 8–9 clearly reflect a sense of resolution. The text does not tell us whether an actual deliverance has already transpired or not. Nevertheless, the psalmist declares his vow to Yhwh, as an act of faith, thereby leading to the element of praise. With the introduction of the lament in vv. 10ff. we are confronted with a sudden unexpected change of mood from praise to lament. The act of juxtaposition creates a "Leer-stelle" which cannot be fully explained. Rather than trying to resolve the tension in the psalm, we should highlight it. For it is the alternation between lament and praise that actually unifies the psalm.[11]

6.2.3.2   *Sudden change of mood from lament to praise*

In vv. 20–23 the psalm alternates once more; this time, it is the other way around: from lament to praise. Like Psalm 28 the psalm moves from imprecations (18b–19; cf. Ps 28:4–5) to a ברכה (22; cf. Ps 28:6). Such a movement lends itself easily to the famous turn from lament to praise. Those who view the psalm as a unity generally explain the sudden shift in terms of an oracle of salvation which has been delivered between vv. 19 and 20.[12] Others view the thanksgiving as having been added later after the prayer has been answered.[13] The problem with the former is that there is nothing in the text which indicates that we have here an oracle of salvation. The latter view needs to explain not

---

[9] Ridderbos, *Die Psalmen*, 226.
[10] Ibid., 227.
[11] Cf. Laberge, "A Literary Analysis of Psalm 31", 165. Craigie, *Psalms 1–50*, 259, demonstrates how the elements of lament and praise alternate: prayer (2–6); trust (7–9); lament (10–14); trust (15); prayer (16–19).
[12] Gunkel, *Die Psalmen*, 131; Anderson, 246; cf. Mandolfo, 72, n. 75.
[13] Anderson, 246.

only the process which the text underwent but more importantly, the text as we have it now.

In its present form, the third section shows correspondence with the preceding two sections. The phrase, "to those who take refuge (חסה) in you" recalls v. 2: "In you, O Yhwh, I take refuge (חסה)". Craigie observes further correlations between the third section and the preceding ones.[14]

Thanksgiving	*Background: prayer/lament*
v. 20 For God's goodness to those who sought refuge...	v. 2 ...as the psalmist had sought refuge in God.
v. 21 God protects his own from conspiracies and the *strife of tongues*...	v. 17 ...as the psalmist experienced conspiracies and verbal attacks (v. 19)
v. 22 God reveals his *lovingkindness*...	v. 17 ...as the psalmist had prayed that he would.
v. 23 God *heard* the prayer of the psalmist...	v. 3 ...as the psalmist had prayed that he would.
v. 24 God loved his saints and hated his enemies...	v. 7 ...as the psalmist hated idolaters and trusted God.

These indicate a close interaction between the three main sections of the psalm. Overall, there is an alternation between lament and praise. The psalm could have ended with v. 23 in a positive note of deliverance. Interestingly, the psalm ended with an admonition.

6.2.3.3 *The admonition at the end of Psalm 31*

Psalm 31 contains in its end an admonition similar to Psalm 27. What is the function of this section? In his study of the didactic role of the Psalms, David Firth explains that "every psalm is at least a model of prayer or praise in practice, which functions to teach those gathered in worship".[15] He cites a number of ways in which the psalms could function didactically. Relevant for the present study is his discussion of 'admonition' as a means of instruction. Belonging to this category are those psalms "marked by a direct appeal made in the second person".[16] Citing as his example the lament in Psalm 130, Firth avers: "Admoni-

---

[14] Craigie, 262.
[15] Firth, "The Teaching of the Psalms", 163.
[16] Ibid., 167.

tion...suggests that the psalmist does not believe that Israel currently acts in the way requested, which is why the climax in vv. 7–8 contains both the admonition proper and additional reasons why Israel should decide to express such hope".[17] He does not mention Psalms 27 and 31 in his discussion, though these two psalms fit very well with those psalms which contain admonitions like Psalm 130.[18] Following Firth's suggestion, we may infer at this point that although Psalm 31 ends on a note of thanksgiving, the presence of an admonition at the very end indicates that the element of lament is sustained not only in the middle part of the psalm but throughout—even till the end. As Curtis remarks, "There is a hint right at the end of the psalm that the road ahead will not necessarily be an easy one".[19] Whilst the psalmist speaks of his own experience of deliverance (Ps 31:23), his admonition at the end reflects an acknowledgment that such is not the case in many of his listeners.[20] This explains why like Psalm 27 the psalm ends with the following admonition: "Be strong...all you who wait on Yhwh".

6.2.4   *Canonical Context*

According to Vesco there are many common expressions between Psalms 31 and 30.[21] In both psalms one finds the same cry for help (Ps 30:3; 31:23), the same petition for mercy (30:11; 31:10). One also observes a similar "internal dialogue": "But I, I said in my ease..." (30:7); "But I, I said in my alarm" (31:23). As Yhwh has established (עמד) the psalmist as a "strong mountain" in Ps 30:8, so in Ps 31:8 he has established/set (עמד) the psalmist's feet in a broad place.[22] Further, like Ps 30:5, Ps 31:24 evokes the faithfulness of Yhwh.[23]

More significantly for the present study, we find an alternation between thanksgiving and lament in Psalm 30. As scholars have rightly

---

[17] Ibid., 168.
[18] See discussion of Psalm 27 above.
[19] Curtis, 70.
[20] As is sometimes the case in church worship, it is difficult for the majority of members to identify with a testimony of triumph and deliverance, for often many find themselves somewhere in between.
[21] Jean-Luc Vesco, *Le Psautier de David* (Paris: Cerf, 2006), 292–3.
[22] Ibid., 292.
[23] Ibid., 293.

observed, Psalm 30 begins and ends with thanksgiving.[24] But in between
the thanksgiving we find a lament (7–11).[25] The waw in v. 7 can be read
adversatively as a way of drawing a contrast between the preceding
thanksgiving (2–4) and exhortation to praise (5–6). The most common interpretation of vv. 7–11 is that these verses recall the situation
before the experience of deliverance.[26] But it is also possible to see
here a juxtaposition of a thanksgiving and a lament. There is in fact a
juxtaposition of a statement of assurance and uncertainty in v. 8: "O
Yhwh, in your favour you have established me as a strong mountain":
"you hid your face, I was terrified". There is no waw that connects
the two cola; they are simply placed side by side, creating a sense of
tension between certainty and uncertainty. We also find a rather sharp
complaint in v. 10: "What profit is there in my death, in my going
down to the Pit? Will dust praise you? Will it declare your faithfulness?"
Surrounding this complaint are two verses which express a petition
(9, 11). The latter indicates a strong sense of urgency: "Hear, O Yhwh
and have mercy on me! O Yhwh, be my help!" When we turn to the
next verse (Ps 30:12) we encounter a sudden change of mood from
the lament to resolution and praise. The sudden shift is comparable
to the change of mood in Ps 6:9–10.[27] We thus find an alternation
between thanksgiving and lament in Psalm 30, which prepares us for
the same feature in Psalm 31.

6.2.5   *Summary*

Psalm 31 contains a series of two alternations between lament and
praise. As shown above, the canonical context of the preceding psalm
introduces this alternation. Psalm 31 begins with a lament which builds
up towards a more confident tone (8–9). But just when the psalm had

---

[24] Gerstenberger, *Psalms Part I*, 133–4; cf. Calvin, *A Commentary of the Psalms*, 343.

[25] Indeed, Psalm 30 has an almost equal number of verses for the lament and
thanksgiving elements. Verses 2–4 and 12–13 constitute the thanksgiving; we may also
include here the exhortation to praise in vv. 5–6. Correspondingly, vv. 7–11 represent
the lament. When we add these verses, the thanksgiving and lament amount to 7 and
5 verses, respectively.

[26] Brueggemann, *The Message of the Psalms*, 127; Kraus, 243, ET 355–6; Broyles,
Psalms, 154; Goldingay, *Psalms I*, 424, 429.

[27] Interestingly, the word בהל which is a key word in Psalm 6 appears in Ps 30:8.
Both psalms also speak of 'going down to the Pit/Sheol' (Ps 30:10; 6:6).

declared an experience of deliverance (9), it suddenly goes back to lament (10ff.). The movement is similar to the return to lament after the vow of praise in Psalm 27. Interspersed with expressions of trust in the middle the lament continues until v. 19. Afterwards, the psalm turns to praise again where it would linger longer (20–23). But then in the final two verses, the psalm turns into an admonition which has the effect of bringing back the tone of lament (see above).

6.3   PSALM 35

6.3.1   *Introduction*

In her discussion of Hebrew poetry, Berlin mentions the importance of becoming sensitive to the movement/s in a psalm. Although it is important to know the various aspects of Hebrew poetry, she admits that often the actual reading or making sense of a particular composition is left to the reader. To make best sense of a particular composition, she advises that we pay attention, among other things, to the *movement* in the psalm: "One might look for the *movement* within the poem, the repeated words or phrases, unexpected expressions or images, and the general tone and effect that it produces".[28] She cites Psalm 13 as an example where we find a movement from "despair to hope".[29]

What makes Psalm 35 particularly interesting in the light of Berlin's comments is that this psalm contains not only one, but three movements from "despair to hope"! We may ask what "general tone and effect" does this type of composition bring out?

The significance of Psalm 35 is further highlighted by the association of this psalm with the whole 'salvation oracle' theory. Begrich sees in the psalm a proof for his 'Heilsorakel' thesis.[30] He believes that Ps 35:3b ("say to my soul, 'I am your salvation'") is a request for a pronouncement of an oracle of salvation.[31] Kraus follows Begrich here.[32]

---

[28] Adele Berlin, "Introduction to Hebrew Poetry", in *NIB* (vol. IV; Nashville: Abingdon Press, 1996), 314, emphasis mine.

[29] Ibid.

[30] Begrich, "Das priesterliche Heilsorakel", 81.

[31] Ibid., 83.

[32] Kraus, 276, ET 393.

As will be seen in the analysis of Psalm 35, one of the problems with Begrich's approach is its tendency to generalise a certain principle and apply it to specific passages without a proper consideration of the passage as a whole. Thus, in the case of Psalm 35, he focuses only on the second half of v. 3 and does not explain his theory in the light of the context of the whole psalm. He readily assumes the presence of an oracle of salvation in Ps 35:3b—a view which cannot be sustained in the passage. But even if we grant that we have an indication of a response in vv. 9–10, one of the questions that Begrich and his camp still need to answer is, why is there a return to lament in vv. 11ff. if the divine response has already been given?[33] What does this imply for the 'certainty of a hearing' theory?

Unfortunately, as is the case in most treatments of Psalm 35, the return to lament after the vow of thanksgiving is left untouched. To my knowledge, only Ridderbos underlines such a movement from praise to lament.[34] But to do justice to the passage one has to consider not only the movement from lament to praise but also the *return* to lament. Since we are presently dealing with the psalm as a whole, it is important to consider the movements in the whole psalm. Whatever literary development the text might have undergone, we are left now with the present form of the passage. And it is to this present form that our discussions revolve.

6.3.2   *Structural Analysis*

Superscription (1a)

1st Part		2nd Part		3rd Part
Lament (1–8)	‖	Lament (11–17)	‖	Lament (19–26)
Praise (9–10)	‖	Praise (18)	‖	Praise (27–28)

---

[33] Although not as explicit as in the other psalms we have looked at, there is in Psalm 35 a shift of mood from lament to thanksgiving, or at least an anticipation that praise/thanksgiving will come (see below).

[34] Ridderbos, *Die Psalmen*, 253.

Psalm 35 is generally recognised by scholars as consisting of three sections—vv. 1–10, 11–18 and 19–28.[35] Ridderbos rightly observes that the three sections are parallel to each other.[36] The division appears to be a natural one in view of the presence of the element of praise at the end of each section (9–10, 18, 28). I use the phrase 'element of praise' to describe these verses primarily because they depict the mood of praise and secondly, to include other elements related to praise such as vow and 'certainty of a hearing'.[37] Begrich distinguishes between vow and 'certainty of a hearing'.[38] In his understanding the vow presupposes the reception of an oracle of salvation and its consequent 'certainty of a hearing'.[39] The vow comes after the reception of an oracle and expression of certainty. Ridderbos, on the other hand, employs the two interchangeably.[40] Gerstenberger regards vv. 9–10 as a "hymnic interlude" and the other two as vow.[41]

6.3.3 Detailed Analysis with Discussion of Canonical Context

6.3.3.1 Direct appeals to Yhwh

The psalm begins with a series of six direct appeals to Yhwh for the psalmist: contend, fight, take hold [of shield…], rise up, draw [the spear…] and say [to my soul] (1–3). The direct petitions are full of military imagery. The six appeals are followed by prayers against the psalmist's enemies (4ff.). They are wishes against the enemies or imprecations. We observe here a shift of direction from the psalmist to his enemies. He prays that they be put to shame. Note the variety of words employed to formulate the petition towards this end: בנש, כלם, סוג and חפר (4). He repeats three of these words towards the end of the third

---

[35] Delitzsch, *Biblischer Commentar über die Psalmen*, 299, ET *Biblical Commentary on the Psalms*, 500; Kirkpatrick, *The Psalms*, 176; Anderson, *Psalms*, 275; Curtis, *Psalms*, 78; Ridderbos, *Die Psalmen*, 251–52. For different division, see Gerstenberger, *Psalms Part I*, 150–53.

[36] Ridderbos, *Die Psalmen*, 252.

[37] See Chapter 2 for discussions of my use of the terms lament and praise in this study.

[38] Begrich, "Das priesterliche Heilsorakel", 81.

[39] Ibid., 82.

[40] Ridderbos, *Die Psalmen*, 251–52.

[41] Gerstenberger, *Psalms Part I with an Introduction to Cultic Poetry*, 151–52.

lament (26), indicating the significance of such a petition as well as the
connection between the three sections (see further below).

6.3.3.2   *Psalm 1 and Psalm 35*

The next imprecation in vv. 5–6 is a clear allusion to Psalm 1.[42] The
occurrence of מץ and דרך betray the connection.[43] The former occurs
only in Psalms 1 and 35 in the whole of the Psalter. More significantly,
both are employed along with the word רוח. In Psalm 1 the wicked
are likened to the "chaff (מץ) which the wind (רוח) drives away" (4). In
Psalm 35, the psalmist wishes that his enemies be like the "chaff (מץ)
before the wind (רוח)" (5). So as not to miss the allusion, he employs
the second word, דרך—a key word in Psalm 1.[44] Drawing on the contrast between the דרך of the righteous and the wicked from Ps 1:6, the
psalmist prays here that the דרך of his enemies be "dark and slippery"
(Ps 35:6).[45] Verse 6 ends with the word רדף, which recalls 3a. What
is striking is the way in which the secure declarations of Psalm 1 are
shaken in Psalm 35 as the latter shifts from praise to lament (see below).
When one reads through Psalm 35 and compares it with Psalm 1,
one gets the impression that the rather black and white presentation

---

[42] By trying to link Psalm 35 to Psalm 1 I am not indicating that the former has been
written later than Psalm 1. It is more likely that Psalm 1 has been added later as an
introduction to the Psalter. My approach here is guided by a canonical reading which
tries to read the Psalter in its present form. As I have noted earlier (see Methodology
in Chapter 1), Brueggemann has tried to establish a connection between Psalms 1
and 25. According to him, Psalm 25 challenges the affirmations of Psalm 1. Similarly,
though with even more definite links, I try to show here a close interplay between
Psalms 1 and 35. Though we have no way of determining whether the connection
is deliberate, at least on the canonical level or *Sitz im Buch* there is close connection
between the two.

[43] In addition to these two important words, see also צדק (Ps 35:24, 27, 28; 1:5, 6)
and the use of a rather unusual word—הגה in Ps 35:28. The same word in used in
Ps 1:1 to speak of the activity of the righteous: meditation. Cf. Kraus, *Psalmen I*, 276,
ET 393, who cites Ps 1:4 in his discussion of Ps 35:5–6.

[44] The word occurs 3x (1, 6 [2x]).

[45] Calvin captures the seriousness of the imprecation here: "As the chaff is driven
with the wind, so also he desires, that, being disquieted by the secret impulse of the
angel of the Lord, they may never have rest. The imprecation which follows is even
more dreadful, and it is this: that wherever they go they may meet with darkness and
slippery places; and that in their doubt and perplexity the angel of the Lord would
pursue them. In fine, whatever they devise, and to whatever side they turn, he prays
that all their counsels and enterprises may come to a disastrous termination". (John
Calvin, *Commentary on the Book of Psalms* [vol. 1; trans. James Anderson; Edinburgh:
Calvin Translation Society, 1845], 578.)

of the life of the righteous in Psalm 1 is not as straightforward as it appears to be. It seems that we have here an attempt to challenge the affirmations of Psalm 1, or at least to make the presentation in Psalm 1 more realistic.

When we consider the canonical context of Psalm 35's adjacent psalms, especially Psalm 34, we observe a similar attempt to challenge the positive assertions about the righteous in Psalm 34. There are numerous points of contact between these two psalms.[46] The most prominent among these is the mentioning of the מלאך יהוה (34:8) which occurs twice in Psalm 35 (vv. 5, 6).[47] Two other significant repetitions are כפיר ('young lion'; 34:11; 35:17) and עצם with כל ('all *his* bones' [34:21]; 'all *my* bones' [35:10]). What makes the contact relevant to the present discussion is the way in which Psalm 35 'reacts' in a sort of a negative fashion to the claims of Psalm 34. Like the laments in Psalms 3–14 [except Psalm 8] which challenge the declarations of Psalm 1, Psalm 35 muddies Psalm 34, presenting a more realistic point of view to the claims made in Psalm 34. Kidner comments: "The deliverance celebrated in that psalm [34] is now seen to be not invariably swift or painless, but subject, if God wills, to agonizing delays".[48] Whilst the presence of the 'angel of the Lord' in Psalm 34 reflects a situation of security, the phrase is used in Psalm 35 in a very insecure situation. Psalm 35 presents an image of conflict, of war whilst Psalm 34 is that of tranquillity. Such a contrast is further seen with the use of the word כפיר. In Psalm 34 the secure status of the righteous is presented as even better than those of young lions: young lions may suffer want, but those who seek the Lord do not lack any good thing (11). In Psalm 35, the word כפיר is employed to bring out the desperate state in which the psalmist has found himself. He cries out to Yhwh: "rescue my only life from the lions!" (35:17). Overall, the tone of Psalm 34 is marked by praise whilst that of Psalm 35 is dominated by lament/complaint.

6.3.3.3 *Motivations for the imprecations*

The imprecations (4–6) are followed by a motivation: "For (כי) 'without cause' (חנם) they have hidden their nets for me" (7). כי can be

---

[46] See Hossfeld, *Die Psalmen I*, 217.
[47] Ibid.
[48] Kidner, *Psalms 1–72*, p. 142.

seen as providing a motivation for the previous imprecations or as a
substantiation for the further imprecation that follows (8). In the latter case, the particle would be translated 'because'. Both are possible.
The word חנם is repeated twice in v. 7 and is employed again later
in the beginning of the third lament (v. 19). As Psalm 1 ends with the
sober statement, "but the way of the wicked will perish" (6b), so the
first lament ends with the following wish: "May ruin come upon him
unawares... (8). The word, 'ruin' is repeated twice in v. 8 for emphasis.
The fate experienced by the psalmist, described as "without cause", is
matched by the imprecation that ruin come to his enemies "unawares".
In Hebrew "unawares" is לא ידע. This phrase plays a significant part
in the second lament.

6.3.3.4   Transition to the element of Praise

The anticipated destruction of the enemy results in the rejoicing (גיל)
of the psalmist (9).[49] The sense of the waw at the beginning of v. 9 is
unclear. Grammatically, it could be translated "but", though this does
not flow well with the preceding context. It could be translated "whilst":
"...in ruin let him fall (8), whilst my soul rejoices in Yhwh". But this
too would not fit well. NASB translates it simply as "and". The majority
of the modern versions translate the waw as "then": "Then my soul
will rejoice in Yhwh".[50] Against this, Curtis notes that the Hebrew
leaves no trace of conditionality, and therefore the word should not
be translated by 'then'. The sense of the text is simply: 'my soul shall
rejoice in Yhwh'. I think Curtis' suggestion is the best option in an
ambiguous case such as this. One can say that the shift to a mood of
rejoicing and praise cannot be fully explained, for it is analogous to a
gift. There is clearly a shift from lament to praise similar to what we
find in Psalms 28 and 31. As shown earlier, there is a movement from
imprecation (Ps 28:4–5; 31:18b–19) to praise (28:6; 31:22) in these two

---

[49] G. A. Anderson, *A Time to Mourn, a Time to Dance: The Expression of Grief and Joy in
Israelite Religion* (University Park, PA: Pennsylvania State University Press, 1991), explains
the significance of this joyful reaction over the defeat of one's enemies as follows: "To
rejoice over the downfall of one's enemies is not simply to take inner delight at someone
else's misfortune, but rather to parade publicly one's lack of solidarity with the party
in question" (73). Conversely, to "fail to show solidarity in such a situation (when one
falls/gets sick)—or even worse, to rejoice while a neighbour was in mourning—was to
declare oneself an enemy rather than a covenantal partner" (94).

[50] JPS, NIV, RSV, NRSV.

psalms. One is struck by a similar transition from an imprecation to praise in Ps 35:8–9. The element of praise becomes more apparent in v. 10: "All my bones will say, 'Yhwh who is like you?'…" Gerstenberger understands this as a hymn.[51]

Verses 9 and 10 employ two words which appeared earlier in 3b. The psalmist asks in the latter: "Say (אמר) to my soul, 'I am your salvation (ישועה)'" (3b). Here, the psalmist declares, "[my soul] exults in your salvation (ישועה). All my bones will say (אמר)….(9–10)". The occurrence of the two words establishes the connection between the petition/lament and the praise. Interestingly, the reversal of the order of the two words in v. 3 and vv. 9–10[52] coincides with the reversal of mood between the lament in vv. 1–8 and the rejoicing and praise in vv. 9–10.

We may recall here Begrich's view that we have in v. 3b a request for an oracle of salvation. There is a clear interaction between vv. 3 and 9f. But to say that what we have in v. 3 is a request for an oracle is way beyond the evidence. There is simply nothing in the text to warrant such a proposal. There is also no explicit statement of a certainty of a hearing in vv. 9f. What we have instead is a declaration of praise. One may assume that a reception of an oracle resulting in a certainty of a hearing may be behind the words of vv. 9–10. But this is not explicit in the text. There is therefore neither a clear oracle nor a 'certainty of a hearing' here.

6.3.3.5   *Return to Lament*

In a typical form-critical framework, the psalm could easily have ended with v. 10. This would have followed the pattern of movement from lament to praise. But just when the song had barely reached the height of praise, it sinks down back to lament in vv. 11ff. With the suddenness with which the lament turned to praise in vv. 9–10, praise turns to lament in vv. 11ff. As if to inform the reader that he is back where he started, the psalmist repeats the word קום from the beginning of the psalm (2). Having cried out, "Rise up (קום) to my help!" (2), he

---

[51] Gerstenberger, *Psalms Part I*, 151.
[52] Taken together, these verses form the following reverse pattern: אמר—ישועה— ישועה—אמר.

now complains, "Malicious witnesses rise up (קוֹם)" (11).[53] Reinforcing
the connection with the earlier lament, the psalmist employs a play on
word with the preceding lament. The phrase לֹא יָדַע (8) recurs in 11b.
The phrase is used as an imprecation in v. 8 that "ruin come upon
him unawares". Here it is used as a complaint for the fate which the
psalmist suffered in the hands of his enemies. They have asked him
something "I do not know" (11b).[54] With these two repetitions (קוֹם and
לֹא יָדַע), the entirety of the preceding lament is taken up as it were in
a sort of an inclusio fashion, implying that the whole of the previous
lament remains (see Table 7 below). The lament in the second section
(11–16) presents a different angle to the preceding lament. The previous
one consists predominantly of prayers of imprecations directed to the
enemies. The present lament can be described more as a complaint to
Yhwh against his enemies. The second lament elaborates on the first
one by providing more bases for the petitions in the first section. It is
directed more at Yhwh, elucidating what the psalmist meant with his
expression, 'without cause' (7).

Anderson sees the three sections of Psalm 35 as a description of the
psalmist's experience "from three different angles".[55] If this is correct
then the second lament can be likened to a more focused close up
with a zoom lens. It basically relates a situation in which the psalmist,
instead of experiencing goodwill from the people concerned, received
'evil' (12). He recounts his acts of kindness to "them" during their
experiences of suffering (13–14). To his amazement, when it was their
turn to complement the kindness he has shown, he received the opposite.[56] At his stumbling, they rejoiced (15). No wonder, earlier, he prays
that their way be slippery (7) and wishes that ruin may fall on them
(8)—an event which occasions the psalmist's rejoicing in v. 9.[57] The
motif of rejoicing—introduced in v. 15—will be the dominant theme
in the third lament. Ridderbos points out the importance of the word

---

[53] The movement shows some affinity to Psalm 12, where one is confronted with
the same problem stated in the beginning even after a divine oracle has already been
given (see v. 9).

[54] The phrase shows up again in v. 15.

[55] Anderson, *The Book of Psalms*, 275.

[56] There is a very good analogy in Filipino culture of this idea of complementing
the good received from another. The term used to express it in our language is 'utang
na loob'.

[57] The word for rejoicing in v. 9 (גִּיל) differs from the more dominant word in the
psalm—שָׂמַח.

'rejoice' in the psalm: "es kann gesagt werden, dass die grosse Frage in diesem Psalm lautet: wer wird frohlocken, die Feinde oder der Dichter und seine Anhänger?"[58] The poet reports that "they rejoiced" over his stumbling (15). This provides the background for the petitions later on in the third section. Rejoicing is connected with the experience of shame along with its related activities of taunting and mocking and physical expressions such as the gnashing of teeth (16).

6.3.3.6   *Psalm 35 and Psalm 22*

Out of his difficult experiences the psalmist turns to Yhwh in a prayer that combines petitions from Psalms 13 and 22.[59] "How long?" (35:17) recalls Ps 13:2–3. The second part of the petition shows striking similarities with Psalm 22, specifically with its final petitions in vv. 21–22. Psalm 35 employs a verb similar to Psalm 22—שׁוּב (Hiphil; cf. נצל in Ps 22:21). נפשׁ and יחידתי occurs in the same order in the two cola of Ps 22:21. יחידתי (from יחיד) occurs in this form nowhere else in the Psalms except in Psalms 35 and 22. Moreover, both psalms use animal imagery to describe their enemies. Though not exactly the same, both refer to 'lions': כפיר (young lion) in Psalm 35 and אריה (lion) in Psalm 22 (v. 22).

The two psalms, at least Ps 35:17, 18 and Ps 22:21–23, resemble each other not only in terms of the words used but also structurally, for like Psalm 22, Psalm 35 suddenly moves to a vow of thanksgiving. From the lament and urgent appeal of v. 17, the psalm shifts to the mood of thanksgiving: "I will give you thanks in the great congregation (קהל); in the mighty throng I will praise you (הלל)" (35:18). As in Psalm 22 the second lament in Psalm 35 suddenly moves upwards to thanksgiving once it reaches its deepest point. Both קהל and הלל occur in Ps 22:23b. The similarity with Psalm 22 not only elucidates the present psalm, it also sheds more light on the textual issue in Ps 22:22.[60] The present analysis proves that it is not unusual for a lament to change to praise in the manner of Psalm 22.[61] At least we have here

---

[58] Ridderbos, *Die Psalmen*, 258.

[59] Weiser, *Die Psalmen I*, 100, ET *The Psalms*, 302, notes the connection between Psalms 35 and 22.

[60] The MT has 'and you answered me' whilst the LXX has 'my afflicted [soul]'.

[61] Here I follow the LXX reading of Ps 22:22b which preserves the tension and leaves the first part of Psalm 22 hanging. See the discussion of the textual problem of Ps 22:22 in Chapter 3.

a clear witness—one which is very much akin to the structure of Psalm 22—which shows a transition from a 'hanging' (i.e. unresolved) petition to thanksgiving. There is therefore no need for the reading found in the MT of Psalm 22A ("and he answered me", v. 22b) to explain the transition to thanksgiving in Psalm 22B.

6.3.3.7   *Sudden change to praise and sudden return to lament*

Psalms 35 and 22 are similar. But they also differ. For unlike Psalm 22, Psalm 35 does not 'explode the limits', to borrow a phrase from Davis.[62] Like a firecracker that fails to take off and produce the expected effect, the thanksgiving in v. 18 quickly dies away and returns to lament. Taking up the word שׂמח from the second section (15), the psalmist appeals to Yhwh *not* to let his enemies "rejoice over me" (19). The negative petition here implies that the psalmist's enemies have been rejoicing over him. In 19b the word חנם, which features prominently in the first section (2x in v. 7), shows up for the last time as a description of the psalmist's enemies. What was earlier described using figurative language is here explicitly set out: notice the variation from "those who hide their nets without cause" (7) to "those who *hate me* without cause" (19b). One can sense a possible heightening here which becomes more apparent when we compare the present section with the preceding ones. My analysis of the three sections shows that this is the first time we see a negative petition in the psalm. All the petitions in the first section are formulated positively. The second consists mainly of a complaint against the enemy; its only direct petition is in v. 17, and this too is formulated positively. But notice the prominence of the negative in this third section. The petition, "Do not let them rejoice over me" is repeated in v. 24. The enemies are described as those who "do *not* speak peace" (20). Twice, the petition "Do *not* let them say" is made in v. 25.

The psalmist continues his complaint against his enemies in vv. 20–21. Employing a play on words with the last part of v. 21 ("our eyes have *seen* it"), the psalmist comes before Yhwh asserting, "[But] you do see, O Yhwh, do not be silent!"[63] Returning to its allusion to Psalm 22, the text continues with the plea: "O Lord, do not be far (רחק) from me"

---

[62] Davis, "Exploding the Limits", *JSOT* 53 (1992): 93–105.
[63] Cf. the contrast in Ps 10:13 and 14 between the claims of the wicked over Yhwh's inaction and the psalmist's assertion that Yhwh "sees".

(22b). רחק is the key word in Psalm 22.[64] Conspicuously, whereas the word occurs before the vow of thanksgiving in Psalm 22, in Psalm 35 the word shows up *after* the vow of thanksgiving. It is as if the psalmist is telling the readers/worshippers: I have already vowed to offer thanks to the Lord, but here I am, back to my lament. As Anderson notes, "troubles do not always come singly, nor are all the word-pictures statements of fact".[65] The psalm seems to be teaching us that the shift to praise is not a guarantee that one will never go back to lament. Such is not always the case. Psalm 22 does not always happen—or at least does not happen too easily/quickly. In the case of Psalm 35, it took three returns to lament. And even when the shift has already occurred, the last praise at the end of Psalm 35 does not reach the same height that Psalm 22 was able to ascend.

Taking up my previous observation on the negative petitions in the present section, one can see a return to the positive petitions in vv. 26–27. The change may be due to the attempt to create a closure by repeating the earlier petitions in v. 4. Verse 26 employs the three words used in v. 4—בוש, חפר and כלם. There is a slight change in v. 26 with the two-fold repetition of בוש. Whereas earlier, the petition is "let them be put to shame" (4); here it is "let them be clothed with shame!" (26b).

6.3.3.8 *Movement to praise for the third time!*

After successfully drawing some form of connection with the first part of the psalm, our passage closes with a prayer wish for those who support the psalmist (27) and a vow of thanksgiving (28).[66] His wish for those who support him contrasts with that of his enemies. He prays that they will shout for joy and rejoice (שׂמח). The last word recalls the rejoicing of his enemies over him (15), his appeal to Yhwh not to allow his enemies to continually rejoice over him (19, 24) and his prayer for those who rejoice over his suffering (26). The difference here is that the experience of rejoicing is on the side of the psalmist. Another important word that the psalmist repeats is אמר. This word featured prominently in the first section. In v. 3, the psalmist asks Yhwh: "Say

---

[64] See Psalm 22 (Chapter 3).
[65] Anderson, *The Book of Psalms*, 275.
[66] The last word in Psalm 35—תהלה (cf. Ps 22:4, 26)—is a further support for the connection between Psalms 35 and 22.

(אמר) to my soul…" At the end of the first section, we find the words,
"all my bones will say (אמר)…" (10). The word is missing entirely in
the second section (11–18). But when it reappears in the last section
(19–28), it 'comes with a vengeance'. As Ridderbos remarked (see above),
the main question in the psalm is "who will rejoice, the enemy or the
poet and his supporters?" Or let me add in order to relate it to the
word אמר, the main concern in the psalm is: "who has the last 'say',
the psalmist or his enemies?" In the third section it has been mostly
the enemies who are having their 'say'. Verse 21b reads: "They *say*
(אמר) 'aha, aha!'…" Twice in v. 25 the psalmist pleads, "Do not let
them *say* (אמר)". But the last occurrence of the word comes from the
psalmist's camp: "Let them *say* (אמר) continually: Yhwh be exalted…"
(27). The movement of the psalm indicates that the psalmist and his
camp have the last 'say'. Yet it is interesting that the contents of their
last 'say' concern not themselves but Yhwh. The word 'exalted' (גדל)
is a play on word with 'those who exalt (גדל) themselves against me'
(26b). Whereas his enemies exalt themselves against him, the psalmist
and his camp exalt Yhwh. The psalmist vows to declare what Yhwh
has done, promising to proclaim his "praise all day long" (28).

6.3.4 *Summary*

As Berlin pointed out (see above), it is important in reading a psalm to
pay close attention to its movement/s. In Psalm 35, we see a threefold
movement from lament to praise (1–10; 11–18; 19–28). The verses are
almost equally distributed between the three sections, each consisting of
8–10 verses. McCann sees the arrangement of Psalm 35 as 'chaotic' and
suggests that the psalm should not be analysed too much in terms of its
literary order. Accordingly, the 'chaotic order' of the psalm is reflective
of the chaotic condition of the psalmist. He writes: "Perhaps it is best
not to attempt to discern too much literary order in the psalm, but to
interpret the apparent literary disarray as an appropriate indication of
the chaotic conditions that prevailed in the life of the psalmist".[67] On
the contrary, as demonstrated above, it is possible to see some sense of
unity in the psalm when one considers the alternation between lament
and praise. A close reading of the literary order of this psalm actually

---

[67] McCann, "Psalms", 818.

brings out the tension that is its central characteristic. There is a close connection between the three sections (see the Table 7 below). The first anticipates the second section. The second lament recalls the lament in the first section by repeating a word from the beginning and end of the first lament (שׁוב and לֹא ידע; see discussions above and the diagram below). The third lament recalls the second one by repeating שׁמח—a central term in the second section. It ends the section by repeating the opening lament on 'shame' (compare vv. 4 and 26). Strikingly, the lament portion occupies a greater part in each section, with the vow of thanksgiving or praise covering at most two verses (two verses in the first and third sections [9–10; 27–28] and one verse in the second [18]).

What makes Psalm 35 particularly significant for the present study is that it *combines* these three sections, along with their respective movements from lament to praise, into one psalm. And I think it is this joining together of the three sections[68] or composing a psalm which moves back and forth from lament to praise that brings out the more dynamic movement between lament and praise. The movement is not just one-way or linear. The alternation between lament and praise brings out the tension between the two elements. For although there is a movement from lament to praise in each of the three sections, the inclusion of the three in one psalm invites one to consider not only the different parts of the psalm but also its entirety. Reading the whole psalm involves not only noticing the movement from lament to praise but also the *return* to lament. One ought to observe not only the movement from lament to praise, but also the return to lament after praise. As Fox stresses, it is not only important to cite the structure of a composition; how one element flows to the next is also important.[69] Citing the case of an introverted structure as an example, he avers that although the repetitions may help, "what may be far more influential will be the way *a* leads into *b* and *b* flows into *c*, then the effect of hearing *c* repeated, and so on".[70]

---

[68] Ridderbos, *Die Psalmen*, 252, compares Psalm 35 with Psalm 31, whose unity has also been called into question because of the return to lament after the praise. As with Psalm 31 he holds Psalm 35 to be a unity, though he is open to the possibility that the first section (Ps 35:1–10) might have been an originally independent composition.

[69] Michael V. Fox, "The Rhetoric of Ezekiel's Vision of the Valley of the Bones", in *The Place Is Too Small for Us: The Israelite Prophets in Recent Scholarship* (ed. Robert P. Gordon; Winona Lake, IN: Eisenbrauns, 1995), 176–90. This article effectively employs a rhetorical method of reading to Ezekiel 37.

[70] Ibid., 178–79.

Table 7: *Structure of Psalm 35*

Section One (1–10)	Section Two (11–18)	Section Three (19–28)
רִיב (1)	"Malicious witnesses rise up (קוּם) Asking me for that which I don't know (לֹא יָדַע)" (11)	"Do not let them rejoice (שָׂמַח) over me… Those who hate me without cause (חִנָּם)" (19)
"Rise up (קוּם) to my help" (2)		"…they say (אָמַר), 'aha, aha!' (21)
"Say (אָמַר)… 'I am your salvation (יְשׁוּעָה)'" (3b)		"Rouse yourself …for my cause (רִיב)" (23)
"Let them be put to shame…" (בּוֹשׁ, כָּלַם) and חָפֵר (4)	"…they rejoiced (שָׂמַח)… I don't know (לֹא יָדַע)" (15)	"Do not let them rejoice (שָׂמַח) over me…" (24)
"For without cause (חִנָּם), they hid a net…" (2x in v. 7)		"Do not let them say (אָמַר)… Do not let them say (אָמַר)…" (25)
לֹא יָדַע (8)		"Let those who rejoice (שָׂמַח) Be put to shame… (בּוֹשׁ [2x], כָּלַם and, חָפֵר) (26)
"…[my soul] shall exult in his salvation (יְשׁוּעָה)" (9)		"Let those who desire my vindication rejoice (שָׂמַח)
		Let them say (אָמַר)…" (27)
"All my bones will say (אָמַר)…" (10)	"I will give you thanks…" (18)	"My tongue will declare your righteousness…" (28)

6.4   Summary and Conclusion

In this chapter we have tried to show that individual lament psalms do alternate between lament and praise. There can be movements back and forth between the two elements. In Psalm 31 we see two series of alternations between lament and praise before finally ending in an admonition. In Psalm 35 we get not just two but three alternations! Indeed, the central feature that brings together these two psalms is the alternation between expressions of hope and despair, confidence and uncertainty. Through this alternation between lament and praise the present discussion is brought further. For now we are able to see that lament is also capable of returning to praise even after it has already shifted back to lament. In a way this goes beyond what we observed in our analysis of Psalms 12 and 28. In these two psalms we pointed out that lament psalms can move back to lament even after praise. Here, in our analysis of Psalms 31 and 35 we have demonstrated that lament psalms can also return to praise after the psalm has already moved to lament. This further proves the dynamic and complex movements between lament and praise.

In the next two chapters we explore other passages outside the Psalter further to strengthen our thesis of the presence of an '*un*certainty of a hearing' in spite of expressions of trust and praise. Specifically, we will examine Jer 20:7–18 and Lamentations 3, respectively.

CHAPTER SEVEN

FROM PRAISE TO 'CURSE': THE TENSION BETWEEN LAMENT AND PRAISE IN JER 20:7–18

7.1 INTRODUCTION

We continue our study on the '*un*certainty of a hearing' in the individual lament psalms by exploring passages outside the Psalter containing tension between lament and praise.[1] Here we focus on Jer 20:7–18. This passage is significant because of its affinity with the individual lament psalms. O'Connor considers the first part of Jeremiah 20 (vv. 7–13) as the closest to the individual lament psalms among the passages known as the 'Confessions of Jeremiah', of which these verses are a part.[2] It follows the classic form-critical structure of the individual lament: invocation (7a), description of the predicament of the speaker (7–10), confession of confidence (11), petition (12) and command to praise (v. 13).[3] More significantly for the present study, Jeremiah 20 contains a sudden shift from praise (v. 13) to a section cursing the day of one's birth (14–18)! We have in vv. 14–18 a *return* to the element of lament *after* praise—a feature I have tried to highlight in the Psalms. This further shows that the reverse movement praise-lament is not confined to the Psalms but can also be found in comparable materials like the

---

[1] In the previous chapters, we have examined psalms which move from lament to praise (Psalms 3, 6, 13), juxtapose lament and praise (Psalms 22), move from praise to lament (9/10, 27, 40), return to lament after the movement to praise (Psalms 12, 28) and alternate between lament and praise (Psalms 31, 35).

[2] Kathleen M. O'Connor, *The Confessions of Jeremiah: Their Interpretation and Role in Chapters 1–25* (SBL Diss Series 94; Atlanta, GA: Scholars Press, 1988), 66. The passages commonly called the 'Confessions of Jeremiah' are: Jer 11:18–23; 12:1–6; 15:10–21; 17:14–18; 18:18–23; 20:7–13 and 14–18. It should be noted, however, that O'Connor does not include vv. 14–18 in her list of the 'Confessions'. She argues that as one reads through the confessions in Jeremiah 11–20, one observes a heightening, a movement towards more confidence until one reaches the peak, which is Jer 20:7–13—a confession ending in praise. It is for this reason that Jer 20:14–18 is excluded from the 'Confessions'. See further below.

[3] O'Connor, *The Confessions of Jeremiah*, 66. Cf. Nancy Lee, *The Singers of Lamentations* (Leiden: Brill, 2002), 167, who believes that "Jeremiah especially employed individual lament more than any other prophet".

one we have in Jeremiah 20. Conversely, because this passage consists
of a return to lament, it provides a good way of demonstrating how
an understanding of the individual lament psalms, which takes into
account its dynamic movements, can be of immense value for the
interpretation of Jer 20:7–18. For as will be seen below, most of the
approaches to this passage have been limited by the form-critical view
of the lament psalms—a view which only sees a one-way movement
from lament to praise. As a result, just as in the case of the psalms
containing the other movements (from praise to lament, return to lament
after praise and alternation between the two), these approaches have
failed to understand and appreciate the dynamic movements of lament
and praise in Jeremiah 20.

In this chapter, I hope to be able to: 1) strengthen my thesis on the
'*un*certainty of a hearing' by showing that such a feature occurs in
Jeremiah as well—a book whose indebtedness to the lament psalms
is widely acknowledged;[4] 2) demonstrate how the form-critical understanding of the lament psalms has led towards a failure to understand
and appreciate Jer 20:7–18; 3) show how a view which considers the
dynamic movements of lament and praise in the lament psalms can
help us understand the movement from praise to lament in Jeremiah
20 and; 4) look into possible ways of how Jer 20:7–18 can contribute
towards our understanding of the psalms which contain a movement
from praise to lament.

7.2   STRUCTURAL ANALYSIS OF JER 20:7–18:
JUXTAPOSITION OF PRAISE AND LAMENT

7.2.1   *The Question Concerning the Unity of the passage*

The composition and division of Jer 20:7–18 have been variously
construed by scholars. These verses are part of what is known as the
'Confessions of Jeremiah'.[5] But whether the whole passage belongs to
this group is a matter of debate. Some consider vv. 7–18 as one con-

---

[4] See Walter Baumgartner, *Die Klagegedichte des Jeremia* (Giessen: A. Töpelmann, 1917),
ET *Jeremiah's Poems of Lament* (trans. David E. Orton; Sheffield: Almond Press, 1988).
[5] See n. 2.

fession, consisting of one whole unit.[6] The difficulty with this view is
how to make sense of the different materials in the passage—vv. 7–13
and vv. 14–18. In the past, those who consider the passage to be a
whole unit usually explain its diversity from a psychological point of
view: what we have in this passage are expressions of Jeremiah's inner
struggle.[7] More recently, Fretheim proposes that we read the passage
as one whole unit on literary grounds. Whatever their original function might have been "[v]erses 7–18 stand together editorially...It is
best to understand vv. 7–18 as a single lament that includes elements
of complaint, confession of trust, petition, certainty of being heard,
and thanksgiving, concluding on a sharp note of questioning".[8] In its
attempt to understand the passage as we now have it, this view is an
interesting development, reflecting canonical readings of the text.

Others consider *only* vv. 7–13 as part of the confessions of Jeremiah.
The language, theme, and the absence of a direct address in vv. 14–18
place this passage outside the range of the other confessions.[9] However,
the question that confronts those who take this position is how to make
sense of vv. 14–18 in its present position, for even if one does not consider these verses as a part of the confessions, the question of why it has
been placed there remains a valid one.[10] There are two main responses
to this issue. On one side are those who consider the question of the
relationship between vv. 7–13 and vv. 14–18 as a separate issue from

---

[6] C.f. Keil, *The Prophecies of Jeremiah* (vols. 40, 41; Clark's Foreign Theological Library,
Fourth Series; Edinburgh: T & T Clark, 1853), 319; Wilhelm Rudolph, *Jeremia* (vol.
1/12; HAT; Tübingen: J. C. B. Mohr, 1958), 119; Cf. Gerald J. Janzen, "Jeremiah
20:7–18", *Int* 37 (1983): 178–83.

[7] Keil, *The Prophecies of Jeremiah*, does not find it strange to have a lament after the
hymn of praise, for psychologically such a move is not inconceivable. He writes: "the
power of the temptation was not finally vanquished by the renewal of his confidence
that the Lord will defend him against all his foes" (319). Rudolph, *Jeremia*, 119, argues
that the question of the prophet's inward struggle, of his sufferings, is very much a
part of the prophet's experience, so that it is not easy to differentiate or distinguish
which bits belong to Jeremiah and which do not (119).

[8] Terence E. Fretheim, *Jeremiah* (Smyth & Helwys Bible Commentary; Macon,
Georgia: Smyth & Helwys, 2002), 289.

[9] Karl-Friedrich Pohlmann, *Die ferne Gottes—Studien zum Jeremiabuch* (BZAW 179;
Berlin: Walter de Gruyter, 1989), 33, n. 13; Norbert Ittmann, *Die Konfessionen Jeremias:
Ihre Bedeutung für die Verkündigung des Propheten* (WMANT 54; Neukirchen-Vluyn: Neu-
kirchener, 1981), 147.

[10] Gisela Fuchs, "Die Klage des Propheten: Beobachtungen zu den Konfessionen
Jeremias im Vergleich mit den Klagen Hiobs (Erster Teil)", *BZ* 41 (1997), 215, writes,
"Doch offenbar ist Jer 20,14–18 'die Summe', das bittere Resume von Jeremias pro-
phetischem Wirken, seiner Leidensgeschichte und seiner Zweifel an YHWH".

that of the confessions of Jeremiah. Intriguingly, three of the monographs devoted to the study of the Confessions of Jeremiah, those by
O'Connor, Pohlmann and Ittmann, do not consider vv. 14–18 as part
of the confessions and do not explain the present arrangement of the
text in Jeremiah 20.[11] On the other side are those who try to combine
the two sections, but they do so by rearranging the order of the verses.
They either move vv. 14–18 before v. 7 or connect the verses with
v. 9. The reason for doing so is that they could not see how a lament
which has already turned to praise can go back to lament.[12] Clearly,
the form-critical framework of a one-way movement from lament to
praise is very much at work here.

Finally, there are those who see two separate compositions in the
passage—vv. 7–13 and vv. 14–18. They discuss each of these separately.
But they go further: they try to address the question, how do we explain
the present arrangement? Rather than altering the order of the verses,
they try to make sense of the passage in its present arrangement. The
outcome is a multi-faceted perspective of reading the text. I follow this
last approach in the present chapter. As I will demonstrate in my own
analysis below, Jer 20:7–18 consists of two distinct materials. That these
two materials have been brought together at some point is clear from
the witness of the MT. How the two have developed into the text that
we now have goes beyond the scope of this study. It is possible that
the text has undergone a process of editing and reworking, but we no
longer have access to such a process.[13] Carroll admits that determining
the specific historical contexts for the confessions is extremely difficult.
He cites possible ways in which these can be interpreted. These include
views that they are the actual pouring out of Jeremiah's soul, that they
arose out of the context of the conflict against false prophets and the
traditional interpretation which sees Jeremiah as a speaker of laments.

---

[11] O'Connor, *The Confessions of Jeremiah*, 3, mentions in her introduction that she
will follow the order of the confessions in the MT which she views to be "generally
correct as they now stand". Yet in her actual treatment of the passages, she excluded
vv. 14–18 from the list of the confessions, thereby contradicting herself. Pohlmann, *Die
ferne Gottes—Studien zum Jeremiabuch*, 33, n. 13, thinks that the present position of vv.
14–18 is a separate issue from the subject of the confessions. Ittmann, *Die Konfessionen
Jeremias*, 147, does not include vv. 14–18 in his discussions of the confessions.

[12] Ewald's proposal is to move vv. 14–18 before vv. 7–13 (cited in Craigie et al.,
Jeremiah 1–25, p. 277); cf. Friedrich Nötscher, *Jeremias, Echter-Bibel* (Würzburg: Echter,
1954), 160.

[13] J. A. Thompson, *The Book of Jeremiah* (Grand Rapids, MI: Eerdmans, 1980), 463,
notes the complex literary history of the passage.

But in the end, he confesses, "I would stress here the fact that this is perhaps the most difficult and, certainly, the most fiercely contested area of interpretation in the study of Jeremiah, and no one viewpoint can be regarded as holding the field".[14]

One of our concerns here is to discern the possible purpose for the bringing together of the two compositions. Fretheim's approach, which views the passage as a unit, could be one way of reading the passage. However, this does not come to grips with the diverse nature of the materials in vv. 7–13 and vv. 14–18. I think it is important to recognise that we have two different passages. Only when we have worked with that should we ask the question of the sense of the text's present arrangement. We hope to address the question of the possible purpose of the bringing together of the two passages in this chapter. But first let us examine the structure and content of the passage.

7.3   Structural Analysis[15] and Detailed Analysis of Jer 20:7–18

7.3.1   From Lament to Praise (vv. 7–13)

The structure of Jer 20:7–18 can be divided into two main separate sections: vv. 7–13 and vv. 14–18. The former is held together by a series of repeated words and structural elements. The word פתה is repeated at the beginning (2x in v. 7) and towards the end (10):

---

[14] Robert P. Carroll, *Jeremiah* (OTG; Sheffield: JSOT Press, 1989), 48–49. In his earlier book, *From Chaos to Covenant: Uses of Prophecy in the Book of Jeremiah* (London: SCM, 1981), 129–30, he tries to argue that the confessions represent the attempts of the traditionists to express the exilic community's struggles. For a critique of this view, see John Day, *Psalms* (OTG; Sheffield: JSOT Press, 1990), 25.

[15] For a different but supplementing analysis of the structure which brings out the element of tension in Jeremiah 20, see Jonathan Magonet, "Jeremiah's Last Confession: Structure, Image and Ambiguity", *HAR* 11 (1987): 303–16. He sees two concentric structures for vv. 7–11 and 14–18, with vv. 12 and 13 in the middle (pp. 314–5). He does not see a direct movement from praise to lament. Rather, his analysis shows a pattern similar to what we find in Psalm 12, where we have a positive statement of faith in the middle juxtaposed by the lament at the beginning and end. He makes the following interesting comment: "Both views, the optimistic and the pessimistic are set side by side, utilizing the familiar concentric framework to give equal weight to both positions...It is for the reader, aware of both sets of information, to decide which view is correct, or even to hold both at once as a genuine paradox of faith" (315).

V. 7—"You have deceived (פתה) me, and I was deceived (פתה)..."
V. 10—"...Perhaps he will be deceived (פתה)..."

Verse 10, in turn, is connected to vv. 11–12 through a partial chiastic structure (see below). This leaves us with v. 13, which appears to be structurally unattached to the preceding verses. However, considering how lament often turns to praise in the lament psalms, the introduction of v. 13 should not be surprising. We should note Lundbom's comment here. Contrary to those who defend the unity of vv. 7–13 on the basis of a similar movement from lament to praise in the lament psalms, he avers that vv. 11–13 do not originally belong to the preceding verses. This is because, according to him, the element of confidence and praise—present in vv. 11–13—is an anomaly in Jeremiah. He explains: "Every other confession either stands alone (15:10–12; 17:14–18; and 18:19–23) or is joined with a divine answer (11:18–23; 12:1–6; 15:15–21; and 20:14–18, with its answer in 1:5)".[16] In response to this, could it be that what we have here is a deliberate attempt to deviate from the other confessions? Is it possible to see here an attempt on the part of the redactor/s to create a stark contrast by introducing the element of praise in v. 13 and immediately following this up with the section on 'curse' (vv. 14–18)? I will say more on this issue below. In the meantime, let us continue our analysis of the structure of the passage.

The first section (vv. 7–13) begins with an extremely strong verb— פתה, accusing God of deceiving Jeremiah: "You have *deceived* me!" (v. 7).[17] As already mentioned, the word פתה is repeated towards the end of the present confession in v. 10, where Jeremiah complains that even his close friends or those who are supposedly his close friends are

---

[16] Lundbom, 853. Cf. Ronald Ernest Clements, *Jeremiah* (Interpretation; Atlanta, GA: John Knox Press, 1989), 120, who notes: "In verse 13 the short invocation to the praise of God, which marks a transition to the bitter personal cry of lamentation, reads strangely and appears to be out of place. It can best be understood perhaps as an addition by a later scribe introducing a note of thanksgiving for the courage and work of Jeremiah".

[17] Abraham J. Heschel, *The Prophets: An Introduction* (vol. 1; NY: Harper and Row, 1962), 113, translates v. 7a as follows: "O Lord, Thou hast seduced me, And I am seduced; Thou hast raped me And I am overcome". He comments: "The call to be a prophet is more than an invitation. It is first of all a feeling of being enticed, of acquiescence or willing surrender. But this winsome feeling is only one aspect of the experience. The other aspect is a sense of being ravished or carried away by violence, of yielding to overpowering force against one's own will. The prophet feels both the attraction and the coercion of God, the appeal and the pressure, the charm and the stress. He is conscious of both voluntary identification and forced capitulation" (114).

conspiring to bring him down. There is an element of expectation in the words, 'my close friends'. Jeremiah may have thought he has done these people well by speaking the truth to them. But instead of receiving something good in return, they conspired to destroy him. This is similar to the thought expressed in Ps 35:12–15.[18] The way in which the confession is constructed intimates a strong sense of vulnerability on the part of Jeremiah: He is helpless before the powerful God; a person 'acted upon'—by God, by events resulting from his prophetic call and by others. In v. 7 he laments: "You have deceived me, O Yahweh, and *I was deceived*!" Notice the passive voice of the verb, "I was deceived". The next statement in v. 7 further shows the prophet's sense of helplessness and vulnerability before his God: "You have overpowered me and 'you were able'". In verses 7b–9b, the structure further betrays the sense of 'being acted upon' by others/events as an outcome of the prophet's ministry of speaking God's message. We may observe here the repetition of the verb דבר and the construction היה + the prep. ל in vv. 7 and 8 and a slight alteration, היה + ב in v. 9:

"I became a laughingstock (ל + היה) all day" (v. 7b)
"For whenever I speak (דבר) I cry out..." (v. 8a)
"For the word (דבר) of Yahweh became to me (ל + היה)..." (v. 8b)
"And if I say...I will no longer speak (דבר) in his name" (v. 9a)
"then it becomes in me (ב + היה) like a burning fire..." (9b)

As can be observed, the word for 'speaking' is prominent in the passage: דבר occurs twice as a verb in vv. 8 and 9 and once as a noun in v. 8. It is because of his 'speaking' that he has become a laughingstock (v. 7). The word of Yahweh itself becomes a "reproach and a derision" for him (v. 8). Such an experience is reported as "כל היום". The word כל shows up a couple of times in the passage: the phrase, "כל היום" twice (vv. 8, 9) and the word כל appears in vv. 7 and 10, both in reference to Jeremiah's opponents. For Jeremiah speaking has consistently become an automatic invitation for hostility. This led him to contemplate ceasing to speak God's word (v. 9a). Unfortunately, even that proved to be oppressively painful as well. For when he resolves no longer to speak, the word becomes within him like a burning fire, which could not be contained (v. 9b). Fretheim's comment is apt: "He

---

[18] See discussions of Psalm 35 in the previous chapter.

suffers if he speaks and he suffers if he does not".[19] Whatever he decides
to do brings suffering: externally, there is hostility if he speaks; inter-
nally, there is agony if he does not. No wonder, at the end of v. 9 he
confesses, 'I am weary...I can no longer carry on ['lit. 'I am not able'
from יכל]". Here the word יכל is repeated to draw a sharp contrast
with the occurrence of the word at the beginning (v. 7): "You are able
(יכל)"[20] (v. 7), Jeremiah tells God. But "I am *not* able (יכל)" (v. 9).

As noted earlier, it is not just Yahweh who is against him; even
his close friends are (v. 10). Jeremiah is constantly threatened by the
"whisperings of many"; there is "terror on every side" and people are
conspiring against him, anticipating, waiting for his fall (v. 10). O how
they wish that he be deceived! The word פתה is repeated in v. 10 to
highlight the strong sense of betrayal that Jeremiah experienced, both
from Yahweh (v. 7) and from the people around him (v. 10). The word
יכל appears again towards the end of v. 10. This time it is those who
are opposing him who are saying, "we will be able" (יכל).[21] Like in v. 9,
the reappearance of the word in v. 10 is followed by another repetition
of the word with the negation לא (v. 11). But unlike the first contrast
between God and Jeremiah, the effect of the people's action on Jeremiah
is different, as the following comparison intimates:

"You are able" (v. 7)
"I am *not* able" (v. 9)
"We will be able" (v. 10)
"They will *not* be able" (v. 11)

Whereas Jeremiah admitted he is not 'able' compared to God who is
'able', here his opponents' claim ("we will be able") is met by the confident declaration, "they will not be able". Why will they not be able?
Because, Jeremiah claims, "Yahweh is with me" (v. 11a). The opening
words of v. 11 come as a real surprise. Jeremiah has just accused God
of deceiving him (v. 7), even thinking of giving up (v. 9). Yet in spite
of this, he still clings on to God. Even though Jeremiah might lament
and utter strong words against God, God remains his only hope, his
deliverance. His enemy is at the same time his redeemer. The language

---

[19] Terence E. Fretheim, *Jeremiah*, 292.
[20] יכל is used here in the sense of 'prevailed'.
[21] Like in v. 7 יכל is used in the sense of 'prevailed'.

is comparable to Job 19: 25–27, where Job addresses God as 'my redeemer' even though he has just lamented bitterly against him in the previous verses.[22] It is also similar to Psalm 22, where the psalmist complains to God, "Why hast thou forsaken me?" yet with the same breath addresses him as "*my* God".

With the confident words of v. 11, some commentators feel the confession could have proceeded directly to v. 13—the high point of the section. They thus view v. 12 as disturbing the flow and suggest it should be transposed before v. 11. Verse 12 contains a petition and thus seems to break the momentum. The verse occurs also in 11:20 and so others think it should be removed from its present context.[23] But if the main reason for deleting v. 12 from Jeremiah 20 is because it causes a return to the mood of lament (i.e. petition), then I would say this is not justified. This is an indication of how much the typical form-critical structure of a movement from lament to praise has so influenced the readings of materials such as we find here. It fails to take into consideration the fact that individual lament psalms also return to petition or lament even after they have moved already to the assurance of resolution.[24] If anything, what makes the petition in v. 12 significant in its present position is that it prepares us—albeit only in small measure—for the big leap from praise (13) to 'curse' in vv. 14–18. Presently, we see that even after the confident affirmation in v. 11, Jeremiah still needs to come to Yahweh and ask for 'vengeance' against those who are wishing the same against him. He asks, "Let me see your vengeance upon them". There is a play on word with the verb 'see' here and in the preceding line where the prophet addresses God as the one "who *sees* the heart and mind". The construction, נקמה plus the prep. מִן, is the same in both vv. 10 and 12. It forms a partial chiastic structure with v. 11 in the centre. The lament (v. 10) and the petition (v. 12) envelope the statement of confidence in v. 11:

---

[22] For a different view on the word 'redeemer' in Job 19, see Marvin H. Pope, *Job* (vol. 15; AB; NY: Doubleday, 1965), 134, who translates the word as 'vindicator' and thinks it is questionable to apply the word to God since he is viewed as the adversary. Cf. David J. A. Clines, *Job 1–20* (vol. 15; WBC; Dallas, TX: Word Books, 1989), 459–60. Based on similarities with Job 16:18–21, Clines argues that the 'redeemer' in Job 19:25 is the same as the 'witness', 'advocate', and 'spokesman' of Job 16.

[23] Baumgartner, *Die Klagegedichte des Jeremia*, 49, ET *Jeremiah's Poems of Lament*, 60, regards v. 12 as not fitting the section.

[24] Cf. the return to petition in Psalm 28 (see above).

"...we will overpower (יכל) him we will take vengeance (נקמה) on him" (v. 10)

But Yahweh is with me...they will not be able (יכל) (v. 11)

"...let me see your vengeance (נקמה) upon them" (v. 12)

Verses 7–13 conclude with a call to sing to Yahweh and praise him. The language is similar to Psalms 22:23 and 35:18,[25] where the psalmist resolves to praise Yahweh in the midst of the congregation. The second part of the verse provides a motivation for the call to praise: "for he has delivered the life of the needy from the hand of the evildoers". The word "delivered" recalls God's promise to Jeremiah when the Lord first called him (Jer 1:8). The series of confessions of Jeremiah which started in Jer 11:18–23 could have ended right here, in a note of deliverance, as a fitting tribute to the God who keeps his promise to his servant. But such was not the case in the text as it has come down to us. For right after the hymn of praise, even whilst one could still hear the sound of victory, the cry of a person in utter hopelessness blows in one's ear so loudly that the sound of victory vanishes right away. Having just moved from lament to praise, the passage turns to lament again, and this time it comes like an enormous body of water gushing from a high mountain.

7.3.2   *Return to Lament: 'Cursed be the day I was born!' (vv. 14–18)*

Jeremiah curses the day of his birth and the man who brought the news of his birth to his father. This passage is outrageously candid. It is hard to know what to make of it. Baumgartner does not consider it as a prayer directed to God, but as a "self-curse".[26] What makes it even more difficult is that this curse follows a hymn of praise, making the transition even more shocking. Compared with the other confessions, it is also the darkest. Von Rad says that here Jeremiah has reached his lowest point, his nadir.[27] Though not entirely different in tone from the previous section, which also contains in its beginning a strong accusation against Yahweh ("You have deceived me" [v. 7]), it is nonetheless

---

[25] Cf. Lundbom, 862.

[26] Baumgartner, *Die Klagegedichte des Jeremia*, 67, ET *Jeremiah's Poems of Lament*, 77.

[27] Gerhard von Rad, *Old Testament Theology* (vol. 2; trans. D. M. G. Stalker; Edinburgh and London: Oliver and Boyd, 1965), 204.

different in that it never advances to praise. Indeed the whole section is the opposite of praise. The first verse highlights the opposite of praise—curse. Forming a chiastic structure, v. 14 reads:

Cursed be
  the day I was born
  the day when my mother bore me
Let it not be blessed!

Verse 14 begins with the word 'cursed' and ends emphatically with the words, 'let it not be blessed!'[28] After wishing that his day of birth be cursed and not be blessed, he wished next that the messenger who brought the news to his father about his birth be cursed as well (vv. 15–17). It seems that Jeremiah was looking for something or some-one on whom he could vent his struggle and sense of injustice, and he found the poor messenger. Beginning from v. 15 to v. 17, Jeremiah hurls his anger on this man. He wishes that this man be like those cities which Yahweh destroyed without pity. He wants this to happen because the man did not kill him from the womb.

With the mentioning of the womb, the lament goes back to the issue of Jeremiah's birth. Even more significantly, the mentioning of the 'womb' recalls the call of Jeremiah in 1:5, functioning as an inclusio to chapters 1–20.[29] These are the only two occasions where the word 'womb' is used in Jeremiah.[30] Lundbom observes that the entire passage of Jer 20:7–18 "hearkens back to the call and commission accounts in chap. 1:

20:7 Jeremiah refers to Yahweh having overpowered him in the call, particularly at the point where Yahweh refused to accept his demur (1:7)

20:11 Jeremiah restates the promises of 1:8 and 1:19, that Yahweh would be *with* Jeremiah and not allow enemies to *overcome* him;

20:13 Jeremiah celebrates his *rescue* as a fulfilment of Yahweh's earlier promise (1:8; 1:19); and

---

[28] Curse, not blessing is the name of the game.
[29] Lundbom, 93.
[30] Although Lundbom cites the repetition of the word 'womb' in both Jeremian 1 and 20, he did not mention that it is only in these two verses that the word is used as a reference to a mother's womb in the whole of Jeremiah.

20:18 Jeremiah refers to his *coming forth from the womb*, mention of which was made at the beginning of the call (1:5)".[31]

This signifies that the whole passage points back to Jeremiah's call and his subsequent ministry or at least to an editorial attempt to relate the whole of Jer 20:7–18, not just of vv. 7–13, to Jeremiah. This will be important when we consider how the whole passage as it now stands in the text can be explained in terms of its overall sense.

With the cry of agony in v. 18, the section ends with the characteristic cry of the lament—the interrogative 'why?': "Why did I come out of my mother's womb to see toil and sorrow and spend my days in shame" (v. 18)? There is nothing here but the darkest of nights. Here the confession reaches its lowest point. Unlike in the previous confessions there is no divine response here—either in the form of a rebuke or an encouragement. Considering the tone and content of vv. 14–18, these verses could have easily solicited divine rebuke like the ones in Jer 12:4–6 and 15:19–21 where God rebukes Jeremiah and asks him to return to him. But we find nothing of that sort. The passage simply ends with a cry of despair, a cry with no answer whatsoever. With the first section having moved to praise in v. 13, the 'curse' that immediately follows it shatters all hope and, even more tragic, leaves the matter unresolved.

How do we explain the movement from praise to 'curse' in Jer 20:7–18?

7.3.3 *Attempts to explain the composition of Jer 20:7–18*

Scholars are at a loss in dealing with the problem of the transition from praise to the section on 'curse' in vv. 14–18. Craigie writes concerning vv. 14–18: "This last section of chap. 20 has caused considerable discussion because of its sudden, dramatic caesura from hymnic praise in v. 13 to the depths of despair that issue in a curse on the day of Jeremiah's birth".[32] Hermisson remarks, "Wie der scheinbar voll befriedigende Abschluss des Zyklus mit der Verfluchung des eigenen Geburtstags fortgesetzt werden kann, das hat noch niemand befriedigend erklärt,

---

[31] Lundbom, 852.
[32] Craigie et al., 277.

und es mag ja sein, dass es gar nicht erklärbar ist".[33] The works on the 'Confessions of Jeremiah' by Pohlmann, Ittmann, Bak and O'Connor find the passage in Jeremiah 20, particularly vv. 14–18 perplexing.

It is debatable, according to Pohlmann whether Jer 20:14–18 should be included in the confessions.[34] He thinks this passage falls short thematically of the other confessions of Jeremiah. He cannot see the reason why the prophet, after gaining confidence in Yahweh, would again recede back to the depths. He thus excises vv. 14–18 and limits his study to Jer 20:7–13.[35] Ittmann also excludes Jer 20:14–18 from the 'confessions' because these verses contain no direct address and thus cannot be interpreted as prayer.[36] Bak is at a loss with the arrangement in Jeremiah 20. He finds it striking "dass die Klage in vv. 14–18 bei der Verbindung mit vv. 7–13 nicht vor die Vertrauensäusserung in vv. 11, 12 und den Aufruf zum Lob in v. 13, sondern hinter sie gestellt wird".[37] This very much reflects a form-critical understanding of the movement between lament and praise.

Following the form-critical understanding of the psalms of individual lament with its movement from lament to praise, O'Connor argues that if we read the confessions as they now stand in the MT, we will observe a heightening, a movement from doubt or despair to confidence and trust and even praise in the fifth confession. Contrary to von Rad's view of a downward movement in the confessions with the last one as the darkest, O'Connor argues the opposite: the confessions turn the brightest at the end. But her thesis works only if vv. 14–18 is not part of the confessions. She thus removes these verses from her discussions of the confessions. She writes that in her study: "the fifth confession (20:7–13) has not been perceived as the nadir of Jeremiah's gloom *because vv. 14–18 have been eliminated from it.* Rather than moving toward an abyss of despair for the prophet and for Israel, the confessions move in the opposite direction from von Rad's assessment—toward

---

[33] Hans-Jürgen Hermisson, "Jahwes und Jeremias Rechtsstreit: zum Thema der Konfessionen Jeremias", in *Altes Testament und christliche Verkündigung: Festschrift für Antonius H. J. Gunneweg* (ed. M. Oeming and A. Graupner; Stuttgart: Verlag W. Kohlhammer, 1987), 335. Although Hermisson admits the difficulty of the passage in Jeremiah 20, he nonetheless tries to explain it, though acknowledging that his own explanation cannot be more than an attempt towards an explanation (see further below).

[34] Pohlmann, *Die Ferne Gottes*, 3, n. 1.

[35] Ibid., 33, n. 1.

[36] Ittmann, *Die Konfessionen Jeremias*, 147.

[37] Dong Hyun Bak, *Klagender Gott—Klagende Menschen* (BZAW 193; Berlin: Walter de Gruyter, 1990), 215.

greater confidence that Yahweh will vindicate the prophet and fulfil
the prophetic word".[38]

O'Connor's work is the clearest example of how the form-critical
understanding of the lament psalms has become determinative for
the way the confessions of Jeremiah are treated. Overall, one has the
impression in reading O'Connor that lament has not been received
on its own terms "simply as lament", to use the words of Balentine.[39]
It seems that for O'Connor lament is essentially praise. Like the other
three works on the confessions of Jeremiah her response to the issue of
the turning of praise into 'curse' in Jeremiah 20 has been dictated by
the form-critical view of a one-way movement from lament to praise.
As a result, 'the return to lament' in Jer 20:14–20 has been construed
as unusual or abnormal. The form-critical understanding of the lament
psalms has simply been imposed on the reading of the confessions. The
expectation is that these confessions should move towards resolution.
In doing so, however, O'Connor and others have to ignore the present
arrangement of the text. Having set out at the beginning of her work to
follow the order that we find in the MT, O'Connor has allowed herself
to be limited by the form-critical framework. She may have succeeded
in conforming the text according to the form-critical perspective, yet
by doing so she has ignored the text itself.[40]

Indeed, the major gap in the study of the confession/s in Jeremiah 20
lies in the failure to consider the dynamic movements in the individual
lament psalms. Leaning heavily on the form-critical understanding
of the structure of the lament, the passage is interpreted narrowly
through the lens of a one-way movement from lament to praise. This
is where an approach which takes into account the polyphonic nature
of the relationship between lament and praise in the Psalms becomes
essential.

---

[38] Ibid., 93, emphasis mine. O'Connor, 145–46, shows ambivalence in connection
with vv. 14–18 which she excised. On the one hand, she removes these verses from
the confessions in her earlier discussions, but later on admits that on literary grounds
these verses form a logical ending of chapters 11–20.

[39] Balentine, *The Hidden God: The Hiding of the Face of God in the Old Testament*, 123.

[40] Interestingly, we find more emphasis on lament in O'Connor's later works on
lament (see her commentary on Lamentations, included in the discussion in the following chapter).

7.4 The Psalms of Lament and Jer 20:7–18

Scholars since Baumgartner have long recognised the value of the lament psalms for Jeremian study, particularly for the passages known as the 'Confessions of Jeremiah'.[41] Baumgartner was on the mark when he said in the conclusion of his book that Jeremiah was influenced not by *"individual psalms"* but by the *"psalm style"*;[42] it is not the individual lament psalms but the particular form that these lament psalms take that points to a better understanding of Jeremiah's confessions. I think what went wrong with Baumgartner's work is in the actual application of his approach. In his discussions of the lament type in the Psalms, he basically follows Gunkel's structural arrangement.[43] What he does is take the different verses from their respective chapters and categorise them according to the common structural elements of a lament. As a result, the uniqueness of each psalm and their present literary context and possible canonical function are sacrificed in favour of generalisation and categorisation. When it comes to his treatment of Jeremiah 20, he performs similar exegetical surgery, dividing the passage into three separate compositions: vv. 10–13 (except v. 12), vv. 7–9 and vv. 14–18. He discusses each of these separately but nowhere do we find an attempt to relate the verses to each other or at least to explain the sense of the passages in their present position. Regarding vv. 14–18 he concludes: "In its form this song differs substantially from the poems of lament. It is not directed to Yahweh and is therefore not a prayer. One might call it a *self-curse*".[44]

Two flaws can be observed in Baumgartner's approach. First, it is limited by Gunkel's form-critical framework, with its concern for generalisation and categorisation together with the one-way view of the movement from lament to praise. Second, arising from this first weakness is the absence of attempts to try to explain the passage in

---

[41] Carroll, *From Chaos to Covenant: Uses of Prophecy in the Book of Jeremiah*, 108, writes: "The careful reader of the sections will be struck by the similarity between the language of the confessions and the language of the book of Psalms". Cf. John Bright, "A Prophet's Lament and Its Answer: Jeremiah 15:10–21", in *A Prophet to the Nations: Essays in Jeremiah Studies* (ed. Leo G. Perdue and Brian W. Kovacs; Winona Lake, IN: Eisenbrauns, 1984), 325; A. R. Diamond, *The Confessions of Jeremiah in Context* (JSOTSup 45; Sheffield: JSOT Press, 1987), 102; O'Connor, *The Confessions of Jeremiah*, 81.

[42] Baumgartner, *Die Klagegedichte des Jeremia*, 92, ET *Jeremiah's Poems of Lament*, 101.

[43] Ibid., 16; see p. 17 for his explicit support for Gunkel's position.

[44] Baumgartner, 67, ET 70; cf. Rudolph, *Jeremia*, 121–22.

Jeremiah in its present position. Thus, rather than looking for whole psalms which have similar movements or patterns to that of Jeremiah 20:7–13, the verses are 'chopped out' and treated independently of the other passages within Jeremiah 20. He is on the right track in seeing the 'type' of lament as a model that influenced the composition of Jeremiah's confessions and Jer 20:7–18 in particular. The question is, "which understanding of the 'type'?" It is not enough to cite related verses from the Psalms to establish the influence of the Psalms on the Jeremian texts. What we need is to consider whole psalms, observe the patterns that we see in these psalms and not be limited by a framework that we can impose on the passage in consideration.

A number of scholars have already observed the similarity between Jeremiah 20 and some psalms, especially Psalms 31 and 35.

7.4.1 Psalms 35 and 31 and Jer 20:7–18

Jones notes that Jer 20:7–18 "leans heavily on Ps. 31".[45] The words "for the word of the Lord has become for me a reproach and derision all day long" in Jer 20:8 employ the same language common in the laments, one of which is Ps 31:11. Furthermore, the words, "terror on every side" are the same as in Ps 31:13 and "my persecutors" (Jer 20:11) also occurs in Ps 31:15 among others.[46] Clines and Gunn also observe a similarity not only with Psalm 31 but also with Psalm 35. Observe the prominence of Psalms 31 and 35 in Jer 20:7–13, in the work of Clines and Gunn:[47]

• "there is no difference between v. 7–9 and...Ps 31:11–14 or 35:11–16".[48]

---

[45] Douglas Rawlinson Jones, *Jeremiah* (NCB; Grand Rapids, MI: Eerdmans, 1992), 272.

[46] Ibid., 273–74. On various attempts to explain the term, מגור מסביב, especially on the occurrence of the phrase in Jeremiah 20 and Psalm 31, see Adrian Curtis, "Terror on Every Side", in *The Book of Jeremiah and Its Reception* (ed. A. H. W. Curtis and T. Römer; Leuven: Leuven University Press, 1997), 111–18. Curtis concludes that we cannot be certain which borrowed from whom, whether Jeremiah 20 or Psalm 31. It is probably that both made use of common liturgical language (p. 118).

[47] David J. A. Clines and David M. Gunn "Form, Occasion and Redaction in Jeremiah 20", *ZAW* 88 (1976): 390–409.

[48] Clines and Gunn, 394.

- "Jeremiah's complaint, 'Thou art stronger (חזק) than I/and thou hast prevailed (יכל)', exemplifies the classical theme of the powerful persecutor that one meets, e.g. in Ps 35:10 ('Thou [Yahweh] dost deliver the weak/from him who is too strong [חזק] for him')".[49]
- Jeremiah's complaint that everyone mocks him (לעג) is also found in Ps 35:16, among other psalms of lament.[50]
- The word reproach (חרף) also occurs in Ps 31:12.[51]

What sets apart the approach of Clines and Gunn from the others already mentioned is that here there is an explicit attempt to explain the juxtaposition of vv. 7–13 and vv. 14–18. They interpret the text not only from its original setting (*Sitz im Leben*) but also in its present literary position (*Sitz im Buch*). Their comment on the effect of the juxtaposition to the passage as a whole is significant:

> The overall meanings of both vv. 14–18 and 7–13 are modified by the juxtaposition…The effect upon the meaning of vv. 14–18 is that it is now to be read as an expression of the prophet's own personal emotion occasioned by his bitter experience in 20:1–6. 'Toil', 'sorrow', and 'shame' have now become primarily what he experienced at the hands of Pashhur, though that was perhaps not the whole horizon of the passage in the eyes of the redactor. But the effect upon the meaning of vv. 7–13 is even more profound: *here the movement towards a climax in confident appeal and praise is reversed and the dominant mood of the whole composition (vv. 7–18) becomes that of distress and lament.*[52]

What is significant about Psalms 31 and 35 is that in these psalms we find a series of 'reversals' from the tone of confidence and praise to lament. Whilst Clines, Gunn and also Jones have noted the similarity between Jer 20:7–18 and Psalms 31 and 35, they did not point out that Psalms 31 and 35 are two psalms in particular which contain a return to lament after praise. As shown earlier, these psalms contain an alternation between lament and praise, not only once but twice (Psalm 31) or even three times in the case of Psalm 35. Psalm 31 in particular, alternates between the elements of lament and praise: prayer (2–6); trust (7–9); lament (10–14); trust (15) and prayer (16–19).[53]

---

[49] Ibid., 395.
[50] Ibid.
[51] Ibid., 395–96.
[52] Ibid., 408, emphasis mine.
[53] Peter C. Craigie, *Psalms 1–50* (WBC; Waco, TX: Word Books, Publisher, 1983), 259.

Particularly conspicuous are the sharp and sudden shifts from praise to lament in Psalm 35 and its affinity to Jeremiah 20. The psalm starts with a typical lament which moves from the element of lament (vv. 1–8) to praise (vv. 9–10).[54] Remarkably, Ps 35:10 contains three words which are also found in Jer 20—עצם (Jer 20:9), נצל (Jer 20:13) and אביון (Jer 20:13). All three words occur in Ps 35:10 in the context of praise. The first word (עצם) occurs in the lament portion in Jer 20 where Jeremiah describes the result of keeping the word within him—it becomes "like a flaming fire, shut up in my bones" (v. 9). But the other two words—נצל and אביון—also occur in the context of praise in Jer 20:13! What is even more conspicuous is that, like Psalm 35, Jeremiah 20 moves back to lament as well. As the praise in Jer 20:13 is followed by an element of lament in the cursing of the day of one's birth, so the praise in Ps 35:10 is immediately followed by another lament (vv. 11–17).

Why are Psalms 31 and 35 particularly close to the confession in Jeremiah 20? I would say that the return to lament which is a prominent feature in these two psalms might have created a lasting appeal to whoever is responsible for the present arrangement of the text in Jeremiah 20. The element of tension, strongly expressed in these two psalms, has become a model for the composition of Jeremiah 20. The editor/s of Jeremian texts has/have been guided by the Psalms of lament. As Baumgartner rightly pointed out, it is not one particular psalm, but the psalm 'type'. But unlike the 'type' of psalm which Baumgartner endorses, the psalm which serves as a model for the confession in Jeremiah 20 is the type of psalm which is capable of moving not only from lament to praise but also *from praise to lament*.

The difference between Psalms 31 and 35 and Jeremiah 20 is that unlike the two psalms the latter does not go back to the element of praise. However, Psalms 31 and 35 belong to a group of psalms where the element of tension between lament and praise is very much present. Closer to the structure of Jer 20:7–18 are those psalms that juxtapose praise/thanksgiving and lament, with the latter as the last word. These psalms are Psalms 9/10, 40 and 27.[55]

---

[54] See analysis of Psalm 35 above (Chapter 6).
[55] For specific discussions of these passages, see Chapter 4. Here I provide only general observations.

7.4.2   *Psalms 9/10, 40, 27 and Jer 20:7–18*

As shown above, Psalm 9/10 begins with thanksgiving which culminates in a confident and hopeful declaration of the poor and needy over the wicked (9:18–19). However, the psalm moves to petition in vv. 20–21 and blasts with a powerful lament in 10:1, completely contradicting the positive tone of the previous thanksgiving. Psalm 40 similarly begins with thanksgiving, recalling what Yahweh has done in the past (vv. 1–11), but then reverts to the element of lament in vv. 12–18. The prayer moves from thanksgiving and confidence to lament in the form of petition (vv. 12ff.). The psalmist, who had just earlier testified about how the Lord has delivered him from the "pit of destruction" (v. 3) and who is confident of help from Yahweh, finds himself in the midst of danger and is in need of deliverance in vv. 13–18.

What makes Psalm 40 especially relevant in relation to Jer 20:7–18 is that the second half of Psalm 40 (vv. 14–18) appears as a separate psalm in Psalm 70. Thus we have a possibility of a deliberate attempt to put together two independent psalms, and even more conspicuously, to do it in such a way that the lament gets the last word. The difference between Psalm 40 and Jer 20:7–18 is that the composition of the former shows a literary attempt to relate the two parts of the psalm.[56] Jeremiah 20:7–13 and vv. 14–18 do not have significant structural and verbal affinities to indicate an artistic joining together of the two. What we find rather is a straightforward juxtaposition of the two passages. In spite of this difference, however, the juxtaposition of thanksgiving/ praise and lament is strikingly similar in the two.

Another relevant psalm is Psalm 27, a psalm which contains a movement from thanksgiving to the element of lament. What makes this particularly relevant to Jeremiah 20 is that with the vow of praise in Ps 27:6 we have a clear mark of an ending of a thanksgiving psalm. Verses 1–6 consist of a complete unit by itself if we follow the usual form-critical understanding of a thanksgiving psalm. Like Jer 20:7–13, Ps 27:1–6 could have ended in a high note, but such was not the case. For immediately after the vow of thanksgiving in v. 6 another unit follows which begins with a cry for mercy (v. 7).

---

[56] For relevant verbal contacts between the two sections, see analysis of Psalm 40 (Chapter 4).

The brief comparative analysis above shows that it is not unusual for a composition to return to lament even after it has already moved to praise. Unfortunately, this has not been mentioned in the discussions of Jeremiah 20. This I believe is due to a limited understanding of the lament psalms—a view which for the most part has been dictated by the form-critical understanding of lament. This demonstrates the importance of having a proper understanding of the interplay between lament and praise in the lament psalms for the interpretation of passages like Jer 20:7–18. This passage fits the individual lament psalms which alternate between lament and praise (Psalms 31, 35) and juxtapose praise and lament (Psalms 9/10, 27, 40). We may also briefly add that the feature of the return to lament after praise is highlighted in Psalm 12—a psalm which contains a return to lament after the 'certainty of a hearing'. My question is, why is Jeremiah 20 close to these psalms and not the psalms which move from lament to praise? Or why would a redactor borrow from such psalms and not the psalms which move from lament to praise?

7.4.3   *Why not the lament psalms that move from lament to praise?*

Will not the lament psalms which move from lament to praise be more relevant to Jeremiah's life and ministry? Hermisson answers in the negative. According to him psalms which move to praise, which are similar to the thanksgiving psalms, would not fit with the experience of Jeremiah.[57] The 'delivered' prophet can fit into this language of praise. But not of Jeremiah who remains a prophet of disaster ('*Unheil*sprophet').[58] The confession at the end marks a big difference from that of the Psalms, specifically the thanksgiving psalms, where the one who has once fallen away from the community has now been

---

[57] Hermisson, *Jahwes und Jeremias Rechtsstreit*, 317–22, in contrast to others who see similarities between Jeremiah 20 and the Psalms, sees the passage in Jeremiah as different from what we find in the Psalms. Specifically, in the case of Jeremiah 20, he finds no psalm like it. I think the reason why he is unable to see the connection is because of the form-critical perspective approach which has dominated the way of looking at these psalms. He thus was not able to see that there are individual lament psalms which move back to lament. He sees the lament psalms which move to praise more like the thanksgiving psalms: the lamenting person is already looking back from the perspective of deliverance.

[58] Ibid., 336. Jeremiah is still very much in the thick of things, in the midst of difficulties.

integrated and thus can already sing praises to Yahweh. What we find in the last confession is a reverse. Hermisson writes:

> So fügte sich auch dieser letzte Text dem prophetischen Verständnis der Konfessionen ein: als die Kehrseite der Rettung des Propheten durch die Bestätigung seiner Unheilsbotschaft. Es ist kein Vergnügen, Prophet zu sein: die Ambivalenz prophetischer Existenz in der Angewiesenheit auf das Jahwewort und in der Vereinsamung durch desselbe Wort, weil Jahwe ihm 'mit Grimm erfüllt', hatte der Prophet schon in 15:16ff ausgesprochen. Das bringt er hier zu einer letzten Konsequenz, und hier erst begreift man, warum seine 'Wunde unheilbar' (15:18) ist.[59]

The psalms which move from lament to praise would certainly not make a good fit for Jeremiah. For as Goldingay explains, Jeremiah is a prophet whose suffering remains deep to the end. Unlike most 'testimonies' that we hear today, Jeremiah's is a testimony which has not yet experienced an answer. Goldingay comments:

> Perhaps the very fact that the last of the confessions (last, that is, in the arrangement of the book), in chapter 20, closes with despair and not confidence warns against our understanding these passages as reflecting an admittedly deep but essentially passing spiritual turmoil. And what was true of the inward affliction, that it ends on a down note, ends in turmoil, is true also of the outward suffering. Of course, Jeremiah does have his good moments. In a paradoxical way the fall of Jerusalem is one, because that is the point at which he is proved right, when it is established that God has not been fooling him. But even then his message is not taken to heart, and the man who had been dragged by his heels in to Jerusalem at the beginning of his ministry...is now dragged by his heels out of Jerusalem at the end of his ministry, taken as a lucky charm by Jews who have decided that the only future lies in refuge in Egypt...As Gerhard von Rad points out..., no ravens feed Jeremiah as they fed Elijah. No angel stops the lions' mouth for him, as one did for Daniel...The story of his outward suffering, like that of his inward affliction, ends in misery.[60]

Heschel describes the "polarity of emotion" that characterises Jeremiah's life:

> Polarity of emotion is a striking fact in the life of Jeremiah. We encounter him in the pit of utter agony and at the height of extreme joy, carried away by divine wrath and aching with supreme compassion. There are

---

[59] Ibid., 337.

[60] John Goldingay, *God's Prophet, God's Servant: A Study in Jeremiah and Isaiah 40–55* (Exeter: Paternoster Press, 1984), 17.

words of railing accusation and denunciation; the lips that pleaded for
mercy utter petitions for retribution, for the destruction of those who
stand in the way of the people's accepting his prophetic word. Indeed,
the commission he received at the time of his call endowed him with the
power to carry out two opposite roles:

> *To pluck up and to break down*
> *To destroy and to overthrow,*
> *To build and to plant*
> *Jeremiah 1:10*[61]

Commenting on Jer 20:14–18 Heschel writes: "The tension of being
caught, heart and soul, in two opposing currents of violent emotion,
was more than a human being could bear".[62]

7.5   The Purpose of the Juxtaposition of Praise and Lament

It is no wonder the redactor/s have seen fit to arrange the confessions
in such a way that the darkest and most depressing bit gets the last
mention. The sense of tension and suffering which characterises much
of Jeremiah's life and ministry is expressed through a composition which
juxtaposes lament and praise and moves from praise to lament. Indeed,
Lundbom may be correct when he said that the element of praise is an
"anomaly" in Jeremiah's confessions. Probably, the element of praise
is introduced in order to create a stronger contrast with the following
'curse'. The juxtaposition brings out a strong sense of contrast, of reversals. Jer 20:14–18 might have existed independently of the preceding
verses, but in their present position, indeed by being joined to vv. 7–13,
the verses' function has been transformed. Although vv. 14–18 are not
explicitly directed to God, its being joined to the prayer in vv. 7–13
meant that it too has become a prayer. As Fretheim explains, "Verses
14–18 are not specifically addressed to God (but neither is 15:10–11),
and there is no petition here...Yet, if vv. 7–18 belong together, the
address to God is probably implicit".[63] In its present position, vv. 14–18
has the important function of reversing the overall direction of vv.
7–13, and indeed even of the whole series of confessions, from being

---

[61] Abraham J. Heschel, *The Prophets: An Introduction* (vol. 1; NY: Harper and Row, 1962), 125.

[62] Ibid.

[63] Fretheim, *Jeremiah*, 296.

an expression of praise, to being an expression of the darkest lament possible.[64]

The application of the insights gained from our analyses of the psalms of lament has helped us appreciate and understand the movements in Jer 20:7–18. Conversely, Jer 20:7–18 provides a window through which we can explore the possible purpose/s of the psalms containing the '*un*certainty of a hearing'. For we have here a clear attempt to adapt this type of psalm to an actual experience of an individual. The literary links between this passage and the call of Jeremiah, noted by Lundbom (see above), demonstrate an application of the psalms which move from praise to lament to the experiences of Jeremiah. It is here that the passage in Jeremiah carves out its own contribution to the psalms containing tension between lament and praise. It suggests that one of the functions of the juxtaposition of praise and lament is to emphasize the sense of tension that often characterises the life of the pious. When one wants to communicate the presence of tension and suffering, and if one does not want anybody to miss the point, one does this by joining a lament immediately after praise.

7.5.1   *The rhetorical effect of the juxtaposition of praise and lament*

Compositions such as we find in Jer 20:7–18 and the lament psalms which move from praise to lament not only bring out the element of tension that characterises the life of the righteous; they also attempt to create a certain effect on the readers[65] by presenting an entirely different way of looking at things. Fox, in an excellent article on the rhetorical effect of Ezekiel's vision of the bones, writes: "The most powerful images are foreign to our everyday experience. Images that conform to everyday experience have didactic value. They are useful in reinforcing accepted truths and in helping the auditor assimilate ideas that are complex or abstract. Strange, shocking, and bizarre images on the other hand are needed when one seeks to break down old frameworks of perception and to create new ones".[66] What we find in Jeremiah

---

[64] Cf. Clines and Gunn, 408 (noted earlier).

[65] I am using the word 'reader' to refer both to the recipients of the book of Jeremiah and to us today who read the text.

[66] Michael V. Fox, "The Rhetoric of Ezekiel's Vision of the Valley of the Bones", in *The Place is too Small for Us: The Israelite Prophets in Recent Scholarship* (ed. Robert P.

belongs to the latter category. There is an attempt to create a sense of
shock and disturbance in order to bring about a change of perspective,
a change of worldview. The worldview presented goes against the usual
expectation. False prophets in Jeremiah are preaching peace and are
teaching that although things may appear bad at the present, everything will be all right: lament will eventually turn to praise. In contrast
to this stands the prophet of doom, preaching the reverse: things will
become even worse! On the part of the redactor/s what better way
of presenting the message of Jeremiah and the reality confronting his
contemporary audience than to end his confessions with that shocking
image of a person cursing the day of his birth, right after the praise?
Indeed, there is no better way of creating disequilibrium, disturbance
and a deep sense of uncertainty.

The 'curse' at the end of the confession in Jeremiah 20 is an important clue to the way in which the composition has been designed to
create a certain effect. Lundbom believes that "those compiling the book
of Jeremiah had definite ideas about what made a suitable beginning
and a suitable end".[67] It is thus striking that we have the passage on
'curse' at the end of the confessions and not at the beginning. In her
comparative study of the passages on the subject of cursing one's day
of birth in Jeremiah and Job, Gisela Fuchs observes that the position
of both passages in their respective books are such that they are made
"exposed".[68] Yet as Hermisson points out, compared with Job the passage in Jeremiah expresses an even more profound sense of tension.
For in the case of the former, the 'curse' stands at the beginning, with
the book ending in resolution. With Jeremiah, the 'curse' stands at the
end of the confessions and is without resolution.[69] Indeed, the entire
book of Jeremiah ends without the certainty of resolution.

For readers then and now the absence of any clear resolution can be
disturbing. But it is a much needed corrective to the overly positivistic
tendencies of all readers. The last 'confession of Jeremiah' provides us
with a realistic way of viewing life's experiences. As Miller remarks:
"The prayer of the faithful moves from lament to praise, from fear to

---

Gordon, Sources for Biblical and Theological Study 5; Winona Lake, IN: Eisenbrauns,
1995), 184. Repr. from *HUCA* 51 (1980): 1–15.

[67] Lundbom, 91. Unfortunately, in his discussions of Jeremiah 20, he does not expati-
ate on the possible "ideas" those who have arranged it might have had.

[68] Gisela Fuchs, "Die Klage des Propheten", 228.

[69] Hermisson, 339.

joy—even for Jeremiah". But he continues: "There may be a certain amount of realism, however, in the movement from 20:13 to 20:14–18. The word of praise is not always the last word. The prophet, like many people, falls back from praise to lament. Deliverance is not necessarily final or even realized. *The logic of faith—and that is the dominant word—is from lament to praise. But life often takes us from the heights back to the depths, as it did for Jeremiah*".[70]

7.6 Conclusion

The present study demonstrates that the movement from praise to lament and the return to lament after praise occurs even outside the Psalms. This is important for it demonstrates the degree of influence such types of composition had in the Old Testament. The study also shows that the failure to see the dynamic nature of the movements between lament and praise in the Psalms has proved to be detrimental to the treatment of Jer 20:7–18. For the most part, the form-critical perspective of a one-way movement from lament to praise has been determinative in the interpretation of Jer 20:71–8 as well as in the confessions of Jeremiah in general. Although some connections were made with Psalms 31 and 35, it has not been pointed out that these two psalms contain a return to lament after praise. I have tried to show in this chapter how a proper understanding of these psalms, along with the psalms that move from thanksgiving/praise to lament (e.g. Psalm 40), can be of immense value in the interpretation of Jer 20:7–18. The individual lament psalms with an '*un*certainty of a hearing' help us appreciate and understand the complexity of the present arrangement of Jeremiah 20.

This study has pointed out not only the significance of the lament psalms which move from praise to lament for Jer 20:7–18. Conversely, this passage helps us see the possible purpose/s of compositions which juxtapose praise and lament. Jer 20:7–18 serves as a window through

---

[70] P. D. Miller, "The Book of Jeremiah", in *NIB* (vol. 6; Nashville: Abingdon Press, 2001), 730, emphasis mine; cf. Rudoph's comment: "Aber es ist ebenso lebenswahr, dass auf Stunden innerer Erhebung auch beim frommen Menschen wieder Zeiten der Depression folgen" (*Jeremia*, 121). Miller's comment is a noticeable development from his earlier remarks in his article, "In Praise and Thanksgiving," *Theology Today* 45 (1988): 180–88, where he stressed the element of praise.

which we can look for the possible purpose/function of such compositions. I have mentioned two: 1) to bring out the sense of tension in the
life of the righteous; 2) to disturb and even shock in order to create a
change of perspective—a perspective which sees life in all its realities.
This reality tells us that the life of faith is marked not only by certainties,
but also by an '*un*certainty of a hearing'. In the next chapter, we explore
one more passage outside the Psalms which contain similar features
to the individual psalms we have examined in the previous chapters,
especially those which contain a return to lament after praise.

CHAPTER EIGHT

THE RETURN TO LAMENT IN LAMENTATIONS 3

8.1 Introduction

In the previous chapter I have tried to demonstrate that the movement *praise-lament* or the *return* to lament after praise can also be found in Jer 20:7–18. Here I try to build on that by further exploring another related text outside the Psalms—Lamentations 3. I chose Lamentations 3 because it is the closest to the individual lament psalms among the five chapters in Lamentations. Though consisting of different genres,[1] the individual lament dominates Lamentations 3.[2] Westermann observes that the first section (1–25) follows the "normal pattern for the genre of the personal lament".[3] By "normal pattern" he means a movement from lament to a more hopeful and confident mood. He explains that although the lament does not contain the usual invocation at the beginning (1), it nonetheless moves from an "accusation against God" (2–17a), "personal complaint" (17b–19), to an "avowal of confidence" (20–25).[4] More importantly for the purpose of this study, Lamentations 3 not only contains a movement from despair to hope (1–24), it also contains a *return* to lament (42ff.).

Unfortunately, as in the case of the psalms we have examined including the passage in Jeremiah, most scholars do not see this *return* to lament *after* praise. Thus, although Westermann noted the movement from despair to hope in the first part of the poem, he did not account

---

[1] Lamentations 3 is a combination of various genres. Paul R. House, *Lamentations* (vol. 23B; WBC; Nashville: Thomas Nelson Publishers, 2004), 404, observes: "Aspects of communal lament, individual lament, wisdom-based psalmic observations, and instructions like those found in Pss 37 and 73 are all in evidence".

[2] Nancy Lee, *The Singers of Lamentations* (Leiden: Brill, 2002), 166.

[3] Claus Westermann, *Die Klagelieder: Forschungsgeschichte und Auslegung* (Neukirchen-Vluyn: Neukirchener, 1990), 143, ET *Lamentations: Issues and Interpretation* (trans. Charles Muenchow; Edinburgh: T & T Clark, 1994), 170. Cf. Nancy Lee, *The Singers of Lamentations*, 169–71, for parallel passages in the Psalms for the first section of Lamentations 3.

[4] Westermann, *Die Klagelieder*, 143, ET *Lamentations*, 169. He sees the last three verses of the chapter (vv. 64–66) as a "(fragmentary) conclusion" to the individual lament.

for the occurrence of the communal lament (42–47) *after* the hymnic affirmations in vv. 22–24. As can be observed above, his understanding of lament is limited by the form-critical view of the movement lament-praise. The focus is on the change of mood from lament to hope, which is often explained in terms of Begrich's salvation oracle theory.

Incidentally, Lamentations 3 occupies a prominent place in Begrich's thesis. Begrich believes that in Lam 3:57b the "wesentliches Moment" of the giving of the oracle of salvation is testified.[5] But as in his application of his theory in Psalm 35:3, the problem with Begrich's approach is that he does not consider the context of the whole of Lamentations 3. Even more problematic, the text is one-sidedly viewed through the lens of the form-critical framework which sees only a one-way movement from lament to praise. The sole emphasis lies on the discovery of the element of certainty in the text, ignoring the element of 'uncertainty' which is at the heart of Lamentations 3.

Lamentations 3 has often been viewed as the 'heart'[6] of the book of Lamentations not only because of its position in the centre of the

---

[5] Begrich, "Das priesterliche Heilsorakel", 83. In their respective analyses of Lam 3:57b Kraus, Rudolph, Westermann, and more recently Knut Heim, follow Begrich's thesis. Kraus, *Klagelieder (Threni)* (vol. 20; 2nd ed; BKAT; Neukirchen: Neukirchener Verlag, 1960), 17, believes that "Wenn der einzelne Beter in seiner Not zu Jahwe schrie und ihn um sein Einschreiten bat, dann durfte er den Zuspruch ,Fürchte dich nicht!' vernehmen". Both Rudolph and Westermann appeal to the article by Begrich in their explanation of v. 57, which they believe contains an oracle of salvation (Wilhelm Rudolph, *Das Buch Ruth. Das Hohe Lied. Die Klagelieder. Die Klagelieder* [vol. 27 (1–3); KAT; Gütersloh: Gütersloher Verlagshaus, 1962], 243; Westermann, *Lamentations*, 186). Knut M. Heim, "The Personification of Jerusalem and the Drama of Her Bereavement in Lamentations", in *Zion, City of Our God* (ed. Richard S. Hess and Gordon J. Wenham; Grand Rapids, MI/Cambridge U.K.: Eerdmans, 1999), 163, strongly endorses this interpretation. Following the form-critical view of a movement from lament to praise, he comments concerning the "fear not" in Lam 3:57: "the significance of this phrase, the only divine utterance in Lamentations, should not be underestimated. 'Fear not!' is the typical opening of the so-called 'salvation oracle' in psalms of lament". He argues that Lamentations 3 is very much like the psalms of lament with its movement towards praise. He understands vv. 22–23 as a hymnic praise. Contrary to many who do not see any response from God in the book as a whole, he sees in v. 57 an 'oracle of salvation', which, even though only a very small part, represents the "heart" of the whole book of Lamentations. He writes: "Here we are at the heart of the book of Lamentations. The author/compiler's purpose is to encourage his fellow citizens, and he achieves his aim magnificently by relating his own experience of a divine oracle in the traditional language of his people's accepted religious lore" (ibid., 163–4).

[6] Writing poetically C. W. Eduard Naegelsbach, "The Lamentations of Jeremiah", in *Lange's Commentary on the Holy Scriptures. Isaiah to Lamentations* (vol. 6; ed. John Peter Lange; Grand Rapids, MI: Zondervan, 1960), 4, describes Lamentations 3 as follows: "As the pyramid of Mont Blanc, seen at sunset from Chamouny, its summit gleaming

book but because of the expressions of hope found in the middle section of the chapter. Scholars who approach Lamentations can be divided into two camps—those who see the book as a hopeful book and those who emphasize the element of lament.[7] The former see the suffering presented in the book as something to be 'mastered';[8] the latter views suffering as something to be expressed. Linafelt observes that those who wish to highlight the element of hope are "eager to move quickly through chapters 1 and 2 in order to light upon chapter 3".[9] For his part, Linafelt focuses on the first two chapters. He believes that

---

with supernal splendours, whilst below, the mountain has already disappeared wrapped in deepest darkness..., so out of the profound night of despair and misery, this middle part of the third song and of the whole book towers upward, radiant with light".

[7] Cf. Linafelt, *Surviving Lamentations: Catastrophe, Lament, and Protest in the Afterlife of a Biblical Book* (Chicago: University of Chicago Press, 2000), 2–3. Specifically for Lamentations 3, among those who see the chapter as highlighting the element of hope and praise are: Kraus, *Klagelieder*; Rudolph, *Das Buch Ruth. Das Hohe Lied. Die Klagelieder. Die Klagelieder*; Renate Brandscheidt, *Gotteszorn und Menschenleid: Die Gerichtsklage des leidenden Gerechten in Klg 3* (vol. 41; Trierer Theologische Studien; Trier: Paulinus Verlag, 1983; Paul S. Re'emi, "A Commentary on the Book of Lamentations", in *God's People in Crisis: A Commentary on the Book of Amos. A Commentary on the Book of Lamentations* (ed. M. A. Robert and S. Paul Re'emi; Grand Rapids, MI: Eerdmans, 1984); Delbert R. Hillers, *Lamentations* (AB; NY: Doubleday, 1992); Westermann, *Die Klagelieder*, ET *Lamentations*; House, *Lamentations* (2004). Recently, there has been a growing number of scholars who seek to emphasize the element of lament in the book of Lamentations: Iain W. Provan, *Lamentations* (NCB; Grand Rapids, MI: Eerdmans, 1991); Linafelt, *Surviving Lamentations* (2000); O'Connor, "The Book of Lamentations: Introduction, Commentary and Reflections" (2001); F. W. Dobbs-Allsopp, *Lamentations* (Interpretation; Louisville: John Knox Press, 2002); Lee, *The Singers of Lamentations* (2002). Between these two camps, J. Middlemas, "The Violent Storm in Lamentations", *JSOT* 29 (2004): 81–97, tries to thread a middle ground. Using the imagery of a violent storm (cyclone) she argues that hope and despair should be held together: "Like the funnel effect of a cyclone that cannot exist without the peaceful eye and raging winds, the two approaches to the book of Lamentations, through the centre and the periphery, co-exist because the very nature of the material insists that they do so" (95). However, in my view the image that she uses breaks down right where it's most needed, for actually what is remembered about cyclones is not their "peaceful eye" in the middle but their destructive effects!

[8] It is striking how often the words 'master', 'overcome' show up in the discussions of the book of Lamentations. Norman K. Gottwald, *Studies in the Book of Lamentations* (vol. 14; Studies in Biblical Theology; London: SCM, 1954), 52, writes: "our book is not an abstract disquisition on suffering, but has for its basic purpose the mastery of pain and doubt in the interests of faith". For Gottwald, Lamentations is like a theological treatise: "The theological significance of Lamentations consists in its bold and forthright statement of the problem of national disaster: what is the meaning of the terrible historical adversities that have overtaken us between 608 and 586 B.C.?" (48). Kraus, *Klagelieder*, 17, sees Lamentations 3 as the 'Herzstück' of the book because it shows the way towards the overcoming of the 'Not': "Hier wird offensichtlich einWeg zur Überwindung der Not gewiesen".

[9] Linafelt, *Surviving Lamentations*, 2.

the book is "more about the *expression* of suffering than the meaning behind it".[10] Here I focus on chapter 3 in order to highlight the element of lament. This chapter might not express the same horror and agony as in the other chapters. But it certainly presents the situation of suffering envisaged in the book in a poignant fashion. For here the experience of lament is set against the backdrop of praise and hope. Like the praise in Jer 20:13 the hymnic affirmations in Lam 3:22–24 highlight the yawning gap between the declared affirmations and present reality. Lamentations 3 is indeed the 'heart' of the book, not because it expresses hope but because it betrays the absence of hope in spite of affirmations of it; it is the centre because it intimates the "tragic vision" which the book as a whole conveys.[11]

The following analysis will examine the overall structure and flow of the poem. The structural analysis will be more extended because of the rather complex nature of the construction of Lamentations 3. As in the other chapters we will focus on the interaction between lament and praise in our detailed analysis of the text. The chapter ends with a summary and conclusion.

8.2 Structural Analysis

8.2.1 *Three Structural Elements*

Three important features figure prominently in the poem: different genres, use of the acrostic and dramatized speech. As mentioned in the Introduction, Lamentations 3 consists of various genres, most prominent of which is the individual lament psalm. Another genre employed is the communal lament which occupies vv. 40–47—the only section in the chapter which is constructed using the first person plural. In between the individual lament (1–24) and the communal lament (40–47) we have a section which resembles what we find in the wisdom traditions (25–39). We hear in these verses instructions like those in wisdom psalms (e.g.

---

[10] Ibid., 4.
[11] The phrase "tragic vision" is discussed in F. W. Dobbs-Allsopp, "Tragedy, Tradition, and Theology in the Book of Lamentations", *JSOT* 74 (1997): 29–60.

Pss 37 and 73).[12] We also hear Job-like dialogues.[13] As Landy observes, "The poet talks like Job one minute, and like one of Job's friends the next".[14] What is significant about all the genres employed is that they all have the potential for creating tension between hope and despair. Individual lament psalms do contain strong elements of tension. Communal laments often end without any resolution.[15] Wisdom poems like Job are full of contrasting views.

What holds these different genres together is the acrostic. House notes, "The acrostic format provides the formal structural cohesion that the poem requires and should be viewed as evidence of careful thought and artistry".[16] Like the other chapters in Lamentations (chapters 1, 2, and 4), the third chapter is composed using the acrostic. In this chapter the acrostic has been most extensively used. In chapters 1 and 2 three lines are devoted to each letter of the alphabet but only the first line begins with the corresponding acrostic. With Lamentations 3 each of the three lines begins with the acrostic. The purpose or function of the acrostic has been much discussed. One of the most common explanations is that the acrostic is employed to convey completeness. According to Renkema, "The A–Z scheme in Lam. 1–4 has been used because they wanted to picture total misery, in every aspect from A–Z".[17] The acrostic is found elsewhere in a number of passages in the OT: Psalms 9/10, 25; 34; 37; 111; 112; 119; 145; Prov 31:10–31.[18] Most relevant of these is Psalm 9/10, for as illustrated in my analysis of the psalm

---

[12] House, *Lamentations*, 404.

[13] Robert Gordis, *The Song of Songs and Lamentations* (revised and augmented edition; NY: KTAV Publishing House, 1974), 175, comments concerning vv. 31–38: "The poet's standpoint is very similar to that of Eliphaz (Job 5:6, 7), who affirms that suffering is not rooted in the universe, but is the result of man's sinful actions".

[14] Francis Landy, "Lamentations", in *The Literary Guide to the Bible* (ed. Robert Alter and Frank Kermode; London: Fontana Press, 1989), 332.

[15] E.g. Psalms 44, 60, 74, 79, 80, 83, 85, 90, 94, 123, 137. Except for Psalms 60 and 94 all of these psalms end in an element of lament, without resolution. Psalm 60 contains an oracle at the middle, though it is conspicuous that right after the oracle the psalm goes back to lament.

[16] House, 404.

[17] Johan Renkema, "The Literary Structure of Lamentations (I–IV)", in *The Structural Analysis of Biblical and Canaanite Poetry* (ed. Willem van der Meer and Johannes C. de Moor; Sheffield: JSOT Press, 1988), 365; cf. Gottwald, *Studies in the Book of Lamentations*, 26–32. Other purposes of the acrostic mentioned are: as a means of magic, an aid to memory, for artistic purposes (Delbert R. Hillers, *Lamentations*, 26).

[18] Kraus, *Klagelieder*, 6. Lee, *The Singers of Lamentations*, 164, adds to the list those psalms which do not have the acrostic but are constructed using the acrostic line: Pss 33, 38 and 94.

we have here an example of the use of the acrostic in a lament psalm which moves from thanksgiving to lament. Similarly, the acrostic holds the entirety of Lamentations 3, which contains among others a lament which moves to praise followed by a communal lament, though in a more complex order.

Another feature important for the interpretation of Lamentations 3 is what Mintz calls "dramatized speech". He has this vital interpretative insight:

> Who speaks to whom about whom as seen from whose point of view? It is in the play of these questions, which defines the rhetorical situation of the text, that the deepest theological business of Lamentations gets transacted. If we can state the theme of Lamentations as an exploration of the traumatized relations between Israel and God in the immediate aftermath of the Destruction, and if we pause to realize that as a poem Lamentations has as its medium dramatized speech and not theological statement, then we must appreciate the significance of the poem's rhetoric.[19]

8.2.2 *Overall Structure*

Overall, the structure can be outlined as follows:

I—From Despair to Hope (1–24)
  Lament (1–20)
  Hope (21–24)
II—Voices from the Wisdom Tradition (25–39)
  Proper response to suffering: quiet submission (25–33)
  A Job-like Objection: "Yhwh does not see" (34–36)
  Counter-argument (37–39)
  Conclusion and Transition: Call for repentance (40–41)
III—*Return* to Lament: Communal lament (40–51)
IV—Past experience of deliverance in the light of present experience of suffering (52–66)
  Past experience of deliverance
  Present crisis
  Petition

---

[19] Alan Mintz, *Hurban: Responses to Catastrophe in Hebrew Literature* (NY: Columbia University Press, 1984), 26.

If we were to describe the overall structure of Lamentations 3 then we would have to agree with Berlin's comment. The poem, according to her "lacks a clear progression of ideas, preferring to alternate between despair and hope".[20] Indeed, it is the tension between the elements of lament and praise that characterise the overall structure of the poem. It begins with an individual lament which moves from grim despair (1–20) to hope (21–24). One sees a clear movement from lament to praise in the passage. As will be shown in the analysis of the passage, however, the hymnic affirmations are brought into conflict with the people's present experience expressed in the communal lament (42–47). The section that follows vv. 1–24 borrows from the wisdom traditions, which is characterised by tension of theological viewpoints such as we find in the book of Job. We have in vv. 25–39 something of the argumentative dialogue common in Job. It is like hearing Job speaking on the one hand and his friends responding with a rebuke on the other. As will be shown below, there is a strong attempt to 'defend' God (31–33) and an equally strong opposition to doubt the assertions being made (34–36).[21] Within the wisdom tradition itself one can sense the tension between hope and despair.

The section that follows (40–51) initially begins with an affirmation of the dominant stance proposed in the wisdom tradition section. Verses 40–41 function as the conclusion to the preceding section and a transition to the following section. Shifting gear to the first person plural, the poet calls for repentance and confession (40–41). In what appears to be a lightning speed response, the poem continues: "We have sinned and rebelled" (v. 42a)—a statement which encapsulates the very essence of confession as an admission of guilt.[22] One can hardly ask for more. These words are the most explicit statement of admission of guilt in the whole poem and indeed in the whole book of Lamentations, of which there is a scarcity.[23] And yet with the same lightning speed as the confession appeared come the words: "you have not forgiven"

---

[20] Adele Berlin, *Lamentations* (OTL; Louisville/London: Westminster John Knox Press, 2002), 86.

[21] See discussions of the relevant verses below.

[22] Cf. the prayers of confessions in Nehemiah 9 and Daniel 9.

[23] Mintz, *Responses to Catastrophe in Hebrew Literature*, 25, points out the conspicuous lack of mention of sin in the book; its only explicit appearance being in chapter 3. But as to the precise nature of what the sin is, the book is silent (25); contra Gottwald, *Studies in the Book of Lamentations*, who argues that the key lies in the admission of guilt and repentance.

(v. 42b). The setting up of the two cola in such a paratactic way creates a tension and contrast between the two that can hardly be missed.[24] One could almost hear the people saying: "We have already done what you were asking: we have repented and have confessed our sins; the problem is that you (Yhwh) did not do your part!" And the communal lament that ensues is so strong in its accusation that it is actually the first time in the chapter where God is ever addressed directly.[25] But whereas addressing him in the second person would have signified a progression in terms of a more hopeful and confident stance resulting from the process of lamenting, the opposite was actually the case. Hope turns back to despair. Confidence shrinks to doubt. Using repetitions of words and similar imagery (compare vv. 43–44 with vv. 5, 7, 8; see discussions below), the communal lament recalls the lament at the beginning. Far from improving, the lament intensifies. With the return to the first person used in v. 48, the prayer expresses its deepest longing, that "Yhwh look and see from heaven" (v. 50).

The first part of the final section (52–66) has often been seen as a recollection of a past experience of deliverance by an individual given at this stage in order to encourage the people who are now suffering.[26] However, the overall context of the chapter and of the whole book for that matter militates against such a view. The lack of resolution at the close of the chapter betrays the purpose of the recollection of past experiences of salvation. They are not recalled in order to serve as an encouragement but to draw a sharp contrast between what God has done in the past and the absence of such in the present; thus the need to plead for mercy from God. It is important to recognize the complexity of the text since it is not easy to discern whether the poet is speaking about the past or the present. Any attempt to iron out the complexity of the text runs counter to the overall effect the poem may be aiming to create. In vv. 52–63 we may refer to what is called a "tension in time".[27] Broyles uses the term to describe the flow of Psalm 31 in which the psalmist speaks about being delivered only to admit in the

---

[24] Paratactic structure is a common feature in Lamentations (see F. W. Dobbs-Allsopp, *Lamentations*, 47).

[25] Yhwh is never addressed directly even in the high point of the individual lament (22–24). The closest it can go to is in the use of the second person pronominal suffix at the end of v. 23: "your faithfulness".

[26] Rudolph, *Die Klagelieder*, 246.

[27] Craig C. Broyles, *Psalms*, 157.

very next verse that he remains in trouble.[28] Past experience of deliverance is narrated in the light of the present experience of suffering. The
structure results in a composition which expresses hope that if Yhwh
has acted in the past he will do the same. At the same time the element
of complaint is preserved: you have done this in the past, why are you
not doing it now? Finally, the passage ends with a series of petitions
and imprecations which correspond to the ending in Lamentations 1.
Although expressions of hope can be found in the middle section of
the poem, a clear resolution to the prayer is lacking at the end. To use
Lee's phrase, Lamentations 3 is an "unanswered lament".[29]

8.2.3   ראה: As a Structural Keyword in Lamentations 3

In my analysis of the passage I observe how the word ראה shows up
in key places in the chapter. First, in v. 1, the word is used as a description of the man: he is the man who 'saw' affliction. On the force of
this statement, Dobbs-Allsopp comments: "In having 'seen affliction'
the man does what God fails to do".[30] The second place the word ראה
appears is in v. 36. Dobbs-Allsopp does not explicitly connect v. 1 with
v. 36, but I think there is a deliberate play on words between the two
verses. In contrast to the man's claim that he has 'seen' the affliction
(1), v. 36 declares, "the Lord does *not* see (ראה)". The words appear
in a difficult section (vv. 34–36), whose translation has proved to be a
real challenge, let alone its sense. But I believe the employment of the
word is deliberate in order to draw connection with v. 1. The third
place where the word shows up is in v. 50.[31] As my analysis below will
show this verse expresses the most intimate concern of the poet. The
poet will not cease in his weeping and crying, brought about by the
destruction of the "daughter of my people" (48), until "Yhwh look and
see (ראה)" (50). Finally, the word occurs towards the end in vv. 59–60.
Here they serve either as a testimony to what God has done, i.e. he has
'seen' or as a petition that Yhwh 'see' the evil done to the petitioner.

---

[28] See discussion of Psalm 31 (Chapter 6).
[29] Lee, *The Singers of Lamentations*, 168, uses the phrase to describe Lam 3:1–24. I
would use the words, "unanswered lament" to describe the whole chapter, for there is
actually no resolution to the lament even up to the end.
[30] Dobbs-Allsopp, *Lamentations*, 110–11.
[31] Again Dobbs-Allsopp does not mention this verse in connection to either v. 36
or v. 1.

The case depends on how we render the perfect verbs in these verses, either as a perfect or a precative (see below).

8.3   Detailed Analysis of Lamentations 3

8.3.1   *From Despair to Hope*

8.3.1.1   *"I am the man"*

Lamentations 3 contrasts sharply with the other chapters of the book, particularly chapters 1, 2 and 4. Instead of the dirge cry, איכה, which occurs at the beginning of each of the other three chapters, Lamentations 3 starts off with a plain statement of identification from the speaker: "I am the man (*geber*)".[32] In place of a female voice, we hear the unmistakeable voice of a male speaker in the word *geber*. The word *geber* occurs 4x in the chapter (1, 27, 35 and 39). O'Connor sees military connotations in the word, translating it as "strong man".[33] But lest the reader be misled into thinking that finally we have one who bears the glad tidings, especially after the gruelling portrayal of suffering and pitch black lament in the previous two chapters, the poet continues, "I am the man *who saw affliction*". Far from being a conquering warrior, this man is a suffering individual, cast down. Probably the choice of the word *geber* is made in order to create the sense of irony: this man who is supposed to be strong is a man of despair. Dobbs-Allsopp draws attention to the close parallel between the statement in v. 1a and the "self-presentation formula of kings in royal inscriptions from the ancient Near East (e.g., 'I am Azitiwada, the blessed one of Baal, a servant of Baal, whom Awarku, king of the Danunians, made

---

[32] For the various views concerning the identification of the *geber*, see House, *Lamentations*, 405–6. Berlin, *Lamentations*, 84, observes that few nowadays attempt to identify the speaker of Lamentations 3 with a historical figure like Jeremiah or Jehoiachin. Such attempts inevitably lead to failure (Mintz, *Hurban: Responses to Catastrophe in Hebrew Literature*, 32). The poem employs traditional and stereotype language common in the Psalms, which do not yield to strict historical analysis (see Patrick D. Miller, Jr. "Trouble and Woe: Interpreting the Biblical Laments." *Int* 37 [1983]: 32–45). Here I follow the position of Hillers, 122 (cf. Dobbs-Allsopp, 106, 109), who interprets the 'I' as a representative of "Everyman".

[33] O'Connor, "The Book of Lamentations: Introduction, Commentary and Reflections", 1046.

powerful'…)".[34] Building on this insight Berlin points out that if it is
true that "the beginning of chapter 3 is imitating an accepted literary convention, then that convention has been turned on its head, for
instead of self-glorification, we find self-abasement".[35] What appeared
to be a statement expressing confidence turns out to be an expression
of despair and dark lament.

So dark is the lament, God is not even mentioned at the beginning
of the poem.[36] Dobbs-Allsopp remarks, "For a poem that draws so self-
consciously on the individual and communal lament genres from the
Psalms, it is remarkable that no other psalm opens in a way analogous
to Lamentations 3".[37] Even Psalm 22 which is known for its strong
words of accusation against God ("My God, my God, why have you
forsaken me?") nonetheless mentions God and calls to him.[38] By contrast, God is not mentioned until towards the end of the first section
(v. 18).[39] This in no way means that God is not talked about in the first
part of the poem. The context of the previous chapter makes it clear
that the antecedent of the pronominal suffix in "*his* wrath" (1b) is God
(see 2:2). Yet the fact that he is not even named or directly mentioned
betrays an attempt to highlight the absence of God, or more specifically
God's failure to 'see' the suffering of the people. One of the central
petitions in the preceding chapters is for God to *see* (1:9, 11; 2:20).[40]
Yet apparently God does not seem to be doing anything. By claiming
that he is "the man who saw affliction", the *geber* "does what God fails
to do".[41] As indicated in the structural analysis, the word ראה is an
important word in Lamentations 3. The occurrence of the word here
anticipates v. 36 which explicitly states: "the Lord does not see (ראה)".
As mentioned earlier, Dobbs-Allsopp does not explicitly connect v. 1
with v. 36, but I think there is a deliberate play on words between the
two verses. In contrast to the man's claim that he has 'seen' the affliction (1), v. 36 declares, "the Lord does not see (ראה)".

---

[34] Dobbs-Allsopp, *Lamentations*, 108.
[35] Berlin, *Lamentations*, 84.
[36] Individual lament psalms usually start with an invocation.
[37] Dobbs-Allsopp, *Lamentations*, 108.
[38] Ibid., 110.
[39] Ibid.
[40] For a discussion of the petition using the verb 'to see' in Lamentations see Heath
Thomas, "Aesthetic Theory of Umberto Eco and Lamentations" (paper delivered at
the SBL meeting; Edinburgh, 2006).
[41] Dobbs-Allsopp, *Lamentations*, 110–11.

8.3.1.2   'Anti-Psalm 23'

The employment of the word 'rod' in v. 1b signals the shift to the use
of shepherd imagery which dominates the initial part of the first section.[42] The poet employs shepherd language to explore his experience
of suffering and despair. The verses talk about guiding, leading (2),
encompassing/surrounding someone (5), causing someone to lie down
(6), setting up walls around (7, 9)—words which depict the protective
and caring role of a shepherd. But in contrast to the good shepherd
that we know from Psalm 23,[43] the shepherd in Lamentations 3 leads
and guides *not* towards "quiet waters and green pastures" but to dark
places where there is no light (2, cf. v. 6). He surrounds and encom-
passes *not* with his presence but with "bitterness and hardship" (5). The
setting up of walls around is not for the purpose of building sheepfolds
to protect the sheep,[44] but to imprison the *geber* so that he will not be
able to escape (7). Instead of leading and guiding, this shepherd blocks
the way, makes the paths crooked (9; cf. 11). Instead of protecting the
sheep from wild animals God himself becomes the bear, the lion in
hiding (10). The sheep becomes the target (12–13). Hillers is certainly
correct in calling the main theme of these verses as the "reversal of
the Twenty-third Psalm".[45]

8.3.1.3   'Pro-Psalm 88'

Interestingly, whilst these verses are 'anti-Psalm 23', the outlook is
'pro-Psalm 88'. Berlin is of the opinion that "Psalm 88 provides an
especially useful background for interpreting this section of Lamentations, for the two texts share not only the same general picture but also
a number of the same phrases".[46] The word חשך occurs twice in the
opening verses of Lamentations 3 (vv. 2 and 6). The word also occurs

---

[42] Hillers, 125, Provan, 85, and Berlin, 86 all see an employment of shepherd language in the initial verses of the chapter.

[43] It should be noted that the verbal contact with Psalm 23 is more thematic rather
than direct.

[44] The nominal form (גדרה) of the verb גדר, used in vv. 7 and 9, has the meaning
"sheepfold" (Holladay, 57).

[45] Hillers, 124; cf. Berlin, 86.

[46] Berlin, 89.

twice in Psalm 88 (vv. 7 and 19).[47] This psalm is so dark it actually
ends with the word מחשך (19). The exact phrase, "in darkness" (lit.
"in dark places"; Lam 3:6) occurs in Ps 88:7. What is significant about
this psalm, which Berlin did not mention, is that it does not move into
the element of praise; the psalm is pure lament.

In addition to Psalm 88, let me draw attention to another psalm,
relevant to the first section in Lamentations 3—Psalm 143. In this psalm
the entire Lam 3:6 appears with a small variation which is probably
due to the employment of the acrostic:

Lam 3:6—במחשכים הושיבני כמתי עולם
Ps 143:3—הושיבני במחשכים כמתי עולם

Interestingly, Psalm 143 is another psalm that lacks any resolution.
Scholars generally see a movement from lament to praise in the Psalter
as a whole. According to them, there are more laments at the beginning but these eventually recede to the background until all we have is
praise. Yet it is noteworthy that we have, even in the last portion of the
last book of the Psalter, a psalm which does not contain a movement to
praise; in fact, a lament which remains a lament until the end. Psalm
143 ends with a series of pleas for God to act on behalf of the psalmist.[48]
I think it is not a coincidence that the word 'steadfast love' features
prominently in the psalm (see vv. 8 and 12). The words 'morning' and
'steadfast love' are linked together as they are in Lam 3:22–23.

As can be observed, there appears to be an attempt to link Lamentations 3 with psalms which do not have any resolution in them. Could it
be that Lamentations 3 is actually commenting on Psalms 88 and 143?
This is possible in view of the verbal and thematic correspondences
between the passages but we cannot be certain.[49] What is clear though
is that the two psalms provide a helpful background for what we find
in Lamentations 3. From the allusions to psalms which end with the

---

[47] Cf. Berlin, 89, who observes other phrases found in both Lamentations 3 and
Psalm 88: "the soul/life being deprived" (Lam 3:17; Ps 88:15), "forgetting" (Lam 3:17;
Ps 88:13), "the deepest cistern" (Lam 3:55; Ps 88:7).

[48] The ESV translates the last verse not as petitions but as statements of confidence
that God will act on behalf of the psalmist. But most translations render v. 12 as
imperatives. The context of v. 11 supports the latter reading.

[49] Where Lamentations 3 differs from Psalms 88 and 143 is in its movement to the
element of praise and subsequent return to lament (see below).

element of lament it should not be surprising to find Lamentations 3 also lacking any resolution even at its last verse.

8.3.1.4 *Lowest point*

In addition to the shepherd imagery and allusions to Psalms 88 and 143, the poet also uses physical and social aspects of experience as a means of exploring the depths of his suffering. In vv. 4 and 16 he describes his suffering in terms of physical affliction such as the "breaking of bones" (4) and "crushing of teeth" (16). In v. 14 he laments about his experience of taunting, becoming a laughingstock among the people—an experience which is extremely difficult for people who place so much value on saving face and community or group.[50] No wonder the poet confesses, "my soul is bereft of shalom" (17a). In contrast to the psalmist who declares that "surely goodness (טוב) and mercy will follow me all the days of my life" (Ps 23:6), the poet sighs, "I have forgotten what happiness (טוב) is" (Lam 3:17b). And by the time he reaches v. 18 he is at the lowest point of his despair.[51] He speaks again in the first person, recalling v. 1. In my analysis, however, I observe that in Lamentations 3 the first person verb אמר is indicative that the speaker has reached rock bottom. Twice in the chapter, when the poet utters the words, "I say" (18a, 54b) he is at the lowest possible state of his situation. Yet it is remarkable that it is precisely at the lowest point of his suffering that he mentions the name Yhwh (see 18b). This marks a development in the poem, which prepares the way for the change of mood in vv. 21ff. The noun 'hope' (18b) is connected structurally to v. 21.[52] That there is a clear movement towards hope is undeniable in vv. 22–24. But that would have to wait a little more. For two more verses (19–20), the poet lingers in the depths, further exploring the anguish of his soul.

Verses 19–20 are a challenge for translation and interpretation.[53] The first word of v. 19 could be translated as an imperative ("remember") or

---

[50] I have in mind here the concept of shame which is very strong in communities like that of Israel in OT times.

[51] Provan, *Lamentations*, 90, comments concerning v. 18: "This is perhaps the lowest point of the whole poem. The catalogue of suffering which the narrator has endured has so taken its toll that even the hope which might make it tolerable seems to have deserted him. He is a man in the deepest despair".

[52] V. 21 employs the verbal form of the word 'hope'.

[53] Provan, 90.

as an infinitive construct ("the remembrance of").[54] If the former, the verse indicates a change from lament to a direct petition—"remember my affliction…" The problem with this view is that we would have to translate v. 20 as an imperative as well, which is unlikely because of the presence of a subject at the end of the verse (נפשי), which functions as the subject for the verbs in v. 20. It is more likely that that v. 20 is a continuation of the poet's expression of distress: he does not forget his affliction but remembers it very well. The temptation is to look into vv. 19–20 for signs of a movement upwards which would somehow facilitate the sudden change of mood in v. 21. Rendering vv. 19–20 as petitions would somehow explain the change of mood in v. 21. But I think it is better to translate the first word of v. 19 as an infinitive construct and interpret vv. 19–20 as still part of the expressions of despair. The text does not signify *how* the transition occurs or what caused it; it simply tells us that a transition has occurred. This feature is not uncommon in the individual psalms of lament (e.g. Ps 13:5, 6; 22:22, 23). In Psalm 13, for instance, when the psalmist has reached his nadir as indicated by the thought of the enemy triumphing over him (5), it is at that point where the way towards trust opens up and he is able to declare, "But I trust in your steadfast love" (6). Similarly, when the poet reaches the depths of his despair, that is also the point where he is able to say, "But this I call to mind, therefore I have hope" (Lam 3:21). I have inserted the adversative at the beginning of the verse because the change of mood that follows calls for it; there is here what O'Connor calls a "sudden emotional reversal".[55]

8.3.1.5   *Sudden change of mood from despair to hope*

The "emotional reversal" is evident in vv. 21–24. In contrast to his earlier cry of despair ("all that I had hoped for from Yhwh has perished" [18]),[56] the poet now proclaims, "I have hope" (21b). In response to the "I say" (אמר) of v. 18a ("I say, my strength is perished"), which expresses a deep sense of hopelessness, v. 24 declares, "my soul says (אמר), 'Yhwh is my portion'; therefore I have hope". The repetition of the words על־כן אוחיל in vv. 21b and 24b marks vv. 21–24 as an

---

[54] Ibid., 90–91.
[55] O'Connor, *The Book of Lamentations*, 1051.
[56] Cf. NIV; lit. "…my hope from Yhwh has perished".

enclosed unit. The basis of his hope is given in vv. 22–23. These verses declare God's steadfast love, mercy and faithfulness. Heim believes that "these verses may be fragments of an unknown hymnic composition".[57] Westermann writes: "These sentences correspond to the motif of praising the goodness of God as found in the psalms of praise".[58]

There is no doubt of the genuineness of these verses as expressions of confidence, hope and even of praise.[59] On the other hand, there are also hints in the passage that we have another element present. The words steadfast love and faithfulness do also appear in psalms of lament.[60] Berlin cites Psalm 88, which, as already shown above, has affinities with Lamentations 3. The words חסד and אמונה appear in Ps 88:12–13.[61] In addition, Dobbs-Allsopp draws a very important connection between Lamentations 3 and the psalm that comes after Psalm 88—Psalm 89. He observes that the "references to 'steadfast love,' 'mercies,' and 'faithfulness' in 3:22–23 allude to God's covenant loyalties as stipulated according to the Davidic grant", expressed in Psalm 89 among other OT texts.[62] The Davidic covenant is unconditional and promissory in nature. "It is this overt promissory aspect of the Davidic covenant that renders the man's hope more than a simple affirmation of confidence in God. By specifically grounding hope in the promises made to David, the man lays claim to those promises and places the onus on God to live up to God's covenantal obligations".[63] Most importantly, as Dobbs-Allsopp later points out, the shift back to the communal lament later in Lamentations 3 (vv. 42ff.) is comparable to the change from hymnic praise to lament in Psalm 89 (see below). Thus, it appears that the affirmations in vv. 21–23 are not tension-free after all.

---

[57] Heim, "The Personification of Jerusalem and the Drama of Her Bereavement in Lamentations", 157.
[58] Westermann, *Die Klagelieder*, 145, ET *Lamentations*, 173.
[59] Provan, 93.
[60] Berlin, 93.
[61] Ibid. Cf. the comparison between Psalm 143 and Lamentations 3 above.
[62] Dobbs-Allsopp, *Lamentations*, 118.
[63] Ibid., 119.

8.3.2   *Tension in the Tradition (25–39)*

8.3.2.1   *Proper response to suffering: quiet submission (25–33)*

Following the affirmations, we hear voices from the wisdom tradition. Verses 25–27 all begin not only with the same letter but with the same word—טוֹב. Verse 25 teaches that Yhwh is good to the one who hopes in him and waits for him. Therefore the ideal posture, even in suffering, is silent waiting and submission (26–27). The word גבר reoccurs in v. 27 recalling and contrasting with v. 1. In v. 1 the *geber* moans in agony, his words with a tint of complaint: "I am the *geber* who has seen affliction". In contrast, v. 27 simply endorses carrying one's yoke (= suffering). There is an implicit rebuke in the latter for the *geber*'s earlier complaint. The rebuke becomes more explicit in v. 39 where גבר appears for the last time. Here the poet argues, "Why should the...*geber* complain...?" Instead of complaining because of his suffering the *geber* should "sit alone in silence" (28a), "put his mouth in the dust" (29; probably a posture of extreme humility), allow others to smite him, becoming satisfied with reproach (30). Then in vv. 31–33 the speaker lays down the basis for his instructions: Yhwh does not reject forever (31); if he afflicts, he will also have compassion (32); he does not "afflict from the heart" (33).

Intriguingly, in spite of all the instructions for submissive suffering and positive statements about God, one can sense in the very construction of the verses and the employment of words an attempt to contradict the very counsel and admonitions being put forward.[64] This is true especially when seen in the light of the context of the whole chapter and the book of Lamentations as a whole. First, as mentioned above, the repetition of the word גבר (27a) creates a tension with the lament in the first section. The *geber* laments (1–20) but is also advised to bear the pain (27) and not to complain (39). The "bearing of the yoke" (27b) which is viewed as having some kind of value for discipline is elsewhere regarded as a "symbol of suffering" (1:114b and 5:5).[65] The usage of

---

[64] Dobbs-Allsopp, *Lamentations*, 105–6, observes: "Many of the individual sentiments expressed throughout this section contradict or conflict with the sentiments and ideas expressed elsewhere in Lamentations. These correspondences are intentional. They force the reader to measure and compare traditional attitudes and dispositions with the suffered reality that comprises the fabric of these poems".

[65] Ibid., 122.

the word בדד (28) contrasts with 1:1. As Dobbs-Allsopp comments, "In the latter, Zion's 'aloneness' is due to abandonment and she is anything but silent".[66] Verse 29 blurs the otherwise confident assertions of hope in vv. 21–24 with its statement, "perhaps there is hope".[67] Hillers cites Luther, who in his translation of v. 29, removes the word 'perhaps', finding it "too fainted-hearted for properly robust faith".[68] But the text as it stands expresses just that: a hesitant confidence. The word שבע (30) recalls the *geber*'s complaint that God has "filled (שבע) me with bitterness" (15). Overall, the verses in the present section reflect tension between the wisdom traditions and present experience of suffering. The poet's denial that God "will reject forever" is directly contradicted in 2:7a (cf. 5:20, 22).[69] "The claim that if God causes suffering he will eventually have compassion (3:32) is refuted in four separate places: 'killing without pity' (3:43), 'the Lord has destroyed without mercy' (2:2a), 'he has demolished without pity' (2:7b), and 'slaughtering without mercy' (2:21c)".[70]

8.3.2.2   *A Job-like Objection: "Yhwh does not see" (34–36)*

The verses that follow (34–36) have proved to be a challenge among commentators and translators. The difficulty is due to the fact that we have here a series of infinitival clauses with the main verb showing up only in v. 36b. The difficulty might have arisen because of the employ-ment of the acrostic which necessitated that each line starts with a ל. Most modern versions translate the verses as one long sentence with the main clause in v. 36b. They either render the main clause as a statement (RSV, NASB, ESV) or a rhetorical question (NRSV, NIV, NJB).[71] I think the key issue here is whether vv. 34–36 affirms *or* objects to the positive statements about God in the preceding verses (31–33). The majority of versions referred to above—whether they translate v.

---

[66] Ibid., 121.

[67] Hans Gottlieb, *A Study on the Text of Lamentations* (trans. John Sturdy; Acta Jutlandica 48; Theology Series 12; Århus: Det laerde Selskab, 1978), 50.

[68] Hillers, 129.

[69] Dobbs-Allsopp, *Lamentations*, 121.

[70] Ibid.

[71] NJPS differs in subordinating v. 34 to the preceding verse ("For He does not willfully bring grief or affliction to man [33], crushing under His feet all the prison-ers of the earth" [34]) leaving only vv. 35 and 36a as the subject clause of the main verb in v. 36b.

36b as a statement or a rhetorical question—support the former: they all interpret vv. 34–36 as positive affirmations about God's compassionate dealing with his people. Interestingly, when v. 36b is translated as a rhetorical question the verb ראה is rendered as "to see" (e.g. "does the Lord not see it?" [NRSV; cf. NJB]). But when it is translated as a statement, the versions deviate from the normal sense of the verb. RSV and ESV have "approve" for ראה; NJPS has "choose".[72] Clearly their interpretation of the verses as positive statements about God necessitated the need for a more 'suitable' sense for ראה: the translation "the Lord does not see" would not make sense if the verses are viewed as affirmations of the previous verses.

Both ways of translating the verses—as a rhetorical question and as a statement—encounter a number of problems. First of all, the construction of a sentence with a series of infinitival clause as a subject of a verb makes a rather awkward reading.[73] The various suggestions for the translation of ראה do not find support from the usage of the Hebrew word in the OT.[74] An alternative way of reading vv. 34–36 is to view these verses as objections to vv. 31–33. The context of the following verses (37–39) supports this interpretation. As Provan explains, "vv. 37–39 seem to be the response to an *objection* to the narrator's speech".[75] He follows Rudolph who sees vv. 34–36 as an objection to the affirmations of the preceding verses.[76] Rudolph explains that these verses represent the viewpoint of the people who have been experiencing extreme suffering. He understands the phrase "prisoners of the land" (34) as a reference to those who have been captured by the Chaldeans, extending the subject of v. 34 to vv. 35 and 36. Accordingly, the assertions of vv. 31–33 do not fit in with the people's experience; the people do not see the reality of the affirmations in their actual experience. What made the people more defiant was that all of their sufferings have taken place "before the face of the Most High" (35b; cf. 34a: "under *his* foot"). The fact that the event occurred with God perfectly aware

---

[72] Hans Gottlieb, *A Study on the Text of Lamentations*, 49, cites other translations of the verb: "find correct", "intend", "want".

[73] Reyburn, *A Handbook on Lamentations*, 91; cf. Hillers, 116.

[74] Cf. Gottlieb, *A Study on the Text of Lamentations*, 49, finds a problem with the translation "approve", arguing that the verb "does not elsewhere have this sense in Biblical Hebrew". He also finds problems with the other suggestions (e.g. the translations "intend" and "want").

[75] Provan, *Lamentations*, 97.

[76] For the summary of Rudolph's view that follows, see Rudolph, 241.

of it makes the objection all the more striking: in spite of all that has happened Yhwh's eyes remained 'closed'. Thus, their lament: "Yhwh does not *see*"; he is not concerned and did not do anything.

Although we may not agree with Rudolph's historical reconstruction here, the advantage of taking vv. 34–36 as an objection to the preceding context is that it preserves the sense of the word ראה reflected in the context of chapter 3 as well as in the whole book. There would be no need to alter the sense of the word in order to make it sound more positive. A straightforward translation of v. 36b is "the Lord does *not* see". The force of the negation results in the meaning of the word in terms of "not concern" or "not act/do anything".[77] This is better than rendering the sentence as "the Lord does not 'approve' or 'choose' which hardly makes sense of the word ראה with the negation. The statement intimates a very strong accusation against God. The picture is that of a people suffering, crying out to God for him to "look and *see*". But God, from their perspective has not 'seen' their awful fate. Dobbs-Allsopp explains that the language of seeing is normally "predicated only of God in the Old Testament (Exod. 3:7; 4:31; Job 10:15; Pss. 9:13; 31:7) and thus specifically calls attention to the repeated unanswered requests for God to 'see' in Lamentations (esp. 1:9a [op. cit.]) and indeed pointedly if subtly indicts God for this divine lapse".[78] Dobbs-Allsopp makes this comment in connection to v. 1 where the poet claims to have seen affliction, implying a contrast with God who fails to do so. But as noted above, I think his comments apply equally well and even better to vv. 34–36. I would say that v. 36b represents the most explicit accusation of God in terms of the people's perceived failure of God to 'see' their situation. Although there have been petitions for God to "look and *see*" (1:9, 11, 20; 2:20; cf. 5:1) this is the first and the only time that we find a direct accusation of God's failure to 'see'. Translating the word as an affirmation misses the point of the passage. We do not have here a one directional train of thought but a series of convergences coming from opposite directions.

---

[77] For the use of ראה in the sense of 'to show concern' and 'to act/do something', see Gen 29:32 (Holladay, 328). Interestingly, Gen 29:32 combines ראה and עני. In the context the word ראה is used in the sense of 'be concerned with' and implies that God has done something on behalf of the person concerned.

[78] Dobbs-Allsopp, *Lamentations*, 111. I think there is a mistake in his Bible reference; it should be 1:9c, not 1:9a.

Further, as scholars point out, we have in the middle section a 'Job-like' construction.[79] It should not surprise us therefore to find differing perspectives presented alongside each other. As Gottlieb rightly observes even the "strong hope of vv. 21–24 has become in v. 29 a hesitant statement 'perhaps there is hope'".[80] Similarly, the claims of vv. 31–33 have not been left unchallenged. The suffering of the people inevitably led them to see the tension between the claims of vv. 31–33 and their present experience. Drawing on from their lament traditions, they did not become silent but expressed their objections. It is important to point out, however, that their objection is not simply a 'voice in the wilderness', but represents the general sentiment not only of the whole chapter but also of the whole book. It is here that I differ from Rudolph. He sees the overall direction of the chapter towards thanksgiving and the main emphasis on hope.[81] Thus the objection represents only a minority view within chapter 3. But as the remaining sections of the chapter will show, the overall emphasis supports the objections of vv. 34–36 rather than the affirmations of vv. 31–33 and the rebuke of vv. 37–39.

8.3.3   *Return to Lament (40–51)*

8.3.3.1   *From Confession to Accusation*

Verses 40–41 form a conclusion to the preceding verses and transition to the section that follows. It supports the previous statements in vv. 37–39. Speaking in the plural form for the first time the poet calls for repentance and confession of sins (40–41): instead of complaining (39) they are to consider their ways and turn to Yhwh (40). The call for repentance is immediately followed by a positive response in the form of confession of sin: "We have transgressed and rebelled" (v. 42a). These words represent the spirit of the prayers of confession expressed in Ezra 9, Nehemiah 9 and Daniel 9. In these passages the prayer of repentance is characterised by admission of guilt (e.g. Dan 9:5) similar to what we find in Lam 3:42. The prayer in Daniel 9 is particularly relevant for the present passage because of the occurrence of the word

---

[79] See discussions above (Structural Analysis).
[80] Gottlieb, 50.
[81] Rudolph, 243, sees the last part of the chapter as a thanksgiving psalm (vv. 52–66).

סלח ("forgive") which also appears in Lam 3:42.[82] Daniel 9 moves from confession of sins (5–15) to petitions, most relevant of which is the petition for forgiveness: "O Lord, forgive" (סלח) (19). In stark contrast to Daniel 9, the confession of sin in Lam 3:42 is followed with the words "you have not forgiven" (42b). Instead of moving from confession to a petition for forgiveness, Lam 3:42 moves from confession to accusation: "but you have not forgiven" (42b).[83] We have here a negation which is even stronger than the one in v. 36b ("the Lord does *not* see"), for here we have a direct address to God.

It is of great consequence that we should pay close attention to the shift in v. 42. Scholars who see (or wish to see) a more hopeful emphasis in Lamentations 3 try to 'soften' the language of this verse. Rudolph follows Luther's translation of v. 42b: "Darum hast du *billig* nicht verschonet".[84] The problem with this is that it gives a rather 'flat' explanation to a more complicated and subtle construction, not to mention the absence of waw in v. 42. The two cola are simply juxtaposed. Naegelsbach's translation aptly represents the Hebrew text through his use of a colon between the two cola: "We have transgressed and have rebelled: thou hast not pardoned".[85] Another problem with Rudolph's translation is that the complexity and tension is explained or ironed out through the doctrine of divine retribution. He explains: "Solange das Volk nur klagte und seine Schuld nicht sehen wollte, musste Jahwe seinen Zorn walten lassen".[86] Similarly, House does not see any incongruity between the two cola in v. 42. He translates v. 42b as 'indeed, you have not forgiven'.[87] In his interpretation, it is the people's acceptance of the consequences of their actions that is highlighted not their accusation of God. House does not agree with Berlin who sees here a crisis of theology in that the expected outcome of repentance is rejected. House reasons that acknowledgment of sin does not automatically mean that the people had actually repented. He cites the case in Jeremiah (Jer

---

[82] In view of the prominence of this word in today's prayers of repentance in church worship, it is surprising that the word 'forgive' does not occur in the other two prayers of confession (Ezra 9 and Nehemiah 9). The petition for forgiveness occurs only in Dan 9:19. For further discussions see Federico Villanueva, "Confession of Sins or Petition for Forgiveness: A Study of the Nature of the Prayers in Nehemiah 1, 9, Daniel 9 and Ezra 9" (ThM thesis; Asia Graduate School of Theology, Philippines, 2002).

[83] I have added the adversative because the context requires it (see further below).

[84] Rudolph, 242.

[85] Naegelsbach, "The Lamentations of Jeremiah", 124.

[86] Rudolph, 242.

[87] House, 421.

15:1–9) where even though the prophet may have already confessed his sin and the people's sin, the Lord had to rebuke him in the form of a call to repentance.[88] House's interpretation implies that the people had not yet properly repented. He sees vv. 42ff. simply as the speaker's *report* about "how things have been as he delivers the early part of his prayer".[89] His explanation is similar to Heim's interpretation who understands v. 42b as a *"description* of how the Lord has afflicted the community".[90] But v. 42 is not simply a "report" or a "description" of how things are; the accusatory nature of the construction of v. 42 and the context of the whole section of which the verse is a part (40–51) clearly indicate that we have here a direct attack against God.[91] The personal pronouns ("we" and "you") in the two cola are emphatic.[92] Dobbs-Allsopp explains: "The adversative sense is communicated through the contrasting or antithetical use of the pronouns *naḥnû* 'we' and *'attâ* 'you', and underscored by the contrast between the positive confession and the negative framing of Yhwh's action".[93] We have here a sudden change of mood. But unlike the shift in the first section which is from despair to hope, the transition here is from hope to lament. We have here a *return* to lament after the expressions of hope in vv. 21–24.[94] What makes the transition conspicuous is that it follows the positive admonitions of the preceding verses. Based on the concluding verse of the preceding section (39) and the call for repentance (40–41) it is just normal for us to expect an 'improvement' from this point on. As Westermann comments on v. 39: "Here, in a concluding admonition based upon the preceding explanation, further lamentation is disallowed".[95] Yet in spite of the instruction that complaining should cease (39); indeed,

---

[88] House, 421–22.

[89] Ibid., 422.

[90] Heim, "The Personification of Jerusalem", 161, emphasis mine.

[91] Westermann, *Die Klagelieder*, 152, ET *Lamentations*, 182, rightly understands v. 42b as the people's "accusation against God".

[92] Naegelsbach, 124; cf. Lee, *The Singers of Lamentations*, 176. Lee, who sees different speakers/singers in Lamentations 3, sees a transition from the second speaker to the third in v. 42. Here Jerusalem's poet responds to the second speaker. Ignoring the "previous singer's advice to keep silent… [s]he turns the previous singer's meek cohortative, 'let us,' into an emphatic, confessional 'we' and an accusing 'you' against YHWH".

[93] F. W. Dobbs-Allsopp, "Tragedy, Tradition, and Theology in the Book of Lamentations", 37.

[94] Whilst Provan, *Lamentations*, 93, recognises the transition from despair to hope in vv. 19–20 and 21–24, he does not mention that we have a return to the element of lament in vv. 42ff. Most scholars do not see the significance of the return to lament here.

[95] Westermann, *Die Klagelieder*, 150, ET *Lamentations*, 179.

even right after the call to repentance and the actual confession of sins, the people complained anyway, their laments growing ever stronger. In v. 42b, we have a sudden change of mood from *hope to lament*. The shift is analogous to Psalm 12 where in spite of the divine response, the affirmations nonetheless returns to lament.

8.3.3.2 *Function of the Hymnic affirmation*

On this return to lament Dobbs-Allsopp makes a very important point. He compares the shift to lament here with the similar transition in Psalm 89: "The section's opening 'But now you' (Ps 89:38) is analogous to the 'but you' in 3:42".[96] Earlier he has drawn attention to the similarity between the language used in Lam 3:22–24 and Ps 89. Here he rightly observes the important similarity in terms of the movement from the element of praise to lament which is found in both passages. This confirms my thesis of the movement from praise to lament which I highlighted in the Psalms. According to Dobbs-Allsopp this feature is not limited to Lamentations 3 but can also be found in the Psalms. He states: "The kind of jarring juxtaposition of hymnic affirmation of God's goodness and the bleak and hurtful reality of historical experience found here in Lamentations 3 is not unique. It appears in other poetic compositions of the Bible as well, especially in the Psalms".[97] Elsewhere Dobbs-Allsopp also makes a similar point to the one I made in my analysis of Jeremiah 20. There, I argued that the element of praise is introduced to highlight the lament.[98] Similarly, for Dobbs-Allsopp the hymnic affirmation in Lamentations 3 actually strengthens the element of lament. Commenting on Lam 3:42, Dobbs-Allsopp writes: "The reality of the situation breaks in and the poet returns once again to complaint and the description of suffering. Hope is never heard from again. The ethical vision is swallowed up by human suffering; it is

---

[96] Dobbs-Allsopp, *Lamentations*, 124.

[97] Ibid. Although he notes the presence of similar movements in the Psalms, however, he only mentions Psalm 89 as an example. My study of Psalms 9/10, 27 and 40 supports Dobbs-Allsopp's statement. As demonstrated in my analysis of these psalms, the element of praise and lament are juxtaposed in a manner comparable to what we find in Psalm 89 and Lamentations 3; though it should be noted that the construction in Lamentations 3 is more complex.

[98] See analysis of Jeremiah 20 in the previous chapter.

unable to contain it. Note, however, that *the tragic point is only made in light of the truth and the appeal of the ethical vision*".[99]

8.3.3.3   *Communal Lament*

Indeed, the movement from the hymnic affirmations in vv. 22–24 and the positive assertions about God in vv. 31–33 to lament can hardly be overemphasized in Lamentations 3. The complaint in vv. 43–44 recalls the lament in the first section. As pointed out earlier, in the first section the poet talks about God encompassing him (5), putting walls around him so he could not escape (7). Here the people complain that God has covered himself "with anger" (43). It is as if God wants to make sure no contact transpires between the two parties, covering both the people and himself. If the poet had earlier complained that God "shuts out my prayer (תפלה)" (8), here the people accuse God of covering himself with a cloud so that no prayer (תפלה) can pass through (44). The word תפלה occurs only in these two verses in the whole of Lamentations. Although there is a shift from individual lament to communal lament the language remains similar.

In v. 48 the poem returns to the first person singular. Although there is a change in voice, however, vv. 48–51 continues the communal lament. The 'I' at this point has reached the status of communal voice; the 'I' is no longer the 'I' of an individual but one who speaks the voice of the community. The significance of the shift to the singular is that the expression of suffering becomes personal. Ewald's comment on the use of the first person singular in chapter 3 is worth quoting here: "Then, suddenly, in the third place, an individual man appears! After all, an individual is able really to lament most deeply what he has experienced personally. The result is an expression of despair—the third, but this is the deepest".[100] This comment can be applied to the shift to the first person singular in v. 48. One can sense an intensification in this verse, as the poet speaks of the destruction of Jerusalem. His eyes flowing like rivers (48), he proclaims that he will not rest "…until Yhwh from

---

[99] Dobbs-Allsopp, "Tragedy, Tradition, and Theology in the Book of Lamentations", 48–9, emphasis mine. This is his comment on v. 42.

[100] Ewald, cited in Hillers, *Lamentations*, 123. Cf. Dobbs-Allsopp, "Tragedy, Tradition, and Theology in the Book of Lamentations", 40: "by embodying the community in the guise of the personified city and the *geber* the poet is able to personalize the suffering in a way that would be unavailable in a more objectively descriptive mode".

heaven looks and *sees*" (50). In my view, this wish represents the central concern of the whole chapter. As noted earlier the word ראה is a very important key word in the chapter. Having made the contrast between the *geber* who "saw" his affliction and Yhwh who has not "seen" (v. 36) the people's suffering, the poet continues to hold on: he will not stop until Yhwh 'sees' their situation.

8.3.4 *Tension between Past and Present Experience (52–66)*

Right next to the impassioned wish for Yhwh to "see" his suffering, the poem moves to an individual's recollection of his experience of deliverance (52–55). The linguistic link and flow of ideas in these verses connect them together.[101] The poet describes his experience of being hunted as a bird by his enemy (52). They have intended to kill him by hurling him into the pit (בור), throwing stones at him (53). The word בור is repeated in v. 55 where the poet narrates how he called from the depths of the pit. In between these two verses the first person verb אמר shows up. As mentioned earlier this verbal form signifies that the speaker has reached the lowest point of his suffering similar to what we saw in v. 18. Interestingly, as in v. 18, it is also at the lowest point of his experience that the way up is opened. For from the 'pit' the poet calls to Yhwh and there testifies that his prayer has been answered: "you have heard my voice" (56a).

Up to this point the text is pretty straightforward. But then comes the imperative in 56b: "do not close your ear..." Suddenly, we are transported into the realm of the present. Most modern versions take 56b as the content of the prayer implied in 56a. RSV translates the verse as, "you heard my plea, 'Do not close your ear to my cry for help, but give me relief!'" (cf. NASB, ESV, NIV). But this construction is rather unusual, if not unheard of, in Hebrew sentence structure. One of the main issues in the discussion of these verses and of the whole of the last section (52–66) is whether we have here only one situation or two, past or present experience?[102] Rudolph and Provan think the verses refer only to one situation of distress. The difference

---

[101] Cf. Heim, 161–2.

[102] Provan, "Past, Present and Future in Lamentations 3:52–66: The Case for a Precative Perfect Re-Examined", *VT* 41 (1991), 168.

is that whereas Rudolph understands the situation to be about a past distress which has already been resolved, Provan thinks the verses are all about present distress.

For Rudolph the main purpose of chapter 3 is to encourage the people in their suffering. One way of doing it is by recalling past experience of divine deliverance. In vv. 52ff. we find just that.[103] The difficulty is with the verses that follow (59–66) which are petitions. In order to sustain his thesis, Rudolph would have to view these verses not as petitions but as a continuation of the preceding verses, declaring what Yhwh has done in the past. These verses would have to be a part of the thanksgiving psalm that commenced in v. 52. Rudolph feels that to do otherwise, to interpret the verbs as precative verbs or as petitions would weaken the goal of the chapter. If after declaring his experience of deliverance 'Jeremiah' would again cry out to God for help, the prayer of thanksgiving would not make sense.[104] Rudolph avers: "Ein Bittgebet hätte hinter dem Danklied nur Sinn".[105] He therefore asserts that the last verses are not petitions but as "Fortsetzung des Dankliedes".[106] He explains that the employment of the acrostic was responsible for the changing of the verbs in vv. 64–66 into the imperfect.[107] This is the second instance where I observe that the acrostic is blamed for the movement back to the element of lament.[108] The first was in Psalm 9/10 where Gunkel explains that the shift to lament in 10:1 is due to the letter ל of the acrostic. But certainly it is not uncommon for a thanksgiving or praise to move back to petitions or lament as my analysis of Psalms 9/10, 27 and 40 (cf. Psalm 12) has tried to demonstrate. Again one can discern here the form-critical view of the movement between lament and praise, a view which tends to enforce a rather narrow perspective on the text. Joyce's comment is apt: "All too often biblical criticism has been hampered by the unrealistic assumption that people react to events with a single consistent emotion or opinion".[109]

---

[103] Rudolph, 236.

[104] Ibid.

[105] Ibid.

[106] Ibid., 236–7.

[107] Ibid., 237. He observes the same in 2:22.

[108] That the acrostic can have an effect in the way in which Lamentations 3 was composed may be illustrated in vv. 34–36. But to apply the same in the case of vv. 64–66 on the supposition that the passage should end in a positive note is a rather weak argument.

[109] Paul Joyce, "Lamentations and the Grief Process: A Psychological Reading", *Biblical Interpretation* 1 (1993), 313.

From Provan's view Rudolph's direction is correct; it is the timing that is wrong. According to him, the text is not about past distress but about a present one. Verses 52–66 pertain to the present experience of distress.[110] He interprets the last verses (64–66) as a "plea for future action".[111] He proposes that we read the perfect verbs in vv. 52–66 as precative. Provan is careful to distinguish between a prophetic perfect and a precative perfect.[112] The former signifies a sense of resolution; the latter pertains to the present situation. His proposal certainly makes the reading of vv. 52–66 more straightforward, albeit an unlikely proposal for those who wish a more positive ending for the poem. However, we need to be careful not to fall into the same trap as Rudolph did by going to the other extreme. I find Provan's proposal too straightforward, eliminating the element of tension which is characteristic not only of the present section but as we have seen of the whole chapter as well. His argument against Zenner and Wiesmann, who both argue that we read the perfects as past action, is revealing. He says that one implication of their view is that on the one hand God has already acted, but on the other hand he is still being asked to do something: "The passage then tells us that though the poet has asked for God's help, and God has initiated such help (vv. 52–62), deliverance has not yet occurred (vv. 63–66)...We now have a passage in which God is said not only to have heard and spoken, but also to have acted already, and yet in which deliverance is still in the future".[113] In Provan's reading such tension is ironed out, since we are only dealing with the present situation. But it is possible that the text is designed in order to express this element of tension. Similar to the 'tension in time' that we find in Psalm 31, my analysis of the structure of Lam 3:55–60 intimates the intertwining of past experience of deliverance and present need for divine action:

What Yhwh has done in the past (55–56a)
    Prayer that Yhwh act in the present: "Do not cover your ears…" (56b)
What Yhwh has done in the past (57)

---

[110] Provan, *Lamentations*, 83, 103. See his article, "Past, Present and Future in Lamentations 3:52–66", for a fuller discussion of his view. His view is followed by Berlin, *Lamentations*, 97; cf. Dobbs-Allsopp, 126.

[111] Provan, "Past, Present and Future in Lamentations 3:52–66", 170.

[112] Ibid., 175. On this point he disagrees with Gottlieb, 173, who uses the two interchangeably reflecting "vacillation of the man praying between trust and hope".

[113] Ibid., 171–72.

What Yhwh has done in the past (58–59a)
   Prayer that Yhwh act in the present: "Judge my cause" (59b)
What Yhwh has done in the past (60)

As can be observed, the petition is enveloped twice by a recollection of what God has done in the past. Verses 55–56a recall how God has responded when the poet cried out to him. In v. 57b, he relates how God drew near to him and told him "do not be afraid". In between these encouraging accounts we hear the cry for help in v. 56b. Similarly, in vv. 58–59a we find a positive declaration of Yhwh's action of deliverance: he has "seen the wrong done to me" (59a). Verse 60 repeats the same word ('to see') and tells how Yhwh has seen "all their vengeance…" Again in between these two positive declarations we find a petition, "Judge my cause!" (59b; cf. 56b). What are we to make of these exchanges? The temptation is to iron out any tension by proposing that we read all the perfect verbs as precative perfects (Provan) or read them as perfect tenses in terms of past actions (Rudolph). The difficulty with the latter is that we have another imperative in v. 63: "See!" The problem with the former is that it lessens the element of tension inherent in the very construction of the structure of the verses. I would therefore follow a translation along the lines of the NEB, which Provan mentions but did not endorse: "thou heardest my voice; do not turn a deaf ear when I cry, 'Come to my relief'" (56).[114] This preserves the element of tension present in the text. More importantly as we have seen in our study of Psalms 31 and 35, the presence of 'tension in time' which we find here is not confined to Lamentations 3.[115] God has already acted and yet he is still being asked to act.

Indeed, even at the end the poet is asking God to do something about his situation. The situation envisaged in the next verses (61–63) points more clearly towards the present. In view of the context of vv. 62–63, the perfect verb in v. 61 may be translated as present: "You hear their reproach".[116] The poet refers to the "lips and musings of those who rise up against him…" (62), in whose resting and rising he

---

[114] Provan, *Lamentations*, 106.
[115] See analysis of Psalms 31 and especially Psalm 35 (Chapter 6).
[116] On the fluidity of the perfect tense, see Diethelm Michel, *Tempora und Satzstellung in den Psalmen* (vol. 1; Abhandlungen zur evangelischen Theologie; Bonn: H. Bouvier u. Co. Verlag, 1960), 79–81.

is the object of their songs of taunts (63), and to which the poet calls for God's attention: "See!" (63a).

The last three verses (64–66) are prayers of imprecation. These verses are similar to the ending of the first chapter (1:21–22). Intimating a deep sense of injustice over the fate that has befallen them, the poet asks God to punish their enemies in the same way that God has done to them. The poet asks that God punish their enemies[117] "according to the work of their hands" (64). The words of v. 65 are rather heavy: the poet asks that God give their enemies a "dullness of heart" and that "your curse" be with them. The last verse alludes to v. 43: As God has "pursued us" (43), so he asks, "pursue [them] in your wrath" (66), recalling the communal lament. Thus, Lamentations 3 ends with the element of lament. Having moved from despair to hope in the first section, the poem nevertheless returns to lament. And even when God's action in the past is recalled in the last section, this becomes an occasion for lament rather than praise. Indeed, the series of imprecations at the end, though they signify an improvement from the earlier laments in the first section and the communal lament,[118] fall short of a proper movement to praise. Lament, not praise remains the main emphasis in Lamentations 3 from beginning to end.

8.4   SUMMARY AND CONCLUSION

Lamentations 3 is a passage akin to the psalms of lament which contain a tension between lament and praise. Like these psalms, the passage moves from despair to hope and returns to the element of lament. Immediately following the hymnic affirmations of vv. 22–24 is a section on wisdom traditions which contains an element of tension between differing perspectives (25–39). This leads in to the communal lament (40–51) which recalls the earlier lament in the first section. The final section (52–66) recalls what Yhwh has done in the past in the light of present experiences of suffering and ends with a series of petitions and imprecations which lack any resolution. We thus have a composition which begins and ends on a note of lament. Even though it contains

---

[117] There is no explicit referent for the "them", but the context implies that this refers to the people's enemies.

[118] This is a positive change from the first section (1–18) which hardly mentions Yhwh in its lament.

a heightening towards the element of praise in the middle (22–24), the poem nevertheless falls back to lament. Like Jer 20:7–13, the element of praise is introduced to highlight the element of lament. Dobbs-Allsopp's comments, drawing attention to the juxtaposition between hymnic affirmations and lament in Lamentations 3 and Psalm 89, support my own analysis of the movement from praise to lament in the Psalms. This shows that the feature is not limited to the Psalter but extends to passages like Jeremiah 20 and now to Lamentations 3.

What makes Lamentations 3 different from the Psalms is how the overall accent falls on lament not only in the third chapter but throughout the whole book.[119] The movement from hope to lament is not confined to Lamentations 3. Close to the movement in Lamentations 3 we have in 4:22 a verse which expresses full assurance that Jerusalem's punishment is over. Yet this verse is immediately followed by the communal lament in chapter 5. Certainty gives way to uncertainty as the people set out to lament (again!) about their sufferings.[120] Within the communal lament itself (chapter 5), we find a hymnic praise in 5:19: "But you, O Yhwh, reign forever, your throne endures from generation to generation". The book as a whole could have ended right here, on this positive note. In this verse, we have "the theme of praise".[121] But the text suddenly moves back to lament; and, as Linafelt comments, "the flicker of praise is extinguished in the final three verses of the chapter".[122] The book thus ends with a strong note of lament (5:20–23).[123]

---

[119] As Provan, *Lamentations*, 22, writes: "[C]hapter 3 is in reality a mixture of hope and despair, and it ends in a plea to God which leaves us balanced on a knife-edge between these two. The reader who reads the chapter to the end does not receive an impression of great hopefulness. Nor is the reader who reads the book to the end left with this impression of the book as a whole. Lamentations does not, after all, end with 3:21–27, but with 5:22; and in spite of many valiant attempts to interpret this verse in a hopeful manner…it cannot plausibly be done".

[120] Cf. the comment of Thomas, "Aesthetic Theory of Umberto Eco and Lamentations", 16: "For the reader, this verse [5:1] jars against 4:22, which preceded it, with its extremely positive statement over the end of Jerusalem's punishment".

[121] Linafelt, *Surviving Lamentations*, 59.

[122] Ibid.

[123] The last verse of the book (5:22) has been much discussed in terms of its 'proper' translation. For various proposals for the translation of the verse, see Robert Gordis, "The Conclusion of the Book of Lamentations (5:22)", *JBL* 93 (1974): 289–91. The difficulty seems to lie with grammatical and syntactical levels, specifically with the problem posed by the first two words of v. 22—כי אם. On a deeper level the issue reflects how one sees the book as a whole. Particularly for Lam 5:22, the decision on the translation of the verse hangs on the issue of whether it makes an 'appropriate' ending or not. Gordis, 289–91, considers as an "inappropriate" conclusion negative

This puts Lamentations 3 in a unique position. For here we have a passage belonging to a book that ultimately ends in lament.[124] Unlike the lament psalms, which although containing a movement from praise to lament nevertheless lead up to praise at the end (Psalm 150), Lamentations 3 belongs to a book which never moves to the "Hallelujahs!" It remains a lament until the end.[125]

When viewed from the perspective of the historical situation out of which the book arose the overall emphasis on lament becomes understandable. There is general agreement among scholars that the historical background behind the composition of the book is the aftermath of the

---

readings such as that of the LXX which deletes the אם ("For you have indeed rejected us") and Hiller's proposal ("But instead you have utterly rejected us, you have been very angry with us"). Gous, "Lamentations 5 and the Translation of Verse 22", *OTE* 3 (1990), 287, follows Gordis' approach: "The translation of Lamentations 5 verse 22 poses a problem to exegetes and translators. This is the case not so much because the words or the construction are obscure; rather, it is a case of what is an appropriate close for the poem". After surveying various proposals, and rejecting them, Gordis (pp. 391–3) suggests we render the difficult phrase, כי אם as "even though". But his suggestion is not without problems. As Provan explains, the position of כי אם "at the beginning of the new line counters Gordis' proposal" (*Lamentations*, 133). Provan, 134, rightly avers, "Whichever rendering is accepted, it is clear... that the poem does not have a confident ending" (cf. Dobbs-Allsopp, *Lamentations*, 149). A translation for 5:22 like that of Linafelt is here endorsed: "For if truly you have rejected us, bitterly raged against us..." (22) (p. 60). This translation preserves the element of tension present in the verse, accounts for the usual sense of כי אם and considers the parallelism between the two cola.

[124] As one scholar remarked, Lamentations is the only book in the OT that does not end on a positive note (the remark was made by John Barton to John Day, who related it to me in a personal conversation). Interestingly, when we compare Lamentations as a whole to related ANE genres like the city laments, Lamentations is decidedly a lament-focused book. In his analysis of Mesopotamian laments, Dobbs-Allsopp, "Tragedy", 32, observes that the twin themes of city laments are divine abandonment and the return of the gods. According to him, Lamentations, in terms of genre, is very similar to the Mesopotamian city laments. But there is one big difference: whereas the Mesopotamian laments end in restoration and in the return of the gods to the temple, we find neither restoration nor the return of God to the temple in the book. He writes: "While there are many differences between Lamentations and the Mesopotamian city laments, a particularly significant and immediately noticeable difference lies precisely in the organizing principle that governs the biblical book. Lamentations does not have a happy ending. In fact, one notes that in place of the twin themes of divine abandonment and the return of the gods, Lamentations is framed by a thematic inclusio involving the divine abandonment theme alone" (ibid., 33).

[125] On a canonical reading, this sets Lamentations 3 apart from the laments in the Psalms. That which we have only in 'miniature' versions in the Psalms is here presented in big strokes and grand scale manner. Could it be that what we have in Lamentations 3 is a well-developed feature of the individual lament psalms which contains a movement from praise to lament?

destruction of Jerusalem.[126] Unfortunately, in spite of the background
of Lamentations, scholars still expected the book to end on a more
positive note. Linafelt observes:

> It is logical to expect that interpretations of the book of Lamentations,
> more than those of any other biblical book, would value the expression
> of pain, if not as a 'condition of truth' then at least as a mode of dis-
> course with merit in and of itself. While this has been the case in the
> history of interpretation of the book (and more specifically the history
> of Jewish interpretation), critical readings in the modern era have almost
> unanimously attempted to tone down, expunge, or belittle the language
> of lament and anguish.[127]

This tendency to interpret the book positively in spite of the clear witness of lament is due in large measure to a lack of a proper understanding of the genre and serious consideration of the context of the poem.
In her book, *Poetic Closure: A Study of How Poems End*, Smith explains
that the determination of the genre of a poem along with its implied
context guide us in determining what constitutes an effective closure
or ending for a poem.[128] Although not specifically about the study of
Biblical poems, her insight is relevant. As shown above, a consideration
of the context of suffering out of which the poem arose assists us in our
interpretation of the text. In addition, a proper understanding of the
genre to which Lamentations 3 belongs assists us in our expectations
as to its appropriate ending. I think the form-critical viewpoint on the
lament psalms has led to the failure to see the significant turns in the
passage. Since individual lament psalms are viewed to have only one

---

[126] Paul M. Joyce, "Sitting Loose to History: Reading the Book of Lamentations
without Primary Reference to its Original Historical Setting", in *In Search of True Wisdom: Essays in Old Testament Interpretation in Honour of Ronald E. Clements* (ed. Edward Ball;
Sheffield: Sheffield Academic Press, 1999), 247, writes that "overwhelmingly the most
common view is that these laments come from the aftermath of the fall of Jerusalem
to the Babylonians in c. 587 B.C.E." (cf. 262). Cf. Dobbs-Allsopp, "Tragedy", 31,
who explains that although Lamentations is not historiography, the situation depicted
in the book portray suffering; "Lamentations...is generally reflective of a disruptive
historical-cultural context".

[127] Linafelt, *Surviving Lamentations*, 2. He cites Brandscheidt and Plöger as examples.
The former writes: "The lament does not concern pain as such; rather, pain is the
backdrop for the recognition of guilt, which is the real issue of a lament" (10). The
latter comments: "In the poem of lament the feature of lamenting, regardless of how
extensive it might be, has no importance in its own right" (11).

[128] Barbara Herrnstein Smith, *Poetic Closure: A Study of How Poems End* (Chicago:
University of Chicago Press, 1968), 18–20. Genre refers to the specific type of literature
to which the poem belongs to. Context refers to the speaker's or audience's situation
envisaged in the poem (20).

movement from lament to praise, the return to lament in Lamentations 3 has not been properly considered. Further, lament psalms are always expected to end on a 'happy' note, resulting in an unrealistic expectation of how a lament ought to end. This is where the psalms which contain a movement from praise to lament become important; they clarify and make us adjust our expectations of Lamentations 3. Understanding Lamentations 3 as a lament which is capable of moving from praise to lament helps us understand the text better.

Another genre under which Lamentations 3 and the book as a whole may fall is the genre of tragedy. The sense of the 'tragic' is implied in the movement, praise to lament as well as in the ending of the book in a lament. Dobbs-Allsopp argues that Lamentations is a tragedy. The five "central ingredients that frequently appear across a wide spectrum of individual tragedies: historical context, trajectory of the organizing pattern, setting, treatment of the problem of evil, and centrality of the tragic hero" can be found in Lamentations.[129] The historical situation surrounding the book as a whole fits in well with this perspective. This may be disturbing for some, especially in the light of the more dominant 'comic' perspective of the biblical literature, but it represents reality as we encounter it. As Exum elucidates:

> The random, the chaotic, the unintelligible, the contingent, are dimensions of reality as we know it, dimensions that the Bible knows also and whose fissures it does not, I have sought to illustrate, try to smooth over. Indeed, the Bible's uncompromising portrayal of reality as embracing dissolution and despair as well as resolution and repair is the source of its extraordinary narrative range and power. Any less expansive, multifaceted, and honest representation of accumulated experience and wisdom would be inadequate and inauthentic.[130]

It is remarkable that Lamentations 3—a poem that is not aimed primarily for encouragement—becomes in the end a source of encouragement through its expressions of pain, agony and suffering engraved in its very words and overall structure. It brings encouragement by embracing the very darkness and struggle which we ourselves have sometimes wished were not there.

---

[129] Dobbs-Allsopp, "Tragedy, Tradition, and Theology", 31–45.
[130] Cheryl J. Exum, *Tragedy and Biblical Narrative* (Cambridge: Cambridge University Press, 1992), 152.

Lamentations 3 therefore provides further evidence for the tension between lament and praise that we find represented in the various movements in the Psalter, particularly those which contain the reverse movement praise to lament and those which return to lament after the movement to praise. Having explored the psalms with the element of the '*un*certainty of a hearing' as well as the two passages outside the Psalter, let us summarise our findings and draw some implications in the following conclusion to the whole study.

CONCLUSION

SUMMARY OF ARGUMENT

Is the sudden change of mood *only* from lament to praise? Do lament psalms *always* move from lament to praise? This has been the main question which the present study has sought to address. As shown in the Introduction (Chapter 1) as well as in the scholarly discussions of the relevant passages, the general assumption has been that lament psalms always move from lament to praise. Although scholars do not explicitly say so, their approach to the subject betrays that their answer to the question is in the affirmative. Influenced by the form-critical framework of a one-way movement from lament to praise, scholars have assumed that the sudden change of mood is only from lament to praise.

This study does not deny that lament does move to praise; the analysis of the psalms which contain this movement affirms this (see Psalms 3, 6, 13 in Chapter 2). But to limit one's understanding of the movement in the lament psalms to this framework does not do justice to what we actually find in the Psalms. There is a sudden change of mood in the Psalms from lament to praise. But the change of mood is not restricted to this movement. As I have tried to demonstrate through my analysis of passages from the Psalms, Jeremiah and Lamentations, the movement between lament and praise is dynamic and multifaceted. Our analysis of Psalm 22 introduces us to the complexity of the relationship between lament and praise. On the one hand, it is possible to read Psalm 22 in terms of the movement lament-praise. Yet, as I have tried to show through my analysis of the psalm, it is also possible to view the movement in terms of a tension between lament and praise. The present form of Psalm 22, in which lament and praise are juxtaposed, creates a certain disjuncture, a tension which makes a straightforward reading in terms of the movement lament-praise rather simplistic.

Psalm 22 forms a bridge between the psalms which move from lament to praise and the psalms which contain the other movements. It is the latter movements that I have tried to highlight in this book. I have identified three of these: 1) the reverse movement from praise to lament; 2) the return to lament after the movement to praise and 3) the alternation between lament and praise.

The first is represented by Psalms 9/10, 27 and 40—three psalms which also juxtapose lament and praise in a manner reminiscent of Psalm 22. The difference is that here the arrangement is the other way around. For instead of the juxtaposition lament//praise as in Psalm 22, we have the reverse, praise//lament. Praise follows the lament! The result is a strong sense of tension between lament and praise. The element of praise is not forgotten, but its function has been transformed: God's act of deliverance which is the subject of thanksgiving is now set against the present experience of suffering.

The second movement further draws out the tension between lament and praise as it carries the movement even further. In Psalms 12 and 28 we have a return to lament even after a movement to praise. In the latter, an imprecation-turned-praise psalm reverts to lament in the form of a petition. Even more conspicuously, in the former, a lament that has turned to praise as a result of a divine response goes back to lament. In spite of the presence of a clear oracle of salvation, Psalm 12 nonetheless ends in a note of uncertainty. There is an '*un*certainty of a hearing' in spite of the 'certainty of a hearing'. This return to lament after praise and the reverse movement from praise to lament run counter to the usual form-critical view which tends to see only a one-way movement from lament to praise and is incapable of envisaging a return to lament after praise.

Finally, we have the alternation between lament and praise in Psalms 31 and 35. These two psalms bring together the different movements, including the movement lament-praise. Here we find the movement lament-praise repeated a couple of times. In Psalm 31 lament moves to praise twice; in Psalm 35, three times. Relevant to the present study, these series of movements are set beside each other in such a way that they resemble those psalms which juxtapose praise and lament. One finds here a 'tension in time'[1] which makes a straightforward, chronological reading limited. And because the different parts of Psalms 31 and 35 have been brought together to form a whole, one is able to observe not only the movement to praise but also the *return* to lament after praise, similar to what we find in Psalm 12. A reading of the whole invites one to undertake the journey of moving back and forth between lament and praise.

---

[1] The phrase is by Broyles (see discussion of Psalm 31 above).

We may conclude then that the sudden change of mood is not only from lament to praise: we also have the reverse movement from praise to lament, return to lament after the movement lament-praise and alternation between lament and praise. We not only have the 'certainty of a hearing' in the Psalter; we also have the '*un*certainty of a hearing'. Our analysis of Jer 20:7–18 and Lamentations 3 further strengthens the presence of this feature in the OT. As shown in our analysis of these two passages, the juxtaposition of lament and praise and the return to lament after a movement to praise is not confined to the Psalter but is more wide-ranging. Indeed, whilst the movement lament-praise is the most common movement in the Psalter, it appears that outside it, it is the other movements that feature more prominently.

IMPORTANCE OF THE STUDY

Lament viewed as merely preliminary to praise

Considering the present climate of research on the sudden change of mood and lament in general, I am increasingly convinced that there is a need to emphasize the other movements in the Psalter. As I have already hinted earlier,[2] the way one understands the relationship between lament and praise affects one's view of lament. An understanding which only sees a one-way movement from lament to praise will tend to devalue lament. Since the direction is always towards praise, lament eventually comes to be viewed simply as a prelude to praise. As Balentine wisely discerned more than two decades ago, Begrich's theory, with its emphasis on the element of certainty and one-way view of the movement from lament to praise, has actually led to the devaluing of lament. Balentine writes: "The most important effect of this theory has been the increasing tendency to understand all laments and questions toward God as preliminary to statements of confidence and praise".[3] This tendency can be seen in the works of Westermann

---

[2] See Introduction, Chapter 1.

[3] Balentine, 122. Balentine observes that "it has become a commonplace in Old Testament studies to argue that lament is related to praise and not to *uncertainty*" (ibid., 121–22). Balentine himself tried to highlight lament. But Balentine's work is not focused on the sudden change of mood; his concern is with the broader concept of the 'hiding

and Brueggemann[4]—two scholars who have sought to highlight the importance of lament. Unfortunately, because their emphasis is only on the movement from lament to praise, lament has actually receded into the background. By highlighting only the movement lament-praise and not taking into account the other movements in the Psalms, they have zoomed in on praise, leaving lament out of focus.[5]

Westermann, for his part, though trying to emphasize the value of lament, nonetheless tended to devalue it as he sees lament as always moving towards praise. He writes: "there is no…such thing as a 'mere' lament and petition in the Psalms. The cry to God is here never one-dimensional, without tension. It is always somewhere in the middle between petition and praise. By nature it cannot be mere petition or lament, but is *always underway from supplication to praise.*"[6] In this statement, one can see how a one-directional view of the movement from lament to praise leads to an overemphasis on the element of praise to the detriment of lament. Although Westermann sees lament as "somewhere in the middle between petition and praise", clearly the accent falls on praise.

In his influential book, *The Message of the Psalms*, Brueggemann basically echoes Westermann's view. He explains that the "life of faith expressed in the Psalms is focused on the two decisive moves of faith that are always *underway*, by which we are regularly surprised and which we regularly resist".[7] His use of the word "underway" recalls Westermann's view of the movement from lament to praise—lament *always* moves to praise.

---

of God' in the Old Testament. In the instances where he tried to address the issue directly, it is the psalms which contain in themselves the movement lament-praise (Psalms 13, 42/43, see above) that he employed to support his argument. This did not advance his argument far enough because these passages—especially Psalm 13—contain a clear movement from lament to praise. I think a better response can be found elsewhere in those psalms which contain the reverse movements from praise to lament.

[4] Cf. Balentine, 122–23.

[5] Gordon Wenham has helped me formulate this metaphor on camera focus.

[6] Westermann, *Lob und Klage*, 56, ET *Praise and Lament*, 75, emphasis mine.

[7] Walter Brueggemann, *The Message of the Psalms* (Minneapolis: Augsburg Publishing House, 1984), 20, emphasis mine. Here Brueggemann talks about the two movements of faith from orientation to disorientation and from disorientation to new orientation.

Lament redefined as petition

As a result of this one-sided emphasis on the movement towards praise, "the merit of lament simply as lament has been on the decline".[8] Since lament is viewed as "always underway" towards praise, lament has come to be regarded simply as something to be done away with, praise being the goal, the more essential element. The overall goal became the overcoming of the distress which leads to praise. But whilst this is true in a number of lament psalms, emphasizing only the element of resolution diminishes the force of the lament; the element of protest and complaint which is at the core of lament loses its force, as lament comes to be understood simply as petition.

This tendency to understand lament in terms of petition aimed at achieving resolution is evident in some scholars' attempts to redefine lament and emphasize praise over lament. For instance, Kraus finds Gunkel's designation, "lament", insufficient, and proposes we use the term "songs of prayer" or plea.[9] He writes: "There is *no lamenting*. Rather, we could speak of two foci that are determinative in given cases, namely, a description of distress, or cry of distress, and a cry for help".[10] Similarly, Seybold prefers the term, "psalm-prayer" over Gunkel's term, "lament". He argues: "In actual fact, we are dealing with prayers of supplication...of a single person in unfortunate circumstances".[11] Broyles explains concerning the nature of the lament: "A lament psalm is *not lamentation*. It does more than simply bemoan current hardship. It seeks change".[12]

To be fair, by defining lament in terms of petition, these scholars are not completely denying the presence of complaint and lament within the lament psalms, and it is important that we be aware of the multilayered nuances represented in their statements. However, one can also observe that in the process of redefining lament, they have overemphasized the element of petition in such a way that lament loses its force. Lament is pushed to the background to give way to petition. This can be seen in Kraus' statement above, which is also expressed by Broyles,

---

[8] Balentine, 123.

[9] Kraus, *Psalmen I*, xlv, ET *Psalms 1–59*, 47.

[10] Ibid., 40, emphasis mine.

[11] Klaus Seybold, *Die Psalmen: Eine Einführung* (Stuttgart: Verlag W. Kohlhammer, 1986), 99, ET *Introducing the Psalms* (trans. R. Graeme Dunphy; Edinburgh: T&T Clark, 1990), 116.

[12] Broyles, *The Conflict of Faith and Experience in the Psalms*, 14, emphasis mine; cf. 29.

that in the lament there is "no lamenting".[13] But whilst it is true that a lament psalm "does more than simply bemoan current hardship", to say that a lament is "not lamentation" leads to the undermining of an important aspect in the lament—the element of protest and sense of struggle. As Goldingay rightly points out, lament psalms "characteristically give rather little space to plea in the sense of requesting Yhwh to act";[14] the major part of the lament is devoted to "expressions of pain and protest".[15] This, according to Goldingay, explains the conventional title "laments" and that is why he prefers the title "protests" as a term to describe these psalms.[16]

Overemphasis on the element of praise

The one-sided emphasis on the movement lament-praise further led to an overemphasis on the element of praise. In more recent discussions on lament, it is revealing how this view has become determinative to how lament is understood. In the book edited by Johnston and Firth, *Interpreting the Psalms: Issues and Approaches*,[17] Johnston and Hutchinson emphasize the element of praise over lament. Johnston writes that "most psalmic clouds of distress have silver linings".[18] Summarizing the different theories on what caused the sudden change of mood, he endorses the recent essay by Williamson.[19] Hutchinson for his part sets the elements of lament and praise in competition with each other with the latter apparently winning the battle. He argues, "Indeed, the form-critical conclusion that individual laments are 'by far the most common type of psalm' [John Day following Gunkel] proves to be misleading, for 'the cry to God...by nature...is *always underway* from

---

[13] Cf. Scott Arthur Ellington, "Reality, Remembrance, and Response: The Presence and Absence of God in the Psalms of Lament" (PhD Diss; University of Sheffield, 1999), 97, who criticises Kraus of reducing "the lament to a mere introduction for praise" in his treatment of Psalm 77.

[14] John Goldingay, *Psalms: Volume 1. Psalms 1–41* (Baker Commentary on the Old Testament Wisdom and Psalms. Grand Rapids, MI: Baker Academic, 2006), 62.

[15] Ibid., 61.

[16] Ibid., 61–2.

[17] Philip S. Johnston and David Firth, *Interpreting the Psalms: Issues and Approaches* (Leicester: Apollos, 2005).

[18] Ibid., 80.

[19] See summary of Williamson's view in Chapter 1.

supplication to praise' [Westermann]".[20] He continues, "Even the gloomiest psalm touches on the importance of seeing Yahweh praised (88:10–11), even if it cannot be said that the psalmist himself emerges from the gloom".[21]

As can be seen, when lament is viewed as "always underway" to praise it becomes too secure, too certain. And I think this is the problem with some scholars' understanding of lament: it is too certain. For instance, Brueggemann maintains that "Israel's insistent lament (which may go unanswered) is finally as much an affirmation of God's *ḥesed* as is the doxology. Israel *does not for a moment* doubt Yahweh's *ḥesed*, nor does Israel doubt its own claim on Yahweh's *ḥesed*".[22] In his book, *The Message of the Psalms*, Brueggemann asserts: "Life may be disoriented, but even in the disorientation, Israel is clear about the place where the problem may be deposited".[23] Similarly, Westermann asserts that in the lament, "the individual may call out in despair, 'God, why have you forsaken me?' but *not once* does the caller say, 'so I shall forsake you too, I shall also turn away from you'".[24] To say that the lamenting person never doubts God or wavers from his/her faith may be true as a reflection *after* the experience of suffering.[25] But this does not represent the actual experience of suffering. Indeed, to say so would be unrealistic, for often the line separating faith and doubt is filament thin. One may not be aware that the line has already been crossed especially during extremely difficult situations.

Moreover, presenting only the movement lament-praise offers false optimism since it fails to take into account the complexities, ambiguities and the untidiness that characterise much of human existence. One value of the Psalms is its capacity to embrace all of life—a charac-

---

[20] Ibid., 95.

[21] Ibid.

[22] Walter Brueggemann, *Psalms and the Life of Faith* (Minneapolis: Fortress Press, 1995), 57, emphasis mine. Commenting on these words by Brueggemann, Ellington, "Reality, Remembrance, and Response", 94–95, writes: "for Brueggemann, all expressions of Israel's doubts and questions are finally relativized in the face of remembered expressions of God's *ḥesed*. But this statement is only possible to make in hindsight and does not fairly represent the full dilemma of the psalmist at the time of the lament. If Yahweh's *ḥesed* is never genuinely doubted, then neither can lament be genuine".

[23] Brueggemann, *The Message of the Psalms*, 56.

[24] Westermann, "The Complaint against God", in *God in the Fray: A Tribute to Walter Brueggemann* (ed. Tod Linafelt; Minneapolis: Fortress Press, 1998), 239, emphasis mine.

[25] Ellington, "Reality, Remembrance, and Response", 94–95.

teristic which is true of the Bible as a whole. As Exum remarks, "the Bible's uncompromising portrayal of reality as embracing dissolution and despair as well as resolution and repair is the source of its extraordinary narrative range and power".[26] Offering only the movement to praise robs us of the Psalter's capacity to embrace both joy and pain, agony and relief, praise and lament.

The Significance of the Lament Psalms with 'Uncertainty of a Hearing'

There is therefore a need to emphasize the psalms containing the other movements. These psalms offer a more widely embracing approach to life's incongruities as they provide opportunities for the suffering individual to process his/her own struggles. In these lament psalms those who are still in situations of lament are able to find a voice to express their struggle and pain. Specifically, the psalms which alternate between lament and praise provide a more realistic perspective of restoration. In contrast to the 'instant' shift from lament to praise influenced by the quick-fix culture in which many today have been brought up, these psalms point the way to a road which can sometimes be long. Restoration and deliverance do occur, but it is not always immediate. For some it may take months, for others years, and even a lifetime.[27] The reverse movement from praise to lament reminds us that the faithful do not always experience deliverance; the movement is not always from lament to praise, from sickness to health, defeat to victory. Sometimes it could be the other way round. As Hebrews 11 reports, whilst some of the faithful have experienced deliverance, others have lost their lives. Finally, the movement back to lament even after praise warns us that even when we have already received an answer or have already experienced victory the element of tension may linger. Answers can turn into questions...praise...into lament.

---

[26] Exum, *Tragedy and Biblical Narrative*, 152; quoted earlier (Chapter 8).
[27] Cf. Janowski, "Das verborgene Angesicht Gottes", 52. For some, the restoration may never come in this side of eternity.

For Further Study

Our journey has taken us, I hope, to new grounds. But it has also opened up other questions and areas for further study. The first area which needs exploring in connection with the subject of the sudden change of mood is the Psalter itself. Because of the limitations of the present study (Book I of the Psalter), I have not been able to include all the relevant psalms. Psalm 86, which is close to the psalms which alternate between lament and praise (e.g. Psalm 35) has not been discussed.[28] Also, the important Psalm 89 has not been given focused attention. This is because the scope of this study is limited not only to Book 1 of the Psalter but also to the individual lament psalms, with the exception of Psalm 12. But a consideration of the communal lament psalms may further strengthen the present thesis, as these emphasize the tension between lament and praise. Unfortunately, in the past, communal lament psalms have been understood in terms of the form-critical view of the structure of the individual lament psalms. The structure of the latter is imposed on the former. As shown in our study of Psalm 12—a communal lament—certainty can turn to uncertainty. But the important shift from praise to lament in the communal lament psalms has not been given the attention it deserves.

Another area where there is a need for further work is in the application of methodology. Since the present study is more of a response to an old problem, I have not focused on applying one method in approaching the subject. Instead, I have sought to provide a critique of the approaches thus far presented on the subject of the sudden change of mood in the Psalms and to give an alternative approach by highlighting the other movements in the Psalter. Although I have employed insights from the canonical method, I have not applied the method systematically. In the future one could do a canonical study of the Psalter from the perspective of the tension between lament and praise in the whole Psalter and perhaps see this as one possible way of explaining the editing of the Psalter. Others may apply a rhetorical method for approaching the tension between lament and praise. As I have shown above, the movement from lament to praise is the most common movement among the individual lament psalms as well as the

---

[28] I have not discussed Psalms 59 and 71 which both contain an alternation between lament and praise.

overall movement in the Psalter. This makes the other movements which I have highlighted a deviation from the more common one. What is the possible rhetorical purpose for this change? In this study I have only barely touched on this issue. My analysis of the passage in Jeremiah suggests that one reason for the employment of a composition which moves from praise to lament is in order to bring out the sense of tension which is at the core of the life of the faithful and to create disturbance or even shock on the part of the hearers in order to effect change.

Outside the Psalter, I have only included Jeremiah and Lamentations. But one may also include the book of Job in a future study. I would not be surprised to find the same tendency among scholars to apply the form-critical framework of the movement lament-praise, along with an overemphasis on the element of praise, in the study of Job.[29] Interestingly, as the study by Alison Lo shows, the differing tone/mood and content as well as the juxtaposition of contradicting viewpoints can be seen as an essential component of the rhetorical message of Job.[30] If we are able to establish that the feature of 'uncertainty of a hearing' can also be found in Job, then it is remarkable indeed that even though the movement lament-praise is the most common movement in the Psalter, it is the other reverse movements that are more common outside the Psalter.

Finally, one may broaden the scope of study further by considering materials from the ANE. Is there an 'uncertainty of a hearing' in the ANE? Can we find a tension between lament and praise comparable to that which we find in the Psalms? There are already a number of works comparing the biblical lament and ANE lament.[31] But there remains no study which focuses on the tension between lament and praise in the ANE. My hunch is that the form-critical framework has also influenced the treatment of this subject.

---

[29] See, for example, the article by Ross, "Job 33:14–30: The Phenomenology of Lament", *JBL* 94 (1975): 38–46, which basically understands lament as thanksgiving.

[30] Alison Lo, *Job 28 as Rhetoric: An Analysis of Job 28 in the Context of Job 22–31*.

[31] See Geo Widengren, *The Accadian and Hebrew Psalms of Lamentation as Religious Documents* (Stockholm: Bokförlags Aktiebolaget Thule, 1937); Walter C. Bouzard, *We Have Heard with Our Ears, O God: Sources of Communal Laments in the Psalms* (vol. 159; SBL Diss. Series; ed. Michael V. Fox; Atlanta: Scholars Press, 1997; cf. W. C. Jr. Gwaltney, "The Biblical Book of Lamentations in the Context of near Eastern Lament Literature", in *Scripture in Context II: More Essays on the Comparative Method* (ed. William Halo et al.; Winona Lake IN: Eisenbrauns, 1983).

BIBLIOGRAPHY

Abbott, T. K. "On the Alphabetical Arrangement of Ps. IX and X with Some Other Emendations." *ZAW* 16 (1896): 292–294.

Achtemeier, E. "Overcoming the World: An Exposition of Psalm 6." *Int* 28 (1974): 75–88.

Aejmelaeus, Anneli. *The Traditional Prayer in the Psalms*. Vol. 167 BZAW, ed. Otto Kaiser. Berlin: Walter de Gruyter, 1986.

Albrektson, Bertil. *Studies in the Text and Theology of Lamentations*. Vol. 21 Studia Theologica Lundensia. Lund: Gleerup, 1963.

Allen, Leslie C. "Psalm 73: An Analysis." *TynBul* 33 (1982): 93–118.

Alter, Robert. *The Art of Biblical Poetry*. NY: Basic Books, 1985.

Anderson, Arnold A. *The Book of Psalms*. Vol. 1. 2 vols. NCB. London: Marshal, Morgan & Scott, 1972.

Anderson, Bernard W. "Sicut Cervus: Evidence in the Psalter of Private Devotion in Ancient Israel." *VT* 30 (1980): 387–97.

———. *Out of the Depths: The Psalms Speak for Us Today*. Philadelphia: Westminster Press, 1983.

Anderson, G. A. *A Time to Mourn, a Time to Dance: The Expression of Grief and Joy in Israelite Religion*. University Park, PA: Pennsylvania State University Press, 1991.

Auffret, Pierre. "Note sur la Structure Littéraire du Psaume 3." *ZAW* 91 (1979): 93–106.

———. "'Tu as Entendu': Étude Structurelle du Psaume 31." *Église et Théologie* 18 (1987): 147–81.

———. "'Il Exultera, Mon Coeur, dan ton Salut': Etude Structurelle du Psaume 13." *BZ* 53 (1990): 7–13.

———. *Que Seulement De Tes Yeux Tu Regardes...: Etude Structurelle de Treize Psaumes*. Vol. 330 BZAW, ed. Otto Kaiser. Berlin: Walter de Gruyter, 2003.

Augustine, Saint. *Expositions on the Book of Psalms*. Vol. 1. 6 vols. Oxford: John Henry Parker; F. and J. Rivington, 1847.

Auld, A. Graeme, ed. *Understanding Poets and Prophets: Essays in Honour of George Wishart Anderson*. Vol. 152 JSOTSup. Sheffield, England: JSOT Press, 1993.

Auwers, Jean-Marie. *La Composition Littéraire du Psautier: Un État de la Question*. Paris: Gabalda, 2000.

Baethgen, F. *Die Psalmen*. HKAT. Göttingen: Vandenhoeck und Ruprecht, 1904.

Bak, Dong Hyun. *Klagender Gott—Klagende Menschen*. Vol. 193 BZAW. Berlin: Walter de Gruyter, 1990.

Balentine, Samuel E. *The Hidden God: The Hiding of the Face of God in the Old Testament*. Oxford Theological Monographs. Oxford: Oxford University Press, 1983.

———. *Prayer in the Hebrew Bible*. MN: Fortress Press, 1993.

Balla, E. *Das Ich der Psalmen*. Vol. 16 FRLANT. Göttingen: Vandenhoeck und Ruprecht, 1912.

Barth, Christoph F. *Introduction to the Psalms*. Translated by R. A. Wilson. Oxford: Basil Blackwell, 1966.

Barton, John. *Reading the Old Testament: Method in Biblical Study*. New ed. London: Darton, Longman, and Todd, 1996.

Baumgartner, Walter. *Die Klagegedichte des Jeremia*. Giessen: A. Töpelmann, 1917. ET *Jeremiah's Poems of Lament*. Translated by David E. Orton. Sheffield: Almond Press, 1988.

Bautch, Richard J. *Developments in Genre between Post-Exilic Penitential Prayers and the Psalms of Communal Lament.* Atlanta: SBL, 2003.

Becker, Joachim. *Israel deutet seine Psalmen: Urform und Neuinterpretation in den Psalmen.* Vol. 18. 2nd ed. Stuttgarter Bibelstudien, ed. H. Haag, N. Lohfink and W. Pesch. Stuttgart: Katholisches Bibelwerk, 1966.

Begrich, Joachim. "Das priesterliche Heilsorakel." *ZAW* 52 (1934): 81–92.

Bellinger, W. H. *Psalmody and Prophecy.* Sheffield: JSOT, 1984.

———. *Psalms: Reading and Studying the Book of Praises.* Peabody, MA: Hendrickson Publishers, 1990.

Berlin, Adele. *The Dynamics of Biblical Parallelism.* Bloomington, IN: Indiana University Press, 1985.

———. "The Rhetoric of Psalm 145." In *Biblical and Related Studies Presented to Samuel Iwry*, ed. Anne Kort and Scott Mors Chauser, 17–22. Winona Lake, IN: Eisenbrauns, 1985.

———. "Introduction to Hebrew Poetry." In *The New Interpreter's Bible*, IV, 301–15. Nashville: Abingdon Press, 1996.

———. *Lamentations* Old Testament Library. Louisville/London: Westminster John Knox Press, 2002.

———. "Psalms and the Literature of Exile: Psalms 137, 44, 69 and 78." In *The Book of Psalms: Composition and Reception*, ed. P. D. Miller and P. W. Flint, 99, 65–86. Vol. 99 VTSup. Leiden: Brill, 2005.

Berry, Donald K. *The Psalms and Their Readers: Interpretive Strategies for Psalm 18.* Vol. 153 JSOTSup. Sheffield, England: JSOT Press, 1993.

Beyerlin, W. "Die Tôda der Heilsverkündigung in den Klageliedern des Einzelner." *ZAW* 79 (1967): 208–24.

Birkeland, Harris. *Ani und Anaw in den Psalmen.* Oslo: I Kommisjon hos Jacob Dybwad, 1933.

Birkeland, H. "Die Einheitlichkeit von Ps 27." *ZAW* 51 (1933): 216–21.

Blank, Sheldon H. "The Confessions of Jeremiah and the Meaning of Prayer." *HUCA* 21 (1948): 331–54.

———. "The Curse, Blasphemy, the Spell, and the Oath." *HUCA* 23 (1950): 73–95.

Boadt, Lawrence. "Review of Ottmar Fuchs, *Die Klage als Gebet: Eine theologische Besinnung am Beispiel des Psalm 22.*" *CBQ* 46 (1984): 536–8.

Bons, Eberhard. *Psalm 31–Rettung Als Paradigma: Eine Synchron-Leserorientierte Analyse.* Vol. 48 Frankfurter Theologische Studien. Frankfurt am Main: Knecht, 1994.

Botterweck, Johannes G. "Klage und Zuversicht der Bedrängten: Auslegung der Psalmen 3 und 6." *BibLeb* III (1962): 184–189.

Bouzard, Walter C. *We Have Heard with Our Ears, O God: Sources of Communal Laments in the Psalms.* Vol. 159 SBL Dissertation Series, ed. Michael V. Fox. Atlanta: Scholars Press, 1997.

Boyce, Richard Nelson. *The Cry to God in the Old Testament.* Vol. 103 SBL Diss Series, ed. J. J. M. Roberts. Atlanta: Scholars Press, 1988.

Bracke, John M. "Jeremiah 15:15–21." *Int* 37 (1983): 174–78.

Brandscheidt, Renate. *Gotteszorn und Menschenleid: Die Gerichtsklage des Leidenden Gerechten in Klg 3.* Vol. 41 Trierer Theologische Studien. Trier: Paulinus Verlag, 1983.

Braulik, Georg. *Psalm 40 und der Gottesknecht.* Vol. 18 Forschung zur Bibel. Würzburg: Echter Verlag, 1975.

Briggs, C. A., and E. G. Briggs. *A Critical and Exegetical Commentary on the Book of Psalms.* Vol. 1. 2 vols. ICC. Edinburgh: T & T Clark, 1906.

Bright, John. *Jeremiah.* Vol. 21 AB. NY: Doubleday, 1965.

———. "A Prophet's Lament and Its Answer: Jeremiah 15:10–21." In *A Prophet to the Nations: Essays in Jeremiah Studies*, ed. Leo G. Perdue and Brian W. Kovacs, 325–37. Winona Lake, IN: Eisenbrauns, 1984.

Brown, Sally A., and Patrick D. Miller, eds. *Lament: Reclaiming Practices in Pulpit, Pew, and Public Square*. Louisville, *KY*: Westminster John Knox Press, 2005.

Brown, William P. *Seeing the Psalms*. Louisville: Westminster John Knox Press, 2002.

Broyles, Craig C. *The Conflict of Faith and Experience in the Psalms: A Form-Critical and Theological Study*. Vol. 52 JSOT Sup. Sheffield: JSOT Press, 1989.

———. *Psalms*. NIBC. Peabody, Massachusetts: Hendrickson Publishers, Inc., 1999.

Brueggemann, Walter. "The Formfulness of Grief." *Int* 31 (1977): 263–75.

———. "Psalms and the Life of Faith: A Suggested Typology of Function." *JSOT* 17 (1980): 3–32.

———. *The Message of the Psalms*. MN: Augsburg Publishing House, 1984.

———. "From Hurt to Joy, from Death to Life." In *The Psalms and the Life of Faith*, ed. P. D. Miller, 67–83. MN: Fortress Press, 1985.

———. "The "Uncared For" Now Cared for (Jer 30:12–17): A Methodological Consideration." *JBL* 104 (1985): 419–28.

———. *Hopeful Imagination: Prophetic Voices in Exile*. 3rd printing ed. Philadelphia: Fortress Press, 1986.

———. *Jeremiah 1–25: To Pluck up, to Tear Down*. ITC. Grand Rapids, MI: Eerdmans, 1988.

———. "Bounded by Obedience and Praise: The Psalms as Canon." *JSOT* 50 (1991): 63–92.

———. *Psalms and the Life of Faith*. MN: Fortress Press, 1995.

Buber, Martin. *Right and Wrong: An Interpretation of Some Psalms*. Translated by Ronald Gregor Smith. London: SCM Press, 1952.

Budde, Karl. "Das hebräische Klagelied." *ZAW* 2 (1882): 1–52.

Buss, Martin. "The Idea of *Sitz Im Leben*—History and Critique." *ZAW* 90 (1978): 157–70.

———. *Biblical Form Criticism in Its Context*. Vol. 274 JSOTSup. Sheffield: JSOT Press, 1999.

Buttenwieser, Moses. *The Psalms Chronologically Treated with a New Translation*. Chicago: University of Chicago, 1938.

Caird, G. B. *The Language and Imagery of the Bible*. Philadelphia: Westminster Press, 1980.

Calvin, John. *Commentary on the Book of Psalms*. Translated by James Anderson. Vols. 1, 2. Edinburgh: Edinburgh Printing Co., 1846.

———. *A Commentary on the Psalms*. Translated by A. Golding. Vol. 1. London: James Clarke & Co. Ltd., 1965.

Carroll, Robert P. *Jeremiah: A Commentary*. OTL. London: SCM, 1986.

———. *From Chaos to Covenant: Uses of Prophecy in the Book of Jeremiah*. London: SCM, 1981.

———. *Jeremiah*. OTL. Sheffield: JSOT Press, 1989.

Cartledge, Tony W. "Conditional Vows in the Psalms of Lament: A New Approach to an Old Problem." In *The Listening Heart*, ed. Kenneth G. Hoglund *et al.*, 77–94. Sheffield: Sheffield, 1987.

Ceresko, Anthony R. "The Sage in the Psalms." In *The Sage in Israel and the Ancient near East*, ed. J. G. Gammie and Leo G. Perdue, 217–30. Winona Lake, IN: Eisenbrauns, 1990.

Cheyne, T. K. *The Book of Psalms: Translated from a Revised Text with Notes and Introduction*. Vol. 1. 2 vols. London: Kegan Paul, Trench, Trübner & Co., 1904.

Childs, Brevard S. *Memory and Tradition in Israel*. Vol. 37 Studies in Biblical Theology. London: SCM, 1962.

———. "Psalms Titles and Midrashic Exegesis." *JSS* 16 (1972): 137–50.

———. "Reflections on the Modern Study of the Psalms." In *Magnalia Dei, the Mighty Acts of God: Essays in Memory of G. Ernest Wright*, ed. F. M. Cross, W. E. Lemke and P. D. Miler Jr. Garden City, NY: Doubleday, 1976.

———. *Introduction to the Old Testament as Scripture*. Philadelphia: Fortress Press, 1979.

Ciardi, John. *How Does a Poem Mean?* Boston: Houghton Mifflin Company, 1959.

Clements, Ronald Ernest. *Jeremiah*. Interpretation. Atlanta: John Knox Press, 1989.

Clifford, Richard J. "Wisdom Meditation or Communal Lament." In *The Book of Psalms: Composition and Reception*, ed. P. D. Miller and P. W. Flint, 190–205. Vol. 99 VTSup. Leiden: Brill, 2005.

Clines, David J. A. *Job 1–20*. Vol. 15 WBC. Dallas, TX: Word Books, 1989.

———. *Interested Parties: The Ideology of Writers and Readers of the Hebrew Bible; Gender, Culture, Theory*. Vol. 205 JSOTSup. Sheffield: Sheffield Academic Press, 1995.

———. ed. *The Dictionary of Classical Hebrew*. Vol. III. Sheffield: Sheffield Academic Press, 1996.

Clines, David J. A. and David M. Gunn. "Form, Occasion and Redaction in Jeremiah 20." *ZAW* 88 (1976): 390–409.

Clines, David J. A., David M. Gunn, and Alan J. Hauser, eds. *Art and Meaning: Rhetoric in Biblical Literature*. Vol. 19 JSOTSup. Sheffield: JSOT Press, 1982.

Coetzee, Johan H. "Politeness Strategies in the So-Called 'Enemy Psalms': An Inquiry into Israelite Prayer Rhetoric." In *Rhetorical Criticism and the Bible*, ed. Stanley E. Porter and Dennis L. Stamps, 195, 209–36. Sheffield: Sheffield Academic Press, 2002.

Conrad, E. W. "Second Isaiah and the Priestly Oracle." *ZAW* 93 (1981): 239–240.

———. *Fear Not Warrior: A Study of 'Al Tîra' Pericopes in the Hebrew Scriptures*. Vol. 75 Brown Judaic Studies. Chico, CA: Scholars Press, 1985.

Cousar, Charles B. *A Theology of the Cross: The Death of Jesus in the Pauline Letters*. Overtures to Biblical Theology. MN: Fortress Press, 1990.

Craghan, John F. *The Psalms: Prayers for the Ups, Downs and in-Betweens of Life*. Wilmington, Delaware: Michael Glazier, Inc., 1985.

Craigie, Peter C. *Psalms 1–50*. Waco, TX: Word Books, Publisher, 1983.

———. et al. *Jeremiah 1–15*. Vol. 26 WBC. Dallas, TX: Word Books, Publishers, 1991.

Creach, Jerome F. D. *Yahweh as Refuge and the Editing of the Hebrew Psalter*. Vol. 217 JSOTSup. Sheffield: Sheffield Academic Press, 1996.

Croft, Steven J. L. *The Identity of the Individual in the Psalms*. Vol. 44 JSOTSup. ed. David J. A. Clines and Philip R. Davis. Sheffield: JSOT Press, 1987.

Crow, Loren D. "The Rhetoric of Psalm 44." *ZAW* 104 (1992): 394–401.

Crüsemann, Frank. *Studien zur Formgeschichte von Hymnus und Danklied in Israel*. Vol. 32 WMANT: Neukirchener Verlag, 1969.

Culley, Robert C. *Oral Formulaic Language in the Biblical Psalms*. Vol. 4 Near and Middle East Series. Toronto: University of Toronto Press, 1967.

Curtis, Adrian. "Terror on Every Side." In *The Book of Jeremiah and Its Reception*, ed. A. H. W. Curtis and T. Römer, 111–18. Leuven: Leuven University Press, 1997.

———. *Psalms*. Epworth Commentaries. Peterborough: Epworth Press, 2004.

Dahood, M. *Psalms I (1–50)*. Vol. 16 AB. Garden City, NY: Doubleday, 1966.

Davidson, Robert. *The Vitality of Worship: A Commentary on the Book of Psalms*. Grand Rapids MI/Cambridge UK: Eerdmans, 1998.

Davis, Ellen F. "Exploding the Limits." *JSOT* 53 (1992): 93–105.

Day, John. *Psalms*. OTG. Sheffield: JSOT Press, 1990.

———. "Review of Cole, Robert L., *The Shape and Message of Book III*." *Society for Old Testament Study Book List* (2001): 59–60.

DeClaissé-Walford, Nancy L. "An Intertextual Reading of Psalms 22, 23 and 24." In *The Book of Psalms: Composition and Reception*, ed. P. W. Flint and P. D. Miller, 140–52. Vol. 99 VTSup. Leiden: Brill, 2005.

Delekat, L. *Asylie und Schutzorakel am Zionheiligtum*. Leiden: Brill, 1967.

Delitzsch, Franz. *Biblischer Commentar über die Psalmen*. Leipzig: Dörffling und Franke, 1883. ET *Biblical Commentary on the Psalms*. Translated by D. Eaton. Vol. 1. 3 vols. London: Hodder and Stoughton, 1887.

———. *Die Psalmen*. 5th ed. Giessen: Brunnen Verlag, 1984.

Diamond, A. R. *The Confessions of Jeremiah in Context*. Vol. 45 JSOTSup. Sheffield: JSOT Press, 1987.

Dillard, Raymond B., and Tremper Longman III. *An Introduction to the Old Testament*. Leicester: Apollos, 1995.

Dion, Paul E. "Stropic Boundaries and Rhetorical Structure in Psalm 31." *Église et Théologie* 18 (1987): 183–92.

Dobbs-Allsopp, F. W. *Weep, O Daughter of Zion: A Study of the City-Lament Genre in the Hebrew Bible* Biblica et Orientalia; 44. Roma: Editrice Pontificio Istituto Biblico, 1993.

———. "Tragedy, Tradition, and Theology in the Book of Lamentations." *JSOT* 74 (1997): 29–60.

———. *Lamentations*. Interpretation. Louisville: John Knox Press, 2002.

Dozeman, Thomas B. "OT Rhetorical Criticism." In *ABD* 5: 712–15.

Driver, S. R. "Lamentations." In *An Introduction to the Literature of the Old Testament*, 456–65. Edinburgh: T & T Clark, 1913.

Duhm, B. *Die Psalmen*. Vol. 14 Kurzer Hand-Kommentar zum Alten Testament. Tübingen: Mohr, 1922.

Eaton, John Herbert. *Psalms: Introduction and Commentary*. London: SCM, 1967.

———. *Kingship and the Psalms*. Vol. 32 SBT. London: SCM Press, 1976.

———. *Psalms of the Way and the Kingdom: A Conference with the Commentators*. Vol. 99 JSOTSup. Sheffield, England: Sheffield Academic Press, 1995.

———. *The Psalms: A Historical and Spiritual Commentary with an Introduction and New Translation*. London, NY: T & T Clark, 2003.

Ehlers, Kathrin. "Wege aus der Vergessenheit." *Jahrbuch für Biblische Theologie* 16 (2001): 383–96.

Ellington, Scott Arthur. "Reality, Remembrance, and Response: The Presence and Absence of God in the Psalms of Lament." PhD, University of Sheffield, 1999.

———. "The Costly Loss of Testimony." *Journal of Pentecostal Theology* 16 (2000): 48–59.

Empson, William. *Seven Types of Ambiguity*. New York: Noonday Press, 1955.

Erbele-Küster, Dorothea. *Lesen als Akt der Betens*. Vol. 87 WMANT. Neukirchen-Vluyn: Neukirchener, 2001.

Etzelmüller, Gregor. "Als Ich den Herrn Suchte, Antwortete er Mir." *Jahrbuch für Biblische Theologie* 16 (2001): 397–406.

Ewald, G. Heinrich A. v. *Prophets of the Old Testament*. Vol. 3. Edinburgh: Williams and Norgate, 1878.

———. *Commentary on the Psalms*. Translated by E. Johnson. London and Edinburgh: Williams and Norgate, 1880.

Exum, Cheryl J. *Tragedy and Biblical Narrative*. Cambridge: Cambridge University Press, 1992.

Farley, Wendy. *Tragic Vision and Divine Compassion: A Contemporary Theodicy*. Louisville, KY: Westminster/John Knox, 1990.

Firth, David G. "The Teaching of the Psalms." In *Interpreting the Psalms: Issues and Approaches*, ed. P. S. Johnston and D. G. Firth, 159–174. Leicester: Apollos, 2005.

Fisch, Harold. *Poetry with a Purpose: Biblical Poetics and Interpretation*. Bloomington Indianapolis: Indiana University Press, 1990.

Flint, P. W., and P. D. Miller, eds. *The Book of Psalms: Composition and Reception*. Vol. 99 VTSup. Leiden: Brill, 2005.

Fohrer, G. *Introduction to the Old Testament*. London: SPCK, 1970.

Follis, Elaine R. *Directions in Biblical Hebrew Poetry* Journal for the Study of the Old Testament. Supplement Series, 40. Sheffield, England: JSOT Press, 1987.

Fox, Michael V. "The Rhetoric of Ezekiel's Vision of the Valley of the Bones." In *The Place Is Too Small for Us: The Israelite Prophets in Recent Scholarship*, ed. Robert P. Gordon, 5, 176–90. Winona Lake, IN: Eisenbrauns, 1995.

Franken, H. J. *The Mystical Communion with Yhwh in the Book of Psalms*. Leiden: E. J. Brill, 1954.

Fretheim, Terence E. *The Suffering of God* Overtures to Biblical Theology, ed. Walter et al. Brueggemann. Philadelphia: Fortress Press, 1984.

——. *Jeremiah*. Smyth & Helwys Bible Commentary. Macon, GA: Smyth & Helwys, 2002.

Frost, S. B. "Asseveration by Thanksgiving." *VT* 8 (1958): 380–90.

Fuchs, Gisela. "Die Klage des Propheten: Beobachtungen zu den Konfessionen Jeremias im Vergleich mit den Klagen Hiobs (Erster Teil)." *BZ* 41 (1997): 212–28.

——. "'Du bist mir zum Trugbach geworden': Verwandte Motive in den Konfessionen Jeremias und den Klagen Hiobs (Zweiter Teil)." *BZ* 42 (1998): 19–38.

Fuchs, Ottmar. *Die Klage als Gebet: Eine Theologische Besinnung am Beispiel des Psalms 22*. Munich: Kösel Verlag, 1982.

Geller, S. A. *Parallelism in Early Biblical Poetry*. Missoula, Mont.: Scholars Press, 1979.

Gerstenberger, E. S. "Psalms." In *Old Testament Form Criticism*, ed. John Hayes. San Antonio: Trinity University Press, 1974.

——. *Der Bittende Mensch*. Neukirchen-Vluyn: Neukirshener Verlag, 1980.

——. *Psalms: Part I with an Introduction to Cultic Poetry*. Vol. 14 FOTL, ed. Rolf Knierim and Gene M. Tucker. Grand Rapids, MI: Eerdmans, 1988.

——. *Psalms Part 2 and Lamentations*. Vol. 15 FOTL. MI/CA: Eerdmans, 2001.

Gese, Hartmut. "Psalm 22 und das Neue Testament." *Zeitschrift für katholische Theologie* 65 (1968): 1–22.

Gibson, J. C. L. *Language and Imagery in the Old Testament*. London: SPCK, 1998.

Gillingham, S. E. *The Poems and Psalms of the Hebrew Bible*. Oxford: Oxford University Press, 1994.

Goldingay, John. "The Dynamic Cycle of Praise and Prayer." *JSOT* 20 (1981): 85–90.

——. *God's Prophet, God's Servant: A Study in Jeremiah and Isaiah 40–55*. Exeter: Paternoster Press, 1984.

——. *Psalms: Psalms 1–41*. Vol. 1 Baker Commentary on the Old Testament Wisdom and Psalms. Grand Rapids, MI: Baker Academic, 2006.

Gordis, Robert. "The Conclusion of the Book of Lamentations (5:22)." *JBL* 93 (1974): 289–93.

——. *The Song of Songs and Lamentations*. Revised and augmented ed. NY: KTAV Publishing House, 1974.

Gottlieb, Hans. *A Study on the Text of Lamentations*. Translated by John Sturdy. Acta Jutlandica 48. Theology Series 12. Århus: Det laerde Selskab, 1978.

Gottwald, Norman K. *Studies in the Book of Lamentations*. Vol. 14 Studies in Biblical Theology. London: SCM, 1954.

——. "The Book of Lamentations Reconsidered." In *The Hebrew Bible in Its Social World and in Ours*. Atlanta: Scholars Press, 1993.

Gous, I. G. P. "Lamentations 5 and the Translation of Verse 22." *OTE* 3 (1990): 287–302.

Gross, Heinrich. *Klagelieder, Baruch, Die Neue Echter Bibel*. Vol. 14, Kommentar zum Alten Testament. Würzburg: Echter Verlag, 1986.

Gunkel, Hermann. *Die Psalmen*. HKAT. Göttingen: Vandenhoeck & Ruprecht, 1926.

Gunkel, Hermann, and Joachim Begrich. *Einleitung in Die Psalmen: Die Gattungen Der Religiösen Lyrik Israels*. Göttingen: Vandenhoeck & Ruprecht, 1933. ET *Introduction to the Psalms: The Genres of the Religious Lyric of Israel*. Translated by James D. Nogalski. Macon, GA: Mercer University Press, 1998.

Gwaltney, W. C. Jr. "The Biblical Book of Lamentations in the Context of near Eastern Lament Literature." In *Scripture in Context Ii: More Essays on the Comparative Method*, ed. Willam Halo et al. Winona Lake IN: Eisenbrauns, 1983.

Haag, H. "יבׄ." *TDOT*, ed. G. Johannes Botterweck and H. Ringgren, II, 159–65. Grand Rapids, MI: Eerdmans, 1975.

Harner, Philip B. "The Salvation Oracle in Second Isaiah." *JBL* 88 (1969): 418–34.

Hatch, Edwin, and Henry Redpath. *A Concordance to the Septuagint and the Other Greek Versions of the Old Testament*. Vol. 3. 3 vols. Graz-Austria: Akademische Druck—U. Verlagsanstalt, 1954.

Hauge, Martin Ravndal. *Between Sheol and Temple: Motif Structure and Function in the I-Psalms* Journal for the Study of the Old Testament. Supplement Series; 178. Sheffield, England: Sheffield Academic Press, 1995.

Heiler, Friedrich. *Das Gebet: Eine Religionsgeschichtliche und Religionspsychologische Untersuchung*. München: Ernst Reinhardt, 1921. ET *Prayer: A Study in the History and Psychology of Religion*. Translated by Samuel McComb. London: Oxford University Press, 1932.

Heim, Knut M. "The Personification of Jerusalem and the Drama of Her Bereavement in Lamentations." In *Zion, City of Our God*, ed. Richard S. Hess and Gordon J. Wenham, 129–69. Grand Rapids, MI/CA U.K.: Eerdmans, 1999.

Herder, J. G. *The Spirit of Hebrew Poetry*. Vol. 2. Burlington: Edward Smith, 1833.

Hermisson, Hans-Jürgen. "Jahwes und Jeremias Rechtsstreit: zum Thema der Konfessionen Jeremias." In *Altes Testament und Christliche Verkündigung: Festschrift Für Antonius H. J. Gunneweg*, ed. M. Oeming and A. Graupner, 309–43. Stuttgart: Verlag W. Kohlhammer, 1987.

Heschel, Abraham J. *The Prophets: An Introduction*. Vol. 1. NY: Harper and Row, 1962.

Hillers, Delbert R. *Lamentations*. Vol. 7A AB. NY: Doubleday, 1992.

——. "Lamentations, Book Of." In *ABD* 4: 137–41.

Hoffman, Y. "The Transition from Despair to Hope in the Individual Psalms of Lament (in Hebrew)." *Tarbiz* 55 (1985): 161–72.

Holladay, William L. *A Concise Hebrew and Aramaic Lexicon of the Old Testament*. Leiden: E. J. Brill, 1971.

——. "The Background of Jeremiah's Self-Understanding: Moses, Samuel, and Psalm 22." In *A Prophet to the Nations: Essays in Jeremiah Studies*, ed. Leo G. Perdue and Brian W. Kovacs, 313–24. Winona Lake, IN: Eisenbrauns, 1984.

——. *Jeremiah 1* Hermeneia. Philadelphia: Fortress Press, 1986.

Hossfeld, Frank-Lothar. "Von der Klage zum Lob—Die Dynamik des Gebets in den Psalmen." *Bibel und Kirche* 56 (2001): 16–20.

Hossfeld, Frank-Lothar and Erich Zenger. *Die Psalmen I. Psalm 1–50* Die Neue Echter Bibel Kommentar zum Alten Testament mit der Einheitsübersetzung (Nechb. AT). Würzburg: Echter, 1993.

——. *Die Psalmen II. Psalm 51–100* Die Neue Echter Bibel Kommentar zum Alten Testament mit der Einheitsübersetzung. Würzburg: Echter, 2002.

——. *Psalms 2*. Translated by Linda M. Maloney Hermeneia. MN: Fortress Press, 2005.

House, Paul R. *Lamentations*. Vol. 23B WBC. Nashville: Thomas Nelson Publishers, 2004.

Howard, David. "The Psalms and Current Study." In *Interpreting the Psalms*, ed. P. S. Johnston and David Firth. Leicester: Apollos, 2005.

Hubmann, Franz D. *Untersuchungen zu den Konfessionen Jer 11:18–12:6 und Jer 15:10–21*. Forschung zur Bibel. Würzburg: Echter Verlag, 1978.

Hutchinson, James Hely. "The Psalms and Praise." In *Interpreting the Psalms*, ed. P. S. Johnston and D. G. Firth. Leicester: Apollos, 2005.

Illmann, Karl-Johan. "Psalm 88: A Lamentation without Answer." *SJOT* 5 (1991): 12–20.

Irsigler, Hubert. "Psalm-Rede als Handlungs-, Wirk- und Aussageprozess. Sprechaktanalyse und Psalmeninterpretation am Beispiel von Psalm 13." In *Neue Wege der Psalmenforschung. Fs W. Beyerlin*, ed. K. Seybold and E. Zenger, 1, 63–103. Freiburg: Herder, 1994.

Ittmann, Norbert. *Die Konfessionen Jeremias: Ihre Bedeutung für die Verkündigung des Propheten.* Vol. 54 WMANT. Neurkirchen-Vluyn: Neukirchener, 1981.
Janowski, Bernd. "Das Verborgene Angesicht Gottes: Psalm 13 als Muster eines Klagelieds des Einzelnen." *Jahrbuch für Biblische Theologie* 16 (2001): 25–53.
———. *Konfliktgesprache Mit Gott: Eine Anthropologie Der Psalmen.* Neukirchen-Vluyn: Neukirchener Verlag, 2003.
Janzen, Gerald J. "Jeremiah 20:7–18." *Int* 37 (1983): 178–83.
Johnson, A. R. "The Psalms." In *The Old Testament and Modern Study*, ed. H. H. Rowley, 162–209. Oxford: Clarendon Press, 1951.
———. *The Cultic Prophet and Israel's Psalmody.* Cardiff: University of Wales Press, 1979.
Johnson, Bo. "Form and Message of Lamentations." *ZAW* 97 (1985): 58–73.
Johnston, Philip S., and David Firth, eds. *Interpreting the Psalms: Issues and Approaches.* Leicester: Apollos, 2005.
Jones, Douglas Rawlinson. *Jeremiah* NCB. Grand Rapids, MI: Eerdmans, 1992.
Joyce, Paul. "Lamentations and the Grief Process: A Psychological Reading." *Biblical Interpretation* 1 (1993): 304–20.
Joyce, Paul M. "Sitting Loose to History: Reading the Book of Lamentations without Primary Reference to Its Original Historical Setting." In *In Search of True Wisdom: Essays in Old Testament Interpretation in Honour of Ronald E. Clements*, ed. Edward Ball, 300, 246–62. Sheffield: Sheffield Academic Press, 1999.
Keel, Othmar. *The Symbolism of the Biblical World.* Translated by Timothy J. Hallett. Winona Lake, IN: Eisenbrauns, 1997.
Keil, C. F. *The Prophecies of Jeremiah.* Vol. 40, 41 Clark's Foreign Theological Library, Fourth Series. Edinburgh: T & T Clark, 1853.
Kidner, Derek. *Psalms 1–72: An Introduction and Commentary on Books I and II of the Psalms* TOTC. London: Inter-Varsity, 1973.
Kilian, Rudolf. "Psalm 22 und das Priesterliche Heilsorakel." *BZ* 12 (1968): 172–85.
Kim, Ee Kon. *The Rapid Change of Mood in the Lament Psalms: A Matrix for the Establishment of a Psalm Theology.* Seoul, Korea: Korea Theological Study Institute, 1985.
———. "'Outcry': Its Context in Biblical Theology." *Int* 42 (1988): 229–39.
———. "Holy War Ideology and the Rapid Change of Mood in Psalm 3." In *On the Way to Nineveh: Studies in Honor of George M. Landes*, ed. Stephen L. Cook and S. C. Winter, 77–93. Atlanta: Scholars Press, 1999.
Kirkpatrick, A. F. *The Book of Psalms.* CA: Cambridge University Press, 1903.
Kissane, E. J. *The Book of Psalms Translated from a Critically Revised Hebrew Text.* Vol. 1. Westminster: Newman, 1953.
Kittel, Rudolf. *Die Psalmen.* 3rd and 4th ed. Leipzig: A. Deichertsche Verlagsbuchhandlung, 1922.
Kleer, Martin. *Der liebliche Sänger der Psalmen Israels.* Vol. 108 Bonner Biblische Beiträge. Bodenheim: Philo, 1996.
Knierim, Rolf. "Old Testament Form Criticism Reconsidered." *Int* 27 (1973): 435–68.
———. "Criticism of Literary Features, Form, Tradition, and Redaction." In *The Hebrew Bible and Its Modern Interpreters*, ed. D. Knight and G. Tucker. Chico, CA: Scholars Press, 1985.
Koehler, Ludwig, and Walter Baumgartner. *The Hebrew and Aramaic Lexicon of the Old Testament.* Vol. 1, 2. 2 vols. Leiden: Brill, 2001.
König, Eduard. *Die Psalmen: Eingeleitet, Übersetzt und Erklärt.* Gütersloh: Druck und Verlag von C. Bertelsmann, 1927.
Krašovec, Jože. "The Source of Hope in the Book of Lamentations." *VT* 42 (1992): 223–33.
Kraus, Hans-Joachim. *Klagelieder (Threni).* Vol. 20. 2 ed. BKAT. Neukirchen: Neukirchener Verlag, 1960.
———. *Worship in Israel.* Translated by Geoffrey Buswell. Oxford: Blackwell, 1966.

——. *Psalmen I*. Vol. 15/1. 4th ed. BKAT. Neukirchen-Vluyn: Neukirchener, 1972. ET *Psalms 1–59*. Translated by H. C. Oswald. MN: Augsburg, 1988.

——. *Theology of the Psalms*. Translated by Keith Crim. MN: Fortress Press, 1992.

Kselman, John. "Psalm 3: A Structural and Literary Study." *CBQ* 49 (1987): 572–80.

Kselman, John S. "'Why Have You Abandoned Me?' A Rhetorical Study of Psalm 22." In *Art and Meaning: Rhetoric in Biblical Literature*, ed. David J. A. Clines, David M. Gunn and Alan J. Hauser, 172–98. Vol. 19 JSOTSup. Sheffield: JSOT Press, 1982.

Kselman, John S. and Michael Barré. "Psalms." In *The New Jerome Biblical Commentary*, ed. Raymond Brown, Joseph Fitzmyer and Roland Murphy. London: Geoffrey Chapman, 1990.

Küchler, Friedrich. "Das Priesterliche Orakel in Israel und Juda." In *Abhandlungen zur semitische Religionskunde und Sprachwissenschaft*, ed. W. Frankenberg and F. Küchler, 285–301. Giessen: A Töpelman, 1918.

Kugel, James L. *The Idea of Biblical Poetry*. New Haven: Yale University Press, 1981.

Kuntz, J Kenneth. "Engaging the Psalms: Gains and Trends in Recent Research." *Currents in Research: Biblical Studies* 2 (1994): 77–106.

——. "Biblical Hebrew Poetry in Recent Research, Part I." *Currents in Research: Biblical Studies* 6 (1998): 31–64.

——. "Biblical Hebrew Poetry in Recent Research, Part II." *Currents in Research: Biblical Studies* 7 (1999): 73–79.

Laberge, Léo. "A Literary Analysis of Psalm 31." *Église et Théologie* 16 (1985): 147–68.

LaCocque, André. "My God, My God, Why Have You Forsaken Me?" In *Thinking Biblically*, ed. André LaCocque and Paul Ricoeur, 187–209. Chicago and London: The University of Chicago Press, 1998.

Lambdin, Thomas O. *Introduction to Biblical Hebrew*. London: Darton, Longman and Todd Ltd, 1973.

Lanahan, William F. "The Speaking Voice in the Book of Lamentations." *JBL* 93 (1974): 41–49.

Landy, Francis. "Recent Developments in Biblical Poetics." *Prooftexts* 7 (1987): 163–78.

——. "Lamentations." In *The Literary Guide to the Bible*, ed. Robert Alter and Frank Kermode, 329–34. London: Fontana Press, 1989.

Lee, Nancy. *The Singers of Lamentations*. Leiden: Brill, 2002.

Lee, Sung-Hun. "The Concept of God's *Hesed* as an Explanatory Feature in the Shift to Praise in the Individual Lament Psalms." PhD, University of Manchester, 1999.

——. "Lament and the Joy of Salvation in the Lament Psalms." In *The Book of Psalms: Composition and Reception*, ed. Peter Flint and P. D. Miller, 224–47. Vol. 99 VTSup. Leiden: Brill, 2005.

Lescow, Theodor. "Psalm 22:2–22 und Psalm 88: Komposition und Dramaturgie." *ZAW* 117 (2005): 217–31.

Leslie, E. A. *The Psalms: Translated and Interpreted in the Light of Hebrew Life and Worship*. NY: Abingdon Press, 1949.

Levenson, Jon D. *Creation and the Persistence of Evil*. Princeton, NJ: Princeton University Press, 1988.

Linafelt, Tod. "Surviving Lamentations." *HBT* 17 (1995): 45–61.

——. *Surviving Lamentations: Catastrophe, Lament, and Protest in the Afterlife of a Biblical Book*. Chicago: University of Chicago Press, 2000.

Lo, Alison. *Job 28 as Rhetoric: An Analysis of Job 28 in the Context of Job 22–31*. Vol. 97 VTSup. Leiden/Boston: Brill, 2003.

Lucas, Ernest. *Exploring the Old Testament: The Psalms and Wisdom Literature*. Vol. 3. London: SPCK, 2003.

Lundbom, Jack R. *Jeremiah 1–20*. Vol. 21A AB. NY: Doubleday, 1999.

Maclaren, Alexander. *The Psalms*. Vol. 1 The Expositor's Bible, ed. W. Robertson Nicoll. London: Hodder and Stoughton, 1893.

Magonet, Jonathan. "Jeremiah's Last Confession: Structure, Image and Ambiguity." *HAR* 11 (1987): 303–17.

Mandolfo, Carleen. *God in the Dock: Dialogic Tension in the Psalms of Lament*. Vol. 357 JSOTSup. London; New York: Sheffield Academic Press, 2002.

March, W. E. "A Note on the Text of Psalm 12:9." *VT* 21 (1971): 610–12.

Markschies, Christoph. "'Ich aber Vertraue auf Dich, Herr!'—Vertrauensäusserungen als Grundmotiv in den Klageliedern des Einzelnen." *ZAW* 103 (1991): 386–98.

Mays, James Luther. "Psalm 13." *Int* 34 (1980): 279–82.

——. *The Lord Reigns: A Theological Handbook to the Psalms*. Louisville: Westminster John Knox Press, 1994.

——. *Psalms*. Interpretation, ed. James Luther Mays. Louisville, KY: John Knox Press, 1994.

McCann, J. Clinton. *A Theological Introduction to the Book of Psalms: The Psalms as Torah*. Nashville: Abingdon Press, 1993.

——. "The Psalms as Instruction." *Int* 46 (1992): 117–28.

——. "Books I–III and the Editorial Purpose of the Hebrew Psalter." In *The Shape and Shaping of the Psalter*, ed. J. Clinton McCann. Vol. 159 JSOTSup. Sheffield: JSOT Press, 1993.

——. *The Shape and Shaping of the Psalter*. Vol. 159 JSOTSup. Sheffield, England: JSOT Press, 1993.

——. "Psalms." In *The New Interpreter's Bible*, IV. Nashville: Abingdon Press, 1996.

McCarter, P. Kyle. *Textual Criticism: Recovering the Text of the Hebrew Bible*. Philadelphia: Fortress Press, 1986.

McConville, J. G. "Statements of Assurance in Psalms of Lament." *IBS* 8 (1986): 64–75.

McKay. "Psalms of Vigil." *ZAW* 91 (1979): 229–47.

Michel, Diethelm. *Tempora und Satzstellung in den Psalmen*. Vol. 1 Abhandlungen zur evangelischen Theologie. Bonn: H. Bouvier u. Co. Verlag, 1960.

Middlemas, Jill. "The Violent Storm in Lamentations." *JSOT* 29 (2004): 81–97.

Millard, Matthias. *Die Komposition des Psalters: Eine Formgeschichtlicher Ansatz*. Tübingen: J.C.B. Mohr, 1994.

Miller, Patrick D. "Yapiah in Psalm XII 6." *VT* 29 (1979): 495–501.

——. *Interpreting the Psalms*. Philadelphia: Fortress Press, 1986.

——. "Book Review: Ee Kon Kim, the Rapid Change of Mood in the Lament Psalms." *Int* 41 (1987): 88–89.

——. "The Beginning of the Psalter." In *The Shape and Shaping of the Psalter*, ed. J. Clinton McCann, 159, 83–92. Sheffield: Sheffield Academic Press, 1993.

——. "The Book of Jeremiah." In *The New Interpreter's Bible*, VI. Nashville: Abingdon Press, 2001.

——. "The Theological Significance of Biblical Poetry." In *Language, Theology, and the Bible: Essays in Honour of James Barr*, eds. Balentine, Samuel E. and John Barton, 213–30. Oxford: Clarendon Press, 1994.

——. "Trouble and Woe: Interpreting the Biblical Laments." *Int* 37 (1983): 32–45.

——. *They Cried to the Lord: The Form and Theology of Biblical Prayer*. MN: Fortress Press, 1994.

Mintz, Alan. *Hurban: Responses to Catastrophe in Hebrew Literature*. NY: Columbia University Press, 1984.

Mowinckel, Sigmund. *Psalmstudien*. Vols. I–II. Amsterdam: Verlag P. Schippers, 1961.

——. *The Psalms in Israel's Worship*. Translated by D. R. Ap-Thomas. Vol. 1 and 2. 2 vols. Nashville: Abingdon Press, 1962. Reprint, 2004.

Müller, Augustin R. "Stimmungsumschwung im Klagepsalm: zu Ottmar Fuchs, 'Die Klage Als Gebet'." *Archiv für Liturgiewissenschaft* 28 (1986): 416–26.

Müller, Hans-Peter. "Gottesfrage und Psalmenexegese: zur Hermeneutik der Klagepsalmen des Einzelnen." In *Neue Wege der Psalmenforschung*, ed. K. Seybold and E. Zenger, 279–99. Freiburg; New York: Herder, 1994.

Muilenburg, James. "Form Criticism and Beyond." *JBL* 88 (1969): 1–18.

Murphy, Roland E. "The Faith of the Psalmist." *Int* 34 (1980): 229–39.

Naegelsbach, C. W. Eduard. "The Lamentations of Jeremiah." In *Lange's Commentary on the Holy Scriptures. Isaiah to Lamentations*, ed. John Peter Lange, 6. Grand Rapids, MI: Zondervan, 1960.

Nasuti, Harry Peter. *Defining the Sacred Songs: Genre, Tradition, and the Post-Critical Interpretation of the Psalms*. Vol. 218 JSOTSup. Sheffield, England: Sheffield Academic Press, 1999.

Niehaus, J. "The Use of *Lûle* in Psalm 27." *JBL* 98 (1979): 88–89.

Nötscher, Friedrich. *Jeremias, Echter-Bibel*. Würzburg: Echter, 1954.

O'Connor, Kathleen M. *The Confessions of Jeremiah: Their Interpretation and Role in Chapters 1–25* SBL Diss Series 94. Atlanta, GA: Scholars Press, 1988.

———. "The Book of Lamentations: Introduction, Commentary and Reflections." In *The New Interpreter's Bible*, VI, 1011–1072. Nashville: Abingdon Press, 2001.

———. *Lamentations and the Tears of the World*. Maryknoll, NY: Orbis Books, 2002.

Oesterley, W. O. E. *The Psalms Translated with Text Critical and Exegetical Notes*. London: SPCK, 1939.

Oswald, Hilton C., ed. *Luther's Works: First Lectures on the Psalms I: Psalms 1–75*. Vol. 10. Saint Louis: Concordia Publishing House, 1974.

Pardee, Dennis. "Yph 'Witness' in Hebrew and Ugaritic." *VT* 28 (1978): 204–13.

Patrick, Dale, and Allen Scult. *Rhetoric and Biblical Interpretation*. Sheffield: Almond Press, 1990.

Pelikan, Jaroslav, ed. *Luther's Works: Selected Psalms III*. Vol. 14. St. Louis, MO: Concordia Publishing House, 1958.

Perowne, J. J. Stewart. *The Book of Psalms*. Vol. 1. CA: Deighton, Bell, & Co., 1864.

Podechard, Emmanuel. *Le Psautier: Traduction Littérale et Explication Historique*. Vol. 1. Lyon: Facultès Catholiques, 1949.

Pohlmann, Karl-Friedrich. *Die ferne Gottes—Studien zum Jeremiabuch*. Vol. 179 BZAW. Berlin: Walter de Gruyter, 1989.

Polk, Timothy. *The Prophetic Persona: Jeremiah and the Language of the Self*. Vol. 32 JSOTSup. Sheffield: JSOT Press, 1984.

Pope, Marvin H. *Job*. Vol. 15 AB. NY: Doubleday, 1965.

Preuss, Horst Dietrich. "Die Frage nach dem Leid des Menschen—Ein Versuch Biblischer Theologie." In *Altes Testament und Christliche Verkündigung: Festschrift für Antonius H.J. Gunneweg*, ed. M. Oeming and A. Graupner, 13–80. Stuttgart: Verlag W. Kohlhammer, 1987.

Provan, Iain W. *Lamentations* New Century Bible Commentary. Grand Rapids, MI: Eerdmans, 1991.

———. "Past, Present and Future in Lamentations 3:52–66: The Case for a Precative Perfect Re-Examined." *VT* 41 (1991): 164–75.

Raabe, Paul R. *Psalm Structures: A Study of Psalms with Refrains*. Vol. 104 JSOTsup. Sheffield: Sheffield Academic Press, 1990.

———. "Deliberate Ambiguity in the Psalter." *JBL* 110 (1991): 213–27.

Raitt, Thomas M. *A Theology of Exile: Judgment/Deliverance in Jeremiah and Ezekiel*. Philadelphia: Fortress Press, 1977.

Re'emi, Paul S. "The Theology of Hope: A Commentary on the Book of Lamentations." In *God's People in Crisis: A Commentary on the Book of Amos. A Commentary on the Book of Lamentations*, ed. R. Martin-Achard and Paul S. Re'emi. Grand Rapids, MI: Eerdmans, 1984.

Reindl, J. "Weisheitliche Bearbeitung von Psalmen. Ein Beitrag zum Verständnis der Sammlung des Psalters." In *Congress Volume, Vienna 1980*, ed. J. A. Emerton, 32, 333–56. Leiden: Brill, 1981.

Renkema, Johan. "The Literary Structure of Lamentations (I–IV)." In *The Structural Analysis of Biblical and Canaanite Poetry*, ed. Willem van der Meer and Johannes C. de Moor, 74, 294–396. Sheffield: JSOT Press, 1988.

———. *Lamentations*. Historical Commentaries on the Old Testament. Leuven: Peeters, 1998.

Reyburn, William D. *A Handbook on Lamentations* UBS Handbook Series. NY: UBS, 1992.

Ricoeur, Paul. "Lamentation as Prayer." In *Thinking Biblically*, ed. André LaCocque and Paul Ricoeur, 211–232. Chicago and London: The University of Chicago Press, 1998.

Ridderbos, N. H. "The Psalms: Style-Figures and Structure." *OTS* 13 (1963): 43–76.

———. "The Structure of Psalm XI." *OTS* 14 (1965): 296–304.

———. *Die Psalmen: Stilistische Verfahren und Aufbau; mit besondere Berücksichtigung von Ps 1–41*. Vol. 117 BZAW, ed. G. Fohrer. Berlin: Walter de Gruyter, 1972.

Ringgren, Helmer. "יָדַס." *TDOT*, ed. G. Johannes Botterweck and H. Ringgren, V, 75–79. Grand Rapids, MI: Eerdmans, 1986.

Roberts, J. J. M. "A New Root for an Old Crux, Ps. 22:17c." *VT* 23 (1973): 247–52.

Rogerson, J. W., and J. W. McKay. *Psalms 1–50*. Cambridge: Cambridge University Press, 1977.

Ross, James F. "Job 33:14–30: The Phenomenology of Lament." *JBL* 94 (1975): 38–46.

Rowley, H. H. *Worship in Ancient Israel: Its Forms and Meaning*. London: SPCK, 1967.

Rudolph, Wilhelm. *Jeremia*. Vol. 1/12 HAT. Tübingen: J. C. B. Mohr, 1958.

———. *Das Buch Ruth. Das Hohe Lied. Die Klagelieder. Die Klagelieder*. Vol. 27 (1–3) Kommentar zum Alten Testament. Gütersloh: Gütersloher Verlagshaus, 1962.

Sager, Dirk. *Polyphonie des Elends: Psalm 9/10 im konzeptionellen Diskurs und literarischen Kontext*. Vol. 21 FAT 2. Reihe. Tübingen: Mohr Siebeck, 2006.

Salters, Robert B. "Searching for Pattern in Lamentations." *OTE* 11 (1998): 93–104.

Schlegel, Juliane. *Psalm 88 als Prüfstein der Exegeses: zu Sinn und Bedeutung eines beispiellosen Psalms*. Vol. 72 Biblische-Theologische Studien. Neukirchen-Vluyn: Neukirchener Verlag, 2005.

Schmidt, Hans. *Das Gebet der Angeklagten im Alten Testament*. Giessen: A. Töpelmann, 1928.

———. *Die Psalmen*. Vol. 15 Handbuch zum Alten Testament. Tübingen: Verlag von J.C.B. Mohr, 1934.

Schroeder, Christoph O. *History, Justice, and the Agency of God*. Vol. 52 Biblical Interpretation Series. Leiden: Brill, 2000.

Seybold, Klaus. *Das Gebet des Kranken im Alten Testament: Untersuchungen zur Bestimmung und Zuordnung der Krankheits- und Heilungspsalmen*. BZWANT: Fünfte Folge, Heft 19 (der ganzen Sammlung Heft 99). Stuttgart: Kohlhammer, 1973.

———. *Die Psalmen: Eine Einführung*. Stuttgart: Verlag W. Kohlhammer, 1986. ET *Introducing the Psalms*. Translated by R. Graeme Dunphy. Edinburgh: T&T Clark, 1990.

———. *Die Psalmen*. Vol. I/15 HAT. Tübingen: J.C.B. Mohr, 1996.

Shea, William H. "The *Qinah* Structure of the Book of Lamentations." *Biblica* 60 (1979): 103–7.

Sheppard, Gerald T. "Theology and the Book of Psalms." *Int* 46 (1992): 143–55.

Smith, Barbara Herrnstein. *Poetic Closure: A Study of How Poems End*. Chicago: University of Chicago Press, 1968.

Soll, Will. *Psalm 119: Matrix, Form, and Setting*. Vol. 23 The Catholic Biblical Quarterly Monograph Series. Washington, DC: The Catholic Biblical Association of America, 1991.

Spieckermann, Hermann. *Heilsgegenwart: Eine Theologie der Psalmen*. Vol. 148 FRLANT. Götingen: Vandenhoeck & Ruprecht, 1989.

Streane, A. W. *The Book of the Prophet Jeremiah (Together with) the Lamentations*. Reprinted ed. Cambridge: Cambridge University Press, 1952.

Strugnell, John, and Hanan Eshel. "Alphabetical Acrostics in Pre-Tannaitic Hebrew." *CBQ* 62 (2000): 441–58.

———. "Psalms 9 and 10 and the Order of the Alphabet." *BibRev* 17 (2001): 41–44.

Stulman, Louis. *Order Amid Chaos: Jeremiah as Symbolic Tapestry*. Vol. 57 The Biblical Seminar. Sheffield: Sheffield Academic Press, 1998.

———. *Jeremiah*. Abingdon Old Testament Commentaries. Nashville, Tenn: Abingdon, 2005.

Szörényi, A. *Psalmen und Kult im Alten Testament*. Budapest: Sankt Stefans Gesellschaft, 1961.

Taylor, R. W, and W. Stewart McCullough. "The Book of Psalms." In *The Interpreter's Bible*, 4. NY: Abingdon Press, 1955.

Terrien, Samuel. *The Psalms: Strophic Structure and Theological Commentary*. Grand Rapids, MI: Eerdmans, 2003.

Thomas, Heath. "Aesthetic Theory of Umberto Eco and Lamentations". Unpublished paper delivered at the SBL meeting; Edinburgh, 2006.

Thompson, J. A. *The Book of Jeremiah*. Grand Rapids, MI: Eerdmans, 1980.

Tov, Emanuel. "Textual Criticism (OT)." In *ABD* 5: 393–412.

Tucker, Gene M. *Form Criticism of the Old Testament*. Philadelphia: Fortress Press, 1971.

Vesco, Jean-Luc. *Le Psautier de David*. Paris: Cerf, 2006.

Villanueva, Federico G. "Confession of Sins or Petition for Forgiveness: A Study of the Nature of the Prayers in Nehemiah 1, 9, Daniel 9 and Ezra 9". Master's Thesis. Asia Graduate School of Theology, Philippines, 2002.

Von Rad, Gerhard. *Old Testament Theology*. Translated by D. M. G. Stalker. Vol. 1. 2 vols. Edinburgh and London: Oliver and Boyd, 1962. Reprint, 1963.

———. *Old Testament Theology*. Translated by D. M. G. Stalker. Vol. 2. 2 vols. Edinburgh and London: Oliver and Boyd, 1965. Reprint, 1963.

———. "The Confessions of Jeremiah." In *Theodicy in the Old Testament*, ed. James L. Crenshaw, 4, 88–99. London: SPCK, 1983.

Waltke, Bruce K. "The *New International Version* and Its Textual Principles in the Book of Psalms." *JETS* 32 (1989): 17–26.

Waltke, Bruce K., and M. O'Connor. *An Introduction to Biblical Hebrew Syntax*. Winona Lake, Indiana: Eisenbrauns, 1990.

Walton, Steve. "Rhetorical Criticism: An Introduction." *Themelios* 21 (1996): 4–9.

Wanke, Gunther. *Jeremia: Teilband 1: Jeremia 1,1–25,14*. Vol. 20 Zürcher Bibelkommentare. Zürich: Theologischer Verlag, 1995.

Watson, Wilfred G. E. *Classical Hebrew Poetry: A Guide to Its Techniques* Vol. 26 JSOTSup. Sheffield, England: JSOT Press Dept. of Biblical Studies University of Sheffield, 1984.

———. *Traditional Techniques in Classical Hebrew Verse* Vol. 170 JSOTSup. Sheffield, England: Sheffield Academic Press, 1994.

Weber, Beat. *Psalmen Werkbuch I: Die Psalmen 1 bis 72*. Stuttgart: Kohlhammer, 2001.

———. "Zum sogenannten 'Stimmungschwung' in Psalm 13." In *The Book of Psalms: Composition and Reception*, ed. P. W. Flint and P. D. Miller, 99, 116–138. Vol. 99 VTSup. Leiden: Brill, 2005.

Weiser, Artur. *Das Buch der Propheten Jeremia, Das Alte Testament Deutsch: Neues Göttinger Bibelwerk*. Vol. 20/21. 4., neubearbeitete Aufl. ed. Göttingen: Vandenhoeck & Ruprecht, 1960.

———. *Die Psalmen I*. Göttingen: Vandenhoeck & Ruprecht, 1950. ET *The Psalms*. Translated by H. Hartwell. Vol. 1 OTL. London: SCM, 1962.

Wenberg-Møller, P. "Two Difficult Passages of the Old Testament: (a) Ps. 12:9." *ZAW* 69 (1957): 69–73.

Wenham, Gordon. "The Ethics of the Psalms." In *Interpreting the Psalms*, ed. P. S. Johnston and D. G. Firth, 175–94. Leicester: Apollos, 2005.

———. "Towards a Canonical Reading of the Psalms." Forthcoming.

———. *"Reading the Psalms Ethically".* Forthcoming.

Westermann, Claus. "The Way of the Promise through the Old Testament." In *Old Testament and Christian Faith*, ed. B. W. Anderson. London: SCM, 1963.

———. *Isaiah 40–66.* Translated by D. M. G. Stalker OTL. London: SCM, 1969.

———. "The Role of Lament in the Theology of the Old Testament." *Int* 28 (1974): 20–38.

———. *Lob und Klage in den Psalmen.* 5., erw. Aufl. Gottingen: Vandenhoeck und Ruprecht, 1977. ET *Praise and Lament in the Psalms.* Translated by Keith R. Crim and Richard N. Soulen. Edinburgh: T&T Clark, 1981.

———. *The Living Psalms.* Translated by J. R. Porter. Edinburgh: T & T Clark, 1989.

———. *Die Klagelieder: Forschungsgeschichte und Auslegung.* Neukirchen-Vluyn: Neukirchener, 1990. ET *Lamentations: Issues and Interpretation.* Translated by Charles Muenchow. Edinburgh: T & T Clark, 1994.

———. "The Complaint against God." In *God in the Fray: A Tribute to Walter Brueggemann*, ed. Tod Linafelt, 233–41. MN: Fortress Press, 1998.

Wevers, J. W. "A Study in the Form Criticism of Individual Complaint Psalms." *VT* 6 (1956): 80–96.

Whybray, Norman. *Reading the Psalms as a Book.* Vol. 222 JSOTSup. Sheffield, England: Sheffield Academic Press, 1996.

Wiessmann, H. "Der Planmässige Aufbau der Klagelieder des Jeremias." *Biblica* 7 (1926): 146–61.

———. "Der Zweck der Klagelieder des Jeremias." *Biblica* 7 (1926): 412–28.

Williamson, H. G. M. "Reading the Lament Psalms Backwards." In *A God So Near: Essays on Old Testament Theology in Honor of Patrick D. Miller*, ed. Brent A. Strawn and Nancy R. Bowen, 3–15. Winona Lake: Eisenbrauns, 2003.

Wilson, Gerald H. *The Editing of the Hebrew Psalter.* Chico: Scholars Press, 1985.

———. "The Shape of the Book of Psalms." *Int* 46 (1992): 129–42.

———. "The Structure of the Psalter." In *Interpreting the Psalms: Issues and Approaches*, ed. P. S. Johnston and D. G. Firth, 229–46. Leicester: Apollos, 2005.

Wittstruck, T. *The Book of Psalm: An Annotated Bibliography.* Vols. 1 and 2. NY and London: Garland Publishing, 1994.

Witvliet, John D. *Worship Seeking Understanding.* Grand Rapids, MI: Baker, 2003.

Wright, N. T. *Simply Christian.* London: SPCK, 2006.

Zenger, Erich. "Was wird anders bei kanonischer Psalmenauslegung?" In *Ein Gott, Eine Offenbarung: Beiträge zur Biblischen Exegese, Theologie und Spiritualität. Festschrift für Notker Füglister.*, ed. Friedrich V. Reiterer. Würzburg: Echter Verlag, 1991.

———. *Die Nacht wird Leuchten wie der Tag: Psalmentauslegungen.* Freiburg: Herder, 1997.

———. "Von der Psalmenexegese zur Psalterexegese." *Bibel und Kirche* 56 (2001): 8–15.

Zyl van, A. H. "The Unity of Psalm 27." In *De Fructu Oris Sui. Festschrift A. Van Selms*, ed. I.H. Eybers et al., 9, 233–51. Leiden: E.J. Brill, 1971.

INDEX OF AUTHORS

INDEX OF BIBLICAL SOURCES

New Testament

INDEX OF SUBJECTS

SUPPLEMENTS TO VETUS TESTAMENTUM

2. POPE, M.H. *El in the Ugaritic texts*. 1955. ISBN 90 04 04000 5
3. *Wisdom in Israel and in the Ancient Near East*. Presented to Harold Henry Rowley by the Editorial Board of Vetus Testamentum in celebration of his 65th birthday, 24 March 1955. Edited by M. NOTH and D. WINTON THOMAS. 2nd reprint of the first (1955) ed. 1969. ISBN 90 04 02326 7
4. *Volume du Congrès* [international pour l'étude de l'Ancien Testament]. *Strasbourg 1956*. 1957. ISBN 90 04 02327 5
8. BERNHARDT, K.-H. *Das Problem der alt-orientalischen Königsideologie im Alten Testament.* Unter besonderer Berücksichtigung der Geschichte der Psalmenexegese dargestellt und kritisch gewürdigt. 1961. ISBN 90 04 02331 3
9. *Congress Volume, Bonn 1962.* 1963. ISBN 90 04 02332 1
11. DONNER, H. *Israel unter den Völkern*. Die Stellung der klassischen Propheten des 8. Jahrhunderts v. Chr. zur Aussenpolitik der Könige von Israel und Juda. 1964. ISBN 90 04 02334 8
12. REIDER, J. *An Index to Aquila*. Completed and revised by N. Turner. 1966. ISBN 90 04 02335 6
13. ROTH, W.M.W. *Numerical sayings in the Old Testament*. A form-critical study. 1965. ISBN 90 04 02336 4
14. ORLINSKY, H.M. *Studies on the second part of the Book of Isaiah.* — The so-called 'Servant of the Lord' and 'Suffering Servant' in Second Isaiah. — SNAITH, N.H. Isaiah 40-66. A study of the teaching of the Second Isaiah and its consequences. Repr. with additions and corrections. 1977. ISBN 90 04 05437 5
15. *Volume du Congrès* [International pour l'étude de l'Ancien Testament]. *Genève 1965.* 1966. ISBN 90 04 02337 2
17. *Congress Volume, Rome 1968.* 1969. ISBN 90 04 02339 9
19. THOMPSON, R.J. *Moses and the Law in a century of criticism since Graf.* 1970. ISBN 90 04 02341 0
20. REDFORD, D.B. *A Study of the Biblical Story of Joseph.* 1970. ISBN 90 04 02342 9
21. AHLSTRÖM, G.W. *Joel and the Temple Cult of Jerusalem.* 1971. ISBN 90 04 02620 7
22. *Congress Volume, Uppsala 1971.* 1972. ISBN 90 04 03521 4
23. *Studies in the Religion of Ancient Israel.* 1972. ISBN 90 04 03525 7
24. SCHOORS, A. *I am God your Saviour.* A form-critical study of the main genres in Is. xl-lv. 1973. ISBN 90 04 03792 2
25. ALLEN, L.C. *The Greek Chronicles.* The relation of the Septuagint I and II Chronicles to the Massoretic text. Part 1. The translator's craft. 1974. ISBN 90 04 03913 9
26. *Studies on prophecy.* A collection of twelve papers. 1974. ISBN 90 04 03877 9
27. ALLEN, L.C. *The Greek Chronicles.* Part 2. Textual criticism. 1974. ISBN 90 04 03933 3
28. *Congress Volume, Edinburgh 1974.* 1975. ISBN 90 04 04321 7
29. *Congress Volume, Göttingen 1977.* 1978. ISBN 90 04 05835 4
30. EMERTON, J.A. (ed.). *Studies in the historical books of the Old Testament.* 1979. ISBN 90 04 06017 0
31. MEREDINO, R.P. *Der Erste und der Letzte.* Eine Untersuchung von Jes 40-48. 1981. ISBN 90 04 06199 1
32. EMERTON, J.A. (ed.). *Congress Volume, Vienna 1980.* 1981. ISBN 90 04 06514 8
33. KOENIG, J. *L'herméneutique analogique du Judaïsme antique d'après les témoins textuels d'Isaïe.* 1982. ISBN 90 04 06762 0

34. BARSTAD, H.M. *The religious polemics of Amos*. Studies in the preachings of Amos ii 7B-8, iv 1-13, v 1-27, vi 4-7, viii 14. 1984. ISBN 90 04 07017 6
35. KRAŠOVEC, J. *Antithetic structure in Biblical Hebrew poetry*. 1984. ISBN 90 04 07244 6
36. EMERTON, J.A. (ed.). *Congress Volume, Salamanca 1983*. 1985. ISBN 90 04 07281 0
37. LEMCHE, N.P. *Early Israel*. Anthropological and historical studies on the Israelite society before the monarchy. 1985. ISBN 90 04 07853 3
38. NIELSEN, K. *Incense in Ancient Israel*. 1986. ISBN 90 04 07702 2
39. PARDEE, D. *Ugaritic and Hebrew poetic parallelism*. A trial cut. 1988. ISBN 90 04 08368 5
40. EMERTON, J.A. (ed.). *Congress Volume, Jerusalem 1986*. 1988. ISBN 90 04 08499 1
41. EMERTON, J.A. (ed.). *Studies in the Pentateuch*. 1990. ISBN 90 04 09195 5
42. McKENZIE, S.L. *The trouble with Kings*. The composition of the Book of Kings in the Deuteronomistic History. 1991. ISBN 90 04 09402 4
43. EMERTON, J.A. (ed.). *Congress Volume, Leuven 1989*. 1991. ISBN 90 04 09398 2
44. HAAK, R.D. *Habakkuk*. 1992. ISBN 90 04 09506 3
45. BEYERLIN, W. *Im Licht der Traditionen*. Psalm LXVII und CXV. Ein Entwicklungszusammenhang. 1992. ISBN 90 04 09635 3
46. MEIER, S.A. *Speaking of Speaking*. Marking direct discourse in the Hebrew Bible. 1992. ISBN 90 04 09602 7
47. KESSLER, R. *Staat und Gesellschaft im vorexilischen Juda*. Vom 8. Jahrhundert bis zum Exil. 1992. ISBN 90 04 09646 9
48. AUFFRET, P. *Voyez de vos yeux*. Étude structurelle de vingt psaumes, dont le psaume 119. 1993. ISBN 90 04 09707 4
49. GARCÍA MARTÍNEZ, F., A. HILHORST and C.J. LABUSCHAGNE (eds.). *The Scriptures and the Scrolls*. Studies in honour of A.S. van der Woude on the occasion of his 65th birthday. 1992. ISBN 90 04 09746 5
50. LEMAIRE, A. and B. OTZEN (eds.). *History and Traditions of Early Israel*. Studies presented to Eduard Nielsen, May 8th, 1993. 1993. ISBN 90 04 09851 8
51. GORDON, R.P. *Studies in the Targum to the Twelve Prophets*. From Nahum to Malachi. 1994. ISBN 90 04 09987 5
52. HUGENBERGER, G.P. *Marriage as a Covenant*. A Study of Biblical Law and Ethics Governing Marriage Developed from the Perspective of Malachi. 1994. ISBN 90 04 09977 8
53. GARCÍA MARTÍNEZ, F., A. HILHORST, J.T.A.G.M. VAN RUITEN, A.S. VAN DER WOUDE. *Studies in Deuteronomy*. In Honour of C.J. Labuschagne on the Occasion of His 65th Birthday. 1994. ISBN 90 04 10052 0
54. FERNÁNDEZ MARCOS, N. *Septuagint and Old Latin in the Book of Kings*. 1994. ISBN 90 04 10043 1
55. SMITH, M.S. *The Ugaritic Baal Cycle. Volume 1*. Introduction with text, translation and commentary of KTU 1.1-1.2. 1994. ISBN 90 04 09995 6
56. DUGUID, I.M. *Ezekiel and the Leaders of Israel*. 1994. ISBN 90 04 10074 1
57. MARX, A. *Les offrandes végétales dans l'Ancien Testament*. Du tribut d'hommage au repas eschatologique. 1994. ISBN 90 04 10136 5
58. SCHÄFER-LICHTENBERGER, C. *Josua und Salomo*. Eine Studie zu Autorität und Legitimität des Nachfolgers im Alten Testament. 1995. ISBN 90 04 10064 4
59. LASSERRE, G. *Synopse des lois du Pentateuque*. 1994. ISBN 90 04 10202 7
60. DOGNIEZ, C. *Bibliography of the Septuagint – Bibliographie de la Septante (1970-1993)*. Avec une préface de PIERRE-MAURICE BOGAERT. 1995. ISBN 90 04 10192 6
61. EMERTON, J.A. (ed.). *Congress Volume, Paris 1992*. 1995. ISBN 90 04 10259 0
62. SMITH, P.A. *Rhetoric and Redaction in Trito-Isaiah*. The Structure, Growth and Authorship of Isaiah 56-66. 1995. ISBN 90 04 10306 6

63. O'CONNELL, R.H. *The Rhetoric of the Book of Judges.* 1996. ISBN 90 04 10104 7
64. HARLAND, P.J. *The Value of Human Life.* A Study of the Story of the Flood (Genesis 6-9). 1996. ISBN 90 04 10534 4
65. ROLAND PAGE JR., H. *The Myth of Cosmic Rebellion.* A Study of its Reflexes in Ugaritic and Biblical Literature. 1996. ISBN 90 04 10563 8
66. EMERTON, J.A. (ed.). *Congress Volume, Cambridge 1995.* 1997. ISBN 90 04 106871
67. JOOSTEN, J. *People and Land in the Holiness Code.* An Exegetical Study of the Ideational Framework of the Law in Leviticus 17–26. 1996. ISBN 90 04 10557 3
68. BEENTJES, P.C. *The Book of Ben Sira in Hebrew.* A Text Edition of all Extant Hebrew Manuscripts and a Synopsis of all Parallel Hebrew Ben Sira Texts. 1997. ISBN 90 04 10767 3
69. COOK, J. *The Septuagint of Proverbs – Jewish and/or Hellenistic Proverbs?* Concerning the Hellenistic Colouring of LXX Proverbs. 1997. ISBN 90 04 10879 3
70,1 BROYLES, G. and C. EVANS (eds.). *Writing and Reading the Scroll of Isaiah.* Studies of an Interpretive Tradition, I. 1997. ISBN 90 04 10936 6 (*Vol.* I); ISBN 90 04 11027 5 (*Set*)
70,2 BROYLES, G. and C. EVANS (eds.). *Writing and Reading the Scroll of Isaiah.* Studies of an Interpretive Tradition, II. 1997. ISBN 90 04 11026 7 (*Vol.* II); ISBN 90 04 11027 5 (*Set*)
71. KOOIJ, A. VAN DER. *The Oracle of Tyre.* The Septuagint of Isaiah 23 as Version and Vision. 1998. ISBN 90 04 11152 2
72. TOV, E. *The Greek and Hebrew Bible.* Collected Essays on the Septuagint. 1999. ISBN 90 04 11309 6
73. GARCÍA MARTÍNEZ, F. and NOORT, E. (eds.). *Perspectives in the Study of the Old Testament and Early Judaism.* A Symposium in honour of Adam S. van der Woude on the occasion of his 70th birthday. 1998. ISBN 90 04 11322 3
74. KASSIS, R.A. *The Book of Proverbs and Arabic Proverbial Works.* 1999. ISBN 90 04 11305 3
75. RÖSEL, H.N. *Von Josua bis Jojachin.* Untersuchungen zu den deuteronomistischen Geschichtsbüchern des Alten Testaments. 1999. ISBN 90 04 11355 5
76. RENZ, Th. *The Rhetorical Function of the Book of Ezekiel.* 1999. ISBN 90 04 11362 2
77. HARLAND, P.J. and HAYWARD, C.T.R. (eds.). *New Heaven and New Earth Prophecy and the Millenium.* Essays in Honour of Anthony Gelston. 1999. ISBN 90 04 10841 6
78. KRAŠOVEC, J. *Reward, Punishment, and Forgiveness.* The Thinking and Beliefs of Ancient Israel in the Light of Greek and Modern Views. 1999. ISBN 90 04 11443 2.
79. KOSSMANN, R. *Die Esthernovelle – Vom Erzählten zur Erzählung.* Studien zur Traditions- und Redaktionsgeschichte des Estherbuches. 2000. ISBN 90 04 11556 0.
80. LEMAIRE, A. and M. SÆBØ (eds.). *Congress Volume, Oslo 1998.* 2000. ISBN 90 04 11598 6.
81. GALIL, G. and M. WEINFELD (eds.). *Studies in Historical Geography and Biblical His-toriography.* Presented to Zecharia Kallai. 2000. ISBN 90 04 11608 7
82. COLLINS, N.L. *The library in Alexandria and the Bible in Greek.* 2001. ISBN 90 04 11866 7
83,1 COLLINS, J.J. and P.W. FLINT (eds.). *The Book of Daniel.* Composition and Reception, I. 2001. ISBN 90 04 11675 3 (*Vol.* I); ISBN 90 04 12202 8 (*Set*).
83,2 COLLINS, J.J. and P.W. FLINT (eds.). *The Book of Daniel.* Composition and Reception, II. 2001. ISBN 90 04 12200 1 (*Vol.* II); ISBN 90 04 12202 8 (*Set*).

84. COHEN, C.H.R. *Contextual Priority in Biblical Hebrew Philology*. An Application of the Held Method for Comparative Semitic Philology. 2001. ISBN 90 04 11670 2 (In preparation).
85. WAGENAAR, J.A. *Judgement and Salvation*. The Composition and Redaction of Micah 2-5. 2001. ISBN 90 04 11936 1
86. McLAUGHLIN, J.L. *The Marzēaḥ in sthe Prophetic Literature*. References and Allusions in Light of the Extra-Biblical Evidence. 2001. ISBN 90 04 12006 8
87. WONG, K.L. *The Idea of Retribution in the Book of Ezekiel* 2001. ISBN 90 04 12256 7
88. BARRICK, W. Boyd. *The King and the Cemeteries*. Toward a New Understanding of Josiah's Reform. 2002. ISBN 90 04 12171 4
89. FRANKEL, D. *The Murmuring Stories of the Priestly School*. A Retrieval of Ancient Sacerdotal Lore. 2002. ISBN 90 04 12368 7
90. FRYDRYCH, T. *Living under the Sun*. Examination of Proverbs and Qoheleth. 2002. ISBN 90 04 12315 6
91. KESSEL, J. *The Book of Haggai*. Prophecy and Society in Early Persian Yehud. 2002. ISBN 90 04 12368 7
92. LEMAIRE, A. (ed.). *Congress Volume, Basel 2001*. 2002. ISBN 90 04 12680 5
93. RENDTORFF, R. and R.A. KUGLER (eds.). *The Book of Leviticus*. Composition and Reception. 2003. ISBN 90 04 12634 1
94. PAUL, S.M., R.A. KRAFT, L.H. SCHIFFMAN and W.W. FIELDS (eds.). *Emanuel*. Studies in Hebrew Bible, Septuagint, and Dead Sea Scrolls in Honor of Emanuel Tov. 2003. ISBN 90 04 13007 1
95. VOS, J.C. DE. *Das Los Judas*. Über Entstehung und Ziele der Landbeschreibung in Josua 15. ISBN 90 04 12953 7
96. LEHNART, B. *Prophet und König im Nordreich Israel*. Studien zur sogenannten vorklassischen Prophetie im Nordreich Israel anhand der Samuel-, Elija- und Elischa-Überlieferungen. 2003. ISBN 90 04 13237 6
97. LO, A. *Job 28 as Rhetoric*. An Analysis of Job 28 in the Context of Job 22-31. 2003. ISBN 90 04 13320 8
98. TRUDINGER, P.L. *The Psalms of the Tamid Service*. A Liturgical Text from the Second Temple. 2004. ISBN 90 04 12968 5
99. FLINT, P.W. and P.D. MILLER, JR. (eds.) with the assistance of A. Brunell. *The Book of Psalms*. Composition and Reception. 2004. ISBN 90 04 13842 8
100. WEINFELD, M. *The Place of the Law in the Religion of Ancient Israel*. 2004. ISBN 90 04 13749 1
101. FLINT, P.W., J.C. VANDERKAM and E. TOV. (eds.) *Studies in the Hebrew Bible, Qumran, and the Septuagint*. Essays Presented to Eugene Ulrich on the Occasion of his Sixty-Fifth Birthday. 2004. ISBN 90 04 13738 6
102. MEER, M.N. VAN DER. *Formation and Reformulation*. The Redaction of the Book of Joshua in the Light of the Oldest Textual Witnesses. 2004. ISBN 90 04 13125 6
103. BERMAN, J.A. *Narrative Analogy in the Hebrew Bible*. Battle Stories and Their Equivalent Non-battle Narratives. 2004. ISBN 90 04 13119 1
104. KEULEN, P.S.F. VAN. *Two Versions of the Solomon Narrative*. An Inquiry into the Relationship between MT 1 Kgs. 2-11 and LXX 3 Reg. 2-11. 2004. ISBN 90 04 13895 1
105. MARX, A. *Les systèmes sacrificiels de l'Ancien Testament*. Forms et fonctions du culte sacrificiel à Yhwh. 2005. ISBN 90 04 14286 X
106. ASSIS, E. *Self-Interest or Communal Interest*. An Ideology of Leadership in the Gideon, Abimelech and Jephthah Narritives (Judg 6-12). 2005. ISBN 90 04 14354 8
107. WEISS, A.L. *Figurative Language in Biblical Prose Narrative*. Metaphor in the Book of Samuel. 2006. ISBN 90 04 14837 X

108. WAGNER, T. *Gottes Herrschaft*. Eine Analyse der Denkschrift (Jes 6, 1-9,6). 2006. ISBN 90 04 14912 0

109. LEMAIRE, A. (ed.). *Congress Volume Leiden 2004*. 2006. ISBN 90 04 14913 9

110. GOLDMAN, Y.A.P., A. van der Kooij and R.D. Weis (eds.). *Sôfer Mahîr*. Essays in Honour of Adrian Schenker Offered by Editors of *Biblia Hebraica Quinta*. 2006. ISBN 90 04 15016 1

111. WONG, G.T.K. *Compositional Strategy of the Book of Judges*. An Inductive, Rhetorical Study. 2006. ISBN 90 04 15086 2

112. HØYLAND LAVIK, M. *A People Tall and Smooth-Skinned*. The Rhetoric of Isaiah 18. 2006. ISBN 90 04 15434 5

113. REZETKO, R., T.H. LIM and W.B. AUCKER (eds.). *Reflection and Refraction*. Studies in Biblical Historiography in Honour of A. Graeme Auld. 2006. ISBN 90 04 14512 5

115. BERGSMA, J.S. *The Jubilee from Leviticus to Qumran*. A History of Interpretation. 2006. ISBN-13 978 90 04 15299 1. ISBN-10 90 04 15299 7

116. GOFF, M.J. *Discerning Wisdom*. The Sapiential Literature of the Dead Sea Scrolls. 2006. ISBN-13 978 90 04 14749 2. ISBN-10 90 04 14749 7

117. DE JONG, M.J. *Isaiah among the Ancient Near Eastern Prophets*. A Comparative Study of the Earliest Stages of the Isaiah Tradition and the Neo-Assyrian Prophecies. 2007. ISBN 978 90 04 16161 0

118. FORTI, T.L. *Animal Imagery in the Book of Proverbs*. 2007. ISBN 978 90 04 16287 7

119. PINÇON, B. *L'énigme du bonheur*. Étude sur le sujet du bien dans le livre de Qohélet. 2008. ISBN 978 90 04 16717 9

120. ZIEGLER, Y. *Promises to Keep*. The Oath in Biblical Narrative. 2008. ISBN 978 90 04 16843 5

121. VILLANUEVA, F.G. *The 'Uncertainty of a Hearing'*. A Study of the Sudden Change of Mood in the Psalms of Lament. 2008. ISBN 978 90 04 16847 3

122. CRANE, A.S. *Israel's Restoration*. A Textual-Comparative Exploration of Ezekiel 36–39. 2008. ISBN 978 90 04 16962 3